A HISTOR RACEHORSE ~~~~~~ ~~ ~ AT EPSOM
(Revised edition)

C000226825

Over 500 trainers, over 60 stables, over 600 big race winners, leading prize-money winners

"There is not a properer place in the world for this sport."
-James Toland 1711

COMPILED BY

BILL EACOTT

Published by C.W. Eacott 2019
Reprinted January 2011
Revised September 2019

ISBN
978-0-9548278-3-0

Sports, General

1

INDEX

INTRODUCTION

"Eclipse first, the rest nowhere!"

Colonel O'Kelly's daring bet, that Eclipse would beat the rest of the field by more than a furlong in a race at Ascot in 1769, set an impossibly high standard for subsequent Epsom-trained racehorses.
It is fitting that one of the great racehorses, and founder of one of the major bloodstock lines should have been trained at the home of Britain's premier race. From Eclipse's success, the thoroughbred breeding industry developed, and the racehorse training industry evolved.

In **Part 2** of this book, trainers' details prior to the publication of the first copy of the Horses In Training Annual in 1893 are inevitably vague. It should also be noted that prior to 1905, trainers (apart from those using Newmarket Heath) did not require a licence, and details of trainers before that date are incomplete. From 1920 onwards the records are near complete and an accurate picture of the racehorse population of Epsom as can be obtained.

The classification of "major" races to be included in **Appendix A** was subjective. For Flat racing the introduction of the Pattern Race system in 1971 provides a fairly accurate guideline. During the period when Epsom was at its peak as a training centre (1950-1970), the handicap was undoubtedly "king". For example when David Hanley trained Weepers Boy to win the Senior Service Handicap at York in 1965 the race was worth £7,065 to the winner, the previous race on the card, the Musidora Stakes; (now a Group 3) was worth £2,454. Races also rise and fall in importance within the Racing Calendar, the two-year-old race; the National Stakes was worth £5,407 to owner Mr Stanley Wootton when Staff Ingham trained Kerrabee to win it in 1960, in comparison the Dewhurst Stakes (now a Group 1 race) was worth £2,406 that year.

Some once important races have simply disappeared, when Staff Ingham won the Brighton Derby Trial in 1961 with Just Great it was worth £3,124, two days later the Dante Stakes (now a Group 2) at York was worth £1,820.

So far as National Hunt racing is concerned the position is equally variable. Jim Beavis in his book "The Croydon Races" sums up prizemoney in Victorian times:

"(In the 1870s) 200 sovereigns were added to the stakes for the Great Surrey Open Steeplechase, making it a handsome Grand National consolation.
This latest large prize consolidated Croydon's position as second only to Liverpool in the National Hunt world.

3

The valuable races such as the Great Metropolitan Handicap had become established landmarks in the Racing Calendar as major Grand National trials or consolation prizes. Croydon was very fashionable among the racing fraternity.
The highlight of the 1876 meeting was the United Kingdom Grand Handicap Steeplechase, with 500 sovereigns added money, won by John Nightingall's Shifnal.
It was not until after World War II that hurdle races gained much prestige and prize money, but Croydon's Grand International Handicap Hurdle was perhaps the most prestigious of its kind at the time with 500 sovereigns added."

Paul Davies in his book "The Grand International Hurdle" writes:

"Croydon was in some respects the course that legitimised hurdling, by framing valuable races at both ends of the year. These races encouraged many owners to send decent flat-race horses over timber, thus improving the quality of the sport, they were also the first hurdling contests to attract large-scale ante-post betting at Tattersalls."

In the 1880s the Grand National was the only "jumps" race worth £1,000, the next three most valuable races were all hurdles; the Grand International at Croydon, the Kempton Grand Hurdle, and the Sandown Grand Prize. The latter two were short-lived, but the Grand International remained the premier hurdles race, until superseded (in prizemoney terms) by the Jubilee Hurdle c.1895, and the Imperial Cup in 1906.

The Cheltenham Festival was of less importance prior to 1950. In the season 1929-1930, the major prize was the Grand National, worth £9,800 to the winner. There were only five other races worth in excess of £1,000; the Champion Chase, the Liverpool Hurdle, and the Grand Sefton Chase, all run at Aintree, the Lancashire Chase at Manchester and the National Hunt Chase at Cheltenham. The Lancashire Chase, worth £1,725 to the winner was the second most valuable race in the National Hunt Calendar. By comparison the Champion Hurdle and Cheltenham Gold Cup were worth £690 each.

Details of who trained some of the 1 big race winners in the 19th century, (even the Grand National), are vague.

In **Appendix C**, "x" indicates that there is documentary evidence that a trainer was at Epsom that year, (usually from the Form Book), "?" indicates that the trainer was believed to operate at Epsom but no documentary evidence has been found.

Prior to 1900, figures for Horses in Training are taken from various publications, and are incomplete. Thanks go to Tim Cox, not only for making his exceptional resources available to me, but also for the amount of research he undertook,.

PART 1.

A BRIEF HISTORY OF RACEHORSE TRAINING AT EPSOM

In 1618 a source of water was found on Epsom Common during a period of drought. The water had an antiseptic quality, and when the water was drunk, the purgative effect was apparent, and thus people came to Epsom to "take the waters."

The area around the spring was enclosed and became known as The Wells. Epsom became a fashionable spa town. Assembly rooms, gaming houses, bowling greens and coffee houses were established for the visitors. Coursing, hunting, hawking, and racing took place. The racing was comparatively rudimentary; the landed gentry would race their horses against each other's, the horses starting on Banstead Downs, and running from or to Carshalton and Epsom Downs. The first meeting on record in England after the Restoration took place on 7th March 1661 on Banstead Downs and was attended by Charles II.

Robert Norden's map of 1694 depicted the four-mile track extending across Banstead Downs between Carshalton and Epsom Downs. In 1711, Toland referred to "... *the new orbicular Race which may be term'd a rural Cirque"* and *"The four mile course over the Warrenhouse to Carshalton, a village abounding in delicious springs..."*; suggesting that more than one "course" was in use.

The Downs were described as running from Croydon to Farnham, and were noted for "*hawking, hunting, and horse-racing...what the middle parts want in riches they supply with pleasures, as being famous for good air, and well stored parks."*

The London Gazette on January 3rd 1695 advertised:

"On Bransted (sic) downs will be two Plates run for yearly 3 times successively, each plate to be 20/- price. The first to be run for the 14 of February next and all others on May-Day and Bartholmew Day in every year, until 3 years are expired. Any horse may run for the said plate that shall be at any of the contributors' stables in Carshalton, Barrowes-hedges, or elsewhere 14 days before the Plate-day".

Barrow Hedges was the site of the stables/hunting lodge now occupied by Carshalton Beeches.

Further advertisements in the London Gazette for races at Banstead Downs appear on various dates between 1696 and 1710.

John Watson appears to be the promoter in 1699 and 1702, and Richard Robinson in October 1707.

In April 1707 the horses are to be entered at Richard Grandy's at Swan in Carshalton, and the contributors are listed as Grandy, Watson, Robinson and Thomas Williams and William Hyde.

In July 1736 the London Evening Post advertised races at Banstead Downs, with Barrow Hedges again designated as the stables for entry.

Advertisements for Epsom Downs appeared in the London Gazette on

20th May 1700 (to be run upon the New Heat at Epsom),5th August 1700 (to be run upon the New Heat at Epsom, the winning rider to have a guinea paid by H.Parkhurst of Epsom), and on 20th October 1701 (on the New Heat. Horses to be entered at Devereux Watson's at the New Stables in Epsom). Then on 4th May 1702, and 19th March 1715. Further details of the "New Stables" can be found on pages 228/229.

From 1702 the "New Heat" is dropped and the venue stated as upon Epsom Downs.

It is clear that racing was taking place from Banstead, and from Epsom during the same period.

Toland's "new orbicular course" referred to in 1711 (see above) was possibly the New Heat i.e. Epsom Downs racecourse referred to in the 1700 and 1701 advertisements.

Mr H. Parkhurst referred to on 5th August 1700, lived at Richmond House, Epsom, the dwelling adjacent to the New Stables (see Epsom's Racing Stables Past and Present (Part 3)

By 1790, the organisation of races was improved; with permanent courses, rules of racing, and the establishment of major races and meetings. In the early days of horseracing, the owner was the most important connection. Record books logged that a horse was, for example, Lord Derby's horse. The name of Lord Derby's head groom or farrier, (in those days the equivalent of his racehorse trainer), was considered of little importance, and rarely recorded.

Gradually it was acknowledged that some "grooms" were better than others in handling horses, and so the "trainer" began to get recognition. Some trainers were good enough to leave the employment of their masters, and set up on their own as a public trainer, *John*

Nightingall and *Ralph Sherwood* being notable local examples; and thus the industry of racehorse training was founded.

Initially the training stables were part of the owner's private estate. Examples of this in Epsom were found at The Durdans, Pitt Place, Woodcote House, Heathcote House, Abele Grove, The Grove, and Down Cottage, (once the stables to Downs Hall).

The first record of the organisation and management of the training grounds appears in the Racing Calendar 1831:

"At a meeting of the Subscribers to the Epsom Race Fund, held at the Spread Eagle Inn, on Thursday December 23, 1830, it was resolved that the sum of ten shillings be paid for every horse that shall be trained or exercised on the Downs from the first of January next to the first of July following, towards the repairing and keeping in order of such Exercise Ground; and for every horse trained or exercised on the said Downs from first of July to the first of January the like sum of ten shillings; and that the sums shall be paid by the trainer or servant having the care of such horses, and be charged by him to the owners thereof; and that this resolution do apply to succeeding years. The money to be paid in advance, or the treasurer to stop all horses going on the exercise ground. Signed T.Scaith treasurer"

One of the earliest lists of Epsom trainers is in The York Herald Saturday 2nd March 1839, listing twelve horses trained by *Sherwood* for Sir Gilbert Heathcote, four horses for Lord Albemarle and one for Lord Tavistock trained by *E. Wright*, six horses trained by *Dockeray*, one trained by *Lambden*, and three horses trained for Mr Stirling by *Boast*.

The York Herald 5th February 1842 notes the training centre as "Epsom, Mickleham, Carshalton, and Sutton"; the training centre, clearly stretching much further than currently.

Gradually parts of the enclosed agricultural land on the edge of the town were turned over to racehorse training, and utilized by the new breed of self-employed trainers, and by 1840, Downs Farm had become Priam Lodge, and South Hatch stables were built.

In 1843, The Sportsman's Gazette published on 26th February details relating to the organization and management of gallops. Signed by Henry Dorling, chairman of the racecourse; *Joseph Farrall*, clerk of the course; and trainers *Ralph Sherwood, George Dockeray, William Smith and Edward Wright*; the group resolved;

"That in consequence of the heavy expense incurred in making the new ploughed sweat, and other new gallops that the sum of 10 shillings be paid by the trainer for every horse exercised over any part of the ground during the year.

7

That Mr Lumley be requested to collect the horse money.
That the thanks of the meeting be given to Mr Barnard for his great exertions already made in improving the gallops; and also to the gentlemen farmers in the neighbourhood for the kind loan of teams, in conveying tan etc."

The "ploughed" gallop was described as the fifth in the country, but the one at Epsom *"in extent and excellence far exceeds them all. This gallop is a mile and a quarter in length, and nearly twelve yards wide. It was dug with the spade, not ploughed unlike the others."*

By the mid-19th century relations between the racecourse management and the trainers were fraught again:

The Morning Post 16th April 1858 stated:

"Mr Dorling makes no secret of his dislike of the Spring Meeting, and his belief that the Derby Day alone would be sufficient for his purposes, and the amusement of those who dwell in the metropolis. He also complains of there being so many horses trained on the Downs, by which they are cut up. The consequence of this feeling has been a declaration of war against him by the Epsom trainers. I trust Mr Dorling will reconsider his determination, and not deprive us of our annual holiday in April."

The training grounds at this time were widespread, with trainers taking their horses to Smitham Bottom, Leatherhead, and Mickleham for work. Bell's Life, 25th January 1863, records that the steeplechasers used the racecourse on Epsom Common for practice. Private "jumps" racecourses were also in use at Tadworth Park, Walton on the Hill, and Walton Heath.

In 1867, Mr Carew sold the Manor of Walton (which included part of the back straight, and the Six Mile Hill gallops) to Mr Edward Studd. The Epsom Grand Stand Association looked at the possibility of re-aligning the course to avoid Walton Manor land, but it was impractical. Mr Carew had received an annual rental of £300 p.a. for the right to race across his land. Mr Studd requested £1,000 p.a., plus a deposit of £2,500. Protracted arguments failed to produce a compromise, and eventually the EGSA agreed to the rental, Mr Studd in turn donating half of the £2,500 to fund two races, the Walton Manor Stakes, and the Six Mile Hill Handicap.

During 1868 local owner/trainer *Mr Thomas Hughes* rented the Six Mile Hill gallops, to make certain that training facilities were available while Epsom Grand Stand Association were in dispute with Mr Studd. The Sporting Gazette in January 1869 indicated that settlement had been reached between the Epsom Grandstand Association, and the Lord of the Manor of Walton over the sale of Walton land to the EGSA. This proved to be false. The York Herald, 23rd January 1869, recorded that agreement had been reached regarding the training fees for Six Mile Hill, but that EGSA's offer of purchase had not been accepted:

"THE TRAINING GROUNDS AT EPSOM. On Thursday week Mr. Baylis, as steward, and Mr. Studd, the Lord of the Manor of Walton, called the Epsom trainers together, and offered the use of Walton Downs, Mr. Studd's portion of Epsom Downs including the Six Mile Hill for the purposes of training; the trainers to pay £2 each for two thirds of the horses in training, the remaining one third not to be charged at all; Mr. Studd is to have the furzes grubbed up, the ground levelled, the rabbits destroyed, and their burrows filled up, and the whole ground made sound and good for training purposes, and kept in repair at Mr. Studd's expense. The trainers unanimously agreed that Mr. Studd's offer was a most liberal one, and consented to the terms proposed. The Epsom Grand Stand Association have, therefore, waited too long."

The Derby Mercury 27th January 1869 confirmed:

"The Epsom Course.
The Sporting Gazette contradicts the statement that the difference between Mr Studd and the EGSA was settled by the purchase of the latter body for £15,500 of Six Mile Hill, which includes a portion of the Derby Course between the mile post and Tattenham Corner. No offer whatever to that effect has been made on the part of Mr Studd; and though the EGSA through their solicitors have within the last day or two, offered to purchase the property in question for that sum, Mr Studd declines to sell at any price. The difficulty there fore is far from settled."

Mr Studd installed *William Puttrell* as his private trainer at Walton, and a note in The Sportsman, 1st March 1871 indicates that Mr Studd was leasing his private gallops to *John Nightingall.*

Meanwhile the Lord of the Manor of Epsom had entered the fray; The Sportsman, 25th May 1869 reported that he was claiming:

"towards defraying the expense of repairing the course and the exercise ground, one guinea be paid annually in respect of every horse…trained at Epsom, and half a guinea for every horse which goes there for any race meeting."

William Reeves had traditionally collected the half guinea, and in turn undertook the maintenance. The Epsom Manor land was used primarily for racing; training mainly being done on Six Mile Hill. The trainers, while happy to negotiate with the Lord of the Manor of Epsom, were adamant that they would not be placed under the control of Mr Dorling, the clerk of the course, and the EGSA.

Mr Studd died in 1877, but before the EGSA could table a bid the estate was sold, and negotiations re-commenced. Finally in 1886 the EGSA completed the purchase of "the famous galloping or training ground for flat races distinguished as Six Mile Hill and a portion of the Derby racecourse adjacent to the far-famed Tattenham Corner."

John Nightingall took the role of renting/administering the use of the Six Mile Hill gallops for £140 p.a.; with the costs of maintaining the land to be borne by the EGSA. *John Jones* took a similar role for the Epsom Manor land for £10 p.a.

Following Nightingall's death the EGSA gave Jones notice to quit, and instigated a plan whereby they administered all of the gallops with the costs remaining the same but divided pro rata.

In the 19th century, Epsom was primarily a centre for training steeplechasers, and at least eight Grand National winners were trained in the area, and several winners of the leading hurdle races. The Prince of Wales was introduced to steeplechasing, and had his horses trained at Epsom by *Rowlands, Jones, Marsh and Arthur Nightingall.*

Such was the interest in National Hunt racing that a course was built on Epsom Common, and several fixtures staged there, (and elsewhere in the area), in the 1850s. See Part 4, National Hunt racing at Epsom.

On the 14th December 1883, The Sporting Life recorded;

"Some few years ago Epsom was the chief centre of steeplechasers, But, alas those good times when Mr. Fothergill Rowlands kept open house at Pitt Place are gone, when the team mustered fifty strong. Each winter Sunday at Pitt Place was gala day. But even in the decline of this hospitable establishment's fortunes steeple chasing prospered elsewhere at Epsom, and perhaps for a few years gained impetus. This was when John Jones set up as private trainer to Lord Marcus Beresford and Captain Paget at Down Cottage, which too has been honoured by a few horses carrying the purple and scarlet jacket of our future King. Poor Jem Potter has gone after a fight for life beyond understanding. Bobby I'Anson of Burgh Heath, is now Mr. Robert I'Anson the starter. Jem Adams has had many a hard knock since his flat days, he has taken Bruce Lodge from Robert Wyatt, and I wish him luck. Death has snatched a good sportsman in Mr Case Walker of Woodcote, and Chandler who had charge of his horses, has now gone to Stockbridge. For some years now Sydney, who began so successfully as Lord Dupplin's private trainer at Epsom, has dwelt at Lewes. Joe Marsh soon after his marriage crossed over to France. John Nightingall is fresh as ever, and so too, for that matter is his respected father."

The *Nightingall* family leased the private National Hunt racecourse on Walton Heath from the Lord of the Manor of Walton. It was in use from the 1870s to the 1930s. *John Jones* used the private steeplechase fences at Tadworth Park.

Sportsman 17th January 1886 noted

"Mr. T.Hughes had the right of galloping his horses on Leatherhead Downs), and he had the right to extend this privilege to Lrd Glasgow, or the latter nobleman paid "a pretty penny" to Mr. Newman the lessee.
John Scott, the Malton trainer stabled his horses at Vale Lodge, Leatherhead in preparation for the Derby, and refused to pay the exorbitant sum of 50/- for three or four morning's work, instead taking his team to Mickleham downs one mile further from Vale Lodge. "a splendid gallop, with a fringe of juniper trees on each side, extending for over two miles on a gentle slope."

Towards the end of the 19th century German owners Baron Topper Laski and Herr Oehlschlager, transferred their best horses from Germany to Epsom for the chasing season, employing a variety of private trainers, including *William Moore*, who after moving to Weyhill with *Patrick Collins* trained three Grand National winners.

The Sheffield Independent 26th February 1889 reported on the German connection:

Saturday last saw the departure from Epsom to Germany of Max Phillips, G. Sopp, Tom McLean, G. Sears, A. Sharp and several others. They will be followed in a few weeks by W. Hunt, A. Hall, W. Sensier and W. Nightingall, each of whom has accepted an engagement to ride in Germany in the ensuing season there.

Sopp had been making the trip since 1873, Arthur Hall, Arthur and William Nightingall all rode the winner of the main steeplechase at Baden-Baden.

The economic sense of sharing gallops, and the availability of labour resulted in the centralisation of training to various centres. Private trainers were still predominant at the start of the 20th century, and the profiles of some of the trainers in **Part 2,** indicates how frequently they moved between employment in Berkshire, Epsom and Sussex.

At the turn of the 20th century, training at Epsom was galvanised by the arrival from Australia of the Wootton family. *Richard Wootton* set up as a trainer at Treadwell House. Despite not having the backing of Jockey Club members with their long-established thoroughbred breeding facilities; he relied on his ability, and eye for a horse, and rapidly became champion trainer. His son Frank won the jockeys championship on four successive occasions while still in his teens. Public perception was that the "Australians" possessed hitherto unknown gifts, and boys moved to Epsom to learn the "secrets".

11

Stanley Wootton succeeded his father Richard, and continued the practice of training jockeys, but did not train such high-quality horses as his father. Epsom was now leaning towards becoming a training centre for racehorses running on the Flat, but the early running of the Imperial Cup (the premier hurdle race prior to the Champion Hurdle), were monopolised by locally trained horses. As late as the 1930s there were still at least ten jockeys based in Epsom purely for the "jumpers", including some who specialised in hurdles races only.

In 1926, the uncertainty over the ownership of the gallops emerged again. EGSA, needing the money to finance the freehold of those parts of the racecourse still under lease, sold to *Stanley Wootton* the freehold of the gallops on Walton Downs, (Six Mile Hill), and *Wootton* took a lease on the gallops within the racecourse. An arrangement that lasted forty years. (See *Stanley Wootton* for further details).

By the 1930s some of the boys who joined the Woottons as apprentice jockeys were now retiring and turning to training. The demand for training premises, coupled with the financial rewards for training (labour was very cheap), resulted in small farms in Beaconsfield Road, the Thirty Acre Farm on Shepherds Walk, Ermyn Lodge, and Woodruff; being converted to equestrian use.

In 1934 the Epsom Trainers Association was formed, the Yorkshire Post, 21st December 1934 announced the formation under the chairmanship of *Mr Arthur Boxall*;

"Mr Percy Allden who organised the gathering referred to the remarkable success of Epsom trainers during the past Flat Season. He pointed out that of about three hundred horses trained there, no less than 177 won races of the total value over £38,000. Including jumpers and ponies there are now nearly 500 horses trained at Epsom"

The Citizen, 29th December 1938, under the headline, "Epsom's Growth as a Training Centre", noted:

"London's suburbs have encroached so greatly on the open country during recent years that it is surprising to find such an important training centre as Epsom just 15 miles from the Metropolis. Epsom has developed from a quiet country town into a popular suburb. Yet the number of horses quartered there has also increased, that now, in that respect it is second only to Newmarket. No doubt the principal factor in producing this unusual position is the introduction of road transport. Racing under Pony Turf Club rules at Northolt has also had its effect, a large number of ponies being trained in Epsom. In fact the two leading trainers Monty Smyth and Pat Donoghue have stables in Epsom.
Epsom also has some of the finest gallops in the country. These gallops, which stretch from Langley Bottom to the top of Six Mile Hill, are nearly a mile and a half in length

and of considerable width. A chalk soil coupled with the fact that they are 500 feet above sea level, means it is a rare occurrence for them to become heavy. Several leading jockeys have set up as trainers at Epsom in recent years notably Johnny Dines, Gerry Hardy, Cecil Ray and Bobby Dick."

For 25 years post 1945, the town was at its peak. Sir Winston Churchill had his horses trained here, and the two largest training strings in the country were based in Burgh Heath Road.

By the 1970s circumstances had changed; employment legislation, coupled with 20 per cent inflation caused overheads to increase rapidly. Property prices also rose sharply, and as the generation of trainers reached retirement age, it became clear that the development value of land that was not protected by the "Green Belt" was far more lucrative for housing than training racehorses. The increased population and vehicle traffic rendered many of the stables in the town inoperable. Stables in the urban area and Langley Vale were demolished.

The the old trainers who could survive on eight to ten horses with a couple of well-executed gambles each year are an anachronism. Building new stables on Green Belt land is fraught with difficulties, particularly because of the need to have living accommodation on site.

Several prominent businessmen have refurbished stables that had appeared lost to racing, and a new generation of young trainers are helping to increase Epsom's racehorse population once more.

PART 2.

RACEHORSE TRAINERS AT EPSOM A-Z

NAME	ADDRESS	KNOWN DATE
ADAMS, Frederick	Pitt Place	1876-1877
(c.1844-1893)	The Parade	1878-1889

Adams was born at Cranbourne in Dorset, and was the elder brother of *William James Adams*. Frederick Adams succeeded *John Jones* as trainer at Pitt Place. He trained Scamp to win the International Hurdle Handicap at Croydon in 1877. The York Herald lists 48 horses in training with Adams in 1877. The Sportsman, 4th January 1878 announced that Adams had commenced training on his own behalf in December 1877. Adams was listed as a trainer at The Parade, Epsom in the 1881 census.

ADAMS, Thomas	Woodcote Road	1911
(1871-1923)		

Son of *William James Adams*; Tom Adams was born at Bourton on the Hill, and rode for his father. He was declared bankrupt in 1896, (his father had cited his sons' gambling debts as a cause of his own bankruptcy the previous year). In the 1911 census Tom Adams is described as a racehorse trainer living in Woodcote Road.

ADAMS, William James	Turf Cottage,	1875-1882
(c.1846-1912)	Bruce Lodge	1883-1897
	The Cottage	1889
	Priam Lodge	1890
	The Cottage	1898-1911

William James Adams was born in Cranbourne, Dorset. Adams appears on four different census returns giving a different year of birth on all four. He always signed documents as Jimmy Adams, and was also known as "Jem", or "Bones" having reputedly broken "every bone" in a series of falls. The Hon. George Lambton in his book "Men and Horses I Have Known" writes:

"If I had a better memory I could write a book of the quaint and witty sayings of Jimmy Adams. He was a little, short-legged man, with the back and shoulders of a prize fighter, and a good bit more below the belt than was convenient for a jockey. But, even then, to see him ride at the last two fences in a close finish was a revelation of what strength, determination and skill could achieve."

An accomplished jockey under both codes, Adams rode in the Derby eight times, and the Grand National nine times; his best finishing position was third in both races. He took up training in 1875 when based at Turf Cottage in Sutton. The York Herald 4th August 1883 noted: *"Jas. Adams has leased Bruce Lodge, Epsom from Robert Wyatt."*

In Kelly's Directory 1889 he is listed at The Cottage, and in 1890 he is at Priam Lodge. In the 1891 census he was employing fourteen staff. In 1892, the Yorkshire Post recorded that Adams had a large string of jumpers for the forthcoming season, and had a private steeplechase course erected on Walton Heath. *"The going is admirable and all the fences made up to regulation pattern."* Financial difficulties led to a decline in his training career.

Adams lived in a time when boys of his class got little education, the lack of education led to business difficulties. In 1895 he appeared at Croydon Bankruptcy Court, where he outlined his problems: Nottingham Evening Post 24th October 1895

"WILLIAM JAMES ADAMS, trainer of racehorses at Bruce Lodge, Epsom, "attributed his insolvency to losses from bad debts, betting, and expenses incurred in connection with the illness if his wife". The accounts showed gross liabilities of £3402, and assets £1541, deficiency £1860. Adams said that he had trained racehorses for 20 years, the last 12 years at Epsom. Sometimes he had 15 – 20 horses in training but he had been unable to get on without borrowing money. His present liabilities had been incurred since 1889. The debtor [Adams] also explained that he had paid at least £500 for betting losses incurred by his sons."

Before his court hearing Adams put Bruce Lodge, comprising a residence, 18 loose boxes, 12 stalled stable and a one acre paddock up for auction, but it failed to reach its reserve, bidding stopping at £2,600.
In the 1898 Ruff's Guide Jim Adams is listed as training at The Cottage, by this time he was only training a few horses.
His son, Robert Adams (1875-1943), moved to mainland Europe and was six times Champion Trainer in Austria and Hungary.

AKEHURST, John	South Hatch	1991
(1961-2012)	Shifnal Cottage	1996-1997
	South Hatch	1998-2004
	Tattenham Corner	2005-2008
	Clear Height	2008-2012

Son of *Reginald Akehurst*, after spells training in Lambourn (1991-1996), and at Shifnal Cottage, Epsom; John Akehurst succeeded his father at South Hatch Stables. He achieved his first Pattern Race success with Mac Love who won the 2004 Supreme Stakes, and also won a Group 3 race in Germany with Capricho. His handicap successes include the 2002 Wokingham Handicap won by Capricho, and with Marsad who won the valuable Ladbroke Handicap at Newmarket in 2001 and 2003.

His last runner was with his own horse Prince of Sorrento, which won at Lingfield on 7th March 2012. He relinquished his licence on 13th March, after a long battle against illness, and died the following day. At the time of his death Akehurst was chairman of Epsom Trainer's Association.

AKEHURST, Reg.	Hillcot	1968-1971
(1929-	South Hatch	1985-1990
	South Hatch	1991-1997

Reginald Peter John Akehurst rode 99 winners under National Hunt rules prior to switching to training. In 1968, Reg Akehurst moved from stables at Wiltshire to take over the lease at Hillcot with some National Hunt horses and a couple of unfashionably bred two-year-olds. Among the juveniles was Gold Rod, who won three races as a two-year-old, and then with Lester Piggott on board won the Greenham Stakes at Newbury, and the Prix du Moulin at Longchamp. In three seasons Gold Rod ran in 31 races, and apart from his debut, was only out of the frame once, he won races from six to ten furlongs, and campaigned against the best in England and France. Notable places included second to Brigadier Gerard in the 1972 Eclipse Stakes, second in the 1971 Prix du Moulin, and second in the 1970 Sussex Stakes.

Akehurst's best National Hunt horses at this time were Moyne Royal who won the 1969 HSS Hire Shops Hurdle, and Rabble Rouser who won the 1969 Tote Placepot Hurdle. Reg Akehurst left Epsom in 1971 and moved to Lambourn, despite saying that he realised it was a mistake after three months; it would be fourteen years before he returned.

After winning the 1973 Coventry Stakes with Doleswood, Akehurst's career slowly declined. In 1984, his tally fell to two winners, however a return to Epsom, where he purchased the historic South Hatch stables, rekindled the passion.

Racehorses of 1994 noted:

"The Epsom handler, who briefly gave up training in the early eighties and at one stage had his string down to nine, is now an acknowledged master in the art of preparing handicappers and setting alight hitherto latent talents. Some of the most striking examples of this have come with animals in the lower grades, but at the 1993 Newmarket Autumn Sales one of his owners purchased the three year old Urgent Request, a colt which has done so well since that he took his connections to top international races on three continents."

Urgent Request, who won the Rose of Lancaster Stakes, was second in the International Vase at Sha Tin, and was beaten two lengths at Woodbine in the Rothmans International. Numerous big handicap winners trained by Akehurst included Sarawat in the 1993 Ebor Handicap, when the owner was reputed to have won £250k by backing the horse, and an even larger amount when Urgent Request was backed from 14-1 into 8-1 for the Northern Dancer Handicap at Epsom. Akehurst resisted the temptation to bet his charges during this successful period, "I have seen too many trainers go broke due to gambling. I am happy with my lot - I make a decent living without gambling."
Other notable handicap wins included the Ascot Stakes, Lincoln, Victoria Cup on three occasions, the Schweppes Golden Mile, the Royal Hunt Cup twice, the Wokingham, the William Hill Cup and the Queen Alexandra.
Over the jumps, Reg Akehurst was equally prolific; winning Grade 1 events with Bimsey in the 1996 Aintree Hurdle, and Dare To Dream in the 1992 Finale Junior Hurdle. Grade 2 successes came with Jazilah in the 1994 Seagram Top Novices Hurdle and the 1994 Dovecote Novices Hurdle, Gaasid in the 1994 Kennel Gate Novices Hurdle; plus the Tote Placepot Hurdle twice, and the Summit Junior Hurdle twice.
Steeplechase successes included Solidasarock in the SGB Chase; and the Welsh National during a year commencing March 1990 that Akehurst spent training at Whitcombe in Dorset.
Seb Sanders, the 2007 champion Flat jockey, served his apprenticeship at South Hatch with Akehurst.
Reg Akehurst retired in 1997; he won with his last runner on the Flat and the last runner over hurdles. His final reflection on his career was: "I love Epsom. It's been good to me. But it's strange they don't send top class horses there. Fashion, I suppose."

ALDRIDGE, Thomas	The Durdans	1889-1891.1910
(1856-1920)		

Born in Staines, Aldridge was primarily a jockey, but briefly trained at The Durdans. The 1901 census shows him as living at Park Cottages, Epsom. His son Private William Aldridge died in 1917, aboard the ship "Transylvania" that was torpedoed en route to

Salonika. The Western Times, 22nd June 1920 recorded:

"Coming off the Downs at Epsom, Mr A. Wildey's Esplanade fell. Tommy Aldridge the old-time jockey who was riding was killed."

Aldridge, who was living at The Durdans stable at the time of his death, is buried in Epsom cemetery.

ALFORD, Ernest George   1898,1903
(1872-1920)

Alford's peripatetic career as groom/jockey/trainer included two spells at Epsom, circa 1898 and 1903, Findon 1900-1902 and 1907, Cranborne 1901 and at Royston in 1903 and from 1908. He served in the Royal Army Veterinary Corps. In 1920, Alford shot himself using a German revolver he had brought back from the Great War. At the time of his death he was estranged from his wife, and working at Shipbourne stables near Tonbridge in Kent.

ALLAM, or ALLUM.T   1869
(1836?-?)

T. Allam is listed in "Special Training Notes" in The Sportsman, 11th December 1869. He appears to have been supervising *George Simpson's* horses.
Thomas Allum born in Brighton in 1836, is shown as a groom living in Church Street in the 1861 census.

ALLDEN, George   Langley Bottom   1922-1923
(1898-1973)   Woodlands   1936-1937

Brother of *Percy Allden*; George was apprenticed to *Thomas Schofield*, who trained at The Cottage for owners including Allden's father. George Allden held a training licence in the early 1920s, and again after Percy left Epsom for Newmarket. George Allden moved to Newmarket after 1945, but lost his licence after one of his horses was found to have been doped (albeit without his knowledge.) He spent much of the rest of his life trying to clear his name, and in 1952 petitioned the Queen. See also *James Russell*, and *Cecil Ray*.

ALLDEN, Percy   Gondola (L'Etoile)   1924-1927
(1900-1978)   1929-1935

When *Stanley Wootton* was negotiating to buy Walton Downs in 1925, his schedule of trainers reveals that Percy Allden, based at L'Etoile, was the only trainer based in

Langley Bottom. The London Gazette, 8th March 1929 records that Allden, of Gondola,

Beaconsfield Road had bought the adjoining Adelaide Farm. The son of a Tattersalls bookmaker and racehorse owner, Percy Allden served his apprenticeship with *Thomas Schofield*. He enlisted in the RAF in 1918, rising to the rank of Pilot Officer. After his service career was completed, Allden commenced his training career at Eastbury in Berkshire in 1921, before moving to Epsom in 1924. In 1927, Allden left Epsom for Chantilly where he was private trainer to Ralph Strassburger for a year.
In 1932 Percy Allden was elected to the Epsom Urban District Council.

Allden sold Gondola to *Bobby Dick*, and moved to premises at Newmarket on 29th June 1935 that he also named Gondola. In World War II, Allden served in the RAF again, leaving as a Squadron Leader.
He died at Newmarket in 1978, leaving effects of £2,862.

AMBLER, Samuel   Down Cottage, Uplands   1903-1906
(1881-1936?)

Ambler, like *James Platt*, spent the early 1900s, as private trainer, or nominee trainer for *James Bell*, moving base between Berkshire and Epsom. Bradford-born Ambler started his career as an apprentice at Malton. In 1903 he trained Mr V. T. Thompson's Rose Wreath to win the Champion Chase, and in 1904 he trained Puerto to win the Grand International Hurdle.
In 1914 he moved to Warwick House, Middleham, and in 1930 moved to France, training at Maisons- Laffitte, before returning to Bradford.

ANSLEY, Thomas (possibly aka John)   1873-76
(1848-c.1912)

Born in Monmouth, Wales; Ansley was a former employee of *William Reeves* at Down Cottage, he is listed in Bell's Life, 11th January 1873 as training 18 horses at Epsom in partnership with *William Gosling*.
("John James Ansley, Epsom trainer," was the father of two children christened at St. Matins Church in 1874 and 1875.)

ARMSTRONG, John   Downs House   1857-1891
(c.1817-1891)

Armstrong was born in Richmond, Yorkshire. His birth date varies from 1816 in the 1871 census to 1825 in the 1881 census. "Downs House"/ "The Downs" referred to the stables next to the Derby Arms. In 1856, The Era lists Armstrong as training at Newmarket, and the following year he was reported to have left Newmarket for stables at Ashtead. In the 1861 census Armstrong is shown as having seven apprentices living in.

19

Training reports in "The Sportsman" in 1866 show Armstrong regularly using Mickleham Downs for working his horses.

ARNOLD, John   1908-1909
(1872-?)

Born in County Down c. 1872, Arnold was previously employed at Southover Stables, Lewes, Sussex. Arnold trained a few winners during 1909 when based at Epsom, usually using *Frank Wootton* as his jockey. He features in Sporting Life gallop reports from September 1908. He left Epsom in 1909 to move to stables at Littleton, Hampshire where he was based at the time of the 1911 census.

ARNULL, Charles   Althorp Lodge   1891-1901
(c.1852- 1924)

Born in Tamworth, Staffordshire, and shown on the 1901 census as a "trainer" based at Althorp Lodge. Arnull was head lad to Richard Sherrard at Newmarket prior to moving to Althorp Lodge in 1891. His great uncle William Arnull rode three Derby winners; and William's father John Arnull, and his uncle, Sam Arnull rode five and four Derby winners respectively.

ASHWORTH, Peter   The Grove   1955-1960
(1924-2002)   Treadwell House   1960-1981
                             The Chalet   1982

Peter Ashworth was born in 1924 in Brussels where his father, Harry Ashworth was working as a jockey. At the age of 12 he signed on as an apprentice jockey with *Stanley Wootton*. World War II interrupted his career as a jockey. *Wootton* sold his horses, and because Ashworth was too young for active service, *Wootton* transferred Ashworth's indentures to *Harold Wallington*. With racing restricted, *Wallington* subsequently moved his horses to Malton. By the time Ashworth was called up for military service in 1942, his riding opportunities had been limited. He served in the Black Watch, seeing active service in Sicily and Italy, but was returned home after his left shoulder was severely injured. Ashworth later rode in Belgium and India before returning to pick up his career in England.

In 1955 he married Janet, the daughter of fellow Epsom jockey Bert Packham, and the same year on *Wootton's* advice, he took out a trainer's licence. Initially he trained from The Grove Stables, where his owners included the jockey Charlie Smirke's brother-in-law. At the time it was assumed that Smirke would eventually take over the stable, but when Smirke retired from riding he left racing completely. In 1961 Ashworth moved to Treadwell House Stables, and the following year trained Lady Senator to win the Irish 1,000 Guineas. Noted as a trainer of fast early two-year-olds, Ashworth trained Lady's

20

View to win the 1968 Seaton Delaval Stakes at Newcastle. Pattern race success came in 1975 when Rorys Rocket won the Queen Mary Stakes. Ashworth also trained a few hurdlers, the best of which was Kas who won the 1977 Phillip Cornes Saddle of Gold Hurdle.

ATKINSON, Christopher	East Street	1871
(1843-?)		

Born in Gloucestershire, Atkinson moved to France where he married, he is shown on the 1871 census, as a "Trainer of Horses" with a French born wife and daughter, and a locally born son, but appears to have returned to France soon after.

ATTWATER, Michael	Racecourse Stables	2007
(1973-	Tattenham Corner	2008-

Michael Attwater rode as a conditional jockey for *Gary Moore*, before working as *John Akehurst's* head lad. He took a training appointment in Nottinghamshire, later spending a brief spell in Lambourn. In 2007, he moved to the Racecourse Stables and subsequently to Tattenham Corner.

BAILEY, Percy R.	The Grove	1947-1954
(1895-?)		

Percy Bailey was formerly headman to *Harry Hedges*, taking over at The Grove Stables from Hedges. Undoubtedly a skilful handler of modest horses, Bailey's name is forever linked with the Francasal coup that eventually cost him his licence.
Bailey's principal owner was William Rook who introduced Bailey to Maurice Williams, who owned horses in France. Williams owned a useful two-year-old named Santa Amara, he also had another two-year-old called Francasal. Although physically similar to Santa Amara, Francasal was quite moderate. On the 8th July 1953 Percy was informed that Williams was sending Francasal from France to Epsom, that he was to trot it, give it two steady canters then take it to Bath where it was entered for a race on 16th July. On the 11th July, both horses arrived in England and were taken to separate yards in Berkshire. On the 13th. July Bailey took delivery of Santa Amara believing that the horse was Francasal. On the morning of the Bath race, the telephone wire to Bath racecourse was cut; a syndicate involving Cardiff bookmaker Gomer Charles, Maurice Williams, and two other men placed £10,000 on the horse.
With telephone communication to the racecourse down, bookmakers off course were unable to hedge money back to the course, and "Francasal" started at 10-1. The horse was taken from the racecourse back to stables in Berkshire, where it was re-united with the real Francasal with a view to shipping the horses back to France immediately.

21

However, the bookmakers' organisations had already advised their members to withhold payment, and the Jockey Club alerted their police.

Percy Bailey insisted that he was not the trainer, but had merely agreed to act for Williams, who he had yet to meet, if he sent horses to England from France.

Maurice Williams, Gomer Charles, William Rook and two other men were charged with conspiracy to defraud. The men's defence was that the horses were unwittingly put in the wrong boxes when they left the stables at Sonning in Berkshire.

Rook was acquitted; Williams and Charles received two-year prison sentences. In 1966 Gomer Charleswas shot dead at his house in Cardiff.

Francasal and Santa Amara were auctioned at Epsom on 26th July 1954. Percy Bailey was warned off.

BAKER, James (1828-?)	West Hill	1871

Born in Maidstone, Baker is described as a farrier of racehorses in the 1871 census.

BALCHIN, Charles (c.1829-1862)	Turf Cottage, Sutton	1851-1862

Born in Paris, Charles Balchin shared the facilities with his brother *William Balchin* at Turf Cottage, Sutton, from c.1852-1854, and was sole trainer from c. 1855 until his death in 1862. In 1861 Balchin trained the Grand National winner Jealousy. Owned by Mr J Bennett and ridden by Joseph Kendall, the seven-year-old carried 9st 12lb when winning at a well-backed 5-1.

Charles Balchin was seriously injured when his horse and cart toppled down an embankment near Mitcham in November 1861, his nose was completely smashed, and his face badly lacerated.

He did not fully recover from the accident and died on 14th October 1862 at Turf Cottage.

The Morning Post recorded:

"Charles Balchin was a very worthy, kind-hearted young man, and in the preparation of horses for hunting and cross country purposes, had obtained wide celebrity. His premature death has caused much sadness among a large circle of friends connected with the turf and the chase."

BALCHIN, Francis A.	The Warren	1860-1867
(c.1823-1880)	South Hatch	1862

Born in Carshalton, Francis Augustus (Gus) Balchin was the third son of *James Balchin* to become a trainer, after a career as a jockey. Balchin trained from The Warren as private trainer for Mr G. Hodgman. Bell's Life 1860 lists him as training 12 horses, and he is shown as employing 11 staff in the 1861 census. The following year he trained Shilleleagh to win the King's Stand Stakes. In Bell's Life 1862 he is shown as training only three horses, and is based at South Hatch. This appears to have been a temporary arrangement, while *Ben Land* trained for Mr George Hodgman; by 1864 Balchin was back at "Warren House". In 1863 he trained Victor to win the Royal Hunt Cup, and in 1865 trained Verdant to win the Ebor Handicap. After leaving The Warren he purchased the stables known as Elm Lodge, at Telscomb, near Lewes for £1,550. He trained at Kentford, Newmarket in 1872, moving to Bloomsbury House, Newmarket in the following year.

BALCHIN, James	Sutton	1841-1851
(1796-1851)	Carshalton	1834-1840, 1851

Father of the three trainers, James Balchin is listed in Ruff's Guide 1851 with his address as Carshalton. He was based at Carshalton in 1834 and 1836 according to church records of his sons' baptism. The census returns for 1841 and 1851 list him as a trainer based at Sutton Village, close to Sutton station.

BALCHIN, William James	Turf Cottage, Sutton	1852-1854
(1824-1893)		

London-born William Balchin, son of *James Balchin*, shared the stables with his brother *Charles Balchin* in 1852-1854. In 1859, he was training at Chantilly in France. His five children were born at Chantilly between 1858 and 1870. Balchin died in France in 1893. He also acted as clerk of the course for race meetings held at Sutton.

BARCLAY, George jnr.	The Paddocks, Ashtead	1905-1907
(1887-1955)	Hillcrest	1921-1928
	Hillcrest	1930-1938

George Shea (1868-1944) is shown in the 1891 census as a sawdust dealer living in Southwark; married to Kate Shea, with children George and Richard. He subsequently became known as George Barclay a theatrical agent, and his wife, is better known as the Music Hall comedienne, Kate Carney. Barclay and Kate Carney had five children. Their sons, *George Barclay junior* and *Richard Barclay* both held a training licence.

George Barclay and Kate Carney for a while held the lease on The Grand in Clapham, a popular Music Hall, where they promoted their own shows. Kate Carney died in 1950, and was performing until shortly before her death. Barclay owned Lord Burleigh, who was strongly fancied for the 1922 Derby, but lost its chance when kicked on the way to start. George Barclay or Shea died in 1944 leaving effects of £10,920, 18 shillings to his widow Katherine Mary Shea.

BARCLAY, Richard Henry   Hillcrest   1930-1939
(1889-1970)

BARKER, Alfred Edgar Vere   1920-1925
(1899-1958))

Barker's family owned the Burnt Stub Mansion in Chessington. Sir Francis Barker sold the property in 1931 and the site was developed as Chessington Zoo, (later Chessington World of Adventures).
Following service in The Lancers "A.E.V. Barker" is shown as holding a licence to train in Ruff's Guide 1920. When *Stanley Wootton* commenced negotiations to purchase the gallops at Epsom "A. Vere Barker" was shown as a trainer using the Downs, by the time of completion Barker was no longer using the Downs.

BARKER, Charles   Heathcote House   1909
(1884-?)

Born in Leeds, Barker took over the training of the horses at Heathcote House in July 1909 following *William Holt's* death.

BARNARD, Herbert   1888
(1858-1889)

H. Barnard appears in Training Intelligence in the Sporting Life between January and April 1888, when he was training two horses, Resin The Bow and The Orangeman for Mr H. Collier. When Resin the Bow won at Plumpton, the Sporting Life noted that the horse was "well handled by H. Barnard, who also trains the horse." The horses subsequently changed ownership, but by the end of the year they were owned by Barnard, but now trained by *Henry May*.
The Sporting Life announced his death on Monday 19th.August 1889. "With much regret we announce the death of this well-known steeplechase rider, which occurred at Epsom at one o'clock on Saturday morning. The deceased, who was a son of Mr John Barnard, the proprietor of the outside stands at Epsom, had been suffering for some time from pleurisy and rheumatism."

However, the Croydon Advertiser and Surrey Reporter announced on, Saturday 24th.August 1889 that Barnard was still alive, and that it was his mother who died. The Sporting Life, 11th.September 1889, reported that Herbert had died on Monday 9th.September.

BARNES, Henry Dennis	Althorp Lodge	1888-1899
(c.1857-1932)	Bush Lodge	1899-1907
	Flint House	1911
		1919-1924

Dorset born Barnes was employed at Stevens' stable in Compton, Berkshire in 1881. Gallop reports for 13th.July 1888, record Barnes's horses working at Epsom. The Sporting Life, 5th.February 1890 lists Barnes as training four horses at Purley. He is listed in Osborne's Two-Year-Olds of 1899 as training at Althorp Lodge. He subsequently trained at Bush Lodge, Windmill Lane, and was at the Flint House in Ashley Road in 1911. In Charlie Smirke's autobiography Finishing Post, he recalls:

"I went to lodge on trial with Mr. Barnes, an Epsom owner-trainer who kept a few horses. I stayed there through the week, returning home at weekends."

BARNETT, C	Turbine Stud	1930-31

BARTON, Edward Irwin		1881
(1839-1884)		

Edward Irwin Barton is described as a trainer at his son's christening at Christ Church, Epsom in 1881.

BARTON, Thomas	Clay Hill	1869-1872
(1842-1914)		

Sheffield-born Barton is shown in Bell's Life as training four horses at Clay Hill in 1870, and two in 1872. He returned to Sheffield shortly after.

BATES, Edward	Althorp Lodge	1905-1909
(1870-?)	Heathcote House	1906
	Downs Lodge	1910
	The Rhodrons, Hook	1911
	Ashtead	1912-1913

Edward Bates, was born in Staffordshire. He held a National Hunt jockey's licence and worked for trainer James Hopwood at Hednesford, prior to commencing training.

25

BELL, Charles	Treadwell House	1940-1948
(1894-1959)		

Charlie Bell, served in the Royal Field Artillery during World War I. He rented Treadwell House stables from *Stanley Wootton* during the 1940s. When Wootton returned to training, Bell moved to Upavon in Wiltshire. He died at Newmarket in March 1959; he was head lad to trainer Harry Thomson Jones at the time of his death.

BELL, Henry or F.	1849
(1824-1870)	

H. Bell is listed in the York Herald, 3rd. March 1849 as training five horses for Mr Nevin at Epsom.
He is also shown as F. Bell in "Movements at Epsom" column in Bell's Life 18th. March 1849, possibly training at Walton Lodge. He also trained at Newmarket.

BELL, James	Down Cottage	1902
(1868-1934)	Uplands	1909
	Priam Lodge	1910-1913
	Woodcote Rise	1914-1929
	Heathcote House	1930-1934

James Mackie Bell was a cross-country jockey whose successes included victory in the 1897 Baden-Baden Steeplechase. He briefly trained at Carlisle before moving south in 1900. He was based at Epsom from 1900 to 1906, for part of that time *Samuel Ambler* was his nominee trainer. The Sporting Life, 23rd. December 1902 noted: "*Mr J.M. Bell has taken the stabling at Downs Cottage, Mr. Merrick's place at Epsom*"
Bell maintained that no man could train more than eight horses and put this into practice by dividing his string between Epsom and premises in Berkshire. From 1900 until 1914 the licences were held by Bell, his brother *Stuart Bell, Samuel Ambler* and *James Platt,* using Priam Lodge as their Epsom base. In 1909, Bell, described as a trainer of Hill House, Links Road, Epsom summoned *Richard Wootton* for assaulting him. During the case *Platt* was also described as Bell's trainer. After a five-hour hearing Wootton was bound over to keep the peace. At the time of the 1911 census James Bell was living at Priam Lodge. In 1914 Bell severed his connections with Berkshire, and moved all of his horses to Epsom where he enjoyed the most successful period of his career. Bell maintained his idiosyncratic methods of training; always keeping a small string that he could tend personally, and having the horses led to the gallops by lads mounted on ponies.
S. Theodore Felstead in the book Racing Romance describes Bell:

"Bell was one of the most enigmatical characters I ever met, impatient of the slightest contradiction, hard on his horses, and intolerant to a degree with the incompetent. No running horses down the course for him. He believed in his horses being fit to win when they ran, and fit they were, trained to the last ounce, superb jumpers, and ridden by nobody but the finest jockeys."

Felstead continued, *"for sheer efficiency in preparing winners, I never knew the equal of Jim Bell of Epsom. Tall, thin, with a weather beaten face, he was utterly ruthless with his horses- and his employees as well, if it comes to that. The horse that could frighten Bell wasn't born."*

Bell trained Trespasser, the greatest hurdler in the first half of the 20th.century. Trespasser won the Imperial Cup (in those days the equivalent of the Champion Hurdle) in three successive years, and the Two Thousand Hurdle at Manchester, a single event that was hurdle racing's richest prize at that time. Bell's first Imperial Cup victory was in 1908 with Perseus, ridden by his brother Stuart. The subsequent victories in the Imperial Cup were all partnered by *George Duller*; Vermouth in 1914, Trespasser in 1920, 1921, 1922, Peeping Tom in 1926 and Hercules in 1929. He trained the winner of the International Hurdle six times.

Jim Bell also trained Vermouth to win the 1915 Lancashire Chase, and the 1916 Grand National (run at Gatwick). He trained numerous winners on the Flat including the winner of the 1919 Queen Alexandra Stakes. In 1930 he moved to Heathcote House stables for the remainder of his career, in 1934 he was training only three horses as ill health took a hold. He died in a London nursing home on 29th. August 1934, and is buried in Epsom cemetery.

BELL, Major Marmaduke	The Grange	1915-1924
(1871-1949)	Reigate Road	

Major Marmaduke Bell, was the cousin of *Ossie Bell*. He trained at The Grange, Ewell. (later known as The Looe).

BELL, Oswald	Priam Lodge	1912-1914
(1871-1949)	The Grange	1913-1915, 1918-19

Captain "Ossie" Bell, was born in County Kildare, he moved to Australia where his father Sir Joshua Bell became Prime Minister of Queensland. After a spell as a trainer in India, Ossie Bell moved to Epsom. He served in the Worcestershire Regiment, and the Royal Flying Corps during the Great War. After leaving the army he trained at Lambourn (1919-1947), where his successes included the 1928 Derby winner Felstead, and the 1938 Oaks and 1,000 Guineas winner Rockfel. *Tommy Gosling* served his apprenticeship with Bell.

Oswald Bell left effects of £54,843.

BELL, Stuart	Woodcote Rise	1909-1912
(c.1866-1912)		

Stuart Bell was the brother of *James Bell*. Both were born at Douglas in Scotland, they rode as amateur jockeys, and commenced training at Carlisle. Stuart Bell remained in the north after his brother moved to Epsom; training at Malton, Middleham, and in Staffordshire, before arriving at Epsom, where he rode for his brother, and shared the training facilities at Woodcote Rise for a few years
He died from pneumonia on 12th.November 1912 at Stafford.

BENNETT		1897-1899

Possibly *Charles Bennett* (1843- ?). He was employed primarily as private trainer to Martin D. Rucker. An early pioneer in the automotive business, Rucker was involved with Daimler, Humber and the Dunlop tyre company. At Rucker's bankruptcy hearing in 1906, £23k of his losses were attributed to buying and selling racehorses. He also purchased Sefton Lodge stables at Newmarket, and a yacht.

BENNETT, Charles	Banstead	1861-1862
(1843-?)		

Bennett's career as a jockey commenced with *Charles Balchin*.
Bell's Life in London, 27th. October 1861 noted that Mr J. Bennett's horses have left C. Balchin's stables and are now trained by C. Bennett at Banstead. The same publication, 24th August 1862 noted:

"The promising young steeplechase rider and trainer, C. Bennett has left Banstead, and taken Englemere House, stables and grounds at Ascot."

BENNETT, Gilbert Nicholls	Shifnal Cottage	1920-1926
(1887-1963)		

Gilbert Bennett was a National Hunt trainer who moved to Sussex in 1926, where he held a licence until 1951, training at Jevington and Polegate. For the 1922 season he retained *Frank Wootton* as his first jockey. His career in Sussex was affected by financial problems in the 1930s that Bennett attributed inter alia to the loss of his principal patron, high overheads, and betting losses. In 1931 he had liabilities of £21,000 and assets of £189.

BENSTEAD, Christopher   Turbine Stud   1941
(1896-1969)

Father of *Ian and C. John Benstead*, Chris Benstead was a leading trainer under Pony Club Rules. He trained ponies at Ruxley Lodge, Claygate, c. 1932-1938, and was later based at the Turbine Stud.

BENSTEAD, C. John	Park Farm, Ashtead	1955-1956
(1928-	Startside	1959
	Hillcot	1960
	The Limes	1961-1998

John Benstead first took out a licence in 1955, training a few National Hunt horses at Park Farm Stables, Ashtead. He was later assistant to *Peter Thrale*; taking over the running of the stables on the latter's death, and moving to The Limes the following year on the retirement of *Johnny Dines*.

John Benstead's first major success on the Flat came with Operatic Society who won the 1959 Manchester November Handicap. The horse became a stable stalwart, winning 30 races in total.

Klondyke Bill, like Operatic Society formerly trained by *Peter Thrale*, won the Ayr Gold Cup, and was second in the 1962 July Cup.

Benstead enjoyed notable success over hurdles with Snuff Box who won the 1962 Oteley Hurdle, and Secret Agent who won the 1967 Feilden Hurdle. He rated Snuff Box as the best National Hunt horse that he trained, and believed it was a Champion Hurdle contender until injury curtailed its career.

John Benstead achieved an unusual feat when winning with Blue Refrain in three successive years at Royal Ascot in three different races. The horse won the Windsor Castle Stakes in 1978, followed by the Jersey Stakes in 1979, and the Queen Anne Stakes in 1980. Blue Refrain also won the 1980 Jubilee Handicap.

Benstead generally gave his two-year-olds plenty of time, but had an outstandingly sharp juvenile filly in Welshwyn who he described as "the second best two-year-old filly in Europe in 1980." Unfortunately, the best filly was the exceptional Marwell, and it was Welshwyn's fate to finish second to Marwell on several occasions, notably in the Cheveley Park Stakes.

Benstead also achieved much success with Baronet, who was a Cambridgeshire specialist, winning the race twice, (in 1978 and 1980), and finishing second twice. Baronet also won the 1980 Rosebery Stakes.

Benstead also had the distinction of training Sheikh Hamdan al Maktoum's first winner in Britain, Shaab, who won a race at Warwick in April 1979.

BENSTEAD, Ian	Fourfields Farm	1958-1966
(1935-		

The brother of *John Benstead*, Ian Benstead was apprenticed to his father, later taking out a licence to train at Fourfields Farm.

BENTLEY, James	The Durdans	1867-1869
(1847-?)	Smitham Bottom	1879

Born in 1847 in Lincoln, Bentley is listed in the Sporting Gazette in 1869 as training 10 horses privately for Mr Arthur Heathcote at The Durdans. Arthur "Squire" Heathcote, who was the son of Sir Gilbert Heathcote, (owner of Derby winner Amato); was Master of the Surrey Staghounds, and steward at the National Hunt meetings on Epsom Common. His most notable coup on the turf was the success of Beeswing, the winner of the 1867 Chester Cup. Squire Heathcote had £2,000 on Beeswing for the Ebor Handicap, the horse was described as "cantering at the distance", but jockey Prior took things too easily, and the horse was beaten on the line. Squire Heathcote died on Thursday 18th March 1869 aged 40.

The Sportsman, October 1879 noted:

"Jem Bentley who was so well known with the Surrey Staghounds, under the mastership of the Late Squire Heathcote, has taken up residence at Smitham Bottom, near Croydon, and will be glad to train for any nobleman or gentleman."

Bentley is described in the 1901, and 1911 census as a Horse Trainer living at The Crescent, Hawthorndene, Leatherhead.

BERG, Horace Samuel	Downs (Derby Arms)	1919-1921
(1868-?)		

Horace Berg's stables were listed as Downs House or The Downs, and were next to the Derby Arms. Berg, was a gullible man whose main owner was the unscrupulous Peter Barrie. Barrie created several fictional identities for horses, ran a three-year-old as a two-year-old, and on more than one occasion dyed a horse with henna to disguise its identity. When Berg discovered Barrie scrubbing a horse to remove the dye, Barrie explained that it was a "new American" treatment.

Barrie had six horses in his wife's name with Berg, and even more under aliases, leaving Berg heavily reliant on his patronage. Berg and Barrie bought an unraced three-year-old, Homs, from *Stanley Wootton*. The horse was with Berg only for a few days before Barrie set about disguising it as the two-year-old Golden Plate and sent it to Chester. However, a poor draw saw the horse defeated.

Barrie, who had been carrying out his frauds for over nine months, was by now under Jockey Club surveillance, and both men were arrested. Berg was eventually sentenced to nine months imprisonment, and Barrie to three years with hard labour.

BIRCH, Arthur   West Hill   1937-42, 1945-46
(c.1900-1993)

Birch was born in Lewes c. 1900. Birch's father, also Arthur Birch, rode Moifaa to victory in the 1904 Grand National. Arthur Birch senior suffered a severe injury after a fall from Black Ivory in 1907. He was left paralysed and died a few years later, leaving £2,846. Birch junior also rode under National Hunt rules. For most of his training career in Epsom, Birch was private trainer to Mr James Hayes. No record has been found as to where he was located, but *"Muddy" King* recalled that at one stage Birch had a couple of horses stabled at West Hill.

BLACKMORE, Michael W.   Myrtle Cottage   1944-1949
(1912-1982)

Michael Blackmore was born in Doncaster, and educated at Ampleforth. He commenced his training career at Letcombe in Berkshire, before moving to Myrtle Cottage stables in Rosebery Road. He moved to the expansive private stables at Whatcombe in Berkshire in October 1946. The adventure was short lived, and Blackmore moved back to Myrtle Cottage stables. Financial problems continued to plague his career, and he was declared bankrupt in 1951.

BLACKMORE, Philip Edward   Worple Road   1904
(1883-1970)

Blackmore was born in Alresford, Hampshire in 1883. He trained a few horses in 1904, but at the time of the 1911 census he was described as a veterinary assistant.

BLOSS, Robert   New Stables   c.1770-1782
(1737-1782)

Former jockey, Robert Bloss arrived in Epsom c. 1770, described as a "Training Groom and Publican", Bloss appears to have combined running the Horse and Groom stables in conjunction with the King's Head pub. Robert Bloss had four children christened at St Martin's, Epsom between 1770 and 1776. He died at Epsom 31st May 1782 "in the 45 year of his age", and is buried at St. Martin's, with his wife Ann Bloss.

BOAST, George   1839-1841
(1786-1867)

George Boast was born in Pocklington, Yorkshire, one of 13 children; and his riding career commenced in pony races around the New Inn in his native village. He moved on to racing stables at Malton, Middleham, and then to Newmarket where he worked in the stables of the Prince of Wales. Boast was riding Mr Stirling's horses trained by J*ames Balchin* in 1838, and rode Orange Boy in the Derby that year. The York Herald in 1839 lists him as training three horses for Mr Stirling at Epsom, a post he held until 1841.

BOOTH, William   Coulsdon   1873
(1850-1924)

William Booth is listed in the 1881 census as a Groom of Godstone Road, Coulsdon, but at the christening of his daughter at St Martins Church, Epsom in 1873 he is described as "trainer, Epsom." He was still based at Coulsdon in 1891, but by 1901 he was a groom based at Mospey, Burgh Heath Road. See also *Charles Lawrence*.

BOXALL, Arthur Stanley   Sandown Lodge   1932-1939
(1894-1939)

Boxall, a North London estate agent, trained a few horses at Sandown Lodge, and let boxes to various trainers. *Harold Wallington* and *Staff Ingham* operated from Sandown Lodge in 1939, and *Pat Donoghue* and *Roland Phillips* trained there under Pony Turf Club rules. When the Epsom Trainers' Association was formed in 1934, Boxall was the secretary, and *Stanley Wootton* the chairman. Boxall served as a councillor for Woodcote Ward in Epsom in 1938.
Boxall also owned a property in Wood Green, and also at East Wittering, Sussex where he died in 1939, leaving effects of £18,000.

BOYCE, Charles Frank   Horse and Groom   1855-1860
(1828-1868)

Boyce was born in Newmarket; where his grandfather, Richard Dixon Boyce (1770-1850), was a racehorse trainer. Charles Boyce rode as a jockey for Tom Oliver who trained at Cheltenham. In 1855, George Hodgman, who owned the Horse and Groom Stables in Church Street, employed Boyce as his trainer-jockey. Hodgman was proprietor of the Horse and Groom from 1855 to 1863, and leased The Warren for 14 years from 1860.

The Sporting Magazine Volume 130, August 1857 recorded:

"Charley Boyce was the trainer and rider of Emigrant, winner of the 1857 Grand National. He was the son of Frank Boyce the jockey. He spent some time with Balchin and with Tom Oliver at Prestbury. He set up for himself at Codford in Wiltshire but he did not stay long. He now appears to be settled on the more congenial soil of Epsom."

In the Spring of 1855, George Hodgman had been staying at the George Hotel, Shrewsbury. *Ben Land* was staying there with two horses - Odiham and Emigrant. Land lost heavily at cards, and remarked 'If things go on like this I shall have to sell Emigrant'. Hodgman was not a participant in the card game, but offered to buy Emigrant. Land wanted £600, Hodgman bargained to £590..

Hodgman recalls in the book 'Sixty Years on the Turf: The Life and Times of George Hodgman 1840 - 1900':

"I kept Emigrant at Epsom part of the summer, until the ground became very hard. Then I sent him to Codford, in Wiltshire, one of my other places. Late in the autumn he returned to Epsom, and commenced a preparation, extending the winter through, for the Grand National."

Boyce severely hurt his right arm when he was out hunting a week before the Grand National and rode in the race with the upper part of his right arm strapped to his side. The 1857 Grand National was run in torrential rain and saw seven false starts before it finally got underway. In an effort to find better ground, Boyce finished up on the canal tow path, and allegedly missed out several fences. *Ben Land,* having sold the winner after a game of cards, ironically owned the second Weathercock.

Hodgman, who described Boyce as *'a splendid specimen of physical development, and, singularly handsome; his manners were charming',* was a fearless gambler. The size of his win can be judged by the present of £1,000 that he gave Boyce. A "Baronet" who was in on the gamble also gave Boyce £500.

Boyce moved to Leicestershire, and bought the Black Swan Inn at Melton Mowbray. In 1860 Boyce, a livery stable keeper from Melton Mowbray, formerly of Epsom was declared bankrupt. He returned to race riding, and in total he rode in 13 Grand Nationals. He died in Hammersmith in 1868 leaving minimal effects.

BOYLE, James R.   South Hatch   2002-
(1973-

Boyle spent five years at Bristol University studying to become a veterinary surgeon. He later joined Paul Cole as an assistant trainer and on-site vet at Cole's yard in Whatcombe, Berkshire. After three years with Cole, he moved to South Hatch, Epsom succeeding *Nigel Hamilton* when taking an appointment working for South Hatch Racing. Initially Boyle shared the facilities with *John Akehurst*, but after improving the stable strength and number of winners, from 2005 he utilised both yards at South Hatch. In 2014 Boyle served as president of the National Trainers' Federation.

BRADLEY, Henry   Down Cottage   1845-1852
(1805-1861)

London-born Henry Bradley was training at Down Cottage, (designated as in Church Street), at the time of the 1851 census, (name given as Bradly), he had eight stable staff including two "visiting" jockeys from Ireland. As a jockey he had twice ridden the winner of Liverpool's Champion Hurdle, in 1843 when there were five runners, and 1844 when three of the six runners had taken part in the Grand National earlier in the afternoon. He trained Tragical to win the 1847 Royal Hunt Cup. He was private trainer to Count Batthyany, originally looking after his hunters. He was with the Count for 33 years until his death. He moved from Melton to Epsom, then in 1852 to Warren House, Newmarket.

BREASLEY, Arthur   South Hatch   1969-1975, 1980
(1914-2006)   Derby Stables   1979

Born in Wagga Wagga, New South Wales, Breasley was given the nickname "Scobie" at the age of six, in deference to the successful trainer James Scobie. Breasley recalled: "He was winning all the big races at the time. He lived in Wagga too. The name just stuck."
In a riding career spanning 40 years, Breasley rode 3,251 winners. He rode his first winner at the age of 14. In Australia, he won four successive Caulfield Cups between 1942 and 1945. Breasley came to Europe in 1950, winning the 2,000 Guineas a year later on Ki Ming. In 1954 he won the 1,000 Guineas on Mr J.A. Dewar's Festoon. In 1958 he rode Ballymoss to success in the Eclipse Stakes and the Prix de l'Arc de Triomphe.
He rode the winner of the Derby twice, in 1964 on Mr J. Ismay's Santa Claus, and in 1966 on Lady Zia Wernher's Charlottown. During his career he was champion jockey in Britain on four occasions.
Breasley retired from race riding in 1968, and purchased the South Hatch stables at Epsom. In 1970 he trained Great Wall and Yellow River to win the King Edward VII Stakes and Ascot Vase respectively.

His Classic success came in 1972 when Steel Pulse won the Irish Derby for Breasley's principal owner, the enigmatic Mr Ravi Tikkoo. Steel Pulse also finished second in the Prince of Wales's Stakes behind Brigadier Gerard and third in the Washington D.C. International. The closest Scobie came to Classic success in England was in 1975 when Hunza Dancer finished third in the Derby behind Grundy.

Breasley had Group 3 winners with Biskrah in the 1972 Doncaster Cup, Kesar Queen in the 1976 Coronation Stakes, and Hanu in the 1979 Cornwallis Stakes.

His handicap successes included Royben, who in 1971 did the Ayr Gold Cup and Portland Handicap double.

Breasley's other major success for Tikkoo was with Hittite Glory who won the Flying Childers Stakes at 100-1, and then went on to win the Middle Park Stakes.

Eight weeks after the Middle Park success, Tikkoo moved all his horses to Chantilly in protest against the imposition of Value Added Tax on bloodstock sales, and Scobie went to France as Tikkoo's private trainer, taking most of the lads from South Hatch with him. Breasley, who was by now 62, rose to the challenge of setting up home and business in a foreign country where he had little knowledge of the language. During an eight-month stay he had 41 winners from a string of 40 horses.

The venture ended in controversial circumstances when Tikkoo's horse, Java Rajah, showed traces of caffeine when tested at Longchamp. Ravi Tikkoo was convinced that the horse and the trainer were being used as some form of retribution for the disqualification of the French horse Trepan at Royal Ascot. Tikkoo promptly moved his horses from Chantilly to the United States, and Breasley moved once more. After training winners on the east coast and in California, Scobie found the lure of England and his family too much. He returned to Epsom with Tikkoo's horses in 1978.

Scobie Breasley retired from training in 1980, and following a spell as Tikkoo's racing manager, he went to live in Barbados, before returning to Wagga Wagga in 1990. His daughter Loretta was the first wife of *Brian Swift*.

| BRETT, Josiah | Field House | 1884 |
| (c.1845-c1915) | | |

Born in Chester, Brett trained at Beverley in 1882-1883. He succeeded Joseph French at Regal Lodge, Stables, Newmarket, in early 1884. Brett moved from Newmarket in November 1884, but moved back within a few weeks. He saddled one winner during his stay at Epsom.

From Newmarket he moved to Cheshire and then Aintree. At Liverpool Assizes in November 1886, he was sentenced to 12 months with hard labour for running the wrong horse in a race at Kelso in April. He was warned off, and on his release moved to Buenos Aires, and re-commenced training. The journalist William Allison visited him there, and described him as "a sterling sort, though inclined to fanciful stories."

BREWER, John Edward   Downs Cottage   1899-1900
(1868-1931)

Born in Victoria, Australia; Brewer moved to England after the death of his wife in 1898. He briefly trained at Lewes, moving to Epsom in April 1899. Brewer married Edith Nightingall (1871-1969), the sister of *William* and *Arthur Nightingall* on 16th June 1900, and then returned to Australia on 22nd June 1900.

An article in the Birmingham Daily Post, 10th January 1900 notes:

"J.E. Brewer, the Epsom trainer, has written to a friend in Melbourne that he would have won a fortune had The Grafter got home in the Cambridgeshire. He had the Melbourne Cup winner backed for a big stake at a long price."

The Grafter subsequently won the 1900 City and Suburban (at that time one of the major handicaps), landing a substantial gamble for Brewer. On Brewer's departure to Australia, The Grafter was transferred to *James Hickey*.

Brewer later returned to train at Park Lodge, Newmarket. In 1911 he purchased, (in partnership with *Richard Wootton*), the stud at the Kiacatoo Station, on the Lachlan river, New South Wales.

He returned to Australia, and in June 1913 sold his half share in the Kiacatoo Stud to *Richard Wootton* for about £40,000. In December 1913 he purchased 17,000 acres of the Merriwee Station near Condobolin, New South Wales for about £48,000.

BRISCOE, G.   Rowland Lodge   1919

The Hull Daily Mail, 24th December 1919 reported;

"G. Briscoe the trainer and jockey has taken up his residence at Rowland Lodge, Epsom, and will in future train Mr. N.M. Rhodes' horses there."

During the period 1919-1924, Briscoe continued to hold a National Hunt jockey's licence, and Rhodes held a trainer's licence.

BRITTLE, Charles   1909-1910
(1871-1932)

Born in Upton Upon Severn, Brittle later worked as a groom in the training stables at Royston, Hertfordshire.

36

BURBRIDGE, Wm. Jas.	South Hatch	1859-1864
(1826-1910?)	Smitham Bottom	1864-1867
	Kenley Hotel, Croydon	1870

William James Burbridge was born in Salisbury, Wiltshire. The Nottingham Guardian, 29th September 1859 noted, *"Burbridge has removed to South Hatch, occupying the stables adjoined by Hammond"*. Burbridge was training at Downs Hall Road, (now known as Burgh Heath Road) in 1861; the census of that year indicates that he employs four grooms.

He appeared in the Debtor's Court, described as "formerly of Ashtead, now of South Hatch, Epsom Downs, Trainer of Racehorses, and occasionally buying and selling racehorses." In 1864 the Sporting Gazette lists nine horses under his care at South Hatch, he was at Smitham Bottom during the latter part of that year. In Ruff's Guide 1870 he is shown as training at Kenley, Surrey. The following year he moved to Sussex, training at Polegate, and then Findon. He was training at Chichester in 1905. Sometimes noted as James Burbridge.

| BUTCHERS, Donald | Priam Lodge | 1956-1963 |
| (1911-1967) | | |

Don Butchers trained at Lewes, prior to moving to Priam Lodge, Epsom in 1956 when Gay Kindersley, the National Hunt enthusiast, and amateur jockey purchased the stables. Butchers trained Saffron Tartan to win the 1960 King George VI Chase, and the 1961 Cheltenham Gold Cup. In 1962 he trained Carrickbeg to win the Kim Muir Memorial Chase at Cheltenham.

He subsequently moved to Kindersley's stable at East Garston, but by now Kindersley was down to two horses. Living with Mr and Mrs Kindersley, Butchers was unsettled by the change in status from a trainer of the likes of Saffron Tartan, to virtual head lad. Despite the mutual strong bond between Kindersley and Butchers, he felt a break was essential, and surprisingly gave up his racing career in 1963. He died from a heart attack four years later. Peter Supple assisted Butchers during his time at Priam Lodge. Supple later trained at Southfleet, and in Hong Kong where he trained the winner of the 1976 Derby. Stable jockey Alan Oughton later trained at Findon, and his son David Oughton trained in Hong Kong.

| CALDICOTE/CALDICOTT, E.J | The Chalet | 1919-21 |
| (1881?-1950?) | | |

An owner/trainer based at The Chalet, he vacated the premises and moved his horses to Lewes in 1921.

CALEY,George Henry   Ashtead   1904
(c.1880-1945)

In the Western Times, 2nd August 1904, "Caley, Epsom" is recorded as the trainer of winning horse Princess Jessie. The Sunderland Echo, 1st September 1904 reported: "H. Caley *who is now training at Ashtead near Epsom has now handed in his riding licence.*" By the time of the 1911 census George Henry Caley, born in Windsor 1880 is described as a groom living in Burgh Heath Road.

CALTON, Henry   East Street   1881-1882
(1851-?)

Henry Calton, (sometimes known as Catton or Cotton), was born at Isleham in Cambridge. After working in stables at Newmarket, he had a brief training career. He was managing a few horses at stables in East Street at the time of the 1881 census. His brother James Calton, born 1845 in Isleham, also worked in the Epsom stables.

CAMERON, William Hunter   Bessa Bungalow   1923-25,
(1879-1959)   Priam Lodge   1925-30, 1933-34

Cameron is shown as living in Rosebery Road in the Electoral Register 1923-25, and subsequently at Priam Lodge.

CANNON, G.   The Warren   1908

G. Cannon was private trainer to *Ben Ellam* for approximately ten weeks during June to August 1908. Possibly T.L.G. Cannon (1872-1945), who subsequently trained in Berkshire.

CAREY, Tommy   Woodruff   1947-1962
(1905-1964)

After completion of his apprenticeship with *Stanley Wootton,* Carey had initially failed to make his mark as a jockey. He rode for *Pat Donoghue* under Pony Club rules, and was leading jockey in 1937 with 49 winners. While riding under Pony Club rules, he formed an alliance with leading owner, the enigmatic Miss Dorothy Paget; and took out a licence to ride under Jockey Club rules, primarily riding for Miss Paget. The crowning moment for the partnership was when Carey rode Miss Paget's Straight Deal to victory in the 1943 Derby.

As a trainer, Tommy Carey enjoyed the distinction of winning with his first runners on the Flat and over hurdles. The best horses Carey trained on the Flat were Le Sage who in 1951 won the Sussex Stakes and the Oxfordshire (now Geoffrey Freer) Stakes, and

Castleton who in 1952 won the King Edward VII Stakes, and the Blue Riband Stakes. He trained Prince Charlemagne to win the 1954 Triumph Hurdle, (the horse was ridden by Lester Piggott). In 1950 Carey's career received a considerable boost when The Gaekwar of Baroda transferred his horses to Carey. The Gaekwar had owned the winners of the St Leger and 2,000 Guineas in previous years, but moved his horses from Sam Armstrong at Newmarket to be nearer his Headley home. Armstrong had been offered the opportunity to move to Epsom but declined as he had recently bought stables at Newmarket. Tommy Carey later moved to train at Godalming, but died after taking an overdose of barbiturates.

CARTER, Herbert J.	Treadwell House	1899-1907	
(1868-1927)	Bruce Lodge	1908-1915	

Born in Carshalton, Surrey, Carter started his career at the age of 12, working for *James Adams* at Sutton. He trained the 1912 Royal Hunt Cup winner Eton Boy. He died 5th January 1927 leaving effects of £157.

CARTER, James	The Warren	1869

James Carter is recorded in Bell's Life training five horses at The Warren in 1869. Possibly James Carter, born 1811 in Cambridge, or James Carter born in Newmarket 1842; both were working in stables at Newmarket at the time of the 1871 census.

CARTER, Lee	Clear Height	2012-
(1969-		

Lee Carter was an apprentice jockey attached to *Reg Akehurst's* yard, and later rode for *Terry Mills*.

He worked for *John Akehurst*, prior to taking over the licence on 13th March 2012, and winning with his first runner, the Akehurst-owned Prince of Sorrento, on the following day.

CARTER, Walter	Loretta Lodge	1989-1992
(1936- 2011)		

Brother of the jockey Tommy Carter, and formerly head lad to *Brian Swift*, Carter trained Poets Cove to win the Group 3 Molecomb Stakes at Goodwood in 1990. Carter later became head lad for *Terry Mills*, and also *David Wilson*.

CARY, W.   1924

Cary was the owner/trainer of a few moderate horses in 1924.

CASTLE, John   The Warren   1872-1874
(1845-1914)

John Castle moved from Letcombe, Berkshire, (where he prepared horses with Tom Parr), to Epsom in 1872 to become private trainer at The Warren to *Benjamin Ellam*. Castle trained 27 horses in 1873, and 13 in 1874. He later moved to Worsley, Lancashire where he managed Lord Ellesmere's stud, and then to Newmarket.

CASWELL, Edward   1878
(1835-1900)

Caswell spent the major part of his career at Lewes, and was temporarily nominee trainer for *Richard Drewitt's* widow. He is shown as training 13 horses at Epsom in the York Herald's "Horses In Training" section 1878.

CHANDLER, James   Woodcote Lodge   1877-1882
(c.1853-1906)   Dorking Road

Chandler was born at Reading in Berkshire. After training in Gloucestershire, he moved to Epsom. His 1881 address is given as Mr Case Walker's training stables, Dorking Road. At this time he managed a large stable with 12 staff living in. He left Epsom in 1882 to move to Lambourn where he spent the remainder of his career. He was living at Lambourn House when he died leaving effects of £2380.

CHARLTON, Henry   Farm Stables   1899-1900
(1873-?)

Training Intelligence in The Sporting Life 15th February 1900, lists him under Epsom Trainers, and he appears in gallops reports in the Sporting Life during 1899. He was private trainer to *John Coleman*, after a spell riding for *Coleman*. Charlton broke his leg while riding at Lewes, he then became a publican in Epsom, prior to moving to Warwickshire as a stud groom.

CHILDERS, Mr.   1877

"Mr. Childers" is shown in the Sporting Clipper, January 1877 as training one horse at Epsom.

CHISMAN, T.W.   Mickleham   1936-?

Horse trader, occasional trainer and riding school proprietor based at Mickleham, his son Peter Chisman was later a jockey and trainer.

CLEMENTS, John Albert   Heath House   1903-1906
(1868-1940)

Born in Devizes, he was private trainer to *Francis Cobb*, subsequently following Cobb to Lambourn.

COBB, Francis   Heath House   1891-1903
(1864-1945)

Born in Kingston-Upon-Thames, Cobb attended Eton College, where he was an outstanding sportsman, particularly excelling at rowing. He trained his own horses at Burgh Heath from 1891, but was residing for part of the time at Hanover Square, London; later moving to Berkshire where he eventually became a farmer. He died at his estate Woodway, Blewbury leaving effects of £50,185.

COLEMAN, John Francis   Farm Stables   1904-1906,1910
(1862-1923)   1917-1918,1920

A veterinary surgeon, Coleman also held a training licence at Farm Stables in Church Street/Downside. He trained and, on occasions, rode his own horses, mainly jumpers. He was also notably successful in the show jumping ring. He was resident at the Farm Stables when he died in 1923 leaving effects of £33,554. Also see *Henry Charlton*.

COLLINS, Patrick W.   York House   1887-1888
(1861-?)

Collins trained for Baron Topper Laski and Herr Oehlschlager, and was one of a succession of private trainers for the gentlemen and their associates, see also *Lutten, Moore, M'Lean* and *W. Jones*. Collins and *W.H. Moore* later moved to Weyhill, where they trained three Grand National winners: Why Not, Soarer, and Manifesto. The Sporting Life credits Collins as trainer, but other sources credit *Willie Moore*. *Arthur Nightingall*, who rode Why Not to victory, confirms *Moore* as the trainer in his book *My Racing Days*.

CONSTABLE, Charles   Primrose Cottage,   1883
(1857-1900)   The Parade

Born in Bayswater, and the brother of *Henry Constable*, Charles Constable resided at Primrose Cottage following his brother's death. At the time of his daughter's baptism in 1883 he was described as a "trainer", but by 1886 a "late trainer", and subsequently as a groom.

CONSTABLE, Henry   The Durdans   1880-1881
(1854-1881)

Henry Constable was born in Paddington, London in 1854; he came to Epsom c. 1868 to work as an apprentice jockey for *William Reeves*, at Down Cottage. In 1874, he purchased 26, The Parade, Epsom, subsequently known as Primrose Cottage in honour of Lord Rosebery.
His successes as a jockey included riding Sefton to win the Derby in 1878. His last ride as a jockey was in 1880 when he finished third in the Cambridgeshire Handicap but was showing signs of weakness.
He was also "supervising the training" of Lord Rosebery's horses by this time.
Constable died in February 1881 of consumption, having already abandoned his career as Lord Rosebery's trainer due to his decreasing health.
He left an estate of £8,000, requesting that Lord Rosebery act as trustee for his mother Mary and sister Ellen. Lord Rosebery was moved by the tragic early death of his loyal and likeable employee, and paid for Henry's elaborate memorial in Epsom cemetery. Protected by a low box hedge, the tombstone is a base of red Balmoral granite, with a suspended memorial stone above. The stone is supported at the four corners by carved angels; the front two face Lord Rosebery's home The Durdans, the back two have their heads turned so that they are looking towards The Durdans also. There is an inscription that says, "Erected by his friend and employer Archibald, Lord Rosebery".
After Constable's mother's death, Lord Rosebery conveyed Primrose Cottage to Constable's daughter Ellen. Henry's brother, *Charles Constable*, also lived there for a short period. Charles Constable was related by marriage to *John Sherrington* and *Robert Wyatt*.

COODE, William   Royal Oak, Purley   1878-1881
(1832-1898?)

Coode is listed in Ruffs Guide, as training at the Royal Oak, where he was licensee. Horses also ran under the name J. Coode training at Caterham. William Coode junior rode most of the runners and later worked as a groom in the Epsom stables. "Goode" is listed as an Epsom-based trainer in the Sheffield and Rotherham Independent 19th June 1879.

COOKSON, Ernest Sawrey   Woodfield, Ashtead   1904-1906
(1867-1948)

Cookson commenced his training career in Yorkshire, and was a Captain in the West Yorkshire Regiment. He was living at Ixworth near Newmarket in 1901, and subsequently moved to Epsom. When the Epsom Grandstand Association introduced a weekly fee for horses using the gallops for training purposes, Cookson objected, claiming that he was allowed free access to the Downs as much as any other Epsom resident. After an acrimonious exchange of correspondence, Sawrey Cookson applied for a licence to train at Newmarket; eventually he moved to Kent. He had married in Australia in 1898 to Amy Coles of Leybourne Stud, West Malling, Kent. For a while Pony racing was held at the West Malling racecourse, in 1931 Cookson was involved in legal action against the Stewards of the Pony Turf Club after being posted on the forfeit list for non-payment of prize money. Cookson's defence was that his wife owned the racecourse not him. Cookson acknowledged his previous business record, which included bankruptcies in 1894 and 1912, and several county court judgements.
He died in 1948 at Welwyn effects of £714 11s. were left to his wife Amy Sawrey-Cookson.

COPPIN, John   Duke of Wellington   1869
(1846- 1908?)

Born in Skipton, Yorkshire in 1846, Coppin worked for *F.A. Balchin*, then moved to become head lad for *James Bentley*. When Mr Heathcote disposed of his bloodstock, Coppin started training in his own right from the "new" Duke of Wellington stables.
The Sportsman 19th March 1869 notes under Epsom Training Reports:

"Skirmish, Dundee colt, Monitress, and Ampleforth did steady work under the care of Coppin."

The Sportsman 12th May 1869 notes:

"Coppin sent Gypsy King a good half speed gallop of a mile."

COTTON, Henry

See CALTON, Henry.

COTTERELL-DORMER, Clement
See *Clement Dormer.*

COTTRILL, Henry L.   South Hatch   1916-17
(1883-1955)

Harry Cottrill, trained at Tarporley in Cheshire and later at Letcombe, Berkshire. During the Great War he leased part of South Hatch from *William Nightingall*.
He moved to Heath House, Newmarket in April 1917; and then, subsequently to Seven Barrows in Lambourn where he later trained Adams Apple to win the 1927 2,000 Guineas, and Lovely Rosa to win the 1936 Oaks.

COVE, Henry J.   Rowland Lodge   1907-08
(1865-1958?)

Originally from Somerford, Wiltshire, Cove was a groom based near Cheltenham in 1901, after a brief stay at Epsom he returned to Gloucestershire.

COVINGTON, Alexander   Bruce Lodge   1899-1900
(1875-?)   Down Cottage   1900-1903

Alex Covington arrived in London, from America, on 21st November 1898, describing himself as a "horseman". *Philip S. Greusel* accompanied him.
Covington and Greusel, appear to have arrived in Epsom as part of a short-lived and relatively unsuccessful "US invasion", (see *Philip S. Greusel* and *C. Riley*).
Covington trained briefly at Bruce Lodge, but The Birmingham Daily Post 15th June 1900 noted:

"Mr. Covington has given up training for Mr McCreery and has moved his horses from Bruce Lodge to Downs Cottage".

CRACKNELL, Thomas   Heathcote House   1905
(1872-1953?)

In 1905 Thomas Cracknell described himself as an "Epsom trainer." He was described as a stableman in the census of 1891, living at Priam Lodge, and a stableman in the 1901 and 1911 census. The 1905 Register of Electors shows him based at Heathcote House with *William Holt*.

CRAVEN, Captain Edward   Wayside, Worple Road   1924-1925
(1862-1942)

Edward Stamford Craven trained in Hertfordshire in 1911, and then at Nepcote Lodge, Findon prior to 1915; taking out a licence again in 1924 to train at Epsom, based in the Caithness Stables.

CROUCH, Frederic   Church Street   1850-1851
(1819?-?)

Born at Six Mile Bottom, Newmarket, Frederic Crouch is shown in the 1851 census as a jockey living in Epsom. Crouch rode in the Derby five times between 1843 and 1850. Sporting Intelligence, April 7th 1851 recorded:

"F. Crouch , the trainer has given up his stables at Epsom and is engaged by the Earl Of Remonstrate with whom he has gone to Mitchell Grove-Count Batthyany now being his second master, and the Earl of Warwick third."

Crouch later worked in stables in Berkshire, and Staffordshire before leaving racing and settling in Essex.

CULLEN, William Parke   Heathcote House   1915
(1861-1937)

A former National Hunt jockey, Cullen was private trainer to Sir William Nelson. He was training at Shrewton in Wiltshire during the early part of the 20th century. He moved to Heathcote House in 1915, but by July of that year left and relocated to Lambourn. Cullen later trained in Ireland, he died in Galway, leaving effects of £891 in England.
His nephew Frank Cullen (1891-1920), was stable jockey for *William Nightingall*, he died after breaking his neck in a fall during a chase.

CURTIS, Roger   Ermyn Lodge   1989-1992
(1949-2018)

Roger Curtis trained mainly National Hunt horses from Ermyn Lodge stables between 1989 and 1992. Either side of this period he was based at New Lodge Stables in Carshalton, also using New Lodge as an overflow during his time at Ermyn Lodge. Other trainers to use New Lodge include David Jermy, and Tommy Masterson. Roger Curtis's major success was with Mister Ed who won the 1993 Midlands Grand National when ridden by *Derek Morris*. While at Ermyn Lodge, Curtis's most prolific horse was St Athans Lad who won nine times at Fontwell during one season. Curtis subsequently moved to Lambourn.

DALE, L. Sid   Startside   1960-1973
(1915-2006)

Sid Dale was the son of David Dale who trained at Seaford. He served in World War II receiving a "mention in dispatches". In 1945 Sid Dale became head lad to Captain Ryan Price at Lavant, and later moved with Price to Findon. When Price lost his licence, Dale moved to Epsom with a number of the horses notably Kilmore, who was beaten favourite for the Grand National while at Epsom.

Sid Dale, made an impressive start to his career at Epsom by winning the Whitbread Gold Cup with Plummer's Plain. The following year he won the Chester Cup with Hoy. Dale also had charge of the great Mill House when the horse first came over from Ireland. Dale trained the winner of the Imperial Cup twice, with Invader in 1964 and Spy Net in 1972. Former stable apprentice Geoff Lawson, who was later assistant trainer to Guy Harwood at Pulborough, rode the latter.

DANIELS, George S.   1869-1870

Probably jockey Samuel Daniels (1844-1881). In December 1869, owner Mr Atkins moved his horses to be trained "privately." Daniels was training and riding them, (occasionally assisted by *Lewin*). From February 1870, the horses ran under the ownership of Mr W. Crook, but were still trained by Daniels until circa April 1870. The core of the horses then moved to *Moreten/ Martin,* and then to *Robinson.*

DAVIES, Jeffrey	Ermyn Lodge	1986
(1947-	Shifnal Cottage	1987

Formerly apprenticed to George Todd at Manton, Davies trained briefly in Epsom before moving to Sussex.

DAVIES, W.   Maidstone House   1882

Listed in The Sporting Life, as private trainer to *Jesse Winfield* in 1882

DAWSON, Peter   Mayfields   1962-1971
(1935-

Peter Dawson was apprenticed to Peter Cazalet at Tonbridge, and took out a licence to train at Mayfields Stable, Kingswood, following a spell training in Sussex. The best horse trained by Dawson was Majetta who finished third in the 1968 July Cup, and third in the Goodwood Mile that year.

DAY, Edward   Lower Ashtead   1871
(c.1834-?)

Son of the Stockbridge trainer John Barham Day (1793-1860), Edward Day is shown in the 1871 census as "A Training Groom", based in Lower Ashtead, with his wife, and three sons including *Ernest Day.*
The Penny Illustrated Paper, 31st October 1881 noted:

"Edward Day, brother of John and William Day, has arrived safely in Australia with the mares and foals purchased in England by Sir Hercules Robinson for the Auckland Stud Company."

Edward Day was living alone in Westminster at the time of the 1881 census, and left for Australia soon afterwards.

DAY, Ernest   The Parade   1901
(1862-?)

Son of *Edward Day*, and shown in the 1901 census as a "Trainer of Racehorses".

Sheffield Evening Telegraph, 12th February 1895 noted:

"Mr. Ernest Day of Epsom, a nephew of the late John and William Day, is the gentleman entrusted to fetch Carbine to England for the Duke of Portland. He is the gentleman who took Ormonde to South America and brought him back again."

DAY, John   Heathcote House   1914-15, 1919-20
(1869-1949)

Grandson of John Barham Day (1793-1860); after two years at Epsom, he moved to Lambourn in 1916, and Newmarket the following year, returning to Epsom briefly in 1919. He was living in Southampton at the time of his death.

DAY, Samuel   poss. Surrey Yeoman,   1844
(1801-1866)   Burgh Heath

Sam Day, brother of John Barham Day, was born at Stockbridge, Hampshire. For much of his career he was known as "Old Sam Day" to differentiate him from his nephew "Young Sam" who rode the 1838 St Leger winner Mango and died a year later following a hunting accident.
"Old Sam" rode the Derby winners in 1821 on Gustavus, and 1830 on Priam. Due to continuing weight problems Day retired and took up farming.

In May 1836 The Sporting Magazine noted:
"Old Sam Day, sick of tilling the land, succeeds Scott in the late W. Day's stables at Ascot Heath."

In July 1843, Day appeared before the bankruptcy courts seeking discharge. The Sportsman's Gazette 19th May1844 noted:

Pedigree and Performance of Derby Runners:

Mr Dixon's Arethusa   *Trained by S. Day at Epsom*

Mr Dixon's Dick Thornton   *Trained by S. Day at Epsom.*

The Era 21st April 1844 records Day as training nine horses for Mr Dixon.
Old Sam Day then shed 3 stone to make his comeback as a jockey, and did the Epsom double in 1846.
He retired from riding once more, and with the patronage of John Gully (for whom he rode the 1846 Derby winner Pyrrhus The First), he recommenced training, this time at Newmarket.
He broke his leg in 1852 after jumping from a cart while travelling to Goodwood, and repeated the accident in 1854 near Denham House, Uxbridge.
John Day junior trainer of Derby winners Andover 1854, and Cossack 1847; and Oaks winners Mincepie 1856, and Cymbra 1848, subsequently used the stables at the rear of the Surrey Yeoman (See Part 3, "Reigate Road") for his Epsom runners, it was possibly here that Sam Day was based during his brief career at Epsom.

DEACON/DEAKIN, J   1875

The York Herald, 22nd January 1875, records J. Deacon as training three horses at Epsom, he had previously been a National Hunt jockey.
Possibly John Deakin b. 1835 Staffordshire, resident at Newmarket c. 1873.

DELLOR, E.   Althorp Lodge   1900

The Birmingham Daily Post, September 8th 1900 noted:

"E. Dellor, son of Mr. A. Dellor, who trains with Charles Arnull at Epsom, has left for Rumania, where he has a two-year engagement to ride for Mr. Phillips."

DENSON, Andrew   The Chalet   1990-1991
(1964-   Caithness   1993

Denson is the son of former National Hunt trainer Bill Denson. He was based at The Chalet, and also had a short spell in Caithness Stables, (renamed Ashley Racing Stables during Denson's stay.)

| DICK, David P. | Glanmire | 1930-41, |
| (1897-1989) | | 1947-61 |

Glasgow-born David P. Dick, came to Epsom to serve his apprenticeship with *Richard Wootton*. He served in the First Dragoon Guards during World War I, and was stationed in India 1916-19, resuming his riding career in 1920. On retiring from riding in 1930 Dave Dick took out a licence to train a small string of horses at Glanmire Farm on Epsom Common. He trained Celibate II to win the 1940 Liverpool Hurdle. His son David V. Dick was apprenticed to him, and rode the winner of many major races including the Lincolnshire Handicap, the Grand National and the Cheltenham Gold Cup. His younger son Jonathan was also apprenticed to him and rode 26 winners.

| DICK, Robert | Mannamead | 1937-1946 |
| (1907-1946) | | |

Bobby Dick was the brother of *David P. Dick*. A third brother, John Dick, worked for *Richard Wootton,* but he died in 1915 after an accident on the gallops, at the age of 11. Bobby Dick was apprenticed to *Stanley Wootton,* and was subsequently the retained jockey for *Walter Nightingall*; and for Lord Astor for whom he won the 1936 2,000 Guineas on Pay Up, and the 1936 Eclipse Stakes on Rhodes Scholar.
Dick rode three winners for Lord Astor at Ascot in 1937 and following a subsequent gift from the owner, purchased Mannamead (named after his favourite horse). Dick died in 1946 after catching pneumonia, leaving £8,712.

| DICKENSON, Thomas W. | | 1907 |

Thomas Dickenson, born 1870 Pontefract, was a National Hunt jockey based at Burgh Heath circa 1900-05. He trained three winners on the Flat in 1907.

| DILLY, John | Horse and Groom Stables | 1797-? |

The Racing Calendar for 1797 contained the following advertisement under 'Training Stables, Epsom':
"John Dilly Begs Leave to inform the Noblemen and Gentlemen of the Turf, that he intends (for the Benefit of his Mother) to Take In Horses To Train, and Hunters To Stand At Livery, at the Stables of his late Father; where Gentlemen may depend on every proper Attention being paid to such Horses, &c. as they may be pleased to fend him, and their Favours will be gratefully acknowledged."
John Dilly, appears to have succeeded his father Thomas. His mother Ann Dilly died in 1825 and is buried in St. Martin's Churchyard, Epsom. Ownership of the Horse and Groom changed on 23rd December 1801, it is unclear if John Dilly remained as tenant to that date.

DILLY, Thomas	Horse and Groom	1796

Thomas Dilly was buried in St. Martins Churchyard in November 1796, and was succeeded at the Horse and Groom Stables by his son *John Dilly* (see above).

DINES, James (Johnny)	Larchfield	1936-40
(1896-1968)		1944-58

"Johnny" Dines, rode the winners of many of the major handicaps as a jockey. He was apprenticed to Irish trainer J. Musker, and rode over 500 winners in five years before relocating to Epsom to ride for *James Killalee*.
Dines trained the winner of the Cambridgeshire, Artists Prince, in his first season as a trainer.
His other major training successes were achieved with Careless Nora the 1948 Nunthorpe Stakes winner; Rose Of Torridge, winner of the 1948 Princess Margaret Stake; and Harwin winner of the 1953 Oxfordshire Stakes and 1954 John Porter Stakes.

DIXON, Mark	Ermyn Lodge	1992-1995
(1961-		

Dixon was formerly assistant trainer to David Oughton at Findon, after leaving Epsom he trained with much success in South Africa.

DIXON, (See NIXON)		1884

DOCKERAY, George Derby	Mickleham	1839-1842
(c.1792-1857)	Horse and Groom	1843-1853
	Mickleham	1853-1855

Carshalton-born George Dockeray was a successful jockey whose numerous victories included the 1826 Derby on Lapdog, and the 1829 Oaks on Green Mantle. After retiring from riding he was initially based at Mickleham, moving to Epsom for approximately ten years when based at Horse and Groom Stables, adjacent to the Kings Head. In the 1851 census he had 11 stable staff resident with him indicating a large training operation for the time. Dockeray trained three, probably four Grand National winners.
In 1839 a Harrow-based horse trainer called John Elmore sent a horse called Lottery to Dockeray. Elmore had raced the horse at the central London racecourse Bayswater Hippodrome, and at Finchley and Kensal Green, before deciding that with proper schooling the horse would jump from "Hell to Harrow."
Lottery won the 1839 Grand National in a canter. The Daily Telegraph, 26th February 1839, under the headline *"New 'chase an outstanding success: Favourite Lottery wins"* recorded:

"They came from far and wide, thousands of visitors pouring into Liverpool by road, rail, and canal, in stately carriages, the new steam trains, and paddle-boats, on horseback and on foot. The attraction was the great steeplechase at Aintree, and the talk for days had been about nothing else.
Ridden by Jem Mason, Lottery was in command as they finally entered the straight, and a prodigious leap at the last left him well clear."

Because of the huge crowds, delays in weighing out, and several false starts, the race went off two hours late.
Lottery went on to win at Cheltenham, Stratford, Maidstone and Dunchurch. Some tracks advertised races as "Open to all except Lottery" or "Entry Fee £10, Lottery £40". In 1839 and 1840 Lottery won the Grand Annual Chase at Cheltenham, on the second occasion carrying over 13 stone. In 1841 Lottery won the Cheltenham Steeplechase, and was allotted an 18lb penalty for the Grand National, but pulled up in the race. Dockeray used Lottery as a hack afterwards, but the horse apparently finished his years pulling a cart at Neasden.
In 1840 John Elmore owned the winner Jerry, although some records give the owner as Lord Suffield or Mr Villebois. In 1842 John Elmore's Gay Lad won the Grand National. However www.aintreegrandnational.co.uk states:

"The winner "Gaylad" was owned by John Elmore, who had also owned "Lottery" when he won the 1839 Grand National along with trainer George Dockeray who won for an impressive third time in 1842 after also training "Lottery" three years ago and "Jerry" when he rode to victory in 1840."

In 1852 Dockeray won the Grand National again with Miss Mowbray. Bells Life 22nd February 1852 has a complete list of trainers for that year's National confirming Dockeray as the trainer. Miss Mowbray was second the following year. In 1854, she was a well-backed favourite, but became the first Grand National favourite to be subject to foul play.
Dockeray trained another great steeplechaser from that era, The British Yeoman, who finished third in the 1848 Grand National, and ran consistently well under big weights. In 1848 the horse won valuable chases at Bath, Windsor, and Newmarket, and in April and November 1849 he won both runnings of the Grand Metropolitan Chase. The British Yeoman was also owned by John Elmore.
There was an illustration of the horse Adine in "The Era" 31st July 1853, described as "Trained by George Dockeray at Epsom" winner of 1852 Ebor Handicap and 1853 Goodwood Stakes. The York Herald lists Dockeray as having 29 horses in training in 1853 including Adine.
On the Flat other prestigious winners were The Conjuror who won the 1846 Ascot Trial Stakes, (now the Queen Anne Stakes), and Mounseer who won the 1850 Chester Cup.

The Conjuror was owned by the financier Edward Rawson Clark, who sometimes raced under the name "D'Orsay". Clark owned many horses in training at Epsom, notably The Conjuror, and six Derby runners trained by Dockeray.

In February 1855 Dockeray arrived at Newmarket to train for Messrs. Greville and Payne.

In 1857 he was training at Newmarket according to Ruffs Guide, he died at Newmarket that year. His first wife Mary, who died on 23rd January 1828; and his second wife Catherine, died 11th November 1850, are buried together in St. Martin's Churchyard, Epsom.

In his will made on 7th November 1850, Dockeray bequeathed all of his "state and effects" to his grandson *Joseph Dockeray.*

DOCKERAY, Joseph	Horse and Groom	1855
(1833-1881)	Mickleham	
	East Street	1871

Born in Epsom, Joseph Dockeray was the grandson of *George Dockeray,* and son of *Thomas Dockeray.* He was apprenticed to his grandfather, about 1857 he moved to Russia to ride, and in 1859 is listed as training 16 horses there.

Kelly's Directory for 1855 shows him as a trainer at Church Street, Epsom, but he was at Mickleham with his father later in the year. After a return to England, he moved to Hungary in 1867. In 1869 he commenced training at Chiseldon, Wiltshire, but was back at Epsom in 1871. He was based in Germany in 1874. At the time of his death in 1881 he was living in St Pancras describing his occupation as Huntsman/Horse Trainer.

DOCKERAY, Thomas	Mickleham	1855
(1808-1874)	Pikes Hill	1871

Son of *George Dockeray;* following his father's move to Newmarket in 1855, a note appeared in the papers that Dockeray's son and grandson had taken over the training grounds and stables at Mickleham, and "will be glad to take any horses entrusted to them." Dockeray's wife Ann, who died on June 29th 1849', is buried in St. Martin's Churchyard, Epsom.

DOGGETT,	1899-1900

Training Intelligence in The Sporting Life 15th February, and 19th October 1900, lists him under Epsom Trainers. He also appears on gallop reports in late 1899. Doggett was training horses for French owners.

DONNELLY, William	Sandown Lodge	1920-1922
(1874-1934?)	Priam Lodge	1923-1924

Former National Hunt jockey William J. Donnelly, was born 1874, in Cheshunt, Herts. Donnelly served his apprenticeship with *Thomas Sherwood*. He became private trainer for *A. Simpson* after riding for him. *Simpson* took out a licence to train his own horses at Priam Lodge in 1922. Donnelly was a witness for the prosecution in the case against Peter Barrie (see *Samuel Berg*.) He described how Shining More was bought to him with her coat so bad he "thought the mare was suffering from skin disease", after Donnelly had cared for the horse Barrie took her away again. Donnelly was living in South Hatch Cottage in 1918.

DONOGHUE, Patrick Joseph	Sandown Lodge	c1935-1936
(1910-1980)	Gondola	1937
	Woodruff	c1938-1939

The son of *Steve Donoghue*, Pat was apprenticed to *Stanley Wootton*. As a jockey he rode in the Derby three times, 1929, 1933, and 1940; on each occasion his father had a mount in the race too. Pat Donoghue trained under Pony Club Rules. He employed *Tommy Carey* as his jockey, and Miss Dorothy Paget became his principal owner. In 1936 he won the Northolt Derby with Ethlestone; and in 1939, he trained Scottish Rifle to win Northolt's top two races; the Metropolitan, (prizemoney £500), and the Northolt Derby (prizemoney £1,000) for Miss Paget. He was leading trainer under Pony Club Rules with 44 winners.
Following Miss Paget's decision to sell her ponies in 1939, Pat Donoghue made a brief comeback as a jockey.

DONOGHUE, Steve	Woodruff	1938-1939
(1884-1945)		

In the 1920s the familiar shout on the racecourse was 'Come on Steve' as British punters urged on their sporting idol. Born in Warrington, Steve Donoghue had his initial rides in France and Ireland. He returned to England with a retainer for *Henry Persse's* Stockbridge stable in 1911, and in 1913 he rode the famous The Tetrach for *Persse*. Donoghue was champion jockey on ten occasions, and rode six Derby winners. By his early twenties he had a large house complete with chauffeur, cook and gardener, and a flat in Park Lane with a valet and a housekeeper.
Steve Donoghue appeared in the 1938 Horses In Training as training 31 horses at Woodruff. The arrangement was short lived, stables at Blewbury, Berkshire became available, and Donoghue moved. Training success was limited partly due to wartime restrictions. He left effects of £19,514.

DONOHUE, William
(?-1910)

William Donohue, described as a trainer, died at Banstead Asylum in 1910, and is buried in Epsom Cemetery.

DORMER, Clement	Burgh Heath	1896-1898
(1863-1906)		

Also known as Clement Cotterell-Dormer.
The York Herald reported in February 1896, that *Thomas Hacking* had been appointed to take charge of Mr Dormer's horses. The arrangement was short lived, and from July onwards, training reports in the Sporting Life make reference to "Mr Dormer's horses." From 1898-1900 Mr Dormer was resident at Uplands, Downs Road. In 1898 the register of Electors lists him as residing at Uplands, and Burgh Heath.
His son Clement was killed at Ypres in 1914, another son Charles was killed in action in 1915.

DOW, Simon	Wendover	1988-1991
(1961-	Clear Height	1992-2015
	Thirty Acre Barn	2015-2016
	Clear Height	2016-

Simon Dow for many years took on the role of chairman of the Epsom Trainer's Association, and was also a founder of the Epsom Training and Development Fund set up to provide living accommodation and support for stable staff. He followed in the tradition of the old Epsom trainers, enjoying success under both codes, and always giving apprentices plenty of opportunities. Paul Doe, and Alan Daly were notably successful apprentices attached to Dow's stable. Simon Dow's best flat horse was Young Ern, an unfashionably bred colt, who won the Prix du Palais Royal at Longchamp, and the Hungerford Stakes at Newbury in 1994, and was beaten a short head in the Group 1 Prix de Maurice Gheest in 1995. Racehorses of 1994 recorded:

"Genuine and consistent....a credit to his trainer...tough and reliable...it's a case of take your pick of complimentary racing epithets when it comes to Young Ern, for all they fit him well enough."

Young Ern's other victories included the 1993 Tote Festival Handicap. Among other prolific handicappers trained by Dow was Gallery God who won the prestigious Vodafone Rated Stakes at Epsom in 2002.
National Hunt stars handled by Dow included Dark Honey who won the Grade 3 Sandown Handicap Hurdle in 1994, and Chiefs Song who won the William Hill

Handicap Hurdle in 1996, plus a succession of valuable two mile chases, notably five wins in successive years at Kempton's October fixture, the last of which was in a race named in his honour.

He moved to Thirty Acre Barn in 2015, but after a lean spell returned to Clear Height, from where, in February 2017 he sent out to Qatar, Mr Scaramanga who won the Group 2 Al Biddah Mile.

DOWLING, Christopher   The Warren   1891, 1900, 1903-1907
(1859-1940)

Born in Ireland at the Curragh, Dowling was stud groom at The Warren, and occasional trainer. In Kelly's Directory 1903 he is listed as Christopher Downing, racehorse trainer, Burgh Heath Road.

DOWNES, J.   1905, 1924

Downes of Epsom is credited with training Mr Poole's Mimist when it won at Worcester in May 1905. J. Downes was recorded as training four horses at Epsom in 1924.

DOYLE, Edward   1928-1929
(1886-1954)

Edward Doyle was born in Dublin in 1886. He served as a Lieutenant in the Royal Army Veterinary Corps. On returning to Britain rode as an amateur jockey until 1925, when he was required to turn professional. He rode in five Grand Nationals, finishing third in 1925 and 1926. He moved to Malaya where he was a racecourse judge, and then trained at Lewes before moving to Epsom. The Yorkshire Evening Post, 23rd. October 1905 credits a winner to "Doyle Epsom."

DREFFIN/DRAFFIN   1896-1897

Dreffin is listed in Ruff's Guide 1896 as training for Mr W.H. Palmer. He is shown as Draffin on 1896 gallop reports in The Sporting Life. Mr W.H. Palmer was a keen amateur jockey, and had horses with several Epsom trainers.

DREWITT, Richard   Mickleham   1845-1853
(c.1816- 1874)

Born in Epsom in c.1816, Drewitt is listed in the York Herald 1st March 1845 as training three horses at Epsom, and in Ruff's Guide 1851 and 1852 as training for Messrs. Douglas, Winstanley, Walker and Lee. He had four apprentice jockeys articled to him including George Fordham (weight 4 st.) Fordham's uncle was Drewitt's travelling head lad. Fordham was champion jockey on 14 occasions between 1855 and 1871. He also rode 15 Classic winners in Britain. Fordham married Drewitt's niece Penelope Hyde. Drewitt trained the 1853 Cambridgeshire winner Little David, ridden by George Fordham. He moved to Spital, Lewes, and was resident at Upper House, Lewes at the time of his death. He left effects of "under £3,000."

DREWITT, T.	Carshalton	1844

Bell's Life and Sporting Chronicle, 24th March 1844 records T. Drewitt as training three horses at Carshalton, and the stallion Oppidan standing at the same stables.

DULLER, George (Senior)	The Chalet	1908-1910
(1863-1930)	Down Cottage	1911
	The Chalet	1912-1917
	Ascot House	1921-1929

Nicknamed "Hoppy", George Duller started his career training trotting horses in Essex. He moved to Epsom and earned the title of the "Selling Plate" king. Concentrating on moderate horses he once trained 61 winners in a season. He was initially based at The Chalet in Burgh Heath Road, but moved temporarily to train the horses of Robert Standish Sievier. However, Sievier's finances were subject to extreme vicissitudes, and he also became embroiled in a legal dispute with *Richard Wootton,* so the arrangement was short lived. Duller took over Ascot House after the Great War.
His son Arthur Duller (b.1893), was also a successful jockey but died in 1914 from enteric fever.
George Duller moved to Brighton on his retirement, and died while attending a race meeting at Brighton Greyhound Stadium, leaving effects of £1,500.

DULLER, George E.	Down Cottage	1929
(1892-1962)	Heathcote House	1934-1938
	St Margaret's	1938-1941
	The White House	1945-1959

Son of *George "Hoppy" Duller,* George was arguably the greatest hurdles jockey of all time. He was the first in a long line of Epsom-based hurdles specialists that included *Frank Wootton, Staff Ingham,* Harry Sprague, John Gilbert, Dennis Dillon and Jimmy Uttley.
During the period when the Imperial Cup was the top hurdles event in the calendar, Duller rode the winner on six occasions. He also rode the winner of the inaugural Champion Hurdle. He rode the winner of the Grand International hurdle on seven

occasions, the County Hurdle and the Gloucestershire Hurdle three times, and the Liverpool Hurdle and the Jubilee Hurdle twice.
His career as a trainer was peripatetic. He took out a licence in 1929 to train for Mr Victor Emanuel and succeeded his father-in-law *George Hyams* at Down Cottage. In 1930 Emmanuel moved him to Letcombe Regis in Berkshire, Duller found the premises at Letcombe too small, and then moved to Aston Tirrold. By the end of 1934 he had moved back to Epsom to train at Heathcote House, where his owners included Prince Aly Khan, (who Duller taught to race-ride), followed by a spell in Beaconsfield Road, where George's patrons now included Lord Rosebery.
Duller's training successes in the pre-war period included the Lingfield Derby Trial with Blandstar in 1938, and the Imperial Cup with Mange Tout in 1939.
In 1939 a Mounted Division of the Home Guard was formed in Langley Vale. The Division included Duller, Mick Dillon, *Tommy Carey, Vic Smyth, Jack Reardon* and *Dave Dick* (junior and senior). *Bobby Dick* was serving as the local Air Raid Warden.
In the season after the war, Duller trained Golden Horus to win the Great Metropolitan, and maintained the yard known as The White House. At this time he divorced his wife Bessie, naming *Walter Nightingall* in the divorce papers. Duller's most successful year was in 1950, when his successes included Babu's Pet in the King Edward VII Stakes, but the following year he lost the patronage of the Maharajah of Rajpipla. He finally retired in 1960, and died on August 6th 1962, at the age of 70. The George Duller Handicap Hurdle, that was staged at the Cheltenham Festival, commemorated him for many years. He was also an accomplished pilot (he served in the Royal Flying Corps in the Great War), and raced motorcars at the Brooklands circuit and Le Mans. He left effects of £5592 1s. 6d.

EDWARDS, Henry F.   South Street   1848-1852
(c.1795-1874)

Newmarket-born Harry Edwards rode the winner of the Oaks in 1820 and 1822, and the winner of the 2,000 Guineas in 1819. He was training in Epsom in the 1851 census at Tag Cottage, South Street, having previously trained in France. By 1861 he was based in the High Street running a small private school. In 1871 he is described as a "professor of music". He is listed in Ruff's Guide 1848 to 1852 as "F. Edwards".
In Bells Life in London and the Sporting Chronicle 1st December 1850, F. Edwards, Epsom; is noted as the trainer of Oaks entry Mary owned by Sir John Hawley, & Mr C. Pitcher.
Henry F. Edwards was one of six jockey sons of Newmarket trainer James "Tiny" Edwards.

EDWARDS, George   New Inn Lane   1851
(1826-?)

George Edwards, a farrier and jockey, born 1826 in Kentish Town, London; is shown as living at New Inn Lane in the 1851 census.

EDWARDS, A. or J.A.   Woodcote Green   1871,1878
(1851-?)

The Sportsman 2nd May 1871 notes:

"Breach of Promise and Jove have arrived at A. Edwards, Woodcote Green to be trained."

Edwards also appears in 1871 Training reports in The Sportsman.
J. Edwards, Epsom had a colt by Joys out of Spec entered in the 1878 Lincoln. Probably J.A. Edwards born 1851 and shown in the 1871 census as a jockey living at Woodcote End.

EDWARDS, James   Uplands   1911
(1859-?)

James Edwards was born in South Africa in 1859; in 1911 he was based at Uplands; training and exporting horses.

EDWARDS, William   Woodcote Lodge   1893-1894

Edwards is shown as living above the stables at York House, Woodcote Lodge in the 1894 Register of Electors.

ELLAM, Benjamin   The Warren   1887-1889,
(1835-1910)

Benjamin Ellam, who had a large saddlery business in Piccadilly, bought The Warren circa 1870. from George Hodgman. Ellam later employed *John Castle*, and *Robert I'Anson Senior* amongst others as his private trainer, and in 1887 held his own training licence. He owned the 1854 Oaks winner Tormentor. Ellam supplied saddlery to many of Europe's nobility, and exported many horses to Russia. His horses raced under the ownership of Mr B. E. Dunbar. He also had an extensive stud at The Warren. Ellam left £38,276 gross on his death in 1910.

ELLAM, Benjamin Jnr.   The Warren   1903

Mr Ellam junior is mentioned in Training Intelligence, The Sporting Life May 13th 1903.

"Mr. Ellam junior gave Armidale, Moaravff, and Broken Eutail schooling at the starting gate, prior to going six furlongs."

ELLIOTT, Edward   The Mays   1880-1881
(c.1816-1894)

Edward Elliott spent most of his career training in Yorkshire. He moved south to Epsom in 1880, moving on to Lambourn a few years later.
The Sporting Life, 19th February 1881 noted:
Syrian Princess has arrived at E.H. Elliott's, The Mays, Epsom to be trained. Elliott has room for several more. His sons Edward Elliott, (age 23), and Albert Elliott (age 28), (both born in Richmond, Yorkshire), and described as "unemployed trainer of racehorses", were living in Ladbroke Road, Epsom in the 1881 census.

ELLIS, Benjamin Thomas   1922-1923
(1876-1946)

Benjamin Ellis, was born in 1876 at Caterham, Surrey, and died in 1946 in Epsom, following an accident while riding out. Previously employed at Weyhill Stables, Hampshire, he held a National Hunt jockey's licence in the 1900s, and was described as a groom at the time of his death. Ben Ellis was booked to ride Moifaa the winner of the 1904 Grand National for *James Hickey*, but missed the mount due to injury. From 1916 to 1918 he served in the army remount service at Redhill. He left effects of £861.

EMERY, Rene   Portland House   1960-1963

Emery was a former National Hunt jockey who rode Meli Melo to victory in the 1950 Grand Steeplechase de Paris, and won Le Prix La Haye Jousselin in 1949 and 1950 on the same horse. After moving to England his victories included Armorial III in the 1954 Cotswold (Arkle) Chase, and Tasmin in the 1954 Gloucestershire (Supreme Novices) Hurdle. Emery was training at Lewes in 1958 prior to moving to Epsom. After leaving Epsom, he returned to Chantilly, where he became private trainer to Monsieur Marcel Boussac.

ESCOTT, Anthony   Uplands   1933-1940
(1896-1973)

Tony Escott was the son of the Lewes trainer *Harry Escott* (b.1859). While riding for his father, Tony won the 1912 Jersey Stakes on Hector. He joined the Scots Guards in February 1915, transferring to the Cavalry in March 1918. As a jockey he had seven Grand National mounts, and one Derby mount. He rode in the United States in the summers of 1924, 1925, and 1926. In 1927, now described as a trainer, he spent the summer in Australia, and the following year returned to the United States. Escott briefly returned to riding, but was forced to retire after sustaining an injury at Cheltenham in 1931. His sister was married to *Victor Smyth,* and Tony moved to Epsom where for a few years he trained a small string of National Hunt horses many owned by Smyth.

ESCOTT, Harry
(1859-1948)

Harry Escott is the father of *Victor Smyth's* wife Grace, and *Anthony Escott.* Harry Escott appears to have spent his entire training career at Astley House, Lewes, Sussex. However, the Nottingham Evening Post credits H. Escott, Epsom with training a winner at Wye on 11th May 1931.
The grandnational.org.uk website notes regarding the 1909 Grand National Winner:

"Lutteur III, noted as a British-trained Grand National victor, held plenty of allegiance to France. His jockey Georges Parfremont and owner James Hennessy were Frenchmen and the horse had only arrived at the Epsom yard of trainer Harry Escott that season to get accustomed to the English style of racing."

However, Harry Escott is shown as training at Lewes in the 1909 Street Directory, and the 1891, 1901 and 1911 census returns. Harry Escott is noted as living at Bruce Lodge, Epsom in the 1935 Register of Electors. He died at his home in Hove in 1948 leaving effects of £30,575.

ESCOTT, John   1851-1857
(c.1791-1869)

Listed in Ruff's Guide 1857 as training for *Mr Mellish.* Bell's Life, 8th February indicates he had 13 horses in his care.

ETHERINGTON,   Banstead   1898

Etherington is listed in Epsom training reports during October to December 1898. He appears to have been training a few horses for stockbroker Mr H.H.D. Seaton.

EUSTACE, Kenneth   The Hermitage   1966-1971
(1918-1981)

Eustace was a Permit trainer based at The Hermitage, Walton Heath, later moving to Sussex.

EVANS, John/Frederick   Pitt Place   1878,1881-1884
(1846-1884)

Wiltshire-born Evans was listed at Pitt Place in the 1881 census.
The York Herald, 4th August 1883 noted:

"Reefer and Cambudsman have joined Evans's team at Epsom."

"Fred" Evans is noted as trainer at Pitt Place in 1878.

FALLON, John "Jack"   The Grange   1924

(c.1869-1936)   1928

As trainer for the notorious Druids Lodge Confederacy, Fallon won the equivalent of a million pounds backing horses. When Hacklers Pride won the 1903 Cambridgeshire the owner reputedly won £250k. Whereas the owners amassed a fortune; trainer Fallon, and jockey Bernard Dillon died in poverty. After leaving Druids Lodge, Fallon bought a farm despite knowing nothing about farming, and returned to Ireland where he spent money profusely with his 'friends' in the local inn. In 1924, he was back in England without a penny; he attempted to rekindle his career by setting up at The Grange, Reigate Road, Ewell, succeeding *Major Bell*, and preceding *Tom Walls*. After *Walls* took over, Fallon moved to Worple Road. He subsequently handed in his licence, and *Herbert Smyth* and *Tom Walls* gave him work. After Fallon's death, Smyth arranged a benefit for his widow.

FANCEY, Edwin J.   Portland House   1951
(1902-1980)

An owner/trainer based at Portland House for one year with *Rene Emery* as his retained jockey. Fancey was a film distributor in the 1930s, later producing a prolific amount of 'B movies' between 1940 and 1960. He served a prison sentence for stabbing his accountant in the leg, after a disagreement regarding Fancey's precarious finances. Edwin Fancey's partner, Olive Negus Fancey, was later an owner with *Ron Smyth*, owning several useful horses including Flash Imp.

61

FARMER, Tommy	Mannamead	1947-1950

A former National Hunt jockey, who rode for *Walter Nightingall*, he later trained at Ascot.

FARRALL/FARRELL, Joseph	Down Cottage	c.1814-1841
(c.1779-1845)

Joseph Farrell was buried at St. Martin's Church, Epsom in April 1845, aged 65. Although he is recorded as Farrell in the church records, his tombstone refers to Joseph "FARRALL who departed this life on 15th April 1845", his wife Mary Farrall pre-deceased him.

Joseph Farrall was clerk of the course at Epsom c. 1839-1845. Prior to that he officiated as the judge at the 1819 Epsom Derby Hunt meeting, and was clerk of the course at Hampton c.1826-1831.

An advertisement in The Era 16th May 1841 shows "FARRELL, EPSOM" as the judge at Hampton and Moulsey races.

Advertisements in The Era on the 3rd and 17th July 1842 shows "JOSEPH FARRELL, EPSOM, judge for "The New City of London Races in Hatcham Park at the back of Henry England's Rising Sun, Old Kent Road."

There is a report in Whyte's History of the British Turf (p440) about Farrall training for Mr Holbrook in Epsom in 1834, with reference to the colt Loutherbourg being entered for the Derby but the pedigree was wrong. A note in 1841 records that "Pathfinder has arrived at Farrall's stable after Ascot."

Farrall had runners at Epsom from c.1814 to c.1837, occasional runners at Ascot, Goodwood, and Newmarket; and also at now defunct tracks Rochester, Chatham, Hastings, Canterbury, Guildford and Reigate inter alia.

He was clerk of the course at Epsom, when the four-year-old Maccabeus was raced under the name of the three-year-old Running Rein in the 1844 Derby.

FARRAN. J		1904-1905

Farran appears in Training Reports in the Sporting Life during 1904 and 1905. He trained several winners during his stay at Epsom for owners including *John Coleman*, and *James Bell*.

FENNING, Bertrand		1905-1906
(1869-1945)

Yorkshire-born Fenning, served his apprenticeship at Falmouth Cottage, Newmarket. He moved from Epsom to Kingsclere racing stables in 1906. During his brief career in Epsom he was training *for J.M. Bell* and *John Coleman*. He left effects of £195, 12s. 1d.

FITZGERALD, William   1921-1929

Fitzgerald was formerly a National Hunt jockey employed by *William Nightingall*. He trained National Hunt horses at Epsom between 1921 and 1929.

FORBES, George   Burley Lodge   1952,1954
(1911-1969)

A veterinary surgeon based at Burley Lodge, Forbes also acted as an auctioneer, bloodstock agent, and breeder. He came to Epsom in 1947, founding the Veterinary Bloodstock Agency. He was a prolific purchaser at the sales, and had clients worldwide. He exported stallions to the US, Australia, and Italy, and many other countries. Forbes was ably assisted by his wife Joan, particularly in the latter years when illness took its toll. He left six daughters including a baby, Nicola; and Fiona, who as Fiona Vigors, became a respected horse photographer. The former trainer Peter Makin, spent a year as an assistant in Forbes' equine enterprise.

FORD, Edward   South Street   1849-1851
(c.1816-1874)

Dorset-born Ford appears in Ruff's Guide 1849 as training for Mr C. Formby and Mr King, and in 1851 as training for Mr Inglefield. In the 1861 and 1871 census he is shown as a "Groom" living in East Street, Epsom. See also *W. Plunner.*

FORDHAM, Charles ?   1869

C. Fordham is listed in "Special Training Notes" in The Sportsman, 11th December 1869. No other record is found for him at Epsom, and he appears to have been supervising *Barton's* horses.

FORSTER, Henry   Clay Hill   1866-1872
(1830-?)   Dewden Castle   1873

Born in Oxford in 1830, he was employed at the Fyfield Stables, Marlborough at the time of the 1851 census. He is listed as H. Foster in the Sporting Gazette 1869 as training eight horses at Epsom, and H. Forster training nine horses at Clay Hill in Bells Life and The Sporting Chronicle. The Liverpool Daily Post 4th June 1868 noted: *"Reeves, Burbridge, Sherwood, Simpson, Potter, H. Forster, Hughes, Nightingale train at Epsom, a few miles from Croydon, their horses generally walk in."*

Forster is listed as training at Dewden Castle, Walton on the Hill in 1873.

FORTH, John   Down Cottage   1808-1825
(c.1773-1848)

Yorkshire-born John Forth, acquired stables at Park Lane, London in 1801; announcing at the same time, that he would continue to run stables at Clandon, Surrey. On the 23rd May1809 he purchased land at Epsom from Edward Harris for £1,943.15, and here he set up Down Hall racing stables. In 1824 he advertised the property in The Times, described as a nine-bedroom mansion occupied by the Earl of Oxford, plus "very superior stabling for twenty four horses" and outbuildings, and upwards of 36 acres occupied by a "celebrated sporting character of the turf".
Forth later moved to Michel Grove in Sussex and trained the Derby winners in 1829, 1840 and 1845. He rode the 1829 Derby winner Frederick claiming to be 60 at the time. Forth retired from training in 1846, and moved to London. His son Henry Forth succeeded him at Michel Grove. Henry Pownall in his book *History of Epsom*, (published 1825), describes a trip up Church Street:

"The road continues by Down Hall, the residence of the Earl of Oxford, a building indicating comfort rather than splendour. Behind this mansion are the stables appropriated for training racehorses, under the care of Mr. Forth, whose knowledge is held in high esteem by the fanciers of the turf. Adjuring to these stables are those occupied by Mr. Farrall, the clerk of the racecourse, and which are likewise appropriated for racehorses."

Forth is buried adjacent to St Martin's Church, Epsom, "Obit the 4th of February 1848, Aetat 74", with his wife Hannah, "Obit the 31st of May 1825, Aetat 56" and their daughter Louisa Evans.

FOSTER, Thomas Albert   St. Margarets   1932-1934
(1881-1934)

Foster started his racing career as a jockey in South Africa. During the 1914-18 war he had charge of *Thomas Hogg's* horses, and later trained at West Horsley near Leatherhead. Foster subsequently trained at the Curragh, moving to Epsom in 1932 to train a few of his own horses. He was living at Newmarket, when he died in a London nursing home on 24th May 1934; his funeral took place at West Horsley. He left effects of £9,896.

FREEMAN, J   Rowland Lodge   1896-1899

Freeman was previously based in Belgium.

FRENCH, Joseph Over   Smitham Bottom   1846-1851
(c.1811-1890)

During the 1840s French trained at Smitham Bottom. French left to take up appointments in Newmarket, Lambourn and France. He died in Newmarket in 1890, leaving effects of £231.

GARDINER. Major   Woodcote Rise   1904

Major Gardiner appears on Epsom gallop reports in The Sporting Life during 1904.

GARRATT, Samuel "Harry"   Bush Lodge   1904-1908
(1876-1953)

Born in Lincoln, Samuel Henry Garratt held a National Hunt jockey's licence c.1890 to c.1907. He trained at Bush Lodge in Windmill Lane, but by 1911 was running a riding school from the same property.

GETHIN, Kenneth   Hillcot   1961-1966
(1911-1978)

Birmingham-born Gethin served his apprenticeship with *Stanley Wootton* at Treadwell House. His major success as a jockey came in 1952 when he won the 1,000 Guineas on Sir Malcolm McAlpine's Zabara, trained by *Vic Smyth*. Ken Gethin was the son-in-law of trainer *Peter Thrale*. He trained with limited success from the Hillcot yard in Beaconsfield Road.

GIBSON, H.   1870-1871

The Sporting Gazette January 1871 lists Gibson as training 12 horses. He was in Epsom prior to that; the York Herald 10th December 1870 refers to a bay filly by Amsterdam, arriving at Gibson's Epsom yard to be trained. He was based at Chantilly prior to moving to Epsom.

GIBSON, James   Eclipse Cottage   1895-1903
(1853-1921)

Formerly head lad at Dawson's stable in Newmarket, died at Epsom in 1921.

GLEESON, Patrick Joseph   Heath House   1908-1913
(1866- ?)

Fulham-born Gleeson employed *Joseph Kelly* as his private trainer, before taking out a licence in 1908.

GOBY, Ernest Grimwood   Heathcote House   1910
(1864-1931)   Badminton   1908-1931
                             Bush Lodge   1909

Ted Goby was the last trainer based at Badminton, which stood in Station Road, his stables were on what is now Upper High Street car park. Goby arrived in Epsom from Sidcup in 1908, trained briefly at Heathcote House, and then returned to Badminton. Meyrick Good wrote of Goby:

"It was the great care that Goby bestowed on his horses that made them. He was humane all the time, and treated them as he did his children."

Good, when editor of The Sporting Life rode out an old chaser called Platonic which he recalled: *"was better cared for than a Derby winner."* Charles Morton, the leading trainer of the day considered that Goby had no equal in stable management or as a feeder. Morton stabled the Derby winners Sunstar and Humorist with Goby.
Goby had some success in Belgium and Denmark, and in December 1917, took charge of 11 horses for Norwegian ship owner Mr Giebelhausen.
Goby (of Badminton House, Epsom) died in Gloucestershire leaving effects of £10,861.

GODFREY, Edward Stanley   Bruce Lodge   1918-1920
(1869–1939)

Like *Horace Berg*, Godfrey was a trainer involved with "Ringer" Barrie. The Times, August 20th 1920 recorded that:

"The Maharajah of Nawangar-known more familiarly as "Ranji" the great cricketer, has chosen Mr. S.E. Godfrey of Bruce Lodge, Epsom, as his private trainer, who will leave for India shortly."

Godfrey died in India in 1939.

GONSALVES, Anson   Cedar Point   1988
(1953-

Gonsalves was formerly apprenticed to *Staff Ingham*.

66

GOODE, See William Coode.

GOODGAMES, Tom   1909

Tom Goodgames, was born St Neots in 1882, he was training at Avebury, Wiltshire in 1911, Horses In Training Annual 1909 shows him as training three horses at Epsom.

GOODMAN, James J.   1920-1924

Goodman trained for Mr A.H. Kempton.

GOSLING, J   The Warren   1885-1886

Possibly *William Gosling.*

GOSLING, Tommy   Priam Lodge   1964-1982
(1926-2008)

Tommy Gosling served his apprenticeship with *Ossie Bell* at Lambourn. As a jockey he was notably associated with Sir Winston Churchill's Colonist II. He took out a training licence in 1964 based at Priam Lodge. His career got off to an exceptional start; his sixth runner Excel won the 1964 Greenham Stakes. In the following year, Ardent Dancer won the 1965 Irish 1,000 Guineas. He won the Yorkshire Cup in 1969 with Quartette, and the 1971 Sandown Classic Trial with L'Apache. Quartette also won the Vaux Gold Tankard, and was second in the Northumberland Plate. His best horse was probably Sol Argent who after winning the 1970 Extel Handicap off a weight of 7st 7lb, improved sufficiently to win the 1972 Geoffrey Freer Stakes.

GOSLING, William   Down Cottage   1871-1873
(1825-1904)   Derby Arms   1873-1875
                                    Pitt Place   1879
                                    Priam Lodge   1891-1892

Formerly Head Lad to *William Reeves* at Down Cottage, Gosling succeeded *Reeves*, following the latter's death. The Sporting Clipper 13th April 1872 notes that: *"Sea Shell has joined W. Gosling's string at Down Cottage"*. Bell's Life 11th January 1873 lists Messrs. Gosling and Ansley as training 18 horses at Epsom. The York Herald 22nd January 1875 lists Gosling as having 27 horses in training at Epsom. The Sheffield and Rotherham Independent, 3rd February 1876, refers to Gosling's Derby string as *"neither strong in quality or quantity"*. In 1881 he was head lad at stables in Newmarket High Street. He trained for *Benjamin Ellam* at Newmarket in 1885-86. Following the illness of

John Jones, Gosling took over the running of Priam Lodge stables for Lord Marcus Beresford.

GOSWELL, Michael   Mannamead   1976-1978

Former National Hunt jockey Goswell trained at Horsham prior to moving to Epsom.

GRAHAM-JACKSON, William   Lyndhurst, College Rd.   1887-1897
(c.1864- c1942)

See *Jackson, William Graham*.

GRAY, George   Heath Farm   1920

Gray, a farmer and trainer from Headley was a witness in the case involving *Horace Berg* and Peter Barrie in 1921. Gray held a National Hunt and Flat trainer's licence in 1920.

GRAY, Robert Elton (see GREY)

GREEN, George   Seabright   1903-1905
(1875-1942)   1911

Born in Berkshire, George Green held a National Hunt Jockey's licence, c.1898-1904, described as a journalist in the 1911 census. G. Green first appears in The Sporting Life gallop reports in 1903.

GREEN, James   The Warren   1909-1910
(1879-?)

James Green rode under National Hunt rules before training at The Warren..

GREGORY, James John   Mickleham   1856-1860
(c.1823-1904?)

Listed in Bell's Life 1858, and the Sporting Life 1859 as training nine horses, by 1861 he had moved to Stoke Lodge Stables, Cobham, and in 1863 was at Hambleton in Yorkshire.

GREGORY, George   Smitham Bottom   1878
(1817- ?)

George Gregory was born in Oxfordshire, and previously worked for *Walter Mullingar* at the Red Lion, Smitham Bottom. The Standard 17th June 1878 records: *"Lady Sebright bought two more lots, and the four that she became possessed of will be trained by Gregory at Smitham Bottom."*

GREUSEL, Philip Henry S.   Burgh Heath Road   1900,1903
(1864 -1905)

The American-born Greusel (aka Greusil) spent some time in Berkshire as head lad to Richard Dawson. He left in 1900 to train at Epsom, (probably as part of Mr Gardner's "US invasion," see *C. Riley*), but later returned to Whatcombe.
Greusel arrived in London on 21st November 1898, aboard the Marquette, he was accompanied by *Alex Covington.*

The Minneapolis Journal March 15th 1905 recorded:

"Philip Greusil, an American, and well known as a trainer at New Market for Lord Carnarvon, Richard Croker, and others, died in Switzerland of consumption."

GREY, Captain Robert Elton   Middle House, Woodcote 1893-1897
(1848-1914)

Born in 1848 in Malta, Grey was a Captain in the 3rd Hussars. E. Gray appears in the 1893 Horses In Training Annual with six horses in his charge, and features in Epsom Gallop Reports in 1895. Captain Grey was resident at Middle House from at least 1890. He died in Dorset in 1914 leaving effects of £1,300.

GRIFFITHS, D.J.   Park Farm, Ashtead   1961-1962

GRIFFITHS, Tom   Woodcote Stud   1947-1955
                       Mayfields   1956-1961

Griffiths was a former jockey who rode for *Herbert Smyth*, and under Pony Club rules for *Monty Smyth.* His major success as a trainer was with Langton Heath, the winner of 1959 Imperial Cup.

GRIFFITHS, Joseph   Woodcote End   1885-86
(1847-1918)

The Sheffield Independent 22nd December 1885 notes under gallop reports, for Epsom, the exercise routines for Nightingall, Jones, Sherwood and Holt, adding that *"Griffiths' Cipollina and the youngsters did serviceable work up Middle Hill"*
Griffiths is also mentioned in Epsom Gallops reports in the Belfast Newsletter 23rd March 1886.
Joseph Griffith, born 1847 in Liverpool, describing himself as a "stud groom" was based at Worlds End, Woodcote, in the 1881 census. He previously worked at Cobham Stud.
Joseph Griffiths subsequently worked as a stud groom in Buckinghamshire.

GRUNDY, Frederick   Heathcote House   1915,1917, 1918

Grundy was based at Epsom during the 1914-18 War. He trained Fil d'Ecosse to win the 1915 Jubilee Hurdle.

GUEST, Walter Nelson   Shifnal Cottage   1994
(1932-

Born in Hampshire, Guest worked for Sir Gordon Richards. Like his elder brothers Joe and Charlie he was primarily a jump jockey. He also rode and trained in Denmark.
Guest had a ten-day stay at Shifnal Cottage during which he had a winner at Plumpton.

GULLY, George   Heath House   1904-1907
(1866-?)

After a brief training career at Burgh Heath, Epsom, George Gully moved to the Nepcote Lodge training stables at Findon, Sussex. He became embroiled in a dispute that culminated in a court case with fellow trainer Bob Gore over rights to use the gallops. The artist Edwin Douglas was the owner of the disputed land at Fox Down and let part of the land to Bob Gore for exercising his racehorses, Gore had erected schooling fences and hurdles on the land.
When Gully took his horses up to Fox Down a fracas took place between the men. Gore subsequently wrote a heated letter to Gully, who responded equally strongly that he believed his lease from Dennis Thirlwell, the owner of Nepcote Lodge, included gallop rights, and that there was room for both of them. Two weeks later after another altercation Gully dismantled Gore's schooling hurdles. In November 1906 the case of Gore and Douglas v Gully was heard in the High Court. Edwin Douglas explained that he had leased the land to Gore for £50 per year for five years, and given permission for the fences to be erected, adding that Gore had "exclusive right and liberty to be there".

Counsel for Gully explained that his client was not in court, and had yet to issue instructions. After seven minutes the case was completed and an injunction, preventing Gully from trespassing, was issued.

HACKETT, James Frederick   Rowland Lodge   1918-20
(c.1873-1949)

Born in Southampton, Hackett rode under National Hunt rules until c.1900. Hackett's training career was mainly spent in Sussex. While based at Telscombe he trained the 1902 Grand National winner, he later trained at Lewes and Alfriston. He also had a spell in Nice, where he assisted *Percy Woodland*.

HACKETT, William   Smitham Bottom   1849-52
(1829- ?)

Originally from Antrim in Northern Ireland, Hackett, a "trainer of racehorses", was resident at the Red Lion, Smitham Bottom at the time of the 1851 census. He also appears in Ruffs Guide 1849, 1851, and 1852.
Harry May was also based at the Red Lion, Smitham Bottom, in 1851.

HACKING, Thomas   Burgh Heath   1896
(1866- ?)

The York Herald, 20th February 1896 reported,

"Tom Hacking who was some time in the Horton Stables at Malton, is now in charge of Mr. Dormer's useful little string at Burgh Heath, Epsom. Hacking has a good knowledge of his work and is a most careful and painstaking trainer."

Hacking was born in Bury, Lancashire, and was working in stables at Newmarket in the census of 1881 and 1901.

HAHN, Ernest   Hill House   1911-14
(1868- 1925)

Born in Venezuela, Ernest Hahn occupied Treadwell House prior to Richard Wootton, and then moved to Hill House, Links Road. Throughout this period he gave his occupation as "Stock Exchange Jobber". The Sunderland Daily Echo records in 1911 that James Nugent sold a nice-looking colt to Mr Hahn, the Epsom trainer.
In 1914 the Sheffield Telegraph reported that:

"Whilst returning from Liverpool races, Mr. E Hahn, the well-known Epsom trainer was taken ill, and on reaching London conveyed to a nursing home."

HALES, John   High Street   1894, 1899
(1850- 1932)

Hales was training and riding his own horses under National Hunt rules during the 1890s.

HALL, Arthur   Pikes Hill   1859-1868
(1838-1870)   Woodcote Green

Locally born Hall served an apprenticeship with *Ralph Sherwood*, before undertaking a brief training career. His principal owner was Mauritius-based Mr R. Couve for whom Hall had much success taking horses to Mauritius. The Liverpool Daily Post 16th September 1864 noted:

"Hall, the Epsom trainer, has been very fortunate in taking horses to Mauritius for Mr R. Couve, having got there safe with five different animals and won the Great Maiden four times."

In 1867, Hall of Woodcote Green was advertising his services to take racehorses on long voyages, drawing attention to eight successful expeditions to Mauritius. His sons *Arthur Henry Hall* (b.1863), and *William Hall* (b.1866)' also trained at Epsom.

HALL, Arthur Henry   1889
(1863-1919)

Arthur Hall, (born in Epsom 1863), was apprenticed to *John Jones*, and son of *Arthur Hall* (1838-1870.) As a jockey Arthur Hall's victories included riding Magic for the Prince of Wales to win the 1888 Grand Sefton Chase, and the 1889 Lancashire Chase. He also rode for the Prince of Wales in the 1888 and 1889 Grand National. A note in the York Herald 16th March 1889 records that:

"Frederick James and Eglanmore have left T.Challoner's stable at Newmarket for Epsom, where A. Hall will train them in future."

Hall left Epsom in 1889 to take up a position in Hoppegarten in Germany, and remained there until 1893. By 1901, now described as a retired jockey, he was living in Worple Road, Epsom.

HALL, Les Montague	Chartwell	1996-2000
(1952-	Ermyn Lodge	2001-2004
	Clear Height	2005-2006
	Chalk Pit	2007-2011

Les Hall was apprenticed to *Peter Ashworth*, and then moved to work for *John Sutcliffe* at Woodruff. An integral part of Sutcliffe's success during the 1970s and 1980s, Hall enjoyed the distinction of leading up eight consecutive Royal Ascot winners while working for Sutcliffe.

| HALL, William | The Grove | 1889-1902 |
| (1866- 1928) | | |

Epsom born Hall, worked at Mr Case Walker's training stable in Dorking Road for James Chandler before training at the Grove Stables. He married Sarah Jane Holt, sister of *William Holt*.

| HAMILTON, Nigel | South Hatch | 1999-2001 |
| (1956- | Woodruff | 2002 |

Nigel Hamilton, former head lad to *Reg Akehurst* and *Geoff Lewis*, was employed by South Hatch Racing to train from the 'new' yard at South Hatch, with *John Akehurst* operating from the old yard. The best horse trained by Hamilton was Parisien Star, a Goodwood specialist, who was beaten a short head in the valuable William Hill Mile Handicap in 2000.

| HAMMOND, William | South Hatch | 1859-1861 |

Hammond is listed in Ruff's Guide 1861 as private trainer for Mr J.C. Smith.
The Birmingham Daily Post 18th July 1859 noted:

"Hammond, the jockey has taken South Hatch stables, at Epsom, formerly occupied by Mr. Mellish and has now five horses in training."

| HAMPSON, Alfred | Hillcrest | 1913-1920 |
| (1868 - 1942) | | |

Salford-born Alfred Hampson worked in stables at Lambourn, and held a licence there in 1911 prior to moving to Epsom. In 1917, because of wartime restrictions in Britain, he took a few horses to race in Ireland. He later retired to Salford.

HANLEY, David L.   Heathcote House   1961-1966
(1928-2008)

Dave Hanley was apprenticed to *Walter Nightingall* at South Hatch, later assisting his father *Sam Hanley*. When at Nightingall's he worked alongside his uncle Bob Hanley, who was associated with Sir Winston Churchill's horse Colonist. David Hanley rode winners on the Flat and under National Hunt rules. He did two year's national service in the Veterinary Corps.

Dave Hanley recalled his time assisting his father. "During this time we were keeping a few horses at Seabright and using the yards at Portland House and Caithness in addition to Heathcote House. In the paddocks opposite The Durdans we had schooling fences and hurdles. Lady Sybil Grant lived at The Durdans, and allowed us access to the Downs via a pretty walk up through the woods past the graves of the Derby winners."

In 1963 he trained Marcher to win the Portland Handicap and the Wokingham Handicap. The following year Marcher finished third in the July Cup. He also trained Weepers Boy to win the valuable Senior Service Handicap at York. In 1966 his lease on Heathcote House expired. The price of property in Epsom put the purchase of a yard out of reach, and rumours suggested that the new London Orbital motorway would cross Six Mile Hill. He moved to Lambourn, subsequently becoming private trainer for his principal owner, Mr A. Richards, and trained with some success in France and in the United States before returning to Berkshire.

HANLEY, Matthew   Downs House (Derby Arms) 1920
                               Turbine Stud, Highfields   1920-1924

Western Daily Press, 2nd December 1920 noted:

"Hanley is shortly removing his horses from Downs House, Epsom, to the Turbine Stud, Highfield, Epsom, having purchased the latter establishment. "

Matthew Hanley was the father of *Sam Hanley*.

HANLEY, Sam   Turbine Stud   1924-1929
(1891-1986)   Seabright   1929-1939
                               Heathcote House   1945-1961

Irish-born Sam Hanley initially trained from the Turbine (later the Woodcote Stud). At the time Hanley used the grounds of the RAC Club to access the Downs. He later had a small yard next to the old police station in Ashley Road before moving to Heathcote House.

Sam Hanley's best horse was Mountraen who finished second in 1949 Irish Oaks. He was a superb judge of horses and for many years worked for the Anglo-Irish Bloodstock Agency. Hanley also trained a few two-year-olds for *Stanley Wootton*.

When Eddie de Mestre, former assistant to fellow Australian *Richard Wootton*, retired from training, he told *Stanley Wootton* that he would like to go out with a bang. Stanley sold him a filly called Martonia, and recommended that Sam Hanley should train it, as they were likely to get a better price as horses trained by Wootton invariably attracted the bookmaker's attention. Ridden by Wootton's apprentice Noel Carroll with the instructions "get right away and don't get caught" Martonia duly won a two-year-old seller at Sandown, with de Mestre having £2,000 each-way through various off course accounts, and hundreds of telegram bets, arriving too late for the off-course bookmakers to hedge; a price of 10-1 obtained.

A similar *modus operandi* was used when Hanley was training for *Charles Stevens*.

| HANSON, Frederick Thomas | | 1925-1926 |
| (1887-1970) | | |

Born in East London, Hanson was employed as a stable lad in Epsom, prior to a brief training career.

| HARDIE, T | Burgh Heath | 1894-1899 |

Hardie is listed in Ruff's Guide 1898; his principal owner was Mr F.D. Neyland. In 1896 he trained Mr Leyland's Westmeath to win the 1896 Great Metropolitan Chase. He left Burgh Heath for Grately in 1899.

| HARDY, Gerald | The Paddocks | 1937-1940 |
| (1907-1993) | Downs Lodge | 1946-1948 |

An outstanding National Hunt jockey, Hardy rode for many years for *Bill Payne,* and was associated with Payne's prolific chaser Colliery Band. Author Roger Mortimer described Hardy as "a consummate horseman", and as "an education and a pleasure to watch." His most important victory as a trainer was with Avignon in 1947 Chesterfield Cup.

| HARPER, Henry George | Madrid Villa, | 1893 |
| (1852-1918) | Lower Downs Road | |

Born in Cheshire, Henry George Harper is shown in the 1893 edition of Horses In Training as training one horse. The census of 1891 shows him as a journalist employing one groom. He wrote under the pseudonym "G,G.", and also wrote several books. His son Harry Harper was an eminent journalist, covering the development of aviation.

HARRISON, James	Clay Hill	1870-1872
(1842- ?)		

Harrison appears in the 1871 census, living at Winchester Cottage in East Street, the Sporting Gazette lists five horses under his care. In The Sportsman, 11th April 1871, Harrison advertises that he is "open to receive a few more horses" at his stables at Clay Hill, Epsom. He is listed in the Sporting Gazette, 21st January 1871, as training five horses.

HARRISON, G.	Stables, Church Street	1826

Listed in the *Racing Calendar 1826*, as standing the stallion Duport at The Stables, Church Street.

HAVELOCK-ALLAN, Alan	Woodcote Rise	1917-1918
(1874-1949)		

When Robert Allan died in 1879, his cousin, Sir Henry Havelock VC, inherited the Blackwell Estate in Durham on the condition that Sir Henry added Allan to his surname. Thus, Sir Henry's son Alan Havelock became Alan Havelock-Allan. He served in the North Yorks Artillery as a lieutenant, and later in the Army Service Corps. He gave his occupation as "racehorse trainer" when enlisting. He briefly trained at Epsom towards the end of the Great War, later training in Wiltshire. His son Anthony Havelock-Allan was an outstanding film producer. He was involved in over 60 productions from 1935 to 1970, including Brief Encounter, and In Which We Serve. He was knighted for his services to the film industry and died in 2003 at the age of 98.

HAYES, James	Worple Road	1911
(1877-1916)		

James Hayes, a former jockey, was born in New Zealand in 1877. He met *Richard Wootton* in Australia circa 1890, and subsequently joined him in Epsom, briefly holding a training licence.

HAYNES, Michael	Tattenham Corner	1974-2004
(1931-2008)		

An apprentice jockey with *Stanley Wootton*, Mick Haynes rode Wootton's last major race success as a trainer when he partnered Bon Mot to victory in the Imperial Cup in 1956. Haynes trained Vorvados to win the 1983 Group 3 Duke of York Stakes, and the 1982 Portland Handicap.

He also won the 1982 Ascot Stakes and the 1980 Cesarewitch with Popsis Joy, who was subsequently second in the Cesarewitch twice. Haynes was assisted for much of his career by his daughter Yvonne, and former stable apprentice David Jeffries.

HEDGES, Harry	The Grove	1923-40, 1944-48
(1884-1948)		

Harry Hedges was apprenticed to his father Mr A.W. Hedges who trained at Windsor Heath; and he later worked for *Joseph Kelly*.

Hedges' major success was when Fet won the Cesarewitch Handicap in 1936 carrying 6st 12lb. At this time, Hedges' modest chasers were ridden by Irish National Hunt jockey Paddy Prendergast. When war broke out, Paddy returned to Ireland. When he returned to Epsom in 1963 it was to win the Oaks with Noblesse. Other trips to England yielded the winners of the 1,000 Guineas, 2,000 Guineas, St Leger, King George V and Queen Elizabeth Stakes twice, and the Eclipse twice. Prendergast was the first Irish- based trainer to be champion trainer in England, achieving the feat in 1963, 1964, and 1965. The education Paddy received riding Epsom's moderate chasers around the 'gaffs' obviously served him well.

Hedges career was spent mainly training modest horses; in 1931 he had eight winners the most expensive of which cost £55. That year he achieved some fame with a moderate horse called Ballyscanlon. Forever looking at ways to 'solve' problem horses, Hedges discovered the horse refused to respond to the whip, but responded to a rattle. Eventually the Jockey Club ruled against this, but as Hedges pointed out "it is more humane than the whip."

He later trained a few horses for Prince Aly Khan, and *Stanley Wootton*. He was landlord of The George Hotel in High Street, Epsom at the time of his death on 4th September 1948. He left effects of £9,444.

HENTON, Reuben W.	Caithness Lodge	1928-1929
(1890-1987)		

Son of a farmer at Gatton, much of Henton's career was based farming in the Reigate area. His son Peter Henton held a jump jockey's licence for four years, riding primarily for Sid Dale, Don Butchers, and Peter Thrale.

HICKEY, James/Joseph	Rowland Lodge	1900-1905
(1867-1911)		

Born in Ireland, Hickey rode in Britain until 1898. He had two mounts in the Grand National in 1897, and 1898 for Mr Spencer Gollan. In 1899 he spent a year in New Zealand before returning to the UK with New Zealand jockeys Webster and *Page*. He trained the 1904 Grand National winner Moifaa for his principal owner Mr Gollan, a horse that was more than 17 hands high. Moifaa won nine races in New Zealand, and on the journey over allegedly survived a shipwreck. At Aintree the horse completed half a circuit after winning before the jockey, Arthur Birch, could pull him up. The Daily Telegraph noted: *"The winner was not in the least distressed and could practically go round again."*

Moifaa was sold to the King prior to the 1905 Grand National, but new trainer *Richard Marsh* reported him "gone in his wind", public support forced him into 4-1 favourite, but he was never going well, and fell at Bechers Brook. Moifaa's jockey Arthur Birch suffered a crushing fall in 1906; he was paralysed and died in 1911.

Hickey was closely involved with the victory of The Grafter in the 1900 City and Suburban Handicap (see *J.E. Brewer.*) When The Grafter won at Manchester, Hickey told all concerned that the horse had too much weight, shortly before entering the betting ring Hickey called over a friend, and handed him a "telegram", it read "Horse won". Hickey then placed his bets, while his friend digested the two words, spread the word, and followed Hickey into the ring, Hickey also trained Australian Star to win the 1901 City and Suburban Handicap.

In 1911, Hickey died in Netherne Hospital, he is buried at Epsom Cemetery, under the name Patrick Joseph Hickey.

HICKEY, Joe/James	Grove Stables	1945
	The Paddocks	1949,1952
HILL, George	Turf Cottage	1875,1887-1891

The York Herald shows George Hill as training two horses at Epsom in 1875. He is listed in the Street Directory for 1887 as a trainer at Turf Cottage, Sutton.

HOGG, Thomas	Caversham House	1911-13, 1916, 1918-19
(1879.1942)	Uplands	
	Everslie, Worple Road	1909
	Caithness, Worple Road	

Scottish-born Captain Thomas Hogg served in the Royal Army Veterinary Corps during the second Boer War.

He settled in South Africa, but returned to England practising as a veterinary surgeon for *Richard Wootton* and others. He was based at Caversham House, Woodcote Side, but also rented Uplands from *Richard Wootton*. He subsequently combined veterinary work with training, before moving to train for Lord Glanely. At one time he was the largest private trainer in the country, having 80 of Lord Glanely's horses in his care at Newmarket with Gordon Richards as retained jockey. During the 1930s he trained the winners of the St. Leger, Oaks and the 2,000 Guineas for Lord Glanely.

He was living at Heath House, Newmarket when he died in 1942 leaving effects of £18,139 19s. 6d.

HOLLAND,   1884

The Belfast Newsletter in its Epsom training Gallops column 5th April 1884 noted: *"Holland's youngsters were cantering."*
Possibly Arthur Gower Holland (1851-1914), who was living at Rose Cottage, The Parade at the time of the 1891 census.

HOLMAN, George Christopher   West Hill   1878
(1842-1896)

George Holman was born in Cheltenham. He is described as a trainer at West Hill at the christening of his daughter at Christ Church in 1878. He was back at Cheltenham by the time of the 1881 census. Holman had nine mounts in the Grand National between 1864 and 1876.

HOLT, William	Eclipse Cottage	1881-1883
(1849- 1909)	Field House	1883
	York House	1884-1886
	Worple Road.	1887
	Lime Tree Cottage	1887-1889
	Woodcote Lodge	1890
	Heathcote House	1891-1909

Born at Coventry, Holt succeeded James Martin at Eclipse Cottage, and was based there at the time of the 1881 census. The next few years saw him moving to various stables in Epsom, in Kelly's Directory 1890 he was based at "Woodcote Lodge Training Stables", (Church Street). In the 1893 Horses In Training Annual, he has 15 horses in his charge. His most prestigious training success was with Skyscraper in the 1887 Liverpool Hurdle. He left effects of £931.

HOPKINS, William Henry	The Paddocks	1907,1908 1918
(1865-?)	Skinners Lane, Ashtead	1911-13

William Henry Hopkins, born in Gloucestershire, was training, and operating as a horse dealer at The Paddocks in Ashtead. Walter Hopkins (born c.1868) operated from the same address.
W. Hopkins is listed at Hooley Lodge, Coulsdon in Trainers and their Addresses, in The Sporting Life, June 21st.1906.

HORNSBY, Fred   c.1899

Fred Hornsby advertised as a tipster c.1899, describing himself as a "famous Epsom and Lewes trainer."

HOWE, G.M.   Hunters Chase, Walton   1963

HOTHAM, W   Smitham Bottom   1853

Hotham is shown in Bell's Life 23rd January 1853 as training four horses at Smitham Bottom.

HOWE, Raymond   Priam Lodge   1985

Ray Howe had a brief training career, including spells at Lewes and Beverley.

HUGHES, David   Church Street   1857-1882
(1835?-1911)   Worple Road & Ashley Road,
                              Ashtead

Born in Glanhaffin, Montgomeryshire, David Hughes rode as a jockey, notably winning the 1857 Chester Cup on Leamington. His brother *Thomas Hughes* reportedly landed a large gamble on the horse. The earliest mention of D Hughes as a trainer is in the York Herald 7th February 1857 where he is reported as having six entries in the Liverpool Steeplechase from his Epsom stable. David Hughes trained primarily for his brother *Thomas Hughes*. David Hughes was sharing stable facilities at Church Street with his brother *John Hughes* in 1861, but later moved to other premises in Epsom. In Bell's Life 1860 David Hughes is listed as training 22 horses, and in 1869 as training 26 horses. Hughes suffered a serious accident while hunting in 1868. In the 1871 census he is listed as a "trainer and jockey" residing at the Church Street stables. The York Herald 1875 notes that Hughes has ten horses in training. He is also listed at Worple Road; he was probably training from Caithness Stables. The 1878 Post Office directory lists him as based at "Ashyead."

Hughes trained Flash-in-the-pan to win the 1864 Chester Cup. He trained The Brewer and Saint Lawrence who won the 1860 and 1864 Liverpool Cup respectively. The Brewer was controversially awarded dead heat second in the 1858 Cesarewitch, when the Hughes stable were convinced that they had won.

80

HUGHES, John   Church Street   1858-1867
(1834-1895)

Elder brother of *David Hughes*, listed in the 1861 census as a trainer of racehorses based in Church Street.

HUGHES, Thomas Edward Horse and Groom   1859-1869
(1827-1910)   Worple Road   1874-1882
          Horse and Groom   1886-1887

The eldest brother of *David and John Hughes,* Hughes is listed in Kelly's Directory 1859 at Church Street.The York Herald 24th March 1860 records:

"T. Hughes has taken the stables lately in the occupation of C. Boyce."

The stables referred to are the Horse and Groom Stables in Church Street; Hughes purchased the stables on 15th April 1863 for £1,102.
The 1861 census shows all three brothers at the Church Street stables; Thomas listed as "gentleman" and his two brothers as "trainers".
In 1868, when the relationship between Lord of the Manor, Edward Studd and the Grandstand Association were at a low point Mr Hughes rented the Six Mile Hill gallops. By 1881, Thomas was living at Salcombe House, Downside, now listed as an "annuitant." Training reports for the period indicate that Hughes often took his horses elsewhere for more secluded work, eg Leatherhead (noted in 1866) where he leased the downs until bought by Baron Rothschild, and Smitham Bottom (noted in 1870).
Thomas Hughes was a notorious heavy backer, winning in excess of £15,000 when his horse Flash-in-the-pan won the 1864 Chester Cup. He reputedly won large sums on the same race when Dalby (owned by his friend and associate William Bennett) won the same race in 1865 and 1866, and when *David Hughes* rode Leamington to victory in 1857.
He died at his home in St John's Wood leaving effects of £2,655 9s.

HUMPAGE, William A.   1902
(1867-1952?)

Born in 1868 at Lewes, Humpage worked at Newmarket in 1891, then trained at East Ilsley c.1901 and moved to Epsom in 1902, but left three months later. He worked at Kingsclere stables c. 1903-1905.

HUTCHINSON, Ray	The Chalet	1985-86
(1954-		

Former amateur jockey and son of Australian jockey Ron Hutchinson.

HYAMS, George	Down Cottage	1912-1931
(1874-1954)		

Hyams was training for the Austrian Royal Family prior to World War I. He had been training the largest string in Europe, and trained the winner of the German Derby in 1903. He was forced to leave hurriedly when the political situation in Europe declined, Hyams later claimed to have left behind a "small" fortune in the banks. He came to Epsom where the bookmaker Martin Benson (known as Dougie Stuart) had bought Down Cottage, and rebuilt the stables with a trainer's cottage, and head lad's cottage. Hyams's reputation as an international trainer helped him to secure a contract to train the English based horses for Rumanian Mr Niculescu in 1916.
Success on the racecourse proved tougher in England than Austria though. At one time Hyams had Shaun Spadah and Sergeant Murphy in his stables; both horses were sold prior to winning the Grand National. In 1923 Hyams was involved in a bizarre court case after one of his horses, Ironore, died in a race and the owner sued the jockey, Michael Beary. George Hyams was asked to value the horse and replied, "£600 to £800 depending on who I was trying to sell it to."
Hyams was married to the sister of Marie Lloyd, the music hall star, (jockey Bernard Dillon later married Marie Lloyd). Hyams had three daughters who were much admired in Epsom. Alice was Charlie Smirke's first wife, and subsequent partner. Bessie married *George Duller junior*, and later married *Walter Nightingall*.

HYDE,		c.1785

The Sporting Magazine, June 1804, in a profile of the horse, Betty Bloss, states:

"Betty Bloss was bred by a smuggler in Kent; her dam was three parts bred, and a winner of small prizes, commonly called Leather Plates. She passed from the hands of this smuggler to Tom Cammell the jockey; from him to Hyde at Epsom; from Hyde to Emmerson, at the Riding School, Mayfair; thence to Bloss the training groom at Epsom."

See also *Robert Bloss*.

HYDE, Stuart J.	Farm Stables	1924-1925
(1884-1961)		

Hyde trained at Sparsholt in Berkshire where he was born, before moving to Epsom.

I'ANSON, Robert, Snr.	Rose Cottage, Mickleham	1847-49, 1851-52, 53-54,
(1818- 1881		61-69,79,80
	The Warren	1869-1872
	Pitt Place	1872
	Walton Heath	1873-1875
	South Hatch	1881

The brother of William I'Anson, the Malton-based trainer who was associated with Derby winners, Blair Athol and Blinkbonny, Robert I'Anson was born on 1st February 1818 at Middleham. He was based in East Lothian in the early 1840s with his brother William. Most of his career was spent in the Epsom area, except for a spell in Ireland between 1849 and 1851, when he was training for the Marquis of Waterford; and various short spells at Middleham, and a brief career in France in 1859, as private trainer to Count Morny. The arrangement with Lord Waterford terminated after a dispute at Brighton; the jockey Robertson had lost his stirrups in a race, and Lord Waterford sacked him in the unsaddling enclosure; I'Anson deemed the decision to be harsh and resigned in protest. In 1859, he moved to Chantilly to take a post as private trainer to Count de Morny. In 1861 he was based at Rose Cottage, Mickleham employing 11 stable staff and one domestic, at this time he was private trainer to Mr S. Jacobs. The relationship ended in 1864 after Sydney Jacobs accused I'Anson of libel after a dispute over outstanding training bills owed by Jacobs. In a letter I'Anson had described Jacobs as "that thief". I'Anson had apologised immediately after Jacobs failed to attend the court, and the jury accepted that "no real damage was done". Damages of a farthing were awarded, effectively both sides paying their own costs. In 1864 Robert I'Anson senior was warned off for two years, and banned from having runners at Newmarket, Epsom, Goodwood and York, after giving his son (*Robert I'Anson junior*) instructions "not to win" on a horse called Telscomb in accordance with the owner's instructions. In 1869 Robert I'Anson appeared in court charged with "violent assault". While travelling on a train in an intoxicated state, I'Anson was involved in an altercation with a fellow traveller and "pulled his beard half out", I'Anson was sentenced to 14 days hard labour. I'Anson moved from Mickleham to The Warren in September 1869, in the 1871 census he was at the lodge at The Warren with seven stable staff and his son Robert as the jockey. After leaving the post at The Warren, he moved briefly to Pitt place (Sporting Life 24th January 1872), and subsequently moved to Walton Heath. In 1873, because the gallops on the Heath were so hard, he sent two horses belonging to Mr Johnstone to his brother at Middleham for 'finishing', they went straight to Goodwood where one of them, Sister Helen won the Stewards Cup. The York

Herald 22nd January 1875 lists 18 horses under the care of R. I'Anson at Epsom. By 1879, I'Anson was back at Mickleham, The Morning Post noting the sale of one of Lord Rosebery's horses to go to I'Anson at Mickleham. By 1881, following the death of his wife, and a period of serious illness, I'Anson had cut back on his training activity and was resident at South Hatch, (his daughter had married *John Nightingall*), where he was training a few horses.

I'ANSON, Robert Jnr.	Heath House	1876-1882, 1886
(1850-1917)	Tadworth Cottage	1873-1876, 1887
	Priam Lodge	1900-1902, 1904, 1907
	Heath House	1891,1903, 1905
	Drumassie. Rosebery Rd.	1911

Robert I'Anson Junior, was born on the Marquis of Waterford's estate where his father was private trainer. Despite being nearly six feet tall, I'Anson was stylish in the saddle, he was described by the King's trainer *Richard Marsh* as "one of the best I ever saw going at a fence."
The Hon. George Lambton wrote: *"no better man over fences and hurdles ever lived. We young men worshipped him. He could give us the best advice about riding in the nicest possible way."*
He rode for the *Nightingall* family, and owned and trained his own chasers. He had his first mount at the age of 11 on Derby Day 1861. At the age of 14, he had his first winner on the Flat, riding Telscombe at Harrow. His debut rides over hurdles and fences both yielded winners. His first major victory was on Packrita when winning the Sefton Chase. He rode the winner of every major steeplechase except for the Grand National where his luck was exceptionally cruel, he was offered the mounts on Shifnal and The Liberator when they won; and when he trained the winner Austerlitz in 1877, he chose to ride Shifnal. Two years later he elected to ride Austerlitz, but the long-term ante-post favourite was found lame on the morning of the race. He rode the Grand National runner up in 1872, and the third in 1876. His best riding records were at Croydon, where on several occasions he won the United Kingdom Steeplechase, Great Metropolitan Steeplechase on three occasions, and Stewards Steeplechase; and at Bromley where over a two-day meeting he once rode seven consecutive winners. His overseas successes included the victory on Wild Monarch in the 1879 Grand Steeplechase de Paris.
I'Anson was married to Julia May on 4th February 1873 at St Clement Danes, Westminster. He later succeeded his father-in-law *Harry May* at Heath House.

The York Herald 22nd February 1873 recorded:

"Robert I'Anson, jun., the steeplechase jockey has taken a house and capital stabling, formerly occupied by Milne, at Walton, near Epsom, and we understand that he will

shortly have a number of horses to train, the property of a well known sporting gentleman."
.

In 1874 I'Anson was involved in a curious court case. Described as a trainer and jockey of Tadworth, I'Anson was riding at Worcester, where before leaving the weighing room he gave the valet £17, a watch and chain, and other articles to look after. On returning to the weighing room, the valet and the money had gone, but the watch was left. The valet was apprehended at the station and sentenced to six months hard labour.

The York Herald 10th May 1876 noted:

"Austerlitz, Hampton, De La Motte, and Last Of The Novelties have left James Nightingall's yard for Robert I'Anson Junior at Tadworth Cottage, Banstead , Epsom to be trained."

Hampton's stay was short-lived, but Austerlitz was trained by I'Anson to win the 1877 Grand National. Other successes during this period included training Bacchus to win Croydon's Great Metropolitan Chase in 1879 and 1880, the 1879 Kempton Park Grand Hurdle, and the 1881 Champion Chase; and in 1882 he trained Mickey to win the Prince of Wales's Steeplechase, ridden by his brother-in-law *Arthur May*.
Following a bad fall in 1881, Robert I'Anson retired from riding and training in 1882 to act as a racecourse official, but returned to training later.
In January 1903 he took up an appointment as private trainer to Baron de Foret near Chantilly, but returned in September that year to train for *Patrick Gleeson* at Heath House. In 1905 he was private trainer to Mr C.T. Garland.
The Kingsclere trainer John Porter who trained six Derby winners, stabled his Epsom runners at I'Anson's Burgh Heath stables, notably 1886 winner Ormonde. I'Anson was also an outstanding cricketer who had to pass over opportunities to play for Surrey because of his riding and training commitments. Following his death at his Ewell home on 5th February 1917, the Sporting Life recorded:

"He was one of the finest jockeys of his time. He prepared Austerlitz to win the Grand National in 1877, and so well had he tried the horse "all of Epsom" was on."

I'ANSON, Thomas   The Warren Lodge   1871
(1843- 1907)

Thomas was the eldest son of *Robert I'Anson* (born 1818).

| INGE, William G. | The Cottage | 1891-1903 |
| (1870-1913) | Rowland Lodge | |

Yorkshire-born Inge gave his address in 1891 as Park Villas, Worple Road, but appears to have been using the facilities at The Cottage/Rowland Lodge during his training career. At one time sharing with *George Vincent,* and in 1901 with *William J. Adams.* Inge's father, Augustus Gladwyn Churchill Inge (1839-1917) was resident at Rowland Lodge circa 1893-95, and prior to that at Eclipse Cottage in 1888. Inge Senior is described as a riding master.

| INGHAM, Stafford W.H. | Bredenbury | 1939,1940, 1946 |
| (1908-1977) | Thirty Acre Barn | 1947-1976 |

Staff Ingham was apprenticed to *Stanley Wootton.* As a jockey he rode the King's horse Weathervane to win the 1923 Royal Hunt Cup, and also rode the winner of the Irish 2,000 Guineas. When his weight increased he became an outstanding hurdles jockey, and won the 1936 Imperial Cup on Negro. He served in the Royal Air Force during World War II leaving as a Squadron Leader. He resumed training at Bredenbury, and then switched to Thirty Acre Barn.
Wootton's former travelling head lad, Charlie Goodwin returned from Lambourn as head lad to Ingham, and William "Scottie" Scott who had been apprenticed at Middleham to the Peacock family, joined from *Johnny Dines* as travelling head lad. Norman Keogh also served for many years as head lad/travelling head lad. At this stage *Stanley Wootton* owned most of the horses in Thirty Acre Barn. In 1947 Ingham trained 27 winners, 18 of then owned by *Wootton.*
Staff Ingham was a noted trainer of hurdlers, winning the Triumph Hurdle twice, with Pundit in 1958, and Englands Glory in 1968, the Imperial Cup with Anglesey in 1948, and the Aurelius Hurdle in 1970 with Fount Of Youth.
His early successes on the Flat were primarily with handicappers, he won the 1952 Cambridgeshire with Richer, and the following year won the Cesarewitch with Chantry, an 85 guinea purchase that started at 4-1 with connections on at prices up to 66-1.
In 1960 Ingham trained probably his best horse in Apostle, whose top performance came when beaten three-quarters of a length by St Paddy in the Great Voltigeur. In the same year he trained the first of several top-class two-year-olds, *Mr Stanley Wootton's* Kerrabee, who won the National Stakes, and finished second in the Nunthorpe Stakes, the Cheveley Park Stakes, and the Molecomb Stakes. His best chance of Classic success was with the Great Voltigeur winner Just Great, who started favourite for the 1961 St Leger but lost the race when the horse spun around at the start and was left several lengths. Just Great's four victories that year included the then valuable Brighton Derby Trial. Ingham finished fifth in the trainers' championship in 1961, with Apostle winning four races including the Jockey Club Cup and the Princess of Wales's Stakes, and Thames Trader winning five races including the Bessborough Stakes. Apostle was

invited to run in the Washington D.C. International, but torrential rain and an unfamiliar surface made the journey fruitless. Overseas success included Le Cordonnier's victory in the Prix Ridgway. As a two-year-old Le Cordonnier had finished second in the Observer Gold Cup, and third in the Dewhurst Stakes.

Another horse just below Classic standard was Soderini, who finished second in the 1963 Dewhurst, and third in the 1964 St Leger. In 1965 Soderini realised his full potential by winning the Hardwicke Stakes, the John Porter Stakes, and was second in the Coronation Cup and the King George and Queen Elizabeth Diamond Stakes.

Ingham specialised in selecting yearlings and training them into good two-year-olds. He relied on his eye for a horse's constitution, and often identified next year's first two-year-old winner in the previous November. His best juvenile was Porto Bello, later a successful stallion, siring numerous winners including future stallions Roman Warrior and Import. Porto Bello won his first six races including the New Stakes at Royal Ascot, finished third in the 1968 King's Stand Stakes, and later won races in America. Another fast two-year-old from this period was Broadway Melody who won three of her first four races before being inexplicably beaten into second place in the Queen Mary Stakes. The following year Broadway Melody won Kempton's 1,000 Guineas Trial.

The mid-1960s saw Ingham at his peak, when victories included the Queen Anne Stakes with Sir Jack Cohen's Tesco Boy. The horse was also placed in the Sussex Stakes, and Champion Stakes. Ingham's health began to deteriorate in the 1970s but successes in that period included Crazy Rhythm's victories in the 1972 Ebor Handicap and 1974 Ormonde Stakes. Lord David, (a son of Tesco Boy), won the Rosebery Stakes in 1972, and finished third in a vintage Champion Stakes beaten by Brigadier Gerard and Riverman.

Like his master *Stanley Wootton*, Ingham was an outstanding tutor of jockeys. His first good apprentice was John Bunker. In the second year of his apprenticeship Bunker rode 25 winners from 98 mounts, including the Zetland Gold Cup; he later worked in racehorse transport and died when a plane crashed at Heathrow as it was bringing seven brood mares and a foal from Deauville on 3rd July 1968. Jimmy Uttley, David Mould, Chris Dwyer, Ronnie Harrison, Alan Watlow, Brian Elder, Michael Kettle, and Bobby Coonan, the six times Irish Champion Jumps jockey, were also apprenticed to Ingham. Coonan later described the experience as "penal servitude". Michael Hole, who rode with great success in the United States, also served his apprenticeship with Ingham. Staff Ingham left an estate valued at £252,370.

INGHAM, Tony	Thirty Acre Barn	1977-1979
(1947-	Mannamead	1980-1989

Tony Ingham was apprenticed to his father, *Stafford Ingham*, and took over the stables at Thirty Acre Barn when *Staff Ingham* died shortly before the start of the 1977 Flat season. In the yard was probably his father's shrewdest purchase, Persian Bold who Ingham had bought for 20,000 guineas. Trained by Tony, the horse won the Richmond Stakes, and was second in the Middle Park and the St James's Palace Stakes. Persian Bold sired the winners of over 1,000 races and £11million in prizemoney, and was twice European-based Champion Stallion.

Tony Ingham also enjoyed success over hurdles, training Levaramoss to win the 1984 Timeform Hurdle and the 1985 Free Handicap Hurdle. Ingham later trained in Macau.

INGRAM, Roger	Shifnal Cottage	1993
(1950-	Wendover	1994-

Apprenticed to *Brian Swift*, Ingram later had spells with Martin Tate, Michael Oliver (where he looked after West Tip in his novice chasing days) and Frank Jordan. He trained at Southwell, before moving back to Epsom. Among his better horses were the useful sprinter Rififi, with whom he won the Ladbroke Racing Sprint at Goodwood, Sky Crusader who won the 2005 Vodafone Group Handicap, and Boule d'Or who won two valuable handicaps in Dubai in 2005.

ISOM, Harold Charles	Holly Lodge	1948-1949
(1897-1962)		

Isom was born in Northamptonshire in 1897. He lived in the Epsom/Banstead area from 1922, taking out a training licence post-war following *Victor Tabor's* retirement. He died in 1962 at Amersham.

JACKSON, Captain John Henry	Downs Lodge/The Chalet	1904-1907
(1865- ?)		

JACKSON, G	1897-1899

Probably *Jackson, William Graham*.

JACKSON, J.	1917

JACKSON, William Graham	Lyndhurst, College Road	1886-1899
(1864- 1942)		

William G. Jackson moved from Wimbledon to Epsom, where he was based between circa 1886 and 1899. During that period he briefly hyphenated his name using Graham-Jackson as the name at his daughter's christening.

By 1901 he had reverted to styling himself William G. Jackson and was a "commission agent" based in Croydon.

JACOBS ,S.   Mickleham   1860,1865, 1866

Probably Sydney Jacobs, one-time owner with *Robert I'Anson Senior*, prior to a dispute that resulted in a court case.

JAGGARD, Abel   1854-1856
(1830-1856)

Jaggard was apprenticed to *Joseph French* at Newmarket in 1851 before training at Epsom. He died at Epsom in August 1856, one month after the birth of his daughter Priscilla.

JARVIS, Alan Peter   South Hatch   1987
(1938-

Formerly apprenticed to *Walter Nightingall*, Alan Jarvis was training at Royston when financial difficulties forced him to move. *John Jenkins* succeeded him at Royston.

JENKINS, John   Woodcote Stud   1984-1987
(1947-

After his apprenticeship to Gordon Smyth, Jenkins became a National Hunt jockey. He initially trained at Horsham, and subsequently moved to the Woodcote Stud, still mainly training National Hunt horses. He trained Wing And A Prayer to win the 1985 Tolworth Hurdle and Victor Ludorum Hurdle, and Beat The Retreat to win the 1984 Summit Junior Hurdle and the Mecca Bookmakers Hurdle Championship. After four years at Epsom he moved to Royston.

JENNINGS, Benjamin   East Street   1889
(c1860-1910)

Born in Northamptonshire, Jennings is listed as "stableman" in 1891 and 1901 census.

JOHNSON, Brett   Cedar Lodge   1998
(1963-   Shifnal Cottage   1999-2000
                          Little Woodruff   2001-2009
                          The Durdans   2010-

New Zealand-born Brett Johnson, rode 360 winners in Australia and New Zealand, before arriving at Epsom. Johnson spent five years working for *Geoff Lewis*, before taking out a licence.

JOHNSON, Edward   Althorp Lodge   1905-1909
(1865- 1945)

Of French/American descent, Johnson was training near Chantilly in 1903 when *Stephen Donoghue* was indentured to him. The relationship was short-lived due to Johnson's dire financial circumstances. Johnson trained at Upper Lambourn in 1905, and then moved to Epsom handling a small string at Althorp Lodge. He later trained at Lingfield, before moving to Newmarket. Johnson was down to two horses by now, and announced at a trainer's meeting: "I am a father of ten and unable to pay rates or school fees." The public appeal raised little apart from sympathy, and Johnson moved back to France.

JONES, John	Pitt Place	1871-1876
(c.1852- 1892)	Down Cottage	1876-1882
	Priam Lodge	1882-1892

Jones was born in 1852 in Cheltenham. He is recorded in the Sporting Gazette 1871 as training 13 horses while head groom to *Fothergill Rowlands* at Pitt Place. Jones left his mentor Rowlands in 1876, and moved to Down Cottage, as private trainer to Lord Paget and Sir Marcus Beresford.
In 1877 Prince Albert sent some horses to Priam Lodge to be trained by Jones. The move was facilitated by Marcus Beresford, the Prince's racing manager. The York Herald 1875 records that Jones had 30 horses in his care in that year, and The Era 5th January 1879 notes that Jones "has over 30 animals under his charge." Jones was an outstanding National Hunt jockey, and while combining riding and training had ridden Shifnal to win the 1878 Grand National. He was also associated with Chimney Sweep, the winner of the Cheltenham Grand Annual Chase in 1877 and the Grand Sefton in 1878; and High Priest, the winner of the 1879 Prince of Wales's Steeplechase. He trained Magic to win the 1888 Grand Sefton, and the 1889 Lancashire Chase. Notable hurdles successes include the winners of the Croydon Grand National Hurdle in 1876 with Woodcock and 1882 with Theophrastus; the Croydon International Hurdle with Lord Clive in 1881 and with Surge II in 1885; and Hungarian in the 1886 Liverpool Hurdle. Theophrastus also won Kempton Park Grand Hurdle in 1882.

A note in the York Herald 18th March 1889 recorded:

"Tycoon, Abbess, Butterscotch, and Primate have joined J. Jones' string at Epsom. On Tuesday morning the Prince of Wales visited Mr John Jones's stable at Tadworth near Epsom, where the horses Magic, Hottie, Hohnelinden and others belonging to his Royal Highness are trained."

The Penny Post, 12th March 1889 recorded:

"THE PRINCE OF WALES accompanied by Lord Alington, Lord Beresford, Lord A. Somerset, and Captain E.R.Owen were at Tadworth private park last Monday, where J. Jones, the Epsom trainer, had several of his cross country horse doing their work. Among them were Coquette (the property of the Prince of Wales); Monolith (the Grand National candidate), Forest King (entered at Kempton Park), and others."

Jones's son Herbert, (born 1880), went to Newmarket to serve his apprenticeship with *Richard Marsh*. He partnered Diamond Jubilee to victory in the 2,000 Guineas, Derby and St Leger. Herbert Jones did not fully recover from the accident in the 1913 Derby when Emily Davison stepped in front of his horse. On 17 July 1951, Jones was found dead in a gas-filled kitchen by his 17-year-old son. The coroner subsequently recorded a verdict of 'suicide while the balance of his mind was disturbed'. Referring to Emily Davison, the former jockey had once said that he was 'haunted by that woman's face' all his life.

John Jones died on November 3rd 1892; according to The Standard, after a long illness from "dropsy and gout", adding that "Until within recent years he had a long string of jumpers under his care at Epsom, and amongst his patrons was the Prince of Wales, for whom he trained The Scot and Magic."

Shortly before his death Jones appeared before Croydon Bankruptcy Court, he blamed his illness, a large family, and general expenses for his debts of £2,000. Jones reported that he had paid £2,600 for Priam Lodge, spent another £1,000 on improving it, and that it was mortgaged for £2,000. He claimed the only presents he had received from "persons of rank" were pictures and he wished to retain these as heirlooms.

John Jones's family suffered a number of tragedies during World War I; his sons Reginald (born 1878 and employed by *Richard Marsh*), Percy (born 1882), and Jack (born 1884) were all killed on the Western Front. Eldest daughter Jessie died in Epsom in 1918.

| JONES, PHILLIP M. | Turf Cottage, Belmont | 1887 |
| (1849- ?) | | |

Jones trained his own horse Resin the Bow at Turf Cottage between March and May 1887.

| JONES, W.H. | Eclipse Cottage | 1895-1896 |

Trained at Eclipse Cottage for Baron Topper Lanski, Baron Koeze, and Mr Oehlschlager. Jones was one of a series of trainers employed by the above owners; see also *Collins, Lutten, William Moore*.

Some of the winners are recoded as trained "privately". Moore returned to Germany in 1897, and rode the winner of the Grossherzog von Badenon on Slusohr, and Nicosia to win the Fursteberg Memorial in 1898.

KELLY, Joseph	Holly Lodge	1902-1908
(1878-1960)	South Hatch	1909-1910
	Derby Arms	1911-1915
	Priam Lodge	1928-1929
	The Haven, College Road	1933-1937

Lancashire-born Joseph Kelly was apprenticed to Alec Taylor at Manton. He came to Epsom to work for *Philip Greusil*. He subsequently worked for *Robert I'Anson* junior, before training at Holly Lodge, Kingswood. He trained for *Mr P Gleeson*, until the latter took out his own licence. Kelly moved to South Hatch in 1909, but by the 1911 census was based at Downs House (The Derby Arms stables). In June 1915 he took a lease on stables at Cheltenham. He later moved to train horses at Southfleet in Kent, returning to train at Priam Lodge in 1928. Kelly, living at 71 College Road, Epsom, died in 1960, leaving effects of £1,342 13s. 9d.

KELLY, T.	1906-1907

Possibly *Joseph Kelly*, or Thomas Kelly (1888-1951?) from Tralee. Based at Myrtle Cottage, Ashtead at the time of the 1911 census.

KEMP, Robert Hamilton	Tattenham Corner	1910
(1877-1933)	Bungalow, Beaconsfield Rd	1911-1915
	Heathcote House	1921-1929

Born in Norfolk, and educated at Winchester College, Kemp trained at Lambourn before taking stables at Ashtead and then Tattenham Corner. Kemp had served in the army from 1904 to 1905; and then again from 1915 to 1919. After the Great War he trained briefly at Portslade in Sussex, before moving back to Epsom. He was subsequently declared bankrupt. He attributed his bankruptcy in 1929 to lack of capital, to unprofitable racing seasons, and to heavy overhead charges of the Epsom stable.

KENNEDY, George	Rowland Lodge	1911-1916
(1866- 1929)		

Born in Durham in 1866, Kennedy was a former jockey riding on the Flat and under National Hunt rules circa 1900. He was based in Richmond, Yorkshire, and trained briefly at Newmarket prior to moving to Epsom.

KILLALEE, James   Portland House   1920-1939
(1887-1950)

Killalee served his apprenticeship in Ireland, and came to Epsom in 1911 as a jockey, taking out a trainer's licence in 1920. Killalee was a director of the Electric Theatre Company, one of Epsom's early cinemas that stood at the junction of Hook Road and East Street. He was instrumental in bringing jockey *Johnny Dines* over from Ireland, and also recommended *Jackie Sirett* and Charlie Smirke to *Stanley Wootton*. He died at Portland House, after sustaining injuries falling from a ladder. He left effects of £1,333.

KING, Walter   Headley Park   1984-85
(c.1917-1999)

Walter King first rode out on the Downs in 1924. Sixty years later he was training horses under permit at Headley. At the age of nine he was riding an old chaser called Tide on the gallops for *Jim Bell* ("the cleverest man to set foot on the Downs"), King fell off into the mud, stood up "all four stone of me", and said "I am muddy." *Jim Bell* picked him up, put him back on the horse and said, "Off you go Muddy"; thereafter he was known as 'Muddy' King.
Muddy served a five-year apprenticeship with *Walter Nightingall*. "We had three training yards, South Hatch. Long Hedge, and Beech Cottage," he said. "All the bad-legged horses he kept over the road at The Chalet." King recalled walking horses to stand in the Horse Pond at Ewell to cool their joints, or travelling down to Seaford to stay at David Dale's so that the horses could swim in the sea. Each lot was out for 90 minutes, often walking to Nightingall's racecourse at Walton Heath.
King recalled riding in three and a half mile gallops on the downs. The gallop involved racing behind Downs House crossing the racecourse at the mile marker, following inside the racecourse to the winning post then back across the Downs and behind Downs House...twice. "That was how we worked the Grand National horses, they would not start pulling till they hit Tattenham Corner then they'd swing on, they'd pull your guts out, wanting to go straight on at Chalky Lane. Imagine that in the sleet and snow."
Such was the strength of National Hunt jockeys in Epsom during the 1930s that King was on his own admission number eight or nine in the pecking order; in good company however, Paddy Prendergast was his rival for the selling chase mounts.
During the war, King served with the Veterinary Corps, the knowledge acquired with tending cavalry horses, plus his reputation for schooling "all sorts of villains," earned him the role of the "leg man" back in racing circles.
Muddy spent the 1950s working for half a dozen different trainers: "I didn't stop anywhere long". In the 1980s he took out a permit to train. With only three horses at a time in his care, Muddy could spend hours with each horse, adhering to the routine he had been taught as a boy. "Different game then." Muddy is credited with training three winners and 12 placed horses: "All old cripples that people wanted to give away."

KINGSTON   1910

Trained two horses at Epsom in July 1910 for Mr. H. O'Rourke.

KIRK, Captain John Charters   1897-1899
(1868-1922)

Born in Belfast, John Charters Kirk was a former Captain in the Royal Artillery. He succeeded R. *Dreffin* as private trainer to Mr W.H. Palmer. Kirk left Epsom in April 1899 to train at Lyddington. At the time of the 1901 census he was living at Hinton, Wiltshire, his occupation stated as racehorse trainer, but by 1903 had moved to Winterbourne, Gloucestershire. At the time of his death he was living in Monmouthshire and left effects of approximately £23,000.

KNIGHT, R.   Down Cottage   1887-1888

Listed under Epsom Trainers in The Sporting Life 11th January 1887. Knight is last mentioned in Training Intelligence in The Sporting Life in January1888. Richard Knight was employed as a stud groom at The Warren,

KNOWLES, Henry   1882-1887
(1842-1918)

Born in Findon, Sussex, Knowles was mainly involved in horse drawn cabs, and breaking horses. Knowles is first mentioned in Training Notes in the Sheffield and Rotherham Independent May 10th 1882; with the additional note that:

"Bones recently purchased by Mr. G.W. Bardrick has left J. Jones' stable for that conducted by H. Knowles at Epsom."

A note in The Cornishman 20th January 1887, records H. Knowles, the Epsom trainer, breaking several bones in his foot. Subsequently he is noted as a cab proprietor, until the time of the 1911 census, when Knowles is described as a "colt breaker."

LAMBDEN George   Leatherhead   1839-1852
(1811- ?)

Lambden is listed in Bell's Life Horses in Training section in 1839 and 1847.

LAND, Benjamin	The Warren	1862
(1815-1872)	Chance Cottage	1870-1872

Ben Land started his training career at East Ilsley, later moving to Englemere Cottage, Ascot Heath. In 1855 he had charge of the 1857 Grand National winner Emigrant, but sold it to George Hodgman for £500, after a losing game of cards.
He was employed as private trainer to Mr George Hodgman at The Warren in 1862, but the York Herald 20th December 1862 noted that the arrangement had finished, and Land returned to Ascot Heath.
In 1867 he took up a position as trainer to Lord Poulett at Droxford, where he trained the 1868 Grand National winner, The Lamb. After four years with Lord Poulett, Land announced that he did not require reengagement.

In 1870 he moved to train at Chance Cottage, Kingswood.

Ben Land's return to the area was noted in the Sporting Life 10th September 1870:

"On Monday last a numerous party met at Mr George Milne's the Red Lion hotel, Smitham Bottom, Coulsdon, Surrey, on the occasion of a dinner to Ben Land who has lately taken training quarters in the neighbourhood."

At the time of the 1871 census his address was in Horley. Land's finances were subject to sudden changes due to his gambling, hence his peripatetic career. It was in the paddocks at Chance Cottage that Land committed suicide by cutting his throat. He left under £1,500. He was the leading steeplechase trainer of his generation, and left two sons Johnny (born 1843), and *Ben Land junior* (born 1839). Both were good steeplechase jockeys.

LAND, Benjamin	Turf Cottage	1866-1868
(1839-1906)		

Son of *Ben Land* (1815-1872), He was an accomplished jockey, riding in the Grand National on nine occasions, recording two seconds and a third.

Sporting Life 3rd February 1866 recorded:

"Agag has gone to Sutton to finish schooling under the tuition of young Ben Land who has taken poor Charley Balchin's stables where Jealousy stood prior to her Grand National coup"

Young Ben was training for Messrs' Leigh, Sheward, Lynton and Willoughby.

95

However, the Sporting Life 13th March 1867 recorded:

"Mr. Sheward's horses have been removed from Ben Land's junior at Sutton and are now trained at the farm near Hendon by Griffiths."

There then followed a dispute over the running of a horse called Old Oswestry; the Sporting Life Wednesday 1st April 1868 summarised the severing of the relationship:

"LAND WITHOUT A COTTAGE-On Friday an action was brought by Mr. Leigh, a gentleman well-known on the turf against Ben Land steeple-chase rider. The object sought was to recover possession of a residence called Turf Cottage at Sutton and the following were the circumstances:- Mr. Leigh engaged Land to train a number of horses agreeing to let him have possession of the cottage in question, and to pay him a salary of £100 a year and ten guineas a mount. Matters went on under this arrangement for some for some time, but owing to the accident that occurred to Old Oswestry and to other circumstances, the plaintiff desired to break off the arrangement that had been entered into with the defendant. A meeting took place, accounts were settled, and it was expected that possession of the cottage would be given up. This however, the defendant refused to do, hence –the present action. Some technical points were raised on behalf of the defendant, but they were overruled, and a verdict was returned for the plaintiff."

The Sporting Life, 15th September 1869 noted:

"Young Ben land advertises for an engagement as trainer or Steeplechase Jockey in England or elsewhere."

After retiring from racing he moved to Islington, and worked as a tram driver.

LANGLANDS, Cecil W.	Hazon House	1922-1929
(1893-1982)	Thirty Acre Barn	1930-1940

Cecil Langlands was the brother of Charles W. Langlands, the clerk of the course at Epsom racecourse. He was educated at Tonbridge School, and served with the Honourable Artillery Company, later transferring to the RAF. In 1923 he married Nancie Lovat (1900-1946), the stage and musical star, they divorced in 1930. Langlands left an estate valued at £506,878.

Thomas Pardy, who assisted Langlands from 1930 to 1934, had previously trained the horses owned by Frank Barbour. Pardy had handled dual Gold Cup winner Easter Hero in its early career. Pardy had been badly gassed in the war, and died in 1934.

LANGLANDS, Geoffrey Stanger   Woodlands   1934-1939, 1948
(1901-1965)

Geoffrey Langlands was educated at Uppingham, after assisting his father in training racehorses on the family estate at Sutton at Hone, Kent, he moved to Epsom in the summer of 1934 after a spell at Lewes, returning to Lewes in 1940. Also known as Jock Langlands.

LANGRIDGE ,George   Golden Ball House, Clay Hill 1846
(1807- 1868?)   Chipstead   1847-1848
                          Headley   1848

At Langridge's Bankruptcy Hearing in 1850, he was described as a trainer of racehorses at Golden-Ball House, Clay Hill, then at Chipstead, then at Headley. He was Chipstead-based in the 1847 Ruff's Guide, and at Headley in the 1848 Ruff's Guide. He was at the time of his hearing working as a cab proprietor in London. The "Horses in Training" section of the York Herald lists Langridge as having four horses in 1846.

LARKIN, William Fraser   Bruce Lodge   1919-1934
(1886- 1965)   1939-1940

Bill Larkin was born in St Helens in 1886. He was apprenticed to William l'Anson and was working as a stableman in Epsom when he enlisted in the Suffolk Regiment, later transferring to the Queens Regiment. He set up as a trainer at Bruce Lodge after the Great War. His principal training success was with Imprudence who won the 1925 Gloucestershire Hurdle at Cheltenham. In 1932 Larkin suffered a severe injury after being kicked in the face by a horse, and was hospitalised for some time. After leaving Epsom, Bill Larkin trained at Lambourn, Seaford, and then at Gatwick. He briefly returned to Epsom in 1939.
In 1942 he accepted the role as private trainer to radio personality and bandleader Vic Oliver at Eastbury, Berkshire. Larkin's owners while at Epsom included the author Edgar Wallace. A prolific writer, Wallace was enamoured with the turf. He was an owner of some moderate horses, but backed them regardless of chance. Wallace frequented with, was respected by, and wrote about turf personalities from both ends of the spectrum. He wrote the racing memoirs for people as diverse as Lord Derby and Peter "Ringer" Barrie. In 1932 Wallace flew to America on a promotional visit, he naturally took in the local race meeting, where a race was named in his honour, shortly after Wallace contracted pneumonia and died aged 57.

LAWRENCE, Charles	Albion Villa, Caterham	1877-1879
(1846-?)	Coulsdon	1880-1881
	Smitham Bottom	1881-1883
	Field House	1883-1884
	Pitt Place	1886

Born in 1846 in Market Harborough, Charles Lawrence is listed in Ruff's Guide 1877 as training for Mr R. Clifford at Albion Villa, Caterham Junction. In the 1881 census he is shown as a groom of Godstone Road, Coulsdon. The Sheffield and Rotherham Independent, 1st December 1881 noted:

"All Mr. F. Frazer's horses are about to leave Clay's training establishment and will in future be trained by C. Lawrence at Smitham Bottom. C. Lawrence has now some useful horses under his charge"

.
The Sporting Life, 10th May 1883 recorded:

"C.LAWRENCE. This well known trainer, having taken the house and stabling recently in the occupation of W. Reeves, at Epsom, will come into residence at once. It is reported that his horses left Smitham Bottom yesterday. On route for their new quarters, where they will be joined by Holt's string. Both teams will be under separate management."

The Sportsman 25th December 1886 noted that *J. Martin* from Eclipse Cottage had succeeded C. Lawrence at Pitt Place. Lawrence subsequently moved to Germany.

LEARY, James	1905

Leary appears in Training Reports in The Sporting Life during the early part of 1905.

LEUTTEN (see LUTTEN)

LEWIN, T.	1870

Lewin is shown in The Sportsman, January 1870, as training three horses; see also *G.S. Daniels.*

LEWIS, Geoff	Thirty Acre Barn	1980-1999
(1935-		

Geoff Lewis arrived in Epsom in 1950 to be apprenticed to *Ron Smyth*. His numerous successes as a jockey included victories in the 1969 2,000 Guineas on Right Tack, the 1971 Oaks on Altesse Royale, and the 1973 1,000 Guineas and Oaks on Mysterious. His most outstanding partnership was with Paul Mellon's Mill Reef, trained by Ian Balding. In 1971 Lewis partnered the horse to victory in the Derby, Eclipse, King George VI and the Queen Elizabeth Stakes, and Prix de l'Arc de Triomphe.

Lewis retired from riding in 1979, and bought Thirty Acre Barn. He trained Rough Pearl to win the 1984 Italian St Leger, and came closest to Classic success in England with Silver Wisp who finished third in the 1992 Derby. Other Group 1 successes abroad included Yawa in the 1983 Grand Prix de Paris and the 1984 Premio Roma.

The best horses he trained were Silver Wisp, and the sprinter Lake Coniston. Unraced as a two-year-old, Lake Coniston won the Diadem Stakes at three, after which Lewis told the press that the horse was a champion, adding that he would "eat Perion and Port Of Light", (his hitherto best sprinters), "for breakfast." His prediction was verified when Lake Coniston won the Group 1 July Cup at Newmarket the following year. Leading from the start, Lake Coniston surged clear to win by four lengths for his owners Highclere Thoroughbred Racing Limited.

Lake Coniston's other victories included the Duke of York Stakes in 1995, and the Prix de Meautry in 1994. Lewis said of Lake Coniston: "He was the fastest I ever had anything to do with." Coincidentally, Persian Bold, the previous champion from Thirty Acre Barn, sired Lake Coniston's dam, Persian Polly.

Other Group winners trained by Lewis included Perion who won the 1988 Palace House Stakes, and Silver Wedge who won the 1994 Queen's Vase. Perion had been sold for 2,100 guineas as a three-year old, hobdayed, and used by Geoff as a hack. In 1987 he returned to racing and won four handicaps in succession, was second in the King's Stand Stakes, and won the Trafalgar House Stakes. Lewis's other smart sprinter Port Of Light had won the 1989 Phoenix Sprint.

In 1992 Lewis trained the two-year-old Silver Wizard who won the Sirenia Stakes, and was second in the Gimcrack. The horse started odds-on for the Middle Park but finished fourth.

In 1991 he landed some large bets for himself and his staff by backing himself to train 40 winners, and again in 1992 to train 50 winners. The string then suffered from a virus during which time Geoff shut the stable for two months. A new star appeared to have been found in Referendum who was beaten in a photo finish by subsequent Irish Derby winner Persian King in a Group 1 in Ireland, however the horse failed to reproduce that form again. After a couple of lean seasons, the costs of running Thirty Acre Barn proved prohibitive, and Lewis announced his intention to scale down the operation. The proposed move to a smaller yard did not come to fruition, and Lewis retired.

Summarising his career, Geoff Lewis said: "Lake Coniston was a great sprinter. I think Silver Wisp who finished third in the Derby may have been the best horse I trained, but he beat himself sometimes because he wanted to look after himself, whereas Lake Coniston was consistent. Obviously, the July Cup was the highlight of his career and probably mine as well. We'd had good sprinters before like Perion, who won a lot of Group 2s, but he was way in front of them, and a lovely horse to train as well."

Ian Balding said of Lewis: "He was always so proud of Epsom, and proved on many occasions that a good horse could be trained there."

LIDDELL,   1884

Belfast Newsletter 25th April 1884 recorded under the heading Epsom gallop reports:

"Liddell's Wild Duck, Tribune and Wokingham, and Mary Hood had good mile work."

LINES, Herbert	Down Cottage	1899-1900
(1872-1927)	Epsom	1914-1916

Born in Essex, by the time of the 1911 census, Lines was based at Clandon Cottage, High Clandon, near Guildford. Lines trained several winners in 1914 that are credited to "Lines, Epsom". He was based at Clandon in 1916 when he trained the winner of the Grand International Hurdle. Lines had moved to Newmarket by the time of his death

LOMAS, George	Burgh Heath	1898-1901
(1861-1909)		

Lomas was born in Manchester. Charles Richardson in his 1901 publication *The English Turf* refers to Lomas having charge of. *C.C. Dormer's* horses at Epsom.

LONGHURST   1902

Mentioned in Sporting Life gallop reports, notably March 1902.

LONGTON, William	Downs Lodge	1905-1907

Nottingham Evening Post 25th January 1905 recorded:

"Another Australian trainer will commence operations in England, W. Longton, who hails from the Antipodes, having arrived at Epsom, where he will take charge of Fleeting Love, Alberto, Chant and Butterwort, which animals were hitherto trained by Love."

Longton arrived at Southampton on 28th May 1904 via South Africa.

LOVE, A.	Downs Lodge	1904-1905

See *William Longton.*

LUMLEY, William Henry   Kings Head   1832-1844
(c.1796-1878)   1847-1863

Kelly's Directory shows William Lumley at The Spread Eagle in 1845, and the King's Head in 1852, and 1855. He was at the King's Head for the 1851 and 1861 census. His father-in-law John Gaston was keeper of the Spread Eagle for some time, and refers to Lumley training racehorses in his will of 1832. Weatherby's Racing Calendar 1844 p117 refers to *Mr Lumley, of Epsom, now trainer to Gen. Wyndham*; and The Horses in Training list in The Era 1844 lists him at Epsom with three horses. However, he subsequently moved to Berkshire, in Ruff's Guide 1847 he is described as moving from Lambourn to Epsom. A note in the Yorkshire Gazette February 1847 notes that Sir Peter Laurie is in training for the St. Leger at Lumley's Epsom yard. Lumley also moved to East Ilsley to train privately for Lord Strathmore, and then to Michel Grove in Sussex. For much of his time at Epsom he is listed as training his own horses. According to The Era in 1855 he had five horses in his care. He is listed in Bell's Life 1858 as training six horses, and in 1860 as training two.

A note in the Leicester Journal 13th November 1863 records:

"Mr. Lumley, Epsom has purchased The Pony, Vengeance for £200 for the Mauritius market."

Lumley's wife Charlotte, niece of Timothy Barnard, shareholder in the Epsom Grandstand Association, died 11th October 1861, and is buried at St. Martin's. Epsom. Lumley later moved to live with his brother-in-law James Gaston, (formerly landlord of the King's Shades in Epsom High Street), who kept the Station Hotel at East Grinstead.

LUTTEN/LEUTTEN   York House   1888-1889

The Sheffield and Rotherham Independent 19th December 1888 records:

"Dartmouth and Magna Charta have arrived at Epsom and joined Leutten's team at York House, where they will be trained in future"

Lutton is mentioned in The Sporting Life gallop reports, notably 16th February 1889: "Lutton's Bronte. Eilcuo, and Calpurnia were sent two miles."

Lutten trained primarily for Baron Topper Lasky. See *W.R. Jones, Collins,* and *W.H. Moore.*

LYNG, William   Priam Lodge   1917-1918

It was announced on 23rd February 1918, that Lieutenant William Lyng, "who trained a few horses at Priam Lodge", had been forced to retire due to severe injuries sustained during the Great War.

MACAW, (M'CAW)   Mickleham   1851-1852

Macaw is recorded in Ruff's Guide as training for Lord Lurgan at Mickleham. He subsequently took up a training appointment in Hamburg.

MacDONALD, William   Woodcote End   1847-1851
(1800-1856)

Shoreditch-born McDonald, aka Macdonald, is listed in the 1851 census, as training at Woodcote End (possibly Heathcote House). He was apprenticed to *Samuel Pearce*, and rode the 1840 Derby winner.

MACKSEY, Henry   Uplands   1888-1889
(1856- 1917)   Priam Lodge   1901-1905

Essex-born Macksey, had spells in Berkshire and at Findon, Sussex (selling the stables there in 1890 to F. Barratt). He spent some time in Chantilly, where in 1885 he married his wife. In 1888 his licence to train at Newmarket was withdrawn after claims that horses that ran in his name were the property of jockey Charlie Wood (see *James Wood*).

The York Herald 24th February 1888 recorded:

"Mr. H. Macksey, the trainer, has taken the Upland stables of Miss Weston at Epsom, and will forthwith recommence training operations there."

The Morning Post 28th July 1899 noted:

th
"The Stewards of the Jockey Club have withdrawn the notice published on July 18 1889 warning Henry Macksey off Newmarket Heath."

Macksey restarted his career at Priam Lodge in 1901. At the time of his death he was living at Twickenham, and left effects of £148.

MAHONEY, Pat	April Cottage Sturts Lane, Walton Heath	1967-1969

MAIRS, David (1878-1947)	Hazelwood Hillcot	1936-1939 1935

David Mairs rose to rank of Major while serving with Royal Army Service Corps in France during the Great War. He temporarily employed *Daniel McKenna* as his private trainer, before taking out his own licence to train during the 1930s, initially training at Lambourn in 1930-1931. An extrovert character, Major Mairs had limited success with his horses, but in 1936 he achieved the distinction of employing Paddy Prendergast, a fellow Langley Vale resident, as his National Hunt jockey. Prendergast became one of the great Irish trainers.

When Mairs returned to England from a trip to Australia in 1933, he gave his address as 127, Queens Gate, London; occupation horse trainer. He died in Bournemouth 1947 leaving effects of £255. 19s. 7d.

MANNING, D	Upperlands,	1893

Manning appears in the first copy of Horses in Training, issued in 1893 listed as training three horses.

MARSH, Joseph Mascal (1853-1926)	Rose Cottage, Ashtead	1878-1881

Marsh is listed as training at Rose Cottage, Ashtead in the Post Office Directory 1878, and appears in the 1881 census. Marsh was the brother of *Richard John Marsh*, trainer to Edward VII. From November 1874 Joseph was private trainer to Mr. Bevill at Findon, Sussex, where he trained the 1877 Oaks winner. His stay at Ashtead was hampered by financial difficulties, resulting in a bankruptcy hearing in 1880. In 1882 he moved to France, and trained there.

Marsh married Anne Page, whose mother Ann Page (nee Sherwood), was the daughter of *Ralph Sherwood*, in 1880.

Marsh was living at East Molesey at the time of his death, and had been working as a "Horse Dentist", and as a starter. He left £1,650.

| MARSH, Richard John | Priam Lodge | 1867-1868 |
| (1851-1933) | Turf Cottage | 1873-1874 |

Richard Marsh was born in Smeeth, Kent on 31st December 1851, and then moved to Priam Cottage (also known as Downs Farm.) In the 1871 census he is listed as a jockey living at Priam Cottage. His father Richard Marsh senior was still living there in 1878. Marsh (possibly Richard senior) is listed in Epsom training reports in 1867 and 1868. The Sportsman noted that in 1871, Marsh was supervising the Down Cottage team during W. Reeves's illness. A note in the York Herald 22nd February 1873 records:

"Marsh, the well known steeplechase jockey has, we believe taken the house and stabling formerly occupied by Henry May, at Sutton, Surrey and previously by the late Charles Balchin when he trained Jealousy, the winner of the Liverpool Grand National."

Marsh recalled in his autobiography schooling the horses on Banstead Downs using the schooling fences of Lord Marcus Beresford, the Prince of Wales's racing manager.

The York Herald 31st August 1874 records:

"R. Marsh has arrived at Newmarket with Farley, Fallero and Jackal, and they will be trained at Six Mile Bottom, where Mr H Blatazzi has taken the house and grounds lately occupied by Sir Wroth Lethbridge."

In 1874, Richard Marsh trained and rode Jackal to win the Grande Course de Haies d'Auteuil. He also trained the winners of the same race in 1882 and 1886.
In The London Gazette, June 22nd 1875, a bankruptcy notice records the liquidation of the partnership of Arthur Beer and Richard John Marsh trading as racehorse trainers of Turf Cottage, Sutton.
In 1892, Marsh was invited to train at Egerton House, Newmarket, for the Prince of Wales, who subsequently became King Edward VII. His successes while training at Newmarket included 14 English Classic winners.
Marsh died at Cambridge in 1933 leaving effects of £383.

MARSH, W.   1873

The York Herald 6th December 1873 noted: *"Queen of the Chase has left Peter Price's stable at Newmarket to be trained by W. Marsh near Epsom for jumping."* Possibly *Richard Marsh.*

MARTIN, Edwin   Rowland Lodge   1921-1926
(1866-1946)

Son of Newmarket trainer Edwin Martin, "Teddy" Martin trained and rode in Germany between 1895 and 1903, where he was champion jockey in 1901, and 1902. He subsequently trained at Royston and Lambourn (1906-1912), before moving to Epsom after the Great War. He left Epsom on 26th March 1926 to train at Ogbourne., but is shown as based at Rowland Lodge in Kelly's directory for 1927.

MARTIN, F.   Woodcote End   1869-1870

The Sportsman notes in 1869 that F. Martin is now training at Woodcote End. Martin appears in the Sporting Gazette 1870 listed as training three horses at Epsom.

MARTIN, James	Beech Cottage	1866-1868
(1828-1911)	Eclipse Cottage	1869-1873, 1883-1886
	The Parade	1874. 1875
	Priam Lodge	1875
	Bordeaux House	1876-1882
	Rowland Lodge	1887-1895
		1900

James Martin was born in 1828 at Maidstone in Kent, and trained from at least six different stables in Epsom. There was a Martin (probably James) at Epsom as early as 1866. The Racing Indicator 1866 records, *"Mr Partner's horses have not yet left Nightingall, Martin has one of the gentleman's, takes others next week."*
James Martin appears in the Sporting Gazette 1870 as training ten horses, six in 1871, 12 in 1873, and seven in 1875 when his address is given as Rose Cottage, but Kelly's Directory lists him at Priam Lodge. The York Herald , 29th December 1877 lists him as having 14 horses.
Martin is credited with training Rosy Cross to win the 1880 Lincolnshire Handicap, the horse later moved to Joseph Dawson at Newmarket for its final gallops. The Sportsman 25th December 1886 records that Martin had moved to Pitt Place, (stables at Rowland Lodge).
Martin's son Sydney enlisted in the army as a horse transport driver in 1903. After two years he returned to Epsom. He became a stable lad at *Richard Wootton's* stables. In the 1911 census he was described as a groom and trainer of racehorses. In 1914 Sydney was called up for service, and two weeks later he was in the front line at the Battle of Aisne. When two officers were wounded, Martin was ordered to go with an officer and an orderly to rescue them. The two officers could not be moved without treatment. Despite being under continue bombardment Martin treated and rescued the men. Two days later he was awarded the Medaille Militaire, (the French equivalent of the Victoria Cross) on

the battlefield by King George V, and the Prince of Wales. Sydney Martin later worked for the council as a road sweeper. His daughter Dorothy married the jockey, Lionel Read, son of trainer *George Read*.

James Martin's sons Albert, John and Herbert were all working in Newmarket stables at the time of the 1901 census. The youngest son Henry Leonard also moved to Newmarket to work for trainer Percy Peck. Henry enlisted with the 20th Hussars, in 1916 he was shot through the neck, and is buried near Ypres in Belgium.

Training Intelligence in The Sporting Life 15th February 1900, lists James Martin under Epsom Trainers.

James Martin was living in South Street at the time of his death. A local newspaper article described him as "a popular, affable man who was training in Epsom for the best part of forty years, and a regular churchgoer."

MASON   1890-91, 1899

Appears in Training Reports c. 1890-91 as a trainer; and also as a work rider for *Thomas Aldridge*, possibly based at The Durdans.

MAY, Arthur   Heath House   1882
(1853-1890)

Bell's Life and Sporting Chronicle, 18th March 1882 recorded,

"Arthur May and Charles Sellars have taken the stables Burgh Heath, Epsom recently occupied by R. I'Anson."

The Sheffield Independent on 2nd April 1890 recorded:

"Arthur May, the jockey, died at Epsom on Sunday morning of consumption after a long illness."

Arthur May, trainer, of College Road, is buried in Epsom cemetery.

MAY, George or J.   Walton Heath   1890-1893

J. May, Epsom is recorded as the trainer of The Saint, winner of a hunter chase, ridden by Arthur Nightingall, at Windsor on 18th February 1890.

106

MAY, Henry E.	Smitham Bottom	1851
(c.1819 –1889)	Turf Cottage, Sutton	1869-1871
	Heath House	1871-1881
	Maidstone House	1881-1884
	Heath House	1887-1889

Born at Moulton in Suffolk, Harry May was training at Redbourne, Hertfordshire in 1850 at the time of the birth of his daughter Julia May, who subsequently married *Robert I'Anson*. He is recorded in the 1851 census as a "Trainer of Racehorses" based at the Red Lion, Smitham Bottom. In 1854 he is listed in Ruff's Guide as training at Cleeve Hill, Cheltenham. May is believed to have trained two Grand National winners, (Little Charley in 1858, and Anatis in 1860). Christopher Capel, who lived at Prestbury Park, owned both horses. Some records credit the training of both horses to William Holman. However, Ruffs Guide records that May trained at Cleeve Hill, Cheltenham from 1854 to at least 1858, with Christopher Capel listed as one of his owners. From 1860 to 1865, May was training at Codford, Wiltshire, with Christopher Capel still listed as one of his owners.

The Sportsman 12th December 1865 noted:

"As is customary at this season of the year, several changes been made noblemen and gentlemen in regard to their trainers. Harry May, so many years with Mr Capel, at Codford is promoted to the charge of Lord Stamford's stud at Enville, vice Smith, retired."

He became private trainer around 1868 to the alias ownership of Mr Lynton/Mr Willoughby/etc which was actually the money of John Gerard Leigh and the expertise of Samuel Brisco Sheward, the West End horse dealer. They ran hunters in the big steeplechase events like the Liverpool and Croydon Grand Nationals. To get Harry May into Turf Cottage at Sutton they had to go to court to evict Mr Lynton's previous trainer, young *Ben Land*, in March 1868. In 1869 the Anderson and Sheward partnership ended, and May left soon after. In 1872 May moved to Heath House, Burgh Heath, where his son-in-law *Robert I'Anson* succeeded him.

In 1877 there were suggestions of raising a subscription for his aid due his suffering from gout 'and other problems'. He continued operating on a smaller scale, assisted by his sons.

At the time of the 1881 census May was still living at Banstead, but around that period he was training from Maidstone House in Chalk Lane, Epsom. May's horses are noted in gallop reports for Epsom on 31st January 1884, and in April 1889.

His sons, HENRY MAY junior, (born in Mickleham in 1848), and EDWARD MAY, (born in Redbourn in 1850); appear on the 1871 census residing at the Surrey Yeoman, Burgh Heath. They are both described as horse trainers. By 1891, Edward May is living in Church Road, Epsom described as groom, training stables. On 29th January 1898,

Edward May, a 47-year-old stableman was admitted to Epsom Union Workhouse, but transferred to Netherne Hospital three days later.

The Sportsman, 3rd April 1889 reported:

"We regret to announce the death of Mr. H.E. May which took place at Belmont. He will be best remembered as having trained Little Charlie, and Anastis, the former carrying off the Grand National in 1858, and the latter winning the same race in 1880."

MAY, William	Mickleham	1841-1842,1848-1850
(1828- ?)	Leatherhead	1853-1855

The 1851 census shows William May, a groom, born in Somerset living at Burford Lodge Mickleham. W. May, is listed as training at "Leatherhead" in Ruff's Guide, 1853 and 1854, and at Mickleham in Ruff's Guide 1848.

"May" is listed in the 1842 York Herald as training four horses, two for Mr Laurence, and two for Mr. Sterling. He was subsequently training for Lord Gratwicke.

MAYLAM, Olivia	Chalk Pit	2011-2013
(1982-		

Formerly based at Newmarket, prior to moving to Epsom.

McALLISTER, William	Woodcote Rise	1905-1911.1916
(1879- ?)		

McAllister trained at Woodcote Rise stables in Hylands Road, where *Percy Woodland's* sister *Ethel Woodland* assisted him. His major success came with Do Be Quick who won the Grand International Steeplechase at Sandown in 1907.

McGRILLAN, Thomas	1870-1871
(1840- ?)	

McGrillan (sometimes recorded as M'Grillane), was working at the East Ilsley stables at the time of the 1861 census. He rode in the 1862 Grand National; from 1863 he was riding in France, and was training there from circa 1865.

The Sportsman 12th April 1870 reported:

"T. McGrillan, Steeplechase trainer to the Nanquette confederacy in France has sent his wife now in a poor state of health to Nice, trusting that this move to a favourable climate may ensure her recovery."

In February 1870 he brought some horses over from France for the Grand National. From December 1870 to March 1871 he was based at Epsom, having runners at local meetings, and appearing in Epsom training reports.

McKENNA, Henry D.	1916,1922-1923,
Hazelwood	1928-1929

McKenna was born in Northern Ireland, and later lived and trained near Maddenstown. At the turn of the century, McKenna was based in Salisbury, (where his son was born), and subsequently at Hednesford and Rottingdean. In 1916 winners are recorded as trained by McKenna, Epsom, *(possibly James McKenna.)* Between 1924 and c.1927 he was at Letcombe Bassett, and was private trainer to *David Mairs* c. 1928-1929.
McKenna's son Daniel Burke McKenna was apprenticed to *Stanley Wootton*. D.B. McKenna (1899-1939) was later private trainer for Mr. D. Kenyon in the early 1920s until Kenyon's death. He was also a playwright, being author of "Van Gogh" which was due to show in the West End until the outbreak of war. D.B. McKenna drowned in 1939; his father-in-law was Senator J. Parkinson, Irish horse trainer and major bloodstock exporter.

McKENNA, James   Down Cottage   1907-1909
(1856- ?)

Born in County Down, McKenna is listed in Kelly's Directory 1909 as a trainer based at Down Cottage, Burgh Heath Road where he was renting from Joseph Merrick. He was training in Shipton, Hampshire at the time of the 1891 census moving to Salisbury in 1892. At the time of the 1911 census he was living at Hammersmith, but was resident at The Amato c. 1922 according to the Register of Electors, (see also *Henry McKenna*). In 1909 he trained 17 winners on the Flat, the second highest number for an Epsom trainer behind *Richard Wootton*. McKenna trained for Essex-based horse dealer George Aston.

McKIE, William A.   Althorp Lodge   1904

McKie previously trained at Wroughton, and first appeared on Epsom Gallop reports in 1904. The Sportsman reported on 6th December 1904 that 21 horses had been transferred to Mckie's Epsom stable from Jevington. The following day The Sporting Life reported that *H.S. Persse* had taken the Althorp Lodge stables recently occupied by McKie.
McKie subsequently moved to Tilshead in Wiltshire.

McLEAN/M'LEAN   1884-1885

Based in Epsom from November 1884 to March 1885, M'Lean trained for German owner Herr Oehlschlager. The Sporting Life 10th November 1884 recorded:

"The following horses have arrived from Germany looking healthy and well and will be trained by McLean. Viz Idea, Halmi, Lady of the Lake, Bell Tower, Sylph, Potosi and Pallas."

See also *Collins, Moore*. He rode for Herr Oehlschlager in Germany in 1874.. In February 1889 Thomas McLean is mentioned among a group of jockeys leaving Epsom for Germany, (see *Max Phillips*).

McNAE, Angus   Ermyn Lodge   1998-1999
(1966-

Angus McNae was assistant trainer to *Joe Naughton*, and was with *Naughton* during the period of Hever Golf Rose's success. He left *Naughton* in 1998 to train at Ermyn Lodge. His best horse was Teofilio who finished third in the Bunbury Cup. He later trained briefly at Compton in Berkshire, and at Wolverhampton Racecourse.
After retiring from training, McNae embarked upon a successful career as a racing broadcaster.

McNAUGHTON, Ben/Bernard   Hillcrest   1920-21
(1876-1924)

Born in County Meath, Ireland, McNaughton was head lad to Richard Dawson at Whatcombe, Berkshire, and for a while nominee trainer for Dawson. In Ruff's Guide 1920 his principal owner is noted as *George Barclay*; McNaughton was probably based at Hillcrest in Burgh Heath Road.

MELLISH, William   South Hatch   1857-1859
(1803-1872)   Woodcote Green   1860-1862

Is listed in The York Herald 1860 as training ten horses at Woodcote Green. See *Ned Smith*. During the period 1851-1857, he employed *J. Escott* as his private trainer.

MILES, H.   1867

H. Miles is listed in "Special Training Notes" in The Sportsman, 2nd November 1867. No other record is found for him at Epsom, and he appears to have been supervising *Reeves'* horses.

110

MILLER, Michael   Bredenbury   1941-1942
(1892–1952)

Miller died at his home Bredenbury in Longdown Lane in 1952 leaving effects of £7,731.

MILLS, Robert   Loretta Lodge   2010-2015
(1972-

Robert Mills succeeded his father *Terry Mills* at Loretta Lodge in 2010.

MILLS, Terry G.   Loretta Lodge   1993-2010
(1939-2010)

After *Brian Swift's* death, Loretta Lodge was sold to Terry Mills who at that time owned some horses in training with *Tony Ingham*. Mills had started life in the scrap metal business in south London, and had built his company into one of the largest waste disposal businesses in the country. In 1993 Terry Mills took out a trainer's licence. His first major success was with Bobzao who won the 1994 Hardwicke Stakes.

In 1999 Mills trained Mitcham to win the Coral Sprint Handicap, and the King's Stand Stakes. Further Pattern Race success followed with Mr. J. Humphreys' Where Or When who won the Somerville Stakes in 2001, and achieved Group 1 success in the Queen Elizabeth II Stakes in 2002. The horse also finished second in the Lockinge Stakes and third in the Queen Anne Stakes.

In 2002 Mills won the Cornwallis Stakes with Peace Offering, and in 2005 trained Resplendent Glory to win the Laurent Perrier Stakes, and Close To You who dead-heated for the Champagne Stakes.

In 2004 Imperial Applause won the Group 3 Prix Eclipse at Chantilly.

Top handicappers from the yard included stable favourite Norton who won the 2002 Royal Hunt Cup, Wannabearound, winner of the 2001 Tote Trifecta Handicap, Boleyn Castle who won the valuable 2002 Hong Kong Jockey Club Sprint, Evaluator winner of the 2005 Summer Stakes, and Greylami who won the 2009 Rosebery Stakes.

Many of the horses that Terry Mills owned or part-owned took were named after Frank Sinatra songs, Mills attributed this to "just being an old romantic."

Mills improved the excellent facilities at Loretta Lodge, extending the property, installing a solarium, equine pool, and buying the 42 acres of gallops at Thirty Acre Barn to install a new 5 furlong all-weather gallop, to add to the 5 furlong oval Polytrack gallop at Loretta Lodge. The total estate at this time extended to 101 acres. Mills also invested considerably in top class horses. Summing up his passion Mills said: "I'm fortunate, I can subsidise it. The thing is I could look at horses, all day, every day, for the rest of my life."

MILNE, George E.	Tadworth Cottage	1855-1862
(1822- ?)	Smitham Bottom	1868-1870

In the York Herald 21st January 1853, Milne is listed with four horses under his care at Epsom. Ruff's Guide 1861 recorded Milne as training at Epsom. "Tiny" Milne, is shown in Bell's Life 1862 as E. Milne, training six horses from Tadworth Cottage. In January 1861, George Milne, "late of Tadworth, near Epsom, trainer of Racehorses"; appeared in the Court for Insolvent Debtors, he was described as being "In the Queen's Prison." His wife Esther appears on the 1861 census alone at Tadworth Cottage. By 1863, Milne was based at Barham, in Kent.
In 1870 Milne's son, H. Milne, left Smitham Bottom to take up a training appointment for Signor. E. Ginistrelli near Naples. In the 1871 census George Milne is the licensee at Red Lion, Smitham Bottom. In 1881, Milne's wife Esther was back at her birthplace Newmarket, where her son George Milne Jnr. (1854-1894) was training.

MITCHELL, C.	1900-1901

Possibly Charles Mitchell, born in 1863 at Wolverhampton, who was based at Newmarket in 1901. Mentioned in Training Intelligence in The Sporting Life 19th October 1900;
"Mitchell's Busby Stoop, and Suspicion cantered five furlongs. Bourton Lass went seven furlongs on the tan."

Also mentioned in Training Intelligence 9th January 1901.

MITCHELL, Cyril	Heath House	1952-1967
(1915-2001)	Downs House	1968-1974

Former *Vic Smyth* apprentice, Cyril Mitchell, took over at Heath House Stables at Burgh Heath in 1952. He trained Golden Lion to win Royal Ascot's top sprint, the King's Stand Stakes in 1954.
Sir Peter O'Sullevan, who had horse with Mitchell for many years, described Mitchell as:

"A former tough, grafting jump jockey, he took an irreverent view of the "art" of training, believing that some horses are naturally better than others and that it is the trainer's job "to see that he doesn't screw up the good ones." His admiration for jockeys was also kept under control."

O'Sullevan recalled a telephone call from Mitchell in March 1966: "It looks as if you've done it this time…bought one that can run, and I do mean run."

The horse was Be Friendly. At that time O'Sullevan wrote a column in the Daily Express, and via his writing communicated the joys and setbacks of racehorse ownership. Be Friendly built up a considerable following, with every racing enthusiast from the Queen Mother down, following the progress of the inexpensive horse trained by an unfashionable trainer from a yard behind a pub.

Be Friendly's final race as a two-year-old was in the Vernon's Sprint at Haydock. The horse won by two lengths, O'Sullevan commentated on the race for BBC television with his customary professionalism, and at no time did his voice betray the sense of personal triumph.

In 1967, Be Friendly won the Kempton 2,000 Guineas Trial over a distance a shade too far, with *Scobie Breasley* nursing him home, but then returned to sprinting.

With give in the ground Be Friendly was the best sprinter of 1967. He won the King's Stand Stakes, the Ayr Gold Cup, and the Vernon's Sprint. Between the latter two races, the horse contested the European sprint championship, the Prix de l'Abbaye, but missed the break.

In October 1968, with *Geoff Lewis* in the saddle, Be Friendly won the Abbaye. In contrast to the previous year, Be Friendly broke well, always led, and won by a comfortable two lengths without coming off the bit.

Be Friendly won the Sceptre Stakes and Palace House Stakes in 1969, but given the odd training setback and unsuitable going, was not up to the previous high standard. Be Friendly retired as the then all-time highest prize-money winner in Europe.

Another good horse from that period was Boysie Boy; a moderate performer at two and three, but as a four-year-old in 1969, he won five races, including a victory over Lorenzaccio-who beat Nijinsky in the Champion Stakes the following season. Boysie Boy produced another fine display when second in the Prix du Moulin.

O'Sullevan's successor to Be Friendly was an unattractive individual, named Attivo, who was beaten in a few selling races as a two-year-old.

The following year, Attivo running off low weights over long distances, eventually won a handicap. Mitchell, like most of the old Epsom trainers, liked to give his suitable three-year-olds a school over hurdles, in Attivo's case this proved to be a turning point. Attivo won the Evesham Hurdle at Cheltenham by 20 lengths with a bold display of front running. Stable apprentice Robert Hughes kept the mount in the Daily Express Triumph Hurdle. At the home turn Attivo went clear, but he ploughed through the last hurdle nearly unseating Hughes in the process. The field closed, but horse and jockey recovered to win by four lengths.

Attivo's hitherto modest form on the Flat had left him on an undemanding handicap mark, and partnered by 7lb claimer Roger Wernham he won the Chester Cup and the Northumberland Plate. At the end of 1974 Mitchell retired and moved to Majorca. Later when asked: "What was your best day in racing?" he replied: "The day I gave it up."

MITCHELL, Phillip   Downs House   1976-2007
(1948-

Cyril Mitchell handed over the reins at Downs House to his son Philip. During an eight-year riding career, Philip Mitchell had been champion amateur on five occasions, and had ridden 65 winners from 128 rides. His training career got off to a bright start when Salado won the John Porter Stakes.

Philip achieved further Group race success with Sylvan Barbarosa who won the 1983 Cork and Orrery Stakes, and Sylvan Express who won Group 3 races in Ireland and Germany. He also won the 1982 Lincoln Handicap with Kings Glory.

In March 1998, Mitchell trained his first major race winner for several years when Mr. Richard Cohen's Running Stag won the inaugural Winter Derby at Lingfield. Mitchell had bought Running Stag from France privately. In August 1998, Running Stag won the Group 3 Prix Gontaut Biron at Deauville, and then went to America where he was third in the Woodward Stakes, and fourth in the Jockey Club Gold Cup, both Grade 1 events.

In 1999, Running Stag returned to America, and won the Grade 2 Brooklyn Handicap, and the Saratoga Breeders Cup Handicap, as well as securing valuable place money on several occasions. In December 1999, Running Stag went to Sha Tin for the Hong Kong Cup. "The Stag" ran a fantastic race to finish second behind course specialist Jim and Tonic, winning prize money of £170,000 pounds in the process. In 2000, "The Stag" won the Masachusetts Handicap, amassing a total career prize-money of £I million.

The Racing Post commented,

"For trainer Philip Mitchell, it provided vindication of his unshakeable faith-and also a chance to answer those critics who have spoken of his globetrotting campaign in patronising terms."

Philip's sons Jack and Freddie Mitchell both became successful jockeys. Philip Mitchell had business problems in 2007, and handed in his licence while the matters were resolved. He left Downs House in 2012, to train at Lambourn.

MOLONEY,   1846, 1852

Recorded in Ruff's Guide 1852 as training at Epsom for Mr. Johnstone. Probably based at the Derby Arms stables.

MONGAN, Laura   Condover   2003-
(1980-

As Laura Sheen, she rode five winners on the Flat as an amateur and had spells with *Brett Johnson* and *Brooke Sanders.* She subsequently married the Group 1-winning jockey Ian Mongan, who had been an integral part of Sir Henry Cecil's team during the Frankel period.

Laura Mongan sprang to public prominence when winning the 2016 St Leger with Mrs. J. Cornwell's Harbour Law. In the process she became the first woman to train a St Leger winner, the first Epsom trainer to train a St Leger winner, and the trainer of Epsom's first English Classic winner since John Sutcliffe's Right Tack in 1969.

Harbour Law had won on his first two starts for Laura Mongan, and then finished second in the Queen's Vase at Royal Ascot, and fourth in a Group 3 race at Newmarket. The horse was then rested prior to his trip to Doncaster where he was sent off a 22-1 chance for the St. Leger.

George Baker rode the horse to maximise its stamina. "Held up towards rear, headway 3f out, driven in final furlong, stayed on well to lead near finish", the Racing Post recorded. "Surreal" was Laura Mongan's reaction, adding "We wouldn't have brought him here if he'd been a 100-1 no-hoper. I don't want to go to make the numbers up. People have said he should be in a bigger yard working with better horses, but we got him there in great shape and he won."

Her husband and assistant trainer, Ian, was more emotional, recalling later: "I lost my voice, I was screaming, I nearly choked poor Olly, (Oliver Jago, the groom leading Harbour Law in), almost broke his shoulder, and I was blubbing away afterwards, but that's how much it mean to us all, not just the day, but everything since we got him. You can't help but worry. We've got one bullet in the gun, and if that goes, that's it gone, so you find yourself looking for imaginary stones that he might tread on, and because we live on the yard and we can hear every little knock and bang, I'll go out and check on him in the middle of the night, and he'll just be standing there looking at me as though I am a lunatic."

Laura Mongan added: "Every morning and every evening you'd look at him and say please be okay. Once I got him there I didn't feel the pressure, because I don't doubt myself, I don't doubt us or the horse and we never doubted we were doing the right thing by going to the Leger."

Ian Mongan recalled his former employer Sir Henry Cecil telling him "Good horses make good trainers." Harbour Law, who added a third in the Ascot Gold Cup in one of just two races after his Leger heroics, proved he was top class, and the Mongans, with only 20 horses, mostly lowly-rated, proved that given the horse they could train it to its peak on the required day.

A successful dual-purpose trainer, Laura Mongan's previous biggest success was with First Avenue, the winner of the 2013 Imperial Cup.

MOONEY, Peter   Ermyn Lodge   1996-1997
(1950-

Peter Mooney took out a licence in 1996 to train his own horses. His most successful horse was Kilcullen Lad who won five races.

MOORE, Garret   1881

Garret Moore was the younger brother of *William H. Moore*, and son of *J.H. Moore*.
Training reports that identify "Moore's horses" make it difficult to identify which of the
three family members was in Epsom at any given time.
Bell's Life, 3rd December 1881 states:

"Mr G. Moore's Lobelia and Woodburn covered three miles over country in Jones's
private grounds. Wild Norah and Athlacca galloped the same distance."

Garret Moore owned and rode the 1879 Grand National winner The Liberator, and was
second with the same horse in 1880.

MOORE, Gary   Ermyn Lodge   1993-1996
(1951-

A former National Hunt jockey, and son of Brighton-based trainer Charlie Moore, Gary
Moore had significant success while training at Epsom with Karinga Bay, who won three
Group 3 races in Germany in 1993. Moore returned to train at Brighton, and he later
moved to Horsham, with *David Wilson* as his assistant trainer. All four of his Gary's
children tasted success as jockeys; Classic-winning Ryan, jump jockeys Jamie and
Joshua, and daughter Hayley, who rode several winners before turning to broadcasting.
Gary quickly outgrew his Brighton yard, moving on to Lower Beeding in Sussex where
he established himself as one of the country's leading dual-purpose trainers. Among his
notable winners was Sire De Grugy whose successes included the Queen Mother
Champion Chase in 2014, and the Tingle Creek Chase in 2103 and 2015.

MOORE, J.H.   Bordeaux House   1882

Father of *William* and *Garret* Moore; J.H. Moore was residing at Bordeaux House when
on April 5th 1882 he wrote to The Sporting Life regarding the objection made by John
Jones, jockey of Theophastus, against Moore's Theodora ridden by Mr. J. Beasley
following a race at Croydon.
J.H. Moore trained the 1879 Grand National winner The Liberator, Bell's Life stated
after the race that the horse was wintered at Ludlow and then bought to Epsom following
his victory at Croydon. However, on 5th April 1879, the paper stated that J.H. Moore had
written to contradict the statement that the horse's preparation was finished at Epsom,
and that be brought him back to Ludlow, the day after the Croydon meeting.

MOORE, William H.   York House   1881-1887
(1857- ?)

Moore is mentioned in Epsom training reports in the Sheffield and Rotherham Independent 28th March 1882;
"Moore was also jumping Theodora, and Lord Liverpool went two miles over hurdles. Vivular went two miles on the flat, and Bold Brennan did healthy exercise."

When Theodora won the Autumn Handicap at Alexandra Park in 1881, and dead-heated in the Croydon Grand Handicap Hurdle in 1882, it was in the ownership of W.H. Moore.

Moore split his time between riding Herr Oehlschlager's horses in Epsom, and in Germany. As a jockey he rode the winner of the Baden-Baden Steeplechase (Altes Badner Jagdreenen) on four occasions for Herr Oehlschlager, in 1883,1884,1886,1887.
Moore, Epsom is listed as the trainer of two Grand National entries in 1884, Lady of the Lake and Idea, both owned by Mr. Oehlschlager. He also trained for Baron Lanski, and Baron Koitze.
After leaving Epsom he trained three Grand National winners, including Why Not, ridden by Arthur Nightingall in 1894. See also *Collins, Lutten, M'Lean.* and *W.R. Jones.*
Described as "cantankerous at the best of times" by the Hon. George Lambton in his book Men and Horses I have known; in April 1899 Moore moved to Stockbridge, and *Collins* who shared the Grand National successes moved with him.
His brother Garret Moore was also involved with riding Herr Oehlschlager's horses.

MOORE,   Heath House   1907

Moore trained one winner in 1907, owned by *Patrick Gleeson.*

MORGAN, Francis   Downs House (Derby Arms) 1934-38
(1888-1970)

Born in Waterford, Frank Morgan won the 1904 Irish Derby on Royal Arch. He was resident in Church Street, Epsom in 1918, with brothers Thomas and Isaac, (both jockeys), and his son Thomas Francis, (later a jockey). He later trained at Stoughton, in Sussex. Together with Richard and Thomas Francis Morgan he was based at the old Downs House stables 1934-1938.

MORGAN, Richard	Badminton	1910-1912
(1882-1944)	The Durdans	1920-1921,1928
	Bredenbury	1929-30
	Kings Head	1922

Born in Waterford, "Dick" Morgan was one of a family of National Hunt jockeys/trainers who spent some time at Epsom. Dick Morgan rode in eight Grand Nationals. Morgan's career was itinerant with spells at Epsom, Tring, Portslade and Lambourn. Financial problems interrupted his career, and he was subject of a Receiving Order in 1922.

He stayed at the King's Head, Epsom in 1922, following several incidents there, he was sent to prison for 14 days on 22nd February 1922 for wilful damage. He re-appeared in court on 15th May 1925 on a drunk and disorderly charge, his wife told the court that she feared for her life, and Morgan was discharged to receive treatment.

His address at the time of his death was St. Pancras Hospital, he is buried in Epsom Cemetery.

MORGAN, Thomas	1912-1914, 1916
(1862- ?)	

A former soldier, born in Dublin, Morgan was a blacksmith in Burgh Heath Road, who trained a few horses.

MORGAN, William	The Warren	19109-1911
(1881-1915)	Woodcote Side	1911

Born in Waterford, Ireland, William is the brother of *Francis* and *Richard Morgan*. He rode the second in the 1902 Grand National. After a bad fall in 1913, he returned to Ireland. He did not fully recover and died in Waterford in 1915.

MORLEY LAWSON, Victor	Longdown House	1955-1963
(1908-1989)		

The lawyer Victor Morley Lawson was married to the daughter of former jockey Otto Madden. Morley Lawson entered the record books in an unusual fashion when he rode Ocean King to victory in 1973; becoming the oldest man to ride his first winner.

MORRIS, Derek W.	Ermyn Lodge	1997-1999
(1963-		

Formerly apprenticed to *John Jenkins*, Morris rode Mister Ed to victory in the Midlands Grand National for *Roger Curtis*. After leaving Ermyn Lodge he trained at Lambourn.

MULLINGAR/MULLENGER, Walter Smitham Bottom   1869-1877
(1831- 1914)

Born in Bungay, Suffolk; in the 1851 census "Mullenger" is working as a "trainer's servant" at Wroughton, Wiltshire. In the 1871 census Mullingar is shown as the trainer at the Red Lion, Smitham Bottom, with *George Gregory* as a stableman, and *George Milne* as the licensed victualler. The York Herald 6th December 1873 noted that the steeplechaser David Copperfield had been presented to Mr. Baylis after a race at Croydon and "joins Mullingar's team at Smitham Bottom." He died at Croydon in 1914, recorded as Walter Mullenger.

NAUGHTON, T.J.   The Durdans   1992-2001
(1963-

Formerly assistant to Barry Hills, Joe Naughton attracted public attention with Hever Golf Rose, a filly that was sent to The Durdans after failing to reach a 6,000 guinea reserve at Doncaster Sales. Hever Golf Rose won a competitive nursery at Newmarket, and then a Listed race in Germany. In the following year Hever Golf Rose really bloomed. *Racehorses Of 1995* states:

"Hever Golf Rose-it is hard to know where to begin. She has had thirty one starts in all and won thirteen of them, eight in 1995 including six pattern races: the epitome of toughness, Hever Golf Rose keeps coming back for more. This has taken her from handicapper to the best five furlong performer in Europe, most of which she seems to have visited."

Hever Golf Rose set a new course record when winning the King George Stakes at Goodwood. She won the Prix de l'Abbaye, Europe's sprint championship, with consummate ease, two and a half lengths clear and pulling up as she crossed the line. Her six Pattern race wins in 1995 were more than those for any other horse, and no older filly trained in Britain since the war can match her total of eight wins in a season. The following year she proved tough as ever but somewhat unlucky, finishing second or third on twelve occasions. In 1997 Hever Golf Rose won the Prix de St. George and the Prix du Couvert in France, and the Taby Sprint in Sweden.

NEAL   1884

Listed in Sporting Life gallop reports in 1884, but was actually head man supervising *Lawrence's* horses.

NEVILL, William	East Street	1897
(1843- ?)		

Employed as a "groom" according to the 1871 census, and a "Turf Correspondent" in 1881, Nevil was described as a horse trainer in 1897 at the marriage of his daughter.

NEWEY, Alfred	South Hatch	1918
(1882- 1940)		

Alfred Newey took out a jockey's licence in 1902. He had his best season in 1905 when he was runner-up in the Jockeys' table. He rode Eremon to win the Grand National in 1907. He later trained at Hednesford, and Cheltenham. He was living at Cheltenham when he died in 1940 leaving personal effects of £2,810.

NEWMAN, C.		1920-21

NIGHTINGALL, Arthur	South Hatch	1892
(1868-1944)	Heath House,	1893-1894
	Priam Lodge	1889, 1894-1901
	Badminton	1904-1907, 1920

Arthur Nightingall, who was born at South Hatch on 1st August 1868, succeeded *John Jones* at Priam Lodge in 1895.
Racing Illustrated, in the January 1896 edition, records,

"As a horseman Arthur Nightingall has acquired very great and thoroughly deserved reputation. In France and Germany, as well as his own country, he is looked upon as a great master of his art."

Arthur Nightingall, in his book *My Racing Adventures* states,

"Riding, as alleged, runs in families, and it certainly seems to have been running very freely in mine for a long time past. We have cultivated a fine natural taste for jockeyship."

Arthur Nightingall rode in 15 Grand Nationals, riding three winners, a second, and four thirds. He also rode the winner of the Scottish Grand National, and in 1901 rode in the Derby. He rode the first of his three Grand National winners on Ilex. He had ridden the horse to a comfortable victory in a hunter chase at Leicester, and recommended to the owner, Mr. G. Masterman, that he sent the horse to his father, *John Nightingall* at Epsom. Eighteen months later the partnership won the Grand National. In Ilex's final gallop Arthur rode him for four miles around the Nightingall's private racecourse at

Walton Heath, and reported him as "a certainty." He noted in his book that Mr. Masterman sent him a cheque for £1,000 after the Grand National.

The Nightingall family were particularly successful at the Croydon racecourse, and *Arthur* was proud to have ridden the last steeplechase winner, and the last Flat race winner before the course closed in 1890. He also rode a hurdle race winner at the last meeting.

In 1893 Arthur moved to Heath House, and was training eight horses there that year, while still riding. His second Grand National success came in 1894, riding Captain C. Fenwick's Why Not, who carried 11st.13lb. The Daily Telegraph recorded,

"That the result of a punishing race was in favour of Why Not was due entirely to the jockeyship of Arthur Nightingall."

In 1896 Arthur rode Count Schomberg to win the Grande Course de Haies d'Auteuil . Arthur's third success in the Grand National came in 1901 on Grudon. The snow was so deep that the race was in doubt. Only five of the original 24 starters finished.

Arthur Nightingall subsequently summed up his career,

"Not being satisfied with being actively employed as a steeplechase jockey which is occupation enough for three men until they are killed. I began to train racehorses, chiefly jumpers towards the back end of 1892. I commenced to train racehorses in the stables formerly occupied by Robert l'Anson at Burgh Heath near Epsom. I had the great honour of training for His Majesty the King. On account of increased patronage and a larger number of horses, I was obliged to move to Priam Lodge, at one time I had no fewer than thirty-two jumpers. What amount of hard work that means for a man who is both a trainer and jockey."

Like several of his Epsom colleagues Nightingall served in the Army Remount Service at Redhill, preparing horses and mules during WWI. Arthur Nightingall stopped training after the death of his wife, and subsequent attempts to revive his career as a trainer were short-lived. He died in 1944, and his ashes were scattered on Epsom racecourse.

THE NIGHTINGALL FAMILY-TRAINERS AT EPSOM

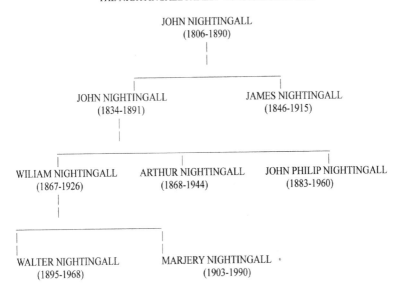

JOHN NIGHTINGALL
(1806-1890)

JOHN NIGHTINGALL   JAMES NIGHTINGALL
(1834-1891)   (1846-1915)

WILIAM NIGHTINGALL   ARTHUR NIGHTINGALL   JOHN PHILIP NIGHTINGALL
(1867-1926)   (1868-1944)   (1883-1960)

WALTER NIGHTINGALL   MARJERY NIGHTINGALL
(1895-1968)   (1903-1990)

NIGHTINGALL, James   South Hatch   1871-1874
(1846-1915)   Beech Cottage   1875-1878,1891

James Nightingall, (born in Welwyn, Hertfordshire), was initially the jockey for his brother *John Nightingall* (b.1834). The horses James trained during his stay at Epsom including Hampton, winner of the Great Metropolitan Handicap in 1875, and subsequent winner of the Doncaster Cup, and the Northumberland Plate. James Nightingall bought Hampton for £200 out of a selling race. Hampton also sired three Derby winners. The York Herald 10th May 1876 noted:

"Austerlitz, Hampton, De La Motte, and Last Of The Novelties have left James Nightingall's yard for Robert I'Anson Junior at Tadworth Cottage, Banstead , Epsom to be trained."

Austerlitz, who had recently won the Prince of Wales Steeplechase at Sandown Park, subsequently won the 1877 Grand National.
Nightingall had 14 horses in his care at South Hatch in 1873; and in 1875, Bell's Life records him moving to the adjoining Beech Cottage with 12 horses. The York Herald records that he had ten horses in 1876. His time at Epsom was interspersed with periods training at Lewes (from 1878), and Hampton Cottage, Robertsbridge in Sussex, and also at Leatherhead. He returned to Lewes in 1893.

NIGHTINGALL, John   Beech Cottage   1867-1882
(1806-1890)

Father of *John Nightingall* (born 1834), Nightingall senior appears on the 1871 census as a trainer, and in Kelly's Directory 1875 and 1882. His grandson, *Arthur Nightingall* recalls riding work with John Nightingall, by which time the old man was in his seventies.

NIGHTINGALL, John   South Hatch   1860-1891
(c.1834-1891)

The Nightingall family arrived at South Hatch in the mid 19th century, having previously been based in Hertfordshire, where John was born in Welwyn. The Manchester Courier, 27th October 1860 noted
:
"J. Nightingall has taken South Hatch stables to which the horses under his care at Welwyn will be removed."

The Nightingall family heirlooms include a presentation whip inscribed, "Thomas Nightingall 1738", and some 230 years later the family were still training winners.

John Nightingall (b.1834) was married first to Mary Ann. Their sons, *William* (b.1867), *Arthur* (b.1868), Robert (b.1874) and John Philip (b.1862) all rode a winner on their first mount over fences. Shortly after his oldest son John's first winner, he was killed in 1876, in a riding accident on Headley Common when his horse hit a tree.

John Nightingall married for a second time to Alice (Annie) I'Anson, the sister of *Robert I'Anson* (b.1850), on 27th March 1877 at Walton on the Hill. By his second marriage he had another son, *John Nightingall* (b.1883). Old John Nightingall observed, "Young Jack will be the best of the lot, his mother is *Robert l'Anson*'s sister." Though the younger John rode many winners, he did not match the achievements of *William* and *Arthur*.

John Nightingall had nine horses in his care in 1861, but the stable grew rapidly with 13 horses in 1863, 24 in 1864, 27 in 1865, 31 in 1869, rising to 37 in 1870, and 29 in 1875.

John Nightingall's first major success was the victory of Cecil in the 1868 Cesarewitch. Cecil went to Newmarket as 5-1 favourite, he won by a length ridden by *Robert Wyatt*, who put up 3lb overweight at 5st 13lbs. The status of the Cesarewitch in those days was such that the field included the Derby winner Blue Gown, and an Oaks winner Tormentor

It was John Nightingall who played a key role in the provision of communal gallops on Epsom Downs, which he supervised strictly (see *Robert Waiting*.) He also had his own private racecourse on Walton Heath.

The York Herald 29th January 1870 noted:

"The Steeplechase training ground at Walton Heath, has lately been thoroughly put in the best possible condition. It is the private property of Mr. Studd over which the grand trial for the Liverpool Steeplechase took place last season."

The same journal on 11th February 1871 recorded:

"We understand that J. Nightingall, the trainer, has taken the training ground at Walton Heath recently occupied by E. Studd."

John Nightingall would only allow his sons *William* and *Arthur* to ride the serious work, and *Arthur* recalled that on occasions they rode 15 to 20 horses between them in a session, sometimes riding work at Sandown Park after, adding: *"The amount of riding we used to do in those days was nothing short of amazing."*

Arthur Nightingall, described the private racecourse:

"The private hurdle and steeplechase course belonging to South Hatch is at Walton Heath about three miles from the stable, and all the fences there are designed of course to the regulation pattern. They are pretty strongly built up in harmony with the finest classical taste. They want "doing", and if they are half done a complete "pearler" is

124

likely to be the result. This is in my opinion one of the best schooling courses in England for young chasers, and the jumping of twenty horses or more there in the morning provides a very sporting spectacular."

John Nightingall trained two Grand National winners at South Hatch. The first was Shifnal in 1878. The early career of Shifnal provides an insight into the training methods at the metropolitan courses at the time. In November 1872, the three-year-old Shifnal finished second in a mile and a half hurdle at Croydon. In February 1873 Shifnal won a maiden hurdle at Bromley, four weeks later Shifnal won the Streatham Steeplechase ridden by *Robert l'Anson*, and a month later won a two-mile chase and a handicap hurdle at Bromley. In 1876, Shifnal won the United Kingdom Grand Steeplechase, and also the Surrey Grand Open Steeplechase, both at Croydon.

Shifnal won the Grand National at the third attempt having previously finished third and sixth. *Robert l'Anson* declined the ride in the belief that the horse had had his chances in the past. Shifnal was owned and trained by John Nightingall, and survived the first ever objection to a Grand National winner.

John Nightingall's second Grand National success came with Ilex, owned by Mr. G. Masterman. Paddock judges who considered him "wrong in the back," derided the former hunter. The horse won the Grand National by ten lengths, but jockey *Arthur Nightingall* recalled that he could have won by much further. Ilex also won the Lancashire Steeplechase at Manchester in 1890.

John Nightingall trained the winner of the Grand International Hurdle twice, Lord Clive in 1881, and Freedom in 1888, and the Liverpool Hurdle in 1890 with Toscano, and the Sandown Grand Prize with Courtier in 1887, and Castilian in 1889.

Other trainers used the Walton course when permitted. *The Sporting Life,* 12th January 1907 noted in the Epsom Gallop reports, *"Captain Jackson's string travelled to Walton for jumping practice." Walter Nightingall* was still using the private racecourse in the 1930s, and the gallops were used for training racehorses in the 1970s.

By the time John Nightingall handed over the reins at South Hatch to *William* and *Arthur,* the gallops on Epsom Downs had become professionally organized and maintained. *Arthur* noted:

"The gallops are kept in excellent order and condition all year round, even in Summer Six Mile Hill affords good going, and as I need scarcely add many winners are trained there every season. Our winter gallops at Epsom are also excellent. The circular two-mile tour represents a delightful journey, starting at the back of Sherwood's and finishing at Tattenham Corner. We soon find out, having slipped along merrily, whether a horse gets the distance."

John Nightingall told his son *Arthur, "All we want is the goods my boy, give us the right sort of horses and then we can win as many races as other people, perhaps more when our circumstances are unusually desperate."*

John Nightingall left a personal estate of £9,141.

NIGHTINGALL, John Philip   Beech Cottage   1911-1917
(1883-1960)   1920-1939

John Nightingall was the son of his father's second marriage, to Annie I'Anson. Nightingall was apprenticed to George Challoner at Newmarket. He retired from race riding after breaking his leg and ankle in a fall at Kempton. He was a member of Epsom Golf Club, and was club captain in 1928. He left effects of £13,751.

NIGHTINGALL, Marjery   South Hatch   1968
(1903-1990)

The daughter of *William Nightingall,* she took over the stables at South Hatch on her brother *Walter*'s death after assisting him throughout his career. She held the licence for the remainder of the 1968 season; from 104 runners, she had 13 winners and 28 places. She was within half a length of an important race winner, when Mr Louis Freedman's Lucyrowe finished second in the Cheveley Park Stakes.
A keen sportswoman, outstanding rider, and good golfer, she was Lady's Captain at Epsom Downs Golf club in 1931, 1949, and 1953.

NIGHTINGALL, Walter   South Hatch   1927-1968
(1895-1968)

Walter Nightingall succeeded his father *William.* Walter's career as a jockey ended at the age of 14 when he fractured his skull in a fall at Windsor. He served in the Royal Army Veterinary Corps during the war, becoming assistant trainer to his father in 1919. Walter became a victim during the 1919 stable lads' strike, when he was assaulted by a group of stable lads while riding work for his father. Three of the defendants were given a conditional discharge; a fourth who had been fined the previous week for assaulting George Pellerin, a French jockey attached to *Stanley Wootton's* stable was fined again.
One of Walter's head lads at South Hatch was a colleague from the Veterinary Corps, Bill Hives. He remained with Walter for 40 years, and was regarded by Walter as *"the finest vet. in the realm."* Essentially remembered as an outstanding Flat racehorse trainer, Walter's early successes were under National Hunt rules. He won the Imperial Cup and the Jubilee Hurdle with Zeno in 1927 within weeks of taking out a licence. He won the Liverpool Hurdle twice, with Arctic Star in 1930, and Advancer in 1934. He was still training with success over jumps in the post-1945 period. He trained the runner up in the Imperial Cup in successive years 1947, 1948, and 1949, and had a winner at the Cheltenham Festival in 1948 with Clare Man who won the Cheltenham Grand Annual Handicap Chase.

Nightingall trained 55 winners in his first season, and had notable success with Jugo, who he had bought out of a selling race. Jugo won 15 races in all including the Great Metropolitan Handicap.

Nightingall's first Classic winner was Rock Star who won the 1930 Irish Derby. Owned by Sir Matthew Wilson; Rock Star ran once as a two-year-old finishing unplaced. As a three-year-old he had three runs prior to finishing second in the Irish 2,000 Guineas. He was still a maiden when winning the Irish Derby by two and a half lengths, at odds of 5-1. The following season Rock Star finished second in both the Coronation Cup and the John Porter Stakes.

On 16th December 1937, the charismatic heiress Miss Dorothy Paget announced that she would not be renewing the lease on her stables at Ogbourne St. Andrew, but would be sending all of her horses (except two) to Walter Nightingall; it was the start of a productive, but turbulent partnership. In 1943, Walter Nightingall won the Derby with Miss Paget's Straight Deal, (due to wartime restrictions the race was run at Newmarket). Between the Guineas and the Derby Straight Deal showed dramatic improvement. His final gallop was outstanding, and Walter phoned Miss Paget, and told her he thought they had the Derby winner. Straight Deal just failed to stay the trip in the St Leger, (also at Newmarket), and finished third beaten less than a length, after leading as they came out of The Dip. Miss Paget regarded wartime restrictions with irritation, and took the view that racing was essential for the morale of the country. In 1942 she came under fierce criticism for sending 22 horses to Nightingall from Ireland, and a question was asked in the House of Commons regarding the appropriateness of her behaviour. A fearless gambler she would arrive at the racecourse at the last minute, and aided by her secretary, Ruth Charlton, (later the third Mrs Charlie Smirke), proceed to back her horse. She demanded daily reports on all her horses, if not racing she rarely rose before 16.30, and was therefore apt to raise her trainer with a telephone call at 02.30 to discuss entries. Walter Nightingall trained over 200 winners for her, he was by nature a mild- mannered man, but eventually gave her immediate notice to remove her horses, following a disagreement at Sandown.

Miss Paget issued a statement:

"A mutual apology for the most inglorious and undignified behaviour on both sides might have been possible, but you have made this impossible through making the private matter public property, so am sending for my ten remaining horses as soon as possible. Regret that having won the Derby together we had to part in such an unnecessary flamboyant and stupid manner, but nevertheless I on my part bear no malice and hope you win another Derby for someone else. Many thanks for the pleasure we used to enjoy in the years gone by."

Such was Nightingall's success, that Lord Derby offered him a formal invitation to move to Newmarket as private trainer. After a great deal of contemplation, Nightingall elected to remain at Epsom as a public trainer.

In 1951 Nightingall was cited in the divorce court by fellow Epsom trainer *George Duller*, whose wife Bessie was a niece of Music Hall star Marie Lloyd, and daughter of Epsom trainer *George Hyams*. Walter Nightingall and Bessie subsequently married.

In 1949 Nightingall commenced a training connection that was to bring him great success and make him a focus of public attention. At the age of 75, Britain's war time leader Sir Winston Churchill was persuaded by his son-in-law to own a racehorse. Nightingall, in partnership with Epsom veterinary surgeon Mr. Carey Foster, had purchased a promising three-year-old called Colonist for £1,650. They sold the horse to Churchill for that price. In 1950 Colonist won on eight occasions from 11 starts, and in 1951 won a further two races. His successes included the Jockey Club Cup, the Winston Churchill Stakes and he was second in the 1951 Ascot Gold Cup. The British public, who followed Colonist's exploits with great enthusiasm, held Churchill in high esteem. Colonist was a tough front-runner, who would often appear beaten, but then draw on extra reserves of strength. "Ran on gamely" or "came again" were frequently used in the formbook to describe his victories. The Daily Telegraph, 26th October 1950 summed up the horse's popularity:

"More than a quarter of a mile from home, Gosling let Colonist II go, and once again we had the gripping spectacle of this grey and gallant horse, flaxen tail flowing in the wind, plugging along in front. There followed the ringing cheers and the familiar scene of hundreds of happy people scampering to the unsaddling enclosure to acclaim horse and owner. Never, surely, has there been a racing partnership the equal of this".

At the end of Colonist's career, Nightingall recommended that Colonist should become a stallion, Churchill remarked that he did not intend to spend his retirement years *"living on the immoral earnings of a horse."* Sir Winston did eventually set up a small successful stud.

The victories achieved with Churchill's horses, helped to make Epsom a fashionable centre, and in 1952 the Queen sent Gay Time to South Hatch to be trained. Nightingall had the largest string of racehorses in the country in 1939, and by 1952 *Vic Smyth* had equal numbers. Colonist's half-brother Le Pretendant was trained by Nightingall to win the 1956 Cumberland Lodge Stakes, and the Churchill Stakes.

Nightingall achieved more success in the early 1960s with two more Churchill-owned horses: High Hat and Vienna. As a three-year-old, Vienna finished third in the St Leger, and won the Blue Riband Stakes, a race Nightingall had won the previous year with My Aladdin. The following year Vienna's three victories included the Lyons Maid Stakes, and at five he won the Prix d'Harcourt and was second in the Prix Ganay. In 1962 he was third in the Champion Stakes. In the Prix de l'Arc de Triomphe he finished fourth, beaten in a photo finish, giving 10lb to the winner Right Royal. High Hat's victories in 1961 included the victory over Petite Etoile in the Aly Khan International Memorial Cup, and, appropriately, the Winston Churchill Stakes.

On 27th October 1964, Winston Churchill wrote to Walter Nightingall from 28 Hyde Park Gate, London:

"My Dear Nightingall,
It is very sad for me to have to end my racing activities owing to the fact that my health does not allow me to attend race meetings any more.
I know that this decision will cause sorrow to you too, since we have had such a long association. My mind goes back to the Spring of 1949, when Christopher persuaded me to buy Colonist. He gave us all great excitement and pleasure, and he was also the forerunner of many successes. I am so grateful to you for the skilful way in which you have trained the horses that I have sent to you from my stud. It does not fall to many people to start a racing career at the age of seventy-five and to reap from it such pleasure.
Yours very sincerely, "

It was thought to be one of the last letters that Churchill sent, and is signed with a shaky, but full signature. "Christopher" is Christopher Soames, Churchill's son-in-law.
In 1960 Nightingall trained another high-class horse in Prolific. The horse had been purchased by *Peter Thrale* for only 400 guineas, was unraced as a two-year-old, and joined Nightingall on Thrale's death. His successes as a three-year-old included five length victories in the Queen's Vase, and the Jockey Club Stakes. Prolific, and *Staff Ingham's* Apostle, were invited to take part in the Washington International at Laurel Park in America, but torrential rain made the going unsuitable for both runners.
In 1965 Nightingall achieved his second British Classic success when Mr. W. Harvey's Niksar won the 2,000 Guineas. Niksar started the season with an effortless six-length victory in the Kempton 2,000 Guineas Trial. At Newmarket, Niksar made all the running in typical Nightingall style. The horse raced relentlessly on the far side, Silly Season, the favourite, was clear leader on the stands' side, but then veered right when challenging at The Dip, leaving Niksar to win by a length. In the Derby that year, Nightingall saddled the third and fourth, I Say and Niksar. The following year I Say won the Coronation Cup.
Ill health was by now affecting Nightingall, and his sister Marjery and head lad Stan Pullen were playing an increasing role in running the stable. Pullen had joined the yard in 1935 as a 5 stone apprentice, and remained at South Hatch as head lad for *Scobie Breasley*. Among many jockeys to serve their apprenticeship at South Hatch were Bill Rees, and Ray Reader, and future trainers *Alan Jarvis*, and *David Hanley*. In 1967 Nightingall finished ninth in the trainers championship, despite training only 18 winners. Shrewd placing captured the Dewhurst Stakes, Greenham Stakes, Imperial Stakes, King George Stakes, Victoria Cup and the City and Suburban.
Nightingall's owners in the latter years included Lady Beaverbrook, whose colours later became famous with horses such as Bustino and Boldboy. Nightingall trained Hametus for her to win the 1967 Dewhurst Stakes. Another recruit to racehorse owning with

129

Nightingall was Louis Freedman, whose yellow with black spots silks were later carried to Derby victory by Reference Point.

Nightingall's reputation for trying with all of his horses, invariably having them running up with the pace, coupled with his success rate in big races earned him much admiration, the popular newspapers dubbed him "The Saturday Specialist".

Walter Nightingall was a keen golfer, and club captain at Epsom Downs Golf Club in 1947. Nightingall died on 6th June 1968, the same day Delabare, owned and trained by him won at Brighton.

Roger Mortimer wrote of Nightingall,

"He was a modest, friendly man of considerable charm whose horses were always out to win, and throughout his career he served the Turf with distinction."

Nightingall's obituary in The Times stated,

"His knowledge, judgement and integrity made him a complete master of his profession."

Walter Nightingall left £110,905 net.

NIGHTINGALL, William   South Hatch   1890-1926
(1867-1926)

William Nightingall rode with some success under National Hunt rules; notable winners included the Liverpool Handicap Hurdle on Hungarian in 1886, the Baden-Baden Steeplechase on Fenelon, and the Aintree Hunt Steeplechase on Cloister in 1888.

He moved to Hoppegarten in Germany to train there in 1889.

He took over as trainer at South Hatch at the time of the death of his father *John Nightingall* on November 13th 1891. William's younger brothers John and Robert were stable jockeys. In 1893 he had 22 horses in training, and by 1898 he was training for Lord Rosebery.

William took over the tenancy of the private racecourse on Walton Heath. A draft contract drawn up in 1896 reveals that the rental agreement was £35 per annum payable in two instalments, and was for renewal every three years. Solicitors for the owner, Henry Padwick Lord of the Manor noted;

"The landlord cannot concur but will not object to any posts, chains, rails, fences or any other erections which for eleven years past have been erected."

Winners trained by William Nightingall on the Flat include Ivor who won the 1895 Manchester November Handicap, and Ambition who won the 1905 Jubilee Handicap. He also won the 1904 Peveril of the Peak Plate at Derby with Marsden, and the

Northamptonshire Stakes with Grand Deacon. Under National Hunt rules his most important successes were with Rory O'Moore who won the 1896 Grand Sefton Chase, Scotch Pearl who won the 1925 Imperial Cup; and Simonson the champion hurdler of 1907/08 after winning the 1907 Great Sandown Hurdle. Nightingall also won the Grand International Hurdle with Lucinda in 1905, and Rassendtyl in 1907.
Simonson won the Duke of York Stakes at Newmarket the following year.

On 23rd July 1914 William Nightingall made his will:

William Nightingall, of South Hatch, Epsom,
To my wife, absolutely all articles of household and domestic use or ornament, which shall at my death be in or about my house South Hatch or the gardens occupied therewith.
To my son, Walter Nightingall, absolutely in the event of his desiring to carry on the business of a trainer of racehorses all my harness, saddlery and stable furniture and other effects used by me in my business as a trainer which were belonged to me at the date of my death.
To my wife Annie Elizabeth Nightingall, £250.

Twelve years later, William Nightingall amended the legacy:

Dated 24th December 1926, I William Nightingall of South Hatch, Epsom, Trainer of racehorses declare this to be a codicil to my last will. I give and bequeath to my wife Annie Nightingall my motorcar and all accessories.
To my son Charles William Nightingall, the sum of £400, to my son Walter Nightingall, the sum of £100, to each of my daughters Violet Elizabeth Nightingall, Dorothy Lockhart Nightingall, Marjory Lucinda Nightingall, and Muriel Helen Nightingall the sum of £100.

William Nightingall died shortly after at the age of 59, he left £29,072 gross, £15,831 net.

NIQUET, Lucien   1915

Also known as Niguet, Lucien Niquet was the proprietor of the *Sport Belge*, the leading Belgian sports paper. As an owner he brought horses to run in England from 1895; and on the outbreak of the Great War, Niquet and several other Belgian sportsmen came to England with their horses. Niquet trained some horses at Epsom, yielding only one winner, and horses were eventually sold. After the war he returned to Belgium.

NIXON, (or DIXON)   1884

The Sheffield and Rotherham Independent 11th January 1884 noted:

"Dixon's Valeureuse. Idea, and Lady of the Lake had two useful spins".

On the 31st January 1884 the same publication reported:

"Nixon's Idea galloped a mile at a useful pace alongside the tan."

The Cheshire Observer, 19th January 1884 noted that Nixon (Epsom) had two entries for that year's Grand National. At the February declaration stage the horses are shown as trained by *Moore* Epsom.
Nixon/Dixon was briefly acting as trainer for Mr. Oemschulberger's horses, see *Collins, Moore, Lutten.*

NUNNELEY, Philip T.B.	Myrtle Cottage	1934-1937
(1913-1993)	Langley Bottom Farm	1937-1939
	Ascot House	1943-1950
	Maidstone House	1951-1953

Nunneley had an itinerant career, training from at least four different stables in Epsom during a 20-year career. For most of his career his address is listed as Maidstone House, in Chalk Lane, and he probably stabled a few horses there. His mother Mrs Phyllis Nunneley was the second wife of Hubert Nicholls (1879-1958), a Lloyd's underwriter who lived at Maidstone House.

O'KELLY, Colonel Dennis	Melision Lodge
(C.1725-1787)	

Colonel Dennis O'Kelly was born in Ireland in 1728. He had worked variously as a sedan chair carrier and a billiard scorer prior to serving a prison sentence for debt. On his release Charlotte Hayes, a lady of dubious repute, financed him and with her backing he established a reputation as a shrewd and fearless gambler. He served in the Middlesex Militia, thereby acquiring (possibly purchasing) the rank of Colonel and established his own racing stables on Epsom Downs. The request to provide a galloping companion for a horse trained at Mickleham changed his life, the horse was Eclipse.
The Duke of Cumberland had bred Eclipse at his stud in Windsor Forest. On the Duke's death in 1765, his bloodstock was offered for sale by auction. *William Wildman*, who had a training yard at Mickleham, went to the sale, and purchased the colt for 75 guineas.
Back at Mickleham, the horse proved to have a fiery temper. *Wildman* sent the horse to Epsom where a local man named George Elton gave Eclipse a lot of work, and focussed

Eclipse's energy on running. The horse was nearly five when Elton sent the horse back to Mickleham, and *Wildman* soon realised he had something special. Eclipse made his racecourse debut on 3rd May 1769 winning at Epsom. On 29th May at Ascot he won two heats without coming off the bit. O'Kelly landed some hefty bets on the first heat, and before the second heat made his now famous boast, "Eclipse first, the rest nowhere." O'Kelly quickly appreciated that the horse would be difficult to back in the future, but he saw the breeding potential and bought a half share from *Wildman* for 650 guineas.

On June 13th at Winchester, Eclipse won both of the four-mile heats, and walked over in the 50 Guinea Plate. On June 29th he walked over in the King's Plate and won the City Bowl at Salisbury. His other outings that year were at Canterbury - walked over, Lewes - won the King's Plate, and Lichfield - won the King's Purse. At the end of the year O'Kelly bought the other half share in Eclipse for 1,100 guineas.

On 17th April 1770, Eclipse ran at Newmarket. O'Kelly bet 600 guineas to win 400 guineas, and for the only time in his career, Eclipse was off the bit to win. Two days later Eclipse landed the King's Purse, winning both heats over 3 and half miles. Eclipse won twice more at Newmarket, and once at Nottingham before winning twice at York. Successes at Lincoln and Guildford followed before a return to Newmarket where O'Kelly obliged a bookmaker who offered 1/70.

Eclipse retired unbeaten. He won 2,149 guineas in prize-money, and on his retirement it was said of Eclipse: "Never had a whip flourished over him, or felt the tickle of a spur, or was ever for a moment distressed."

Eclipse retired to O'Kelly's stud at Clay Hill, Epsom. Over the next 14 years O'Kelly took £25,000 in stud fees for Eclipse. He kept more than 50 mares at Clay Hill, and two other stallions, Volunteer and Dungannon.

Following Eclipse's retirement and the inauguration of the Derby and the Oaks, horses trained at the stables adjacent to the Derby start by Dennis O'Kelly and his grooms were dominant in the Epsom classics:

1780	Boudron	2nd in the Derby
1781	Young Eclipse	Won the Derby
1783	Dungannon	2nd in the Derby
	Primrose	3rd in the Oaks
1784	Serjeant	Won the Derby
1786	Scotia	3rd in the Oaks
1787	Gunpowder	2nd in the Derby
	Augusta	2nd in the Oaks

In addition to the stables on the Downs, the house and stud at Clay Hill Stud, and a house to the south of Clay Hill (now the site of West Hill House), O'Kelly had acquired a townhouse in Piccadilly, and an estate called The Cannons near Edgware. O'Kelly stated that "keeping company" was one of his pleasures, and in this respect seems to have kept open house at Clay Hill. O'Kelly enjoyed entertaining jockeys, trainers and some shady characters alongside nobility, and recorded his delight in seeing them "circulating the same bottle with equal familiarity and merriment." Despite socialising with distinguished guests, O'Kelly was refused admission to the Jockey Club probably because of his dubious early life. Dennis O'Kelly died on 28th December 1787.

Dated 11th October 1786, the main points of O'Kelly's will were:

1. Thomas Birch of Bond Street, and William Atkinson of Pall Mall were the executors, and Andrew Dennis O'Kelly (his nephew) the sole administrator.
2. Charlotte Hayes, "called Mrs O'Kelly", was granted use of the Cannons and an annuity of £400.
3. After her death, the freehold of The Cannons and all the furniture and effects pass to Andrew Dennis O'Kelly
4. Charlotte Hayes was left O'Kelly's "large diamond ring and also all and every of the diamonds jewels watches rings and other personal ornaments"
5. £1,000 to his niece Mary Harvey
6. Eclipse was left in trust with all profits to be shared equally between Charlotte Hayes, his brother Philip O'Kelly and nephew Dennis O'Kelly.
7. Charlotte Hayes was left the chariot, the coach and the coach horses
8. £20 and a mourning ring was left to each executor
9. Any item not already covered was left to Charlotte Hayes and Andrew and Phillip O'Kelly.

Dennis O'Kelly then added a clause that if "Andrew or Phillip O'Kelly lay any bet or make any matches" or "be engaged or concerned in any such matters in any shape or manner" they forfeit five hundred pounds. This clause was extraordinary for a man who had founded his life on gambling, but marked his aversion to his earlier lifestyle.

Andrew and Phillip O' Kelly continued to run the stud, and manage the property at Clay Hill. Andrew O'Kelly was resident in Paris at the time of his death in 1820.

On 11th February 1788 at Hyde Park, Messrs. Tattersalls conducted the dispersal sale of the bloodstock of Colonel O'Kelly. The 14 lots (12 of which were sired by Eclipse) raised £8,321.

Eclipse retired in 1788, he was taken to The Cannons in a van drawn by two horses, the first recorded instance of a mobile horsebox. He died of colic on 27th February 1789, and after his death was subject to detailed scrutiny by the London Veterinary College to discover the reasons for his exceptional speed. Eclipse's skeleton is currently located at the Horse Racing Museum in Newmarket.

OLIVER, W.L.   Heathcote House   1909-1912

The Sporting Life, 7th July 1909 records:

"W.L .Oliver is getting a string together at Heathcote House, Holt's place at Epsom. Oliver who is well known in this country, is a native of Scotland, and has trained and owned horses in America for upwards of twenty years."

ORRELL/ORBELL, J.   Heath House   1900-1902

Probably George Orbell (1862?-1928?), based at Heath House, Burgh Heath, described as a "stableman" in the 1901 census. Listed as J. Orbell in Training Intelligence in The Sporting Life January 1901.

OSBORNE,   1887

Osborne is mentioned in Gallops reports in the Sheffield and Rotherham Independent, 11th November 1887.

O'SULLIVAN, Roland   Cedar Point   1999-2003
(1943-

Roland O'Sullivan trained in Sussex prior to moving to Cedar Point Stables in 1999. He was based there until retiring in 2003.

PAGE,   David   c.1824-1840
(C.1785–1843)

Page was the uncle of jockey and trainer "Black" Tom Olliver (1812-1874).

The History of Steeplechasing by Michael Seth-Smith records:

"Tom [Olliver] sneaked off from home whilst his family were at a fete celebrating the coming-of-age of Mr Gratwicke – the son of a local squire – and went to his uncle Mr Page, the Epsom trainer...To his credit his uncle soon got him a job riding the lightweights for Lord Mountcharles."

Olliver rode in 17 Grand Nationals riding the winner on three occasions. Known as "Black" Tom because of his dark appearance, Olliver's love of the good life eventually led him to debtor's prison. He later trained in Wiltshire, where he prepared George Frederick for the 1874 Derby, but he died prior to the horse's success.

David Page was made bankrupt in 1830. Page died in 1843 aged 58, and is interred at St. Martin's Church, Epsom. Following Page's death, his widow was involved in the case, Curlewis v Page. The Times noted:

"This was an action for the restoration of certain goods and chattels, alleged to be the property of the plaintiff, a tailor in Hanover Square, but now in the possession of the defendant, the widow of a horse-trainer at Epsom."

Page had trained horses for Mr Curlewis, and had occasionally bought items of sportswear, saddles etc. from the "sporting tailor". Following Mr. Page's death, Mrs Page was operating as a lodging-house keeper. Mr Curlewis had from time to time recommended potential guests to Mrs Page; including a Mrs Carr who it later transpired was Mr. Curlewis' mistress. The lodging house became a rendezvous for Curlewis and Mrs Carr, and, dissatisfied with some of the furnishings, Curlewis had provided his own, notably a sofa. He was now suing Mrs Page for their return. The case was complicated by the appearance of a Mrs Bartlett, Curlewis' cook, claiming that the furniture was hers. Mrs Page's defence was that she had paid Curlewis by exchanging items of horse clothing, and saddles for the furniture; and that the case had only been bought after she had sued Curlewis for outstanding rents.

Witnesses were produced to testify that an exchange had been agreed, and that the furniture was worth far less than the saddles and clothing; and the jury found for Mrs Page.

| PAGE, Daniel | Rowland Lodge | 1905-1906 |
| (1871-1912) | | |

A New Zealand-born jump jockey, Page travelled over in September 1895 with fellow jockeys *James Hickey*, and J. Webster. Page held the training licence for a year succeeding *Hickey*. He later moved to Lewes.   He died in Netherne hospital in 1912, one year after *Hickey*, and is interred at Epsom Cemetery.

| PARKER, Evan | Shifnal Cottage | 1940-1968 |
| (1900-1994) | | |

Evan "Snowy" Parker trained at Shifnal Cottage from 1940 to 1968. Parker rode under National Hunt rules until injury forced his retirement. He commenced training from a yard at Cheltenham, before moving to a yard at Shifnal in Staffordshire. He never trained more than ten winners in a year, using other yards cast-offs, and spending years nursing horses back to fitness, but from his small unfashionable operation he won the 1947 Portland Handicap with Good View, and in 1949 he trained Fidonia to win the Manchester November Handicap at 40-1.

Parker also won Royal Ascot's King George V Handicap with Vinca.

In April 1957, following the defeat of Parker's odds-on favourite High Fidelity in a Brighton selling race, the stewards interviewed jockey, Lester Piggott, and asked Parker if he was satisfied with Piggott's riding. "I was quite satisfied with the ride, and I had

£4,000 on it", Parker replied. He retired in 1968 and died on the 28th March 1994 at the age of 94.

PARKES, Albert/Alfred William	The Cottage	1905-1908
(1867-1920)	Hovedene	

Formerly a clergyman, with degrees in Divinity and Theology from Trinity College Dublin and Durham; Parkes was also a keen sportsman, playing rugby at a high level, and was close to playing for Ireland. He also took part in cricket, boxing, coursing and hunting. His interest in sports plus his passionate sermons made him popular in his first parish at Bolsover. He hated Puritanism and Socialism, and had a tendency to settle disputes with his fists, or anything else that came to hand. Eventually his lifestyle was in conflict with his profession and he quit the clergy.

He began training at Cooksbridge, near Lewes from 1899, he trained privately for Mr. Edward Bleakley, achieving over 100 winners in three years. With his employer, ageing Parkes moved to Epsom. He trained at The Cottage, Ashley Road, (at that time also known as Hovedene). Parkes announced his dislike of Australian and South African trainers which immediately put him at odds with some of Epsom's other recent arrivals. Parkes was playing billiards in a room above the Spread Eagle, when a deputation arrived to put him in his place, with the advantage of a billiard cue, and "pole positon" at the top of a single starircase, "The Parson" saw off his attackers. He was also a fearless gambler, on one occasion having three winners at 3-1 11-2, and 9-2, the fourth runner was fifteen lengths clear when it split a pastern. Parkes was training at Chitterne, Wiltshire at the time of the 1911 census. He stopped training on the outbreak of war, declaring that anybody who continued training was "unpatriotic." During the war he designed a method of producing horses shoes from sheet metal, rather than individually on a forge, and won a contract to supply the British Army. Post war he purchased twenty two-year-olds and commenced training at Tilshead. He backed one of his early runners from 10-1 to 11-2 at Newmarket but was beaten a short head. He contracted pneumonia shortly after..He died in 1920 leaving effects of £541.

In his last sermon before leaving the church, Parkes told his congregation, "Always run straight, but if you can't do that run as straight as you can."

Recorded on the Register of Electors as Alfred Parkes during his stay at Epsom.

PARKES, J.   1904

There was a "Parkes" training at Epsom as early as 1899, possibly Albert or J.Parkes.

PATTERSEN, J.   1860

Listed in Ruff's Guide as J. Patterson possibly *Pattison H.* Frederick Patterson was living at South Hatch in 1855.

PATTINSON, Mark Ian   Tattenham Corner   2016-

Formerly employed by *Reg* and *John Akehurst*, and *Jim Boyle*, Pattinson also worked in New Zealand prior to joining *Lee Carter* as head lad. He took out a training licence in 2016.

PATTISON, or PATTERSON Henry South Hatch   1857-1859, 1861
(? - 1862)

The Morning Chronicle 3rd February 1857 records that Mr. Pattison has moved his stud from Brighton to Epsom. Pattison is listed in Bell's Life 1858 as training six horses. H. Pattison is listed in Ruff's Guide 1861 as training for Major Bringhurst, and Mr. Roland's, (possibly *John F. Rowlands*). Listed as Henry Pattersen of South Hatch in Kelly's Directory 1859.

PAY, F.W.   Copthill, Burgh Heath   1962

PAYNE, William   Heath House   1922-1947
(1891-1961)

From an Essex hunting and farming family, Payne had spent his early career riding at his local tracks, many like Rugby and Ipswich are now defunct. Payne was champion National Hunt jockey in 1911 with 70 wins.
Bill Payne trained Blaris to win the first Champion Hurdle in 1927, and won the Scottish Grand National three times, with Harrismith in 1923, Clydesdale in 1932, and Libourg in 1933. He won the 1932 Imperial Cup with Last of the Dandies, the 1933 Cotswold Chase (now the Arkle Trophy) with Ready Cash, and the 1936 Victory Chase with Argental. Ready Cash was partnered by his son, Bill Payne junior, as was Blaris when it won the 1930 Coventry Cup at the Cheltenham main meeting.
In 1928, he came close to winning the Grand National with Great Span, ridden by "Young Bill" Payne, who was then just 17, the horse was well clear when the saddle slipped at the second last.
A long-standing owner of Bill Payne's was Mrs H. M. Hollins. The relationship suffered because of Mrs Hollins erratic behaviour, but despite several threats to part ways, owner and trainer enjoyed great success together; Blaris won 22 races, Turkey Buzzard won 20 races, and Colliery Band won the Grand Sefton Chase, and the Champion Chase.
Bill Payne moved to Seven Barrows at Lambourn after the war, where he trained with some success prior to finding the overheads of that large establishment too much of a burden. He left an estate valued at £67.

138

"Young Bill" served with distinction in the 1939-45 War, winning the Military Cross and rising to the rank of major; and later trained at Eastbury in Berkshire. "Pip" Payne, the son of "Young Bill", trained at Newmarket.

PEARCE, Samuel	Smitham Bottom	1822-32
(1759-1842)		

An article in The American Farmer by John Skinner, January 1829 refers to a trotting match in which the "roan horse" was stabled with Mr. Pearce at Smitham Bottom.
The Racing Calendar 1826, lists the stallion Eryx, bred by the Earl of Derby, standing at Mr. Pearce's, Red Lion, Smitham Bottom.
The Morning Post, 11th October 1822 notes, *"Pearce, the renowned Smitham Bottom trainer bought Prosody"* (a winner the previous day at Enfield).
Bell's Life 12th June 1842 noted:

"Died on the 5th inst., in the 83rd year of his age, Mr Samuel Pearce of Smitham Bottom. He was well known in the sporting world, many years ago under the cognomen "Bristol Sam", as a very successful jockey, and through a long life he maintained an upright and unimpeachable character."

PENDARVES, John S.	Birches/Farm Stables	1923-33
(1894-1938)	High Ridge	1934
	Priam Lodge	1935-37

John Stackhouse Pendarves was born at the family estate near Camborne in Cornwall, where the family reputedly owned a tin mine. Educated at Harrow, he served in the Life Guards during the Great War, rising to the rank of Lieutenant. He briefly trained at Wantage, prior to buying The Birches, the former home of the Dorling family in Downs Road. At this stage he had 40 horses in his care, and his owners included Lord Astor. He later moved to Priam Lodge with a smaller string. He trained mainly National Hunt horses, and was regarded as a "gentleman trainer", i.e. impeccably mannered and dressed, and ran his horses on merit purely for the sport with no interest in betting.
He was taken ill at the Epsom summer meeting in 1937, and left to convalesce in Switzerland; he was preparing to return to Epsom when he died on 22nd January 1938. Pendarves left an estate of £125,000 gross.
In Pendarves' obituary, The Times noted:

"As a man Jack Pendarves was a delightful and amusing companion who had innumerable friends and no enemies. He early got the reputation of being very clever with bad horses, and it is certain that he won innumerable races with horses which had been discarded by other trainers. He was a most capable member of his profession."

PERSSE, H.S.   Althorpe Lodge   1904-1906
(1870-1960)

Henry Seymour "Atty" Persse was born in Galway. After a short spell at Epsom he moved to Stockbridge, Hampshire. Persse trained the winner of the 2,000 Guineas on three occasions, the 1,000 Guineas once, the Irish Derby, and the July Cup. He was Champion trainer in 1930. Shortly before his death he rekindled his links with Epsom, owning Thames Trader, a useful handicapper trained by *Staff Ingham*. He left effects of £152,668.

PHELAN, Patrick   Ermyn Lodge   2007-
(1950-

In 2007 Ermyn Lodge combined facilities as a stud with approximately twelve broodmares plus a training base. Former Irish Army officer Pat Phelan was appointed manager of both operations, having previously trained in Ireland and spent two years at the Highclere Stud.

PHILLIPS, George   The Paddocks, Mill Road 1904-1905

Listed in Trainers and their addresses, The Sporting Life, 31st March 1905, and featured in Training Reports in The Sporting Life in1904, and1 905.

PHILLIPS, Henry Charles (Harry) Althorpe Lodge   1908-09
(1863-1939?)

Born in Bow, London, Harry Phillips worked in the Burgh Heath stables, prior to moving to Epsom. In the 1911 census he is described as a groom based in Burgh Heath Road.

PHILLIPS, James   Woodcote Rise   1912-1915,1917-1918
(1873-1953)   Rowland Lodge   1905-1911

Born at West Malling, Kent, Phillips rode under National Hunt rules c.1890-1906. He shared the yard at Rowland Lodge with *Hickey*, c. 1905; Phillips temporarily called his part of the stables Uplands.

The Sportsman, 24th July 1909 noted:

Phillips has the fullest knowledge of all that pertains to bloodstock breeding, riding on the flat and over country, and training."

The Newcastle Journal, 28th July 1916 recorded:

Lieutenant J. Phillips of the Durham Light Infantry, the Epsom Trainer, has been badly wounded in the face and eyes. "

He died at his home in Worple Road, Epsom on 13th October 1953, described as a retired Racehorse Trainer, he left an estate of £6,865.

PHILLIPS, Max   1888-1889

Max Phillips was private trainer for Count Esterhazy, he prepared Et Cetera for the 1889 Grand National. In December 1888 Phillips rode and trained Et Cetera to win the valuable Manchester Handicap Steeplechase, but was disqualified due to a technicality regarding registration.

Phillips attended the Epsom Trainer's Dinner at the Spread Eagle, the Sporting Life noted that the "ever genial" trainer entertained the gathering with some comedy songs. The Cambridgeshire Daily News, Monday 28th January 1889 stated:

It is reported in Newmarket that Et Cetera who is at present in most demand for the Grand National, and who is under the care of Max Phillips at Epsom, will shortly arrive at Head quarters to be prepared by J. Cannon for the big steeplechase.

Phillips left for Germany a month later.

PHILLIPS, Rowland   Sandown Lodge   1932-1934
(1886-1945)

Phillips trained under Pony Club rules at Sandown Lodge. Phillips died at Haverfordwest in Wales, but is buried in Epsom Cemetery.

PICKLES, Albert   Hillcrest   1929-1930
(1879- ?)

Born in Lancashire, Pickles was formerly head lad to *Victor Tabor*; before acting as private trainer to *George Barclay*.

PITT, Arthur   Manor Farm   1966-1968
(1935-2016)   Wendover   1969-1986

Arthur and Heather Pitt bought "Nightingall's top yard" in 1969; they rebuilt the yard and built a trainer's house, naming the property Wendover. Pitt had previously trained

National Hunt horses at Manor Farm in Kingswood. His major success came in 1970. Given charge of Persian War, at the tail end of the champion hurdler's career he won the Irish Sweeps Hurdle. Other hurdles success came with Bowies Brig who won the 1970 HSS Hire Shops Hurdle, and the veteran Moyne Royal whose successes included the 1973 Ascot Hurdle, the 1973 Cheltenham Stayers Hurdle, and the 1974 Keith Prowse Long   Distance   Hurdle.

Pitt's training successes on the Flat included Redden in the 1985 City and Suburban Handicap, and Ocean King in the 1973 Cesarewitch. The jockey, Joe Blanks served an apprenticeship with Pitt, and was tragically killed in a race riding accident at Brighton. During the 1980s, Pitt's wife Heather purchased the house at South Hatch and converted it into a racing club and museum. During the next 20 years Heather Pitt was a popular hostess, and a staunch supporter of Racing Welfare, notably hosting regular tea parties for retired stable staff.

PLATT, Alfred   1902-1904, 1912-1914
(1865-1946)

A former jockey; Platt was apprenticed to Charles Archer at Newmarket. He was based in Epsom in 1891, marrying his wife Minnie Edwards in Ewell in 1892. He later worked in stables at Newmarket and Berkshire, before spells training at Epsom. In 1911 he worked at Lord Derby's stud, Coworth Park near Ascot.

PLATT, James W.   Priam Lodge   1909-1911
(1883-1928)

Son of jockey James W. Platt, Yorkshire-born James Platt was an apprentice jockey prior to becoming private trainer/licence holder for *James Bell*. In this role he trained for Bell in Berkshire and at Priam Lodge. After leaving Bell, he trained at Winchester and at Newmarket.

In 1911, Platt discovered a body on the Downs, and was described at the court hearing as "Head man to an Epsom trainer." He was residing at The Chalet, Burgh Heath Road at the time.

Walter Hopkins, a trainer, living at Ashtead, told the court that the woman had been at his house, but had left about 8.45 for an appointment. He had known her for ten or 12 years, and described her as "excitable" when she left. Death by natural causes was the inquest verdict.

PLUMB, Arthur   The Warren   1905
(1879- ?)

Former jockey, trained for *B. Ellam* at The Warren. Listed in Trainers and their addresses, The Sporting Life, 31st March 1905.

142

PLUNNER/PLANNER, W.   1849

Shown in Ruff's Guide 1849 as training for Mr. C. Formby, and Mr. King. *Edward Ford* is shown as training for the same two owners. Possibly William Planner, born at Newmarket in 1831.

POOLEY, Albert   Clay Hill   1868-1877
(1843-1915)

Born in Isleham near Newmarket, Pooley was based in Epsom from 1868-1877. He subsequently moved to Royston, Hertfordshire; following the death of his wife, Pooley was publican at the Coach and Horse with his seven children; and continued to work in local stables. He later moved to Marylebone.

POOLE, A.   1911-1913

Possibly Albert Poole born 1892, son of *William Poole* of Glanmire Farm.

POOLE, William   Glanmire Farm   1901, 1909
(1851-1924)

Born in Derby, Poole is listed as a hunts man of Acre Hill Farm House in the 1891 census, but as a horse trainer in 1901, by which time the property is known as Glanmire. His son Robert worked in racing stables at Jevington and Newmarket. William Poole died in 1924 leaving effects of £4,152.

POTTER, James   Eclipse Cottage   1865-1870
(1841-1881)   York House, Woodcote End 1871-1881

James Potter was born in Manchester in 1841. His career started with *Robert I'Anson* at Mickleham. In December 1865 Potter advertised a horse for sale at his stables at Clay Hill. He had four horses in 1867, but had increased to 21 by 1869. Kelly's Directory 1867 shows him at South Street. In Ruff's Guide 1870 he is shown as training at Eclipse Cottage, Clay Hill, In March 1881, Potter achieved a major success by riding (and probably training) Mr. Reed's Northfleet to win Sandown's Grand Prize. However, he suffered a bad fall in a race at Bromley on 31st March 1881, fractured his spine, and was admitted to Bromley Cottage hospital, returning to Epsom on 11th June. It was clear that he would not return to work, and "The Potter Fund" was started for his wife and children, with Lord Rosebery donating £50. He died at York House on 5th August 1881, leaving effects of £1,148.

PRIESTLEY, Francis Vickerman   Caversham House   1913- 1915
(1872-1945)

Priestley trained at Lambourn (1907-1912) before exchanging stables with *Thomas Hogg*. He served as a lieutenant in the army during the Great War, and did not return to horse training thereafter.

PRINCE, G.   Smitham Bottom   1870,1889

PUTTRELL, William   Burgh Heath   1868-1870
(1840- ?)   Walton on the Hill   1871-1872

The Sporting Gazette, January 1869, records him as training six horses at Epsom. The Manchester Times 2nd January 1869 records a horse being sent to him at Burgh Heath, Epsom, and he had Grand National entries in 1870 and 1871.
Puttrell was private trainer to Mr. Edward Studd, the owner of the Six Mile Hill Gallops, and part of Epsom racecourse.
In 1871, Mr. Blackman engaged Puttrell as private trainer, based at Dowding Castle, Walton-on-the-Hill.

RANDELL, Charles E.   1918-1919
(1866-1941)

Born in Cheltenham, Randell was apprenticed to Sam Darling. After his riding career finished, Randell trained at Avebury, Wiltshire in 1901, and then at Lambourn. He was based at Whitewall Stables, Malton in 1911. He moved to Epsom during the latter part of the Great War, but left in 1920 for stables at Blewbury, near Didcot.

RAY, Cecil Cameron   Hillcot   1937-1942
(1894-1948)

Cecil Ray was born in Kent, and emigrated to South Africa, where he was apprenticed to T. Johnson, the brother-in-law of *Richard Wootton*. Between 1926 and 1934, he spent the winter months riding in South Africa, returning to the UK for the start of the Flat racing season. After a successful career as a jockey that included a spell as first jockey for Lord Carnarvon, Cecil Ray commenced training at the Hillcot yard in Langley Vale. His head lad was Jack Dillon, brother of numerous jockeys (notably Bernard), and father of jockeys Dennis and Mick Dillon. Jack had previously been head lad to *Percy Allden*.
Phil Bull, the founder of the Timeform service was one of Cecil's main owners. Mick Dillon recalls Bull arriving at the yard with a bushy, bright red beard. (Later Bull's trademark beard was as white as snow). At the time Bull was working as a maths teacher at Putney, providing tips under the name of William K. Temple, and building his

reputation as a shrewd backer of horses. Bull ran his horses under the name of W. Richardson.

After the outbreak of war in 1939, Cecil Ray, in common with *Harold Wallington* decided to move to the North where there were more opportunities for average horses. When Bull returned to Halifax, Ray's move North became permanent. The Jockey Club declined to register Bull as an owner until 1946 telling him: "So long as you are connected with the business of "Temple', the stewards will not be prepared to give any trainer permission to train your horses." Bull remained an opponent of the Jockey Club all his life.

In 1946, after moving to Malton Ray had his licence withdrawn after one of his horses was found to have been doped. The event left Ray devastated, and he died a few years later. Phil Bull was appalled by the handling of the case, and campaigned to clear Ray's name, and to change the Jockey Club policy of using draconian sentencing when dealing with small trainers.

On 10th June 1952, Bull wrote reassuringly to Cecil Ray junior who had emigrated to South Africa. "No stigma now attaches to your father's name...I sent all the papers to the Jockey Club...I know that they have accepted the evidence in the documents. It appears from your letter that you are not aware just how conclusively these documents did in fact pin the job on one of the lads in your father's stable."

In 1977 in Bull's submission to the Royal Commission on Gambling, he referred to the Cecil Ray case, accusing the Jockey Club of dispensing an "Alice in Wonderland off-with-his-head-sentence." He added the verdicts were "published in words calculated to take away not merely a man's livelihood but his good name as well." Bull described Ray and two other trainers warned off at the same time as "completely innocent of anything but notional negligence." Bull also described attending "the farcical charade that passed as an inquiry, and the way Cecil and I were treated. I remember Cecil's distress. I remember how the loss of his licence, took all life out of him."

Probably the best horse handled by Ray was Lady Electra, who won five times for Bull and Ray, including a war time Lincoln. Stable apprentice Mick Dillon won three races on her, including one while on a 36 hour leave pass from RAF Hendon.

Dillon worked for *Bobby Dick, George Duller, Cecil Ray, Jack Reardon* and *Vic Smyth* during his time in racing. He also took an active part in the Epsom Lads Gang Show, and became a full-time actor and stuntman. His many credits included the part of Ringo Starr's stuntman in "Help".

Cecil Ray died at Epsom in 1948 leaving £11,308.

RAYNER, Samuel   The Hermitage, Walton   1856-1861

Bell's Life in London and Sporting Chronicle, 3rd February 1856, carried and advertisement for the stallion Sir Tatton Sykes that stood at The Hermitage, Walton on the Hill.

The same journal, 21st April 1861 reported:

"Mr. Ford's horses will in future be trained at Epsom under the care of S. Rayner."

READ, George Gilbert   Heathcote House   1934
(1878-?)

Born in Winchester, after working in several Epsom stables, Read became head lad to *James Bell*, he left in 1924 to train in Berkshire. He returned to work for Bell in 1931, and temporarily took over the stables on Bell's death. His son Lionel was apprenticed to *Percy Allden*, and rode the 1926 Cesarewitch winner.

REARDON, Dennis   Abele Villas   1920-1922
(1893-1931)

Dennis Reardon, brother of *Jack Reardon*, served in the army service corps, and subsequently died after a racing accident at Sandown Park on 20th March 1931.

REARDON, John M.   Chelmer   1922-1927
(1891-1974)   Ermyn Lodge   1930-1964

Waterford-born Jack Reardon was apprenticed to George Lambton, and later rode in Holland and Belgium. He served in the Army Remount Service at Redhill during World War I, which enabled him to maintain his career as a jockey, His principal success as a jockey was on Vermouth, winner of the 1916 Grand National, ran at Gatwick. He rarely had more than 12 horses under his care, preferring to rely on a few well-planned gambles to finance the operation. David Nicholson in his autobiography "The Duke" recalls how his father Frenchie had ridden a horse for Reardon that was not "off". Going down to the start Frenchie discovered that all the other jockeys had similar instructions, and he was unable to do anything but win. Frenchie avoided a furious Reardon after the race and that evening cycled up to Ermyn Lodge to explain. Frenchie waited in the hall, suddenly Jack appeared, (still wearing his bowler hat), and hurled a bread roll at Frenchie, the jockey ducked, and the roll smashed a glass cabinet in the hall, Frenchie made a hasty retreat. Mick Dillon worked for Reardon in the late 1940s, and recalled: "He was as shrewd as they come, and everything had to be right including the price before he put his money down." Trainer Derek Kent worked for Reardon prior to training at Chichester; as did Newmarket trainer Bill Holden.
Brian Swift, and jockeys Harry Sprague, and Jock Wilson served their apprenticeships with Reardon. Sprague recalled arriving at Epsom weighing 3st 10lb, after his mother saw him on the train at Exeter. Like many of his generation the war interrupted his career, and on discharge he weighed over 12 stone. He spent all 25 years of his career with Reardon, later Sprague recalled "he came to rely on me too much." Although primarily remembered as a hurdles jockey, his major success came on Done Up in the

Whitbread Gold Cup. It was the last mount of his career, Sprague had already decided to retire, and was persuaded by trainer Captain Ryan Price to come out of retirement for the ride.

John Reardon left an estate of £93,780.

REARDON, Michael   Abele Villas   1920-32
(1852-1942)

Michael Reardon was the father of *Jack Reardon* and *Dennis Reardon*. He trained under Pony Club rules, but was a licensed trainer under Jockey Club rules when operating from Abele Villas in South Street during the 1920s. He made a brief comeback in 1932 when he trained a winner at Gatwick for his daughter-in-law. Reardon was 80 at the time.

REDMAN, Henry   The Warren   1881-1884
(1827-?)   1891-1896

Born in 1827 at Arundel, Redman was stud manager at The Warren, intermittently combining the job with training. In 1881 he employed six stable staff including three of his sons. In 1893 he was training four horses at The Warren.

REEVES, J.   Beddington Corner   1846, 1850-1851
                              Epsom   1852

According to Ruff's Guide 1851, Reeves trained at Beddington Park for Mr Carew. In the following year's Annual he is listed as a Public Trainer at Epsom. Probably *William Reeves* (1819-1872).

REEVES, Oliver   Leatherhead   1861
(1829-1900?)   Downs Road   1867-1870

Born in Hampshire, Oliver Reeves was the brother of *William Reeves* (b.1819). Oliver Reeves rode for his brother, and is listed in the 1861 census as training at Vale Lodge Farm, Leatherhead. During the latter part of the 1860s he was training at "Downs Road", (possibly sharing facilities at Down Cottage with his brother). He was subsequently head lad to Matthew Dawson at Newmarket, prior to taking an appointment as private trainer to Baron Schickler in Chantilly, France in September 1872. He returned to Epsom in 1877, announcing in Baily's Gazette that he was living in East Street, and seeking employment as a trainer, at the time of the 1881 census he was described as Trainer of Horses (out of work.)

REEVES, Samuel William Pitt Place   1867-71
(1845-1885)

Son of William Reeves (1819-1872), he is listed in the 1871 census as a "trainer of Racehorses." Samuel Reeves listed his occupation as "Trainer" when he married Mary Jane Marsh, sister of *Richard Marsh*, in 1869. S.W. Reeves appears on Training Reports from Epsom in The Sportsman between 1867 and 1871. He may have been deputising for his father at this time, as he was also training at Belmont House, Rottingdean, Sussex. At the time of the 1881 census he was living at Thames Ditton, Surrey and gave his occupation as "journalist".

REEVES, William	Church Street	1851
(1819-1872)	Down Cottage	1852-1871

Bell's Life 12th September 1852, carried the following advertisement:

EPSOM- DOWN COTTAGE-WILLIAM REEVES
Many years lightweight to Mr. John Day, and late trainer to Sir Edward Baker, bart., and Mr. Carew, begs to inform the nobility, gentry and the public that he has taken the above extensive Stabling and Premises lately occupied by Mr. Bradly, and most desirably situated at the foot of Epsom Downs, (which is greatly improved, and is now an excellent training ground, and that he is enabled to afford every accommodation that gentlemen having HORSES TO TRAIN may require; and he trusts from the experience he has had, with unremitting attention, to obtain a part of their support and interest, which it will be his study to deserve.

William Reeves was born in Meddesford, Hampshire. At the time of the 1851 census he was listed as training in Church Street. Reeves had ten stable staff including his brother *Oliver Reeves* as jockey.

The Sporting Life 1868 lists Reeves as having 51 horses under his care, and in that year trained Roving Maid to win the Sefton Chase. The jockey Harry Constable who rode Sefton to victory in the 1878 Derby was apprenticed to Reeves.
The latter part of his career was interrupted by illness, during this time his son *Samuel Reeves*, his head lad *William Gosling*, and *Richard Marsh* had been supervising the horses. William Reeves died 4th May 1872, and is interred in St. Martins Churchyard with his wife Harriet, (died 10th March 1869.)

REEVES, William   Pitt Place   1868
(1838-1913)   Field House, Ashley Road 1869-1882

Born in Gloucester in 1838, Reeves moved to Epsom with *Fothergill Rowlands*, and married the maid at Pitt Place. Kelly's Directory 1878 lists him at Field House, Ashley Road; as does the 1881 census. Kelly's Directory for 1882 places Field House in Worple Road.

In 1875 Bell's Life lists him as having 18 horses, and in 1876 the York Herald records that he had 19 horses under his care. In 1876 he trained Pathfinder to win the Grand National. "Mr Thomas" (Tommy Pickernel) was the jockey. The Daily Telegraph recorded that the horse was unnoticed in the race until approaching the last, and *was "declared the winner, to the surprise of all, and the disgust of a few. An objection on the grounds of insufficient description fell to the ground, being frivolous and the Stewards ordered the £5 to be forfeited."*

Pathfinder was of modest pedigree, and was originally sold for ten sovereigns and six dozen bottles of beer. The best Flat horse trained by Reeves was Mr. H. Bird's Lowlander who won the Royal Hunt Cup in 1874, the All-Aged (now Diamond Jubilee) Stakes in 1875 and 1876, and the 1876 Queen's Stand (now King's Stand Stakes).

In 1879 he trained Military to win the Scottish Grand National. In 1877 Reeves trained Sir John Kaye's Citizen to win the Grand National Hurdle, (a race he had won in 1873 with Dr. Temple), and the Grand Sefton Chase. He trained the winner of the Liverpool Hurdle twice, with Lowlander in 1874, and Whitebait in 1876. Whitebait also won the Ascot Stakes that year.

In the 1881 census, William Reeves had eight stable staff living in. In 1882 Reeves petitioned for voluntary liquidation, and he left Epsom shortly after, initially moving some horses to Lewes, but eventually to take a position as a private trainer in Scotland during 1883 and 1884. The Sporting Life 29th April 1899, announced:

"TESTIMONIAL FOR WILLIAM REEVES AND FAMILY
This well-known old trainer and steeplechase jockey whose name will be remembered in connection with such horses as Whitbait, Ciize, Lowlander , and Pathfinder, having the misfortune to become in straitened circumstances, Mr C. W. Golding, the trainer, organised a subscription on his behalf. "

He subsequently retired to Lambourn.

RHODES, Murgatroyd Northrop   Rowland Lodge   1912,17,19-1922
(1859-1924)

The Hull Daily Mail, 24th.December 1919, announced that:

"G. Briscoe the trainer and jockey has taken up his residence at Rowland Lodge, Epsom, and will in future train Mr. N.M. Rhodes' horses there."

There is no other record of Briscoe in Epsom. Rhodes, however, trained several winners in his own name in 1920-1922. Formerly of Chessington Hall, Murgatroyd Rhodes is shown at 2 College Road, Epsom in the 1921 Register of Electors.

Horses in Training Annuals for 1920-1924 gives his address variously as Chessington, Leatherhead, and East Horsley. Winners for Rhodes, Epsom are also recorded in 1912, 1917.

He was residing at Manor Farm, East Horsley at the time of his death. Leaving effects of £37,514.

RHYS, Edward A.W. Horton   Rose Cottage, The Parade   1885
(c.1850-1906)

Rhys was described as a "Horse Trainer" at a bankruptcy hearing in 1886, and also a "Retired Army Officer". Rhys left effects of £29, 4s.8d.

RILEY, C.   Bruce Lodge   1900

Riley was part of a much-heralded but short-lived "US invasion".

Pall Mall Gazette 1st November 1900 recorded:

"Twenty-seven yearlings from America have arrived at Bruce Lodge, Epsom in the charge of C. Riley".

The Standard 7th November 1900 noted:

"Another American invasion -Sloan to manage Racing Stable

Mr Gardner, the American racing gentleman, has opened a racing establishment at Bruce Lodge, Epsom, and it is understood Tod Sloan is to have management. About seventy horses and a number of American stable lads have arrived."

American trainer *Philip S. Greusil*, who had spent two years at Whatcombe, Oxford moved to Epsom at the same time. His compatriot *Alex Covington* was already based in Burgh Heath Road. However, Mr Gardner's scheme involving the great American jockey Tod Sloan, and 70 horses was short lived.

Leeds Mercury 19th December 1900 noted:

"Mr. Gardner will remove his establishment from Bruce Lodge, Epsom to Foxhill, Wiltshire at the commencement of next month".

There is no record of Riley, Greusil, Covington or Gardner at Foxhill. W.T. Robinson trained there from 1895 to 1918.

RINTOUL, Thomas W.	Heath House	1913-15, 1917-22
(1874- 1942)	Bungalow, Mannamead	1931-1935

Thomas Rintoul was assistant trainer to *Jack Fallon*, when the latter was training for the Druids Lodge Confederacy on Salisbury Plain. He trained at Burgh Heath from 1913 to 1922, briefly leaving to manage Frederick Pratt's stable during the War. In the early 1930s, he was renting the bungalow, and smaller yard at Mannamead from *Percy Allden*, but then moved to train at Wantage, where he was living at the time of his death. His major win while at Epsom was with Old Riley in the 1934 King George Stakes at Goodwood.

RISTE, Jonathan	The Holt, Ashtead	1905
(c.1845-1926)	Station Road	1906
	Priam Lodge	1908-1925

Born in Cheltenham; while working as a stable boy Riste was involved in a riding accident that left him with multiple fractures. Jonathan Riste trained many winners for the journalist "Larry Lynx", who under the name "Lotinga" produced the sporting journal Lotinga's Weekly, but the relationship finished with some acrimony and litigation, when Riste sued Mr Lotinga and the proprietors and printers of The People newspaper for defamation. Prior to moving to the Epsom area, Riste trained at Heath House, Lewes. He was declared bankrupt at Lewes Court in 1903, where it was noted that gambling "had brought on or contributed to his bankruptcy."
After an altercation on Epsom Downs between Riste and *Richard Wootton*, both men appeared in court on December 4th 1910 and were bound over in the sum of £60 to keep

the peace for six months. Additionally, Riste was fined £2. Riste told the court that he had been a publican at Cheltenham for 25 years, and had been a "gentleman jockey" for 25 years.

Riste had the future champion National Hunt jockey Billy Stott as an apprentice, but Stott's indentures were subsequently transferred to *Stanley Wootton*'s stable, where there were more opportunities for him.

Riste moved to Sutton on retirement, but died the following year leaving effects of £1,127.

ROBINSON, Walter   1870-1871
(1845-1873)

Born in Croydon, Robinson's horses are mentioned in various gallop reports in The Sportsman between October 1870 and November 1871. Robinson was admitted to Bromley Hospital, after a fall when riding Cardinal Wolsey at Bromley and died the next day. See also *George Daniels*.

ROE, Robert   Pound Cottage, Banstead 1866-1871
(1813-?)

Robert Roe (b.1813) formerly a trainer based at Stockbridge, and Robert Roe (b.1850), are both listed as trainers in the 1871 census.

ROE, William   Pound Cottage, Banstead   1869-1871
(1844- ?)

Son of Robert Roe (b.1813), and brother of Robert Roe (b.1850); The Sporting Gazette 1871 lists Roe as training three horses at Epsom. William Roe left Epsom to train at Chantilly in 1871.

ROGERS, Benjamin   Mickleham

Benjamin Roger was a farmer, stud-owner and trainer based at Mickleham. He is noted for his success with the racehorse Babraham.

ROWLANDS, Abraham Cecil F.F. Pitt Place   1878-79
(1856-1914)

The Glasgow Herald 24th February 1879 noted:

"Pitt Place is now under the management of Mr. Cecil Rowlands, son of Fothergill Rowlands, and young though he is, he already has a large stable of horses."

Cecil Rowlands had been training the horses during his father's long illness. Also known as Cecil Raleigh, he was an actor and playwright, he died at his home in Regents Park leaving effects of £8,575.

ROWLANDS, John Fothergill   Pitt Place   1867-78
(1822-1878)   Rowland Lodge

The son of a Monmouth chemist, "Fogo" often rode for Lord Strathmore, and is the jockey on Lord Strathmore's The Switcher in Herring's painting "Steeplechase Cracks". His major success as a jockey was on his own horse Medora, the winner of the Grand Steeplechase at Baden-Baden. Steeplechase racing was unregulated in the early part of the 19th century. In 1860 Rowlands, training at Prestbury, organised a Grand National Hunt Steeplechase over four miles at Cheltenham. The race survives today as the National Hunt Chase. Rowlands' rules, known as the Harborough Act, became the basis for steeplechase racing, and the Grand National Hunt Steeplechase Committee became the sport's ruling body.
The History of Steeplechasing by W.C.A. Blew records:

"About 1857 or 1858 it occurred to several people, Mr. Fothergill Rowlands amongst the number, that something should be done to encourage farmers to breed high class horses, and that some step should be taken to found a steeplechase in which bona fide hunters should compete.....so Mr. Fothergill Rowlands and his friends addressed themselves to the task of carrying out the idea. The different hunts were asked to subscribe; but the project met with scant support. The experimental race took place at Market Harborough in 1859, the added money, £250, being guaranteed by Mr. Fothergill Rowlands and his friends."

After winning the 1866 Grand Annual Chase, he moved to Pitt Place, Epsom, 13-year-old *John Jones,* the son of Rowlands' gardener, came with him and later became jockey, head land and trainer to his mentor. Rowlands took a 21-year lease in 1867 starting at £400 p.a. At Pitt Place his owners included the Duke of Hamilton and Lord Marcus Beresford, and it was through the latter that Rowlands encouraged the Prince of Wales to become involved with National Hunt horses.
Rowlands employed *John Jones, Jeffrey Tomlinson, William Reeves,* and later *Frederick Adams* as his trainers, preferring the role as overseer of the stables, but took particular interest in some of his horses, notably Woodcock winner of the 1876 Croydon Hurdle.
The Sheffield and Rotherham Independent 8th January 1878, notes under the list of entries for the Croydon International Hurdle:

"The Pitt Place team, over which Mr. Fothergill Rowlands presides is the most numerous of the lot."

A charismatic figure, famed for his philosophies, when one of his "certs" got beat Rowlands observed, "Experience is nothing unless you pay for it," adding after a pause, "But the less you pay the better."

The Sporting Times, 27th April 1878, in Rowland's obituary stated:

"Mr. Rowlands was one of the finest gentleman riders of his time. In the management of the large stud of horses Mr .Rowlands had at Pitt Place,, he brought intelligence to bear in training them, and won good races with animals whose condition had been considered hopeless. His great fault as head of al large training establishment was that he always liked to see his friends win, and he was one of the few men who would go out of his way to put those whom he knew on the "good things.. This open policy did not commend itself favourably to some of his friends who had horses with him.. Sir John Aysley on the other hand,who remained true to the stable, and fast friend to the end, was enabled to win with Scamp one of the best races he ever secure, and with his commission worked on the most favourable terms."

Rowlands lived in grand style at Pitt Place but left an estate of less than £800. Revised Probate in 1911 valued his estate at £1,130.

RUSSELL, James   Treadwell House   1932-1934
(?-1961)

After two seasons renting Treadwell House stables, South African-born Russell moved to Mabelthorpe, Lincolnshire. He lost his licence in the 1940s when one of his horses was found to have been doped. See also *George Allden*, and *Cecil Ray*. The banning of Russell provoked convicted fraudster Peter Barrie (see *Horace Berg*) to announce that he was behind the spate of dopings, and that the trainers had no knowledge of his activities, but they were being unfairly punished. Russell sued the Jockey Club, but the litigation costs left him bankrupt.

SAIT, Alfred/George	Smitham Bottom	1847-1849
(1815-1886)	Waddon	1851-1852
	Old Wells, Epsom	1853-1862
	Common	
	Croydon	1855, 1881

Alfred Sait was born in Chichester in 1816, he is listed in Ruff's Guide 1847 and 1848 as training at Kingston Bottom, (possibly Smitham Bottom), but according to Ruff's Guide in 1851 and 1852, he had moved to Waddon, nr. Croydon. He subsequently moved to the Old Wells where he trained the 1853 Chester Cup winner Goldfinder. The 1851 census lists him as a racehorse trainer at Croydon.

'The London Gazette', records under 'Court for the relief of Insolvent Debtors' 3rd Jan 1855:

"Alfred Sait formerly of The Hare and Hounds Waddon near Croydon, Surrey next of the Old Wells, Epsom Common and now of 3 Tamworth Rd Croydon, both in Surrey, trainer, owner of Steeple Chase horses and Steeple Chase Rider."

Sait later trained at Merrow near the old racecourse at Guildford, and was based there at the time of the 1871 census. He was back in Croydon operating as a racehorse trainer at the time of the 1881 census.

He is recorded in Kelly's Directory 1855 as George Sait, trainer at Old Wells. Ruff's Guide 1853,1854 and 1861 records A. Sait as training at Old Wells, Epsom.

SANDERS, Brooke	Nohome	1982-1983
(1948-	Chalk Pit	1986-2005
	Thirty Acre Barn	2006

Brooke Sanders was one of the first lady jockeys, obtaining her licence while working for *Brian Swift*. She held a Permit to train a few horses in the early 1980s, eventually taking out a full licence in 1986 when moving to Chalk Pit Stables. Her best horse was Pearl Angel who won the 1991 Sweet Solera Stakes, and was third in the Oaks. Initially she also trained National Hunt horses, the best of which was Calapaez, whose victories included the Aurelius Hurdle in 1987, and the 1989 Daily Telegraph Hurdle.

| SAXTON, James William | Lime Tree Cottage | 1884-87 |
| (1858-1924) | | |

The Belfast News Letter noted Saxton's horses working in "Epsom Gallop Reports" during 1884.

The Sheffield Independent 22nd December 1885 notes under gallop reports, Epsom, the exercise routines for Nightingall, Jones, Sherwood and Holt adding that *"Saxton's Cambusdoon and Real Jam gelding traversed a mile steadily."*
The Manchester Courier 1st October 1884 records Saxton J., Epsom as having entries in the Cesarewitch and the Cambridgeshire.
Saxton is shown as living at Lime Tree Cottage in Mr. Hughes yard in the Register of Electors for 1886 and 1887. Also known as William James Saxton; born in Birmingham, he resided in East Street in 1891, and then at Bromley Hurst Stables, Church Street in 1918-24. He is recorded as James William Sexton at Epsom Cemetery.

Sayers was training four horses for Major Hardinge for the military races, including Scotland Yard who won the United Services Steeplechase.

| SCAITH, Thomas | Horse and Groom | c.1813-1832 |
| (c.1778-1836) | a.k.a. New Stables, Church Street | |

Thomas Scaith trained his own horses from c. 1813 to c.1832. Primarily he ran his horses at the local tracks Egham, and Hampton; but often had runners at the main Ascot and Epsom meetings. In 1824 he trained Blunder to win "His Majesty's" Plate at Guildford. In 1826 he trained El Dorado to win the Duke of York's Plate at Ascot, and won a valuable match there in 1830. He had unplaced runners in the 1816 Derby, and 1828 Oaks. His victories at Epsom included winners of the Craven Stakes, and Metropolitan Stakes. He trained the second in the 1825 Epsom Gold Cup.
In 1823 he trained Netherfield to win the Oxford Gold Cup worth 100 sovs.
An article in the The Sporting Magazine 1822, states that he was based in the stables kept by the "*late Robert Bloss*". The article continues:

"I had some conversation with Scaith, then a stranger to me, who appears to be a well-informed and careful man in his line, completely free from the all the old destructive prejudices of working and physicking horses to death. The expense of training, I understood, was last year at Newmarket, two pounds six shillings per week for horse and boy; at Epsom two pounds two, which has been reduced to thirty-six shillings. The number of horses in training on Epsom downs, of which the Duke of Grafton's, I believe were the most considerable part, did not exceed five-and-twenty; but many more were expected against the meeting. In former years, at a similar number has stood at one hundred, or upwards. They have always trained at Mickleham likewise; and I was sorry to hear that his Royal Highness the Duke of York's horses stood at a private gentleman's stable, hoping that his Royal Highness, on his gracious consideration, would, in future, determine to patronize those who have a living to make as public training grooms. Indeed old Epsom stands much in need of the patronage of our sporting nobility and gentry."

The Racing Calendar 1831 records a meeting of the Epsom Race Fund, (see Part 1), whereby trainers paid ten shillings half-yearly towards the maintenance of the training ground; T. Scaith was the treasurer.
Thomas Scaith was buried at St. Martin's Church, Epsom on 21st October 1836.

SCHOFIELD, Thomas   The Cottage   1911-1915
(1869- 1957)   Hovedene, Ashley Road

Percy Allden and *George Allden* were apprenticed to Lancashire-born Schofield. Their father owned horses trained by Schofield.
Music Hall entertainer George Formby, (George Booth); spent a year with Schofield 1913-1914 when he had his first mount in public. Formby made his first film shortly after, and moved with Schofield to Ireland when the Great War disrupted the British racing season.
Schofield returned to train at Newmarket 1919-1920, subsequently emigrating to Australia.

SCHWIND, Walter H.   1895-1899
(1867-1955)

Schwind was born at Altrincham, Cheshire. He farmed at Long Ditton, Surrey, before moving to Berkshire. Schwind is featured in Epsom gallop reports during this period, He was residing at Newbury at the time of his death. *George E. Duller* was apprenticed to him.

SCOTT   1899

Possibly Henry Scott (born 1875), and recorded as a stud groom at High Farm, Headley Road in the 1911 census; or John James Scott (born 1874), who was a stud groom employed by *William Nightingall* at the time of the 1911 census.

SCOTT William H.   Smitham Bottom
(1821- ?)

The Sporting Life, 2nd February 1870, in an article on Smitham Bottom noted:

"W. Scott, who now trains at Holywell, also tried his hand here for a time,"

Scott was based at Holywell in the 1861 and 1871 Census returns.

Jockey Brian Jago (left) with trainer Victor Smyth (right) at Caithness
Stables c.1960
Photo courtesy of Brian and Sandra Jago,

Stanley Wootton and his jockeys and apprentice jockeys. 1928

Back Row: S.Ingham, poss. J.Warren, C.Smirke, R.Dick, J.Marshall, S.Magee, poss. F.Feltham, A.Jack
Middle Row: J.McGonigal, ?, ?, K.Gethin, poss.A.Smirke, poss. S.Cordell, ? ? ?, S.Carroll, A.Wragg
Front Row: P.Donoghue, J.Caldwell, L.Cordell, S.Wootton, B.Turtle, F.Field, J.Sirett

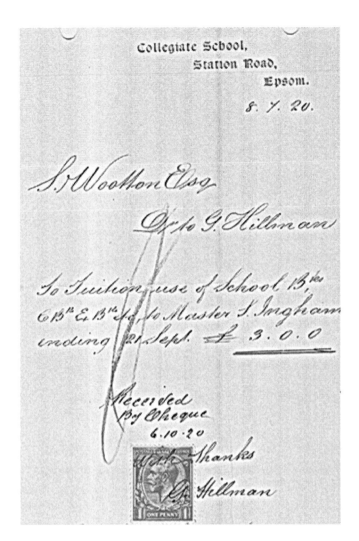

Collegiate School,
Station Road,
Epsom.

8. 7. 20.

S. Wootton Esq.

Dr. to G. Hillman

To Tuition, use of School 13/-
6/13 & 13/4, to Master S. Ingham
ending 21 Sept. £ 3 . 0 . 0

Received
By Cheque
6.10.20

with thanks
G Hillman

Trainers were required to provide education for apprentices below school leaving age. Philip Welsh in his book Stable Rat recalls that a friend of Herbert Smyth's provided his education; English by reading out the results, and mathematics by calculating handicap weights.

The receipt above indicates that Stanley Wootton was prepared to invest in a more formal education for Staff Ingham. The above receipt was rescued from a builder's skip, and passed to the author, who in turn forwarded the original to Stanley Wootton's daughter, Catherine Remond in Australia.

Left to right; Unknown, Stella Wootton, Frank Wootton, Brenda Wootton, Dave Dick Senior.
Photo Courtesy of Judy Dick

Stella and Brenda Wootton with the kangaroo, Treadwell House c. 1930.
The emu outlived the kangaroo, and was still in the paddock c. 1940, it
was a popular attraction with the local children.
Photo courtesy of Catherine Remond

SHERWOOD'S COTTAGE c.1890 Racing Illustrated

Renamed Downs House, when bought by Epsom and Ewell Council in 1944, and sold on leasehold in 2016 for refurbishment. Photograph c. 2005.

n.b. Pre 1944 "Downs House" generally referred to the stables next to The Derby Arms.

picture courtesy of The Cox Library

Stable lads and apprentice jockeys at Stanley Wootton's stable, Shifnal
Cottage c.1937
L.to Right. German jockey Helfort?, J. Hunter, unknown, M. Hunter, F.
Hunter, A. Sharples, J. Crouch, T. Thompson (Cat unknown).
Identified by Mick Dillon
Alfie Sharples was killed following a fall at Windsor races on 5th
November 1938
Jackie Crouch was killed in a plane crash flying to Newcastle races on
20th June 1939

Shifnal Cottage, c. 1937

The Chalet, Burgh Heath Road c.1911

The grave of the Derby winner AMATO is in the woods at The Durdans, adjacent to the graves of Lord Rosebery's Derby winners Ladas, Sir Visto and Cicero.
Sir Gilbert Heathcote Amato's owner, was the owner of The Durdans prior to Lord Rosebery.

Priam Lodge 1893. Note the Prince of Wales' Feathers above the clock.

The stable yard was demolished in 2018 and replaced by housing known as College View.

Racing Illustrated (The Cox Library)

SEARLE, Charles J.	Clay Hill,	1853
(1823-1870)	Smitham Bottom	1854-1857
	Waddon	1857,1859
	High Street, Epsom	1857-1867

Born in Lewes, Sussex; after a short spell at Clay Hill, Charles Searle moved to Smitham Bottom, on the Downs to the south of Croydon. By 1857 he was training at Waddon, near Croydon. The Morning Chronicle 3rd February 1857 records that Searle has moved from Smitham Bottom to Epsom. Searle's three sons *John*, George and Charles C., all rode for him. In Bell's Life 1858 he is listed as training two horses, and in 1859 training eight horses at Brighton Road. In Ruff's Guide 1861 he is listed as having the patronage of three owners. At his bankruptcy hearing in 1859 he was described as a "Livery Stable Keeper and Trainer of Racehorses, late of High Street, Epsom."

| SEARLE, John C. | Common Fields | 1868-1876 |
| (1843-1919) | Maidstone House | 1877-1881 |

Born in Paddington, the son of *Charles J. Searle*, John Searle trained from Field Park Cottages on the Common Fields near the junction of Ashley and Worple Road, possibly the site of The Cottage. He was apprenticed to *Henry Wycherly* at South Hatch, and after a spell as a private trainer in Mauritius returned to Epsom.
The Sportsman 7th February 1879 reports that Searle had over 30 horses "*scattered all over the town,*" in the main using the stables attached to Maidstone House, Jess Winfield still occupied the house, and owned many of the horses under Searle's charge.

| SELLERS/SELLARS, Charles | Burgh Heath | 1882 |
| (1851-?) | | |

Sellers is mentioned in gallop reports in the Sheffield and Rotherham Independent on the 23rd and 28th March 1881:

"Sellers sent Printer and Trierman a mile at a good pace: Melville and Moira followed steadily."

The horses mentioned are trained by *R. I'Anson*; and Charles Seller, living at Burgh Heath, described in the 1881 census as a "Foreman of Racehorses" was I'Anson's head lad.

Bell's Life and Sporting Chronicle, 18th March 1882 recorded:
"Arthur May and Charles Sellars have taken the stables Burgh Heath, Epsom recently occupied by R. I'Anson."

Sellers, (also recorded as Seller or Sellar), was born in Yorkshire and started work at the age of 12 in the stables of William I'Anson at Malton, after leaving Epsom he worked as a stud groom at Melton Mowbray.

SHERRARD, Frank. R.   Treadwell House   1918-1919
(1875-1965)

Son of Newmarket trainer Richard G. Sherrard, Frank Sherrard held the licence at Treadwell House for a time when *Frank Wootton* and *Stanley Wootton* were on military service. He subsequently moved to become head lad for Peter Peck at Newmarket.

SHERRINGTON, John   West Hill   1879-1882
(1849-1890)

Born in Salford, he is the son of jockey John Sherrington (born 1822). John Sherrington junior started his racing career with *James Potter*. Sherrington married Ellen Blake, and was thus related by marriage to *Robert Wyatt*, who had married her sister Jane Blake. Other Blake sisters were married to Henry Booty, a Newmarket trainer/jockey; Charles Constable, jockey and brother of Derby-winning jockey *Henry Constable*: and Sydney Barnard, whose father and grandfather had substantial interests in Epsom racecourse.

SHERWOOD, Louis/Lewis Tom   Sherwood's Cottage   1922-1923
(1883-1970)

Louis was the son of *Tom Sherwood*, and grandson of *Ralph Sherwood* (b.1803) the trainer of Amato. He attended Epsom College leaving in 1894, to assist his father. He served as a sergeant in the Surrey Yeomanry in the 1914-1918 war.

SHERWOOD, Ralph   Sherwood's Cottage   1830-1882
(c. 1803-1883)

The stables on the Downs adjacent to the Derby start, were purchased by Sir Gilbert Heathcote in the 1830s, and thereafter passed to the Sherwood family, prior to purchase by Epsom Council in the 1940s. Ralph Sherwood (who was born in Yorkshire) was for many years private trainer to Sir Gilbert Heathcote. On 30th May 1838, Ralph and Sir Gilbert had their greatest success when the unraced colt Amato won the Derby and was promptly retired.
"Dorling's Genuine and Correct Card" records the terms:

"A renewal of the DERBY STAKES of 50 sovs. Each, half forfeit, for three years old colts, 8st.7lb. and fillies 8st. 2 lb. Last Mile and Half. The Owner of the second horse to receive 100 sovs. Out of the stakes, and the winner to pay 100 sovs. Towards the expenses of additional Police Officers, START AT TWO. Value of the Stakes 3975."

The card also noted that in the betting at Lumley's betting room in the Spread Eagle, Epsom on Tuesday night, Amato was available at 40-1. There were only three other races on the card that day, and no trainers' names are recorded.

On three occasions Ralph Sherwood trained the winner of the King Edward VII Stakes, (then the Ascot Derby), with Bokhara in 1840, Amorino in 1843, and Bravissimo in 1846, all three horses were ridden by J. Chapple (Amato's jockey) and owned by Sir Gilbert Heathcote. In 1843 Ralph trained La Stimata to win Ascot's Coronation Stakes. Bell's Life for that year lists him as "Private Trainer to Sir Gilbert Heathcote" with 12 horses.

The York Herald, February 1842 lists Sherwood as training 11 horses, in 1843, and in 1845 14 horses. According to Ruff's Guide 1851, Sherwood was still private trainer to Sir Gilbert Heathcote, and the census that year shows him as employing 13 staff.

Following Sir Gilbert Heathcote's death, Sherwood trained a few horses for French owner Monsieur Lupin, and performed a unique training feat when Monsieur Lupin's filly Jouvence won the French Derby and French Oaks, Ralph's son Robert rode her. After returning to England Jouvence won the Goodwood Cup. In 1855 Ralph is listed as training for Monsieur Lupin, and Monsieur Fould.

The stable strength dropped to three in the mid-1840s, but rose again by the end of the decade.

In 1869 he trained Temple, ridden by 17-year-old *Richard Marsh*), to win the New Stakes at Ascot. At the time of the 1871 census, Ralph was described as age 65, born in 1806. He employed 12 stable staff and listed his sons Ralph Henry, Robert W., and Thomas as trainers. According to the Sporting Gazette he had 20 horses in training. The York Herald lists "R. and T. Sherwood as training 12 horses in partnership. By 1881 he was apparently 78, now giving his birth year as 1803, and Thomas was still resident listed as trainer. About this time, Ralph retired and was succeeded by his son Tom.

SHERWOOD, Ralph Henry   1871
(1834 – 1873)

Brother of *Thomas and Robert W. Sherwood* , Ralph H. Sherwood was originally articled to an attorney, but all three brothers are shown as sharing the training with their father in the 1871 census.

SHERWOOD, Ralph Howard   Sherwood's Cottage   1911
(1882-1963)

Son of *Thomas Sherwood,* He attended Epsom College leaving in 1893. He was primarily involved in commerce but is shown as a racehorse trainer in the 1911 census.

SHERWOOD, Robert W.   South Hatch   1861-1862
(1835-1894)

Robert Sherwood had a short career as a jockey. In 1851 his first retainer was to Sir Gilbert Heathcote, and his second retainer to Mr Carew who had his horses trained at Beddington Park. In addition to the French Classic wins on Jouvence in 1853, he won the Derby in 1855 on Wild Dayrell. After a brief career training in Epsom, he left England to train in Hong Kong. He returned 17 years later, and in 1884 he trained St Gatien to dead-heat in the Derby, and named his Newmarket stable after the horse. Robert Sherwood died in 1894 after suffering a fit while supervising his horses on Newmarket Heath. He left effects of £13,000. His son Robert Louis Voduz Sherwood succeeded him at Newmarket.

SHERWOOD, Thomas   Sherwood's Cottage   1871-1911,1919
(1839-1923)

Tom Sherwood worked for his father Ralph at Epsom before taking over as trainer. Bell's Life in January 1875 accredits the 12 horses to be being trained by R and T Sherwood. He did not enjoy the same success on the racecourse as his brother or father. In the 1891 census he is shown as employing 12 staff. In the 1893 Horses In Training he has 27 horses in his stable. He died in 1923, leaving effects of £4,000. His son Louis succeeded him. Tom's wife lived at Downs House from her marriage in 1888 until her death in 1942. She was a popular hostess, and Downs House was open to jockeys and trainers during the Derby meeting. Alec Taylor and Joe Lawson the former Manton trainers, stabled their horses and resided there for the Derby meeting. Spearmint, Pretty Polly, and Lemberg are among the famous horses that boarded there. Fred Archer also stayed there, and Mrs Sherwood recalled that the day before her wedding Archer had taken her for a ride in a pony and trap and "nearly broke my neck." "You may be a good rider but you are a dunderhead when it comes to a carriage," the future Mrs Sherwood told the great jockey. Mrs Sherwood saw every Derby for 66 years apart from the Newmarket races during World War I. Her five children always joined her, and in later years she gave up her grandstand seat to watch from her front garden.

SILKSTONE, H   Burgh Heath   1873

Bells Life, 29th March 1873 recorded:

"We recently stated by mistake that Preserpose and Hard Times are now trained by R. Marsh at Sutton. The above named horses are under the charge of H. Silkstone, of Burgh Heath, Epsom, formerly headman to Alec Taylor."

Bells Life 19th April 1873 noted:

"Preserpose and Hard Times have left H. Silkstone Burgh Heath, Epsom."

SIMPSON, A.   Priam Lodge   1922

Owner of horses with several Epsom trainers, Simpson took out a licence to train his own horses in 1922, *W. Donnelly* was also employed as his private trainer.

SIMPSON, George   Smitham Bottom   1861-1864
(1827-1894)   South Hatch   1864-1869
                                     Woodcote Green   1869-1882

Former jockey George Simpson was born in Pickering, Yorkshire, and originally based at the Red Lion, Smitham Bottom, (he is listed in Ruff's Guide 1861 and 1862 as training near Croydon.) He moved to South Hatch where he is recorded as training six horses in 1869. He had moved to Woodcote Green by the time of 1871 census, training from The Cottage on Stone House estate, later known as Althorp Lodge. The York Herald 1875 lists him as having three horses. He trained Jove to win the Manchester Cup in 1869.

SIMPSON, Rodney   South Hatch   1982-1983
(1945-

Formerly apprenticed to *Cyril Mitchell*, Rodney Simpson, had a spell at South Hatch in 1982 and 1983. He won the 1982 City and Suburban Handicap with African Pearl, and the 1983 Cesarewitch with Bajan Sunshine. Simpson's career later took him to Lambourn (three times), Buckingham, Wokingham, Wales, and Dubai.

SIPPLE, William   1903-1904
(1875-1932)

London-born Sipple worked in stables at Letcombe Regis, Berkshire prior to a spell at Epsom, where he featured in Training Reports in The Sporting Life in September 1904.

SIRETT, Jack   The Durdans   1954
(1908-1987)   Portland House   1955-1959
                                     Treadwell House   1960
                                     Burnside   1961-1973

After serving an apprenticeship with *Stanley Wootton*, Jackie Sirett established himself as the country's leading lightweight jockey. Such were the demands for Sirett's services,

172

that when *Wootton* negotiated Sirett's first retainer with an outside stable it was on condition that Wootton retained the right to negotiate Sirett's mounts in the major handicaps.

After spells training at several yards in Epsom, Sirett moved to the stables formerly occupied by *George Duller*, which he renamed Burnside after a favourite horse from the 1920s. Sirett achieved notable success with the sprinter St Alphage, and with the filly Pulchra who won the Nassau Stakes, and the Lingfield Oaks Trial.

St Alphage broke the track record at Brighton, when carrying 10st 3lb, and was second to So Blessed in the King George Stakes conceding 6lb. St Alphage won a total of ten races, and became a top stallion notably siring Sandford Lad.

Arthur Pitt was Sirett's travelling head lad prior to taking out a training licence.

SKILTON/SKELTON, Thomas　　High Street　　　　　1899, 1900
(1857-1918)

Also known as Thomas Skelton, he was a veterinary surgeon who served Epsom District Council, in addition to many local thoroughbred stables. He left effects of £12,589.

SKILBECK, George/Joseph　　Badminton House　　　1893-1899
(1846-

Also known as Shilbeck, he trained at East Hill House, later known as Badminton House. He appears on Epsom gallop reports in the Sheffield and Rotherham Independent in 1893. In 1900 Joseph Skilbeck, a trainer of Bishopstone, Sussex, lately "carrying on business at Badminton House, Epsom" appeared in
Lewes Court for Public Examination of his finances. The 1901 census shows Joseph Skilbeck, born in Stockton in 1846 training at Bishopstone.

SMITH, Ned　　　　　　South Hatch　　　　　　1856-1859

Jockey Henry Custance in his book "Riding Recollections and Turf Stories" records:

"I went to live at Epsom with "Mr Mellish"-he will perhaps be better known as Mr. Ned Smith. I lived with him at South Hatch, Epsom for just over three years, and a jolly though rather a rough time I had of it. Mr. Smith had nearly forty horses in training at one time."

Custance recalls that after taking some horses from South Hatch to Yarmouth, Ned Smith announced that he was leaving for York. Custance asked for some money to get the horses back to Epsom and Smith replied, "Win some races, or walk." Custance recalls he won four races, "so we finished up a great meeting for the South Hatch horses, and returned to Epsom laden with bloaters."

173

SMITH, R. J	Tattenham Corner	2008-2011
(1961-	Chipstead	2012-2016
	Little Woodruff	2016-

Formerly apprenticed to Ian Balding, Ralph "Jack" Smith trained in Spain prior to returning to England in 2008 to share facilities at Tattenham Corner Stables, moving to Chipstead in 2012.
In April 2016 he returned to Epsom training from part of the yard at Woodruff.

SMITH, William	Downs Farm	1841-1845
(1811- 1867?)		

Smith is listed in Bell's Life 1843 as private trainer to Mr. Goodman with ten horses. Abraham Levi Goodman, owned a two-year-old called Running Rein and a three-year-old called Maccabeus. By constantly switching their stables, he managed to confuse their identities. When "Running Rein" won a two-year-old race in 1843, after Levy had backed him from 10-1 to 3-1, many judges thought him to be the best developed two-year-old they had ever seen, and the Duke of Rutland, who owned the second horse, objected to him.
It could not be proved that the horse was not Running Rein, and Levy collected his money. However, Lord George Bentinck was convinced that Running Rein was really Maccabeus, and during the winter he collected evidence to support his view. Running Rein ran in the Derby and Levy backed him to win £50,000. The bookmakers refused to pay, Colonel Peel, the owner of the second horse objected, and the horse was subsequently disqualified.
The Dublin Monitor, 16th December 1841 refers to a horse called Croxby who was *"not up to the mark"* and was sent to "Mr. Smith *at Epsom who brought him to the scratch apparently in excellent condition."*
The York Herald lists Smith as having one horse in 1842, nine in 1843, and The Era as having seven in 1844. He is listed in the 1841 census as a farrier based "near the Downs".
The Era, 14th September 1845, lists St Leger entrant, Clear The Way, as trained by Smith at Epsom.

SMITH, William Griffin	St. Margarets	1944-1945
(1912-1971)	Thirty Acre Barn	1946

SMYTH, A. M.	Rowland Lodge	1934-1938
(1903-1981)		

Alfred Mornington (Monty) Smyth was apprenticed to *Stanley Wootton.* After retiring from race-riding he enjoyed prolific success as a trainer under Pony Turf Club Rules;

particularly at Northolt, and also at Portsmouth Park. He took out a P.T.C. licence in June 1934 with a few ponies under his care, and had 20 by mid-1935. *Tom Griffiths* was his stable jockey. In 1937 he trained the most winners (48) under P.T.C. Rules, and in 1938 over 60 winners.

Following the cessation of Pony Racing in 1939, Monty assisted his brother *Herbert Smyth*.

After the war, with Northolt not reopening, Monty Smyth trained under Jockey Club rules; initially at the William Hill stud at Whitsbury, and later in Berkshire.

SMYTH, Herbert E.	Down Cottage	1951-1976
(1911-1996)		

Herbert Edwin "Ted" Smyth, was the eldest son of *Herbert G. Smyth*. He succeeded his father at Down Cottage, and was assisted for much of his career by his younger brother Tony. The best horse that Ted trained was Crimson, who in 1953 won the Lowther Stakes. Ted's fastest two-year-old was Cerise who clocked a record of an average 40.76 m.p.h. when winning at Epsom in 1954.

He was an exceptional trainer of jockeys. Duncan Keith spent six years at Down Cottage, and recalls Ted as "a good teacher, very strict but a super fellow." Keith was later jockey to *Walter Nightingall* at South Hatch, and won the 1965 2,000 Guineas on Niksar.

Brian Rouse was another graduate from Down Cottage, he won the 1980 2,000 Guineas on Quick As Lightning, and the 1983 Japan Cup on Stanerra. Recalling his time with Ted Smyth he said: "He was strict alright - thorough, he taught me everything I know. It was the best learning process any apprentice could ever have." Alan Bond (1974-75), and Richard Dicey (1968), were both champion apprentices during their time with Ted Smyth. Noel Flanagan, Jimmy Tulloch and Michael Kettle were other good jockeys to learn their trade under Smyth.

SMYTH, Herbert G. T.	Downs House (Derby Arms)	1922-1930
(1885-1952)	Down Cottage	1930-1950

George Smyth was a steeplejack from Blankney, Lincolnshire who moved to Woolwich in the latter part of the 19th century. George had 13 children. Four of George's sons and four grandsons held trainer's licences, and a fifth son, George Junior, was a jockey's valet and an outstanding work rider.

Herbert G. "Nat" Smyth, who was apprenticed to Mornington Cannon on Salisbury Plain, was the first of the family to enter racing. Herbert won the 1920 Welsh Grand National on Mark Back, prior to retiring from riding, and moving to Epsom.

Herbert took over the yard next to the Derby Arms, where he trained Victor Noir to win the Broadway Novices Chase at Cheltenham (now the RSA Chase).

He relocated to Down Cottage in February 1930. Herbert Smyth worked hard at winning races with moderate, injured horses using tack and blankets that were borrowed from or were donated by fellow trainers. Herbert is noted as one of Epsom's most colourful characters and raconteurs, a man with a wry sense of humour. On one occasion he was entertaining a prospective new owner, and the conversation turned to racing colours. "Easy, come into the morgue," said Herbert. The new owner entered the tack room, "Are all these people dead?" he asked. "No, some of them went broke as well", laughed Smyth.

Philip Welsh in his book Stable Rat described his times as an apprentice at Smyth's. Welsh discovered that the job involved not just stable work, but also painting, bricklaying, decorating, cleaning the shoes and house, and picking up stones on the gallops under *Stanley Wootton's* supervision.

Lodgings were found for Welsh with Mrs Kildea in Treadwell Road where he shared a room with jockey *"Manch" Taylor.* Welsh described Herbert as "typical of the racing scene at that time. He practised what had been practised on him." (This included a clip round the ear or a kick up the backside.) Welsh acknowledged that Herbert himself had "come up the hard way." The quality of his horses improved, and he trained for some nouveau riche owners, as well as being retained by the Astor family. Herbert viewed the change in owners with wry amusement, "They come in all shapes and sizes these days, like liquorice allsorts, and often the richer they are, the queerer they look." He was by now getting a better class of horse in the yard. In 1936 he trained William Of Valence to win the Chesterfield Cup, and the City and Suburban Handicap the following year. His son *Ted Smyth*, by then assistant to his father, named his house in Downs Road "Valence" after the horse. When racing resumed after 1945, Smyth had a full yard and some good owners. He won the 1946 Gloucestershire Hurdle with Prince Rupert, the 1948 Champion Chase with Luan Cascar, and the 1948 Free Handicap with Rear Admiral. That year he trained the best horse of his career, Solar Slipper who won the Greenham Stakes, and was a Derby contender, but was found cast in his box on the morning of the race. Solar Slipper subsequently finished third in the St Leger, and won the Champion Stakes. "Racehorses of 1948" described Solar Slipper as a *"Tip top classic horse, and one of the best in the country."*

Among those jockeys apprenticed to Herbert were his sons *Ron Smyth, Ted Smyth, Albert "Manch" Taylor,* and Bert Packham. He left an estate of £81,000.

SMYTH, Paul   Caithness   1965-1974
(1936-2016)

Educated at Haileybury School, *Victor Smyth's* son Paul Smyth, served in the East Surrey Regiment, before training from the Caithness stables in Worple Road.

SMYTH. Ronald   Ascot House   1948-1957
(1914-1997)   Clear Height   1958-1991

After serving an apprenticeship with his father *Herbert Smyth*, Ron was an outstanding National Hunt jockey. In 1942 he was champion National Hunt jockey. He rode three Champion Hurdle winners, all trained by his uncle *Victor Smyth*.
As a trainer Ron never quite reached the heights achieved by Victor in the Champion Hurdle. He twice handled the second; Boxer in 1972 and Flash Imp in 1975. Towards the end of his career he trained another high-class hurdler in Wishlon, who won the Tolworth Hurdle and the New Years Day Hurdle.
Similarly, on the Flat Ron just failed to achieve success at Classic level. His best horses were H.V.C., who beat Tulyar (the last time that Tulyar was beaten on a racecourse), in the Horris Hill Stakes, and Convamore who in 1965 won the King Edward VII Stakes and finished second in the Irish Derby.
Ron commenced his training career in 1948 at Ascot House stables, he continued riding for another year, notably winning the Stayers' Hurdle on Mytholm for fellow Epsom trainer *Walter Nightingall*. In 1951 he had his first Cheltenham Festival success as a trainer when Red Stranger won the Gloucestershire Hurdle, and in that same year he won the Imperial Cup with Master Bidar. He was to win the race again with Irish Imp in 1962, and Flash Imp in 1974.
By 1958, the old Ascot House yard was becoming difficult to work from due to increased traffic and its distance from the Downs. Ron bought some land at the back of the Derby stables, adjacent to where his father had started training, and built Clear Height. Ron credited the financing of the operation to an old dual-purpose horse called Harrowful that landed several touches for the trainer. Ron had bought the old horse from *Walter Nightingall* for £120. "Old 'Arrerful used to get himself ready every year," Ron recalled modestly. At Clear Height, the Classic success proved equally elusive. In 1960 Filipepi won the Greenham Stakes, Racehorses of 1960 recorded:

"Filipepi's success on his debut suggested that he would be very hard to beat in the 2,0000 Guineas, but he ran a disappointing race."

In 1976 Ron had a Group winner with Heaven Knows who won the Lingfield Oaks Trial, and the Earl of Sefton Stakes in 1977.
Ron Smyth is best remembered as an outstanding trainer of handicappers. He won the 1966 Stewards Cup with Patient Constable, and was unlucky not to win the race three years later when subsequent winner Royal Smoke was removed from his stable four days before the race. In 1973 he achieved a notable autumn handicap double when stable apprentice Terry Cain rode Flash Imp to win the Cesarewitch, and fellow apprentice Ian Jenkinson rode Only For Jo to win the November Handicap. Jenkinson was also associated with Sin Y Sin who carried top weight to win the 1973 Tattersalls Nursery, and was rated by Ron as one of his best three Flat horses.

177

Towards the end of his career, Ron Smyth trained a few horses for Prince Khalid Abdulla. In 1985, Tremblant won the Victoria Cup, the Bunbury Cup, and then the Cambridgeshire carrying 9st 8lb for Prince Khalid. It was a remarkable training feat, particularly by a man of 70. Jonathan Powell of the BBC drew attention to the art of a trainer who could improve a horse to win three top handicaps over a five-month period, and suggested an autobiography might be well received. "You'll have to speak to my brother Ted, he's the one who can read and write", replied Ron.

Over fences, Ron's successes included Ragafan in the 1984 Game Spirit Chase, and Mazurka in the 1960 Cotswold (now the Arkle) Chase. Ron was a genius with his novice hurdlers, notably winning the Triumph Hurdle with Blarney Beacon in 1965, and Boxer in 1971.

Ron was also an outstanding tutor of jockeys. Geordie Ramshaw, Peter Skelton, Pompey Beasant, Terry Cain, John Sharman, Philip Cheese, Paul Elliott, Ron Forsyth, Ian Jenkinson and Nat Newman all partnered big race winners for the stable while claiming the apprentice's allowance. The 'star' of Ron's boys, was undoubtedly *Geoff Lewis*, who in 1971 won the Derby, Prix de l'Arc de Triomphe, and the King George on Mill Reef. His other classic victories included the 2,000 Guineas on Right Tack, and the Oaks on Altesse Royale and Mysterious. Lewis recalled: "He was very loyal and gave every kid a chance. I doubt if I would have got the same opportunities anywhere else. The standards he set were of the highest order and he expected his staff to conform. He was brought up tough and didn't suffer fools at all."

Ron was never impressed with fashionable jockeys. His view was that the trainer and staff did the hard bit, the jockey only had to do was what he was paid to do: follow instructions and keep out of trouble. Geordie Ramshaw noted that Ron would have been unimpressed by the air punching and whip-waving of some of the current breed. "He was a hard man who kept very high standards. If you made a mistake Ron would let you know. Everything had to be done in a professional way."

Ron Smyth retired in 1991. He observed, "I don't envy the young. There's much more paperwork and good labour is difficult to find. If a lad used to do more than two it was a crime. Even with motorways the travelling's no easier."

The horses remained the same though. The skill developed in his formative years with his father "Nat", and later with his uncle Victor enabled him to handle the most awkward of the breed. Ron Smyth's retirement was blighted by tragedy. His elder brother Ted died in 1996, and in the same year Ron's daughter Dian died. She had been his assistant in the latter years, driving him to the races, doing the entries, dealing with the owners. Ron was left to concentrate on "What I'm happiest at, just training horses."

Ron's younger brother Tony died in June 1997, and Ron died in his sleep at Clear Height on Friday 4th July 1997. For nearly 70 years in true, extended family fashion, the three brothers had lived and worked within a few hundred yards of each other, and had died within a year.

John Rickman wrote of the Smyth family:

"They have not moved easily into the racing game from notable cavalry regiments, the leisured world, or from homes backed by massive fortunes. Virtually all of the Smyths have had to make their way the hard way, and are to be admired."

Richard Onslow wrote of Ron Smyth:

"He leaves the memory of a genial man, who made a huge contribution to maintaining the prestige of Epsom as a training centre. Every kind of horse came alike to him, and he was an exemplary tutor of young horses."

SMYTH, Victor	Mospey	1926-1964
(1901-1984)	Rowland Lodge, Priam Lodge, Bruce Lodge	

Victor Smyth followed his brothers William and Monty to be apprenticed to the Wootton family at Treadwell House. He was champion apprentice jockey in 1915 and 1916. He retired as a jockey in 1925, after a career that included a victory in the 1923 Oaks on Brownhylda. Vic took out a trainers licence and was based at Mospey in Burgh Heath Road.

He trained Prince Oxendon to win the Goodwood Stakes in 1933, and in 1937 achieved an unusual double at Ascot winning races on successive days with Diplomat. By 1939 when Allure won the Molecomb Stakes, Vic had established a reputation as one of the country's finest trainers. He had outgrown Mospey and extended by buying the yard next door at Bruce Lodge in 1934. Victor Smyth announced in 1939 that he was sending some of his horses to Ireland, but eventually he was one of the few Epsom trainers with sufficient patronage to sustain operations throughout the war, and won the Champion Hurdle in 1941 with Seneca and 1942 with Forestation, both horses were ridden by his nephew *Ron Smyth*. They were the last four-year-olds to win the Champion Hurdle, and Seneca was running for only the second time.

Vic continued to expand using Rowland Lodge in College Road, and Priam Lodge in Burgh Heath Road after the war, and by 1952 his string was the second largest in the country.

Vic Smyth trained the winner of the Champion Hurdle on two more occasions with National Spirit, who won in 1947 and 1948. Invariably equipped with blinkers and bandages, what National Spirit lacked in looks he more than compensated for with courage. He won 32 of his 85 races, and captured the spirit of the post-war Britain to such an extent, that when he fell in a race it was front-page news. Vic Smyth's steeplechasing winners include Bronze Angel who won the 1948 Lancashire Chase.

On the Flat, Vic trained Mombassa to win the 1947 Princess Royal Stakes, and in 1948 did the Epsom Double with Kings Counsel in the Blue Riband, and Now Or Never in the Great Metropolitan Handicap. He also won the Imperial Stakes, (in those days a premier two-year-old event), on three occasions: Lovers Path in 1936, Clutha in 1950, and

Zabara in 1951. Zabara went on to win the Cheveley Park Stakes. The following year, Sir Malcolm McAlpine's Zabara won the 1,000 Guineas ridden by Ken Gethin. Zabara won Lingfield's Oaks Trial, but in the Oaks just failed to stay and finished second. Returning to a mile, she then won Royal Ascot's Coronation Stakes. In 1952, Vic also trained Sir Malcolm McAlpine's Blarney Stone to win the Jockey Club Cup.
The following year Vic Smyth added to his Royal Ascot tally with Absolve who won the Queen's Vase, and also won the Cherry Hinton Stakes with Eastern Venture. The McAlpine family were the principal owners at Mospey; other successes with horses that they owned included Infatuation who won the Dewhurst Stakes and Royal Lodge Stakes in 1953, followed by the Greenham Stakes in 1954, Ratification who won the Coventry Stakes and Richmond Stakes in 1955 and also the Greenham the following year, and Clarification who won the 1955 Horris Hill Stakes. Infatuation was among the market leaders for the Derby, but following a final workout at Sandown, sustained an injury in the horsebox on the way back. Despite Vic's assertion - "This horse is good enough to win the Derby on three legs" - Infatuation was retired.
Apprentices who served their time with Vic Smyth included *Cyril Mitchell*, Dennis Dillon and Brian Jago.
Victor Smyth left an estate of £282,862

| SMYTH, William | Woodcote Rise | 1929-1938 |
| (1884-1970) | Down Cottage | 1940-1944 |

Attracted by the successes of the Wootton family, who had recently arrived from Australia, *William Smyth* made the journey from Woolwich to Epsom to be apprenticed to Richard Wootton. He served in the Army Veterinary Corps in the Great War. After a career as a jockey, he took out a trainer's licence, and trained a small string from Woodcote Rise stables in Hylands Road. During the war he shared the yard at Down Cottage with his brother Herbert. He won the Nunthorpe Stakes in successive years with Linklater. He also trained Kingsway as a two-year-old, but the horse moved to another stable before winning the 1942 2,000 Guineas. After World War II he moved to Arundel, where he was private trainer to the Duke of Norfolk. His son Gordon succeeded him, and subsequently moved to Lewes where he trained Charlottown to win the Derby.

| SOLLOWAY, Henry | Rowland Lodge | 1894-1895,1899 |

Henry Solloway, trained at Hoppegarten, Germany for most of his career, He is listed as training at Epsom in the Yorkshire Evening Post, 15th April 1895.
He was training a few moderate horses for Mr. F. Simon between November 1894 and March 1895, and had a winner at Lingfield on March 12th 1895. He is listed in Training Reports in The Sporting Life during 1899. When local racing correspondent Tom White died in 1902 following an accident while returning from Kempton, "H. Solloway" was

noted in the Dorking and Leatherhead Post as being among the many mourners at the funeral from Epsom's racing fraternity.

In November 1914 there were arrests of British subjects in Germany, with many jockeys, and trainers interned at Ruhleben concentration camp, (which was in fact the stables at Hoppegarten racecourse). The Western Mail, November 9th 1914 reported that among the few not interned were H. and F. Solloway, who having passed the age limit for military service were not liable to confinement.

Harry Walter Solloway, a chauffeur born in 1885 in Vienna, and resident in London, (presumably visiting the Solloways) was interned and detained until 1918.

Trainer Montague Aylin who was engaged to Henry Solloway's daughter Alma who was a German national, despite owning his own property in Berlin, Aylin was also interned. See also *Frederick Winter.*

STAINTON,   Lambourn House   1916

Possibly former jockey Joseph W. Stainton born in Islington c.1870, and previously employed by *John Jones;* or Harry Stainton, (1869-1926), who married *John Jones'* daughter Jessica in 1897.

STEVENS, Charles H.   Downs Lodge   1925
(1880-1942)   1932-1933

Major Charles Stevens was a shrewd gambler and businessman. He trained his horses at Eastbury in Berkshire, and Rottingdean in Sussex, before training briefly at Downs Lodge, Epsom in 1925. His business at Wimbledon, (several properties and a chemical laboratory) was becoming increasingly time-consuming so Stevens sent his horses to be trained by *Sam Hanley.*

David Hanley recalled: "My father trained a lot of winners for a shrewd gambler called Major Stevens, who for a time trained his own horses. The Major landed one spectacular coup by placing his bets by telegram, the bookmakers did not receive the bets until after the 'off', but the telegram was timed before the race so the bets stood. The following day my father told the Major that he had a few more in the yard that were even better, Major Stevens asked: "Can you keep them for a while, it will take me six months to get paid for yesterday's winner."

Charles Henry Stevens died in Brighton in 1942, leaving effects of £140,525.

STEVENS, George   1899-1900
(1860-1919)

Possibly George Stevens, born 1860 in Cheltenham, stableman resident in South Street at the time of 1901 and 1911 census, formerly employed by Matthew Dawson at Newmarket. Featured in Sporting Life gallop reports in 1899.

STEVENS, Joseph   Grove Stables   1961-1971
(1922-2018)

Former *Johnny Dines* apprentice Joe Stevens took out a licence in 1961. One of Stevens'
horses, Solway Cross, became a minor celebrity, not because of his exploits on the turf,
but because of his owners. Two East London twins, Reggie and Ronnie Kray bought the
horse for their mother Mrs Violet Kray. In 1968 both brothers received life sentences,
Ronnie for the murder of George Cornell in the Blind Beggar pub, and Reggie for the
murder of Jack McVitie. Both brothers served over 30 years and were never released. A
biography written by the twin's brother Charlie Kray includes a photograph of Ronnie
and Joe Stevens with the horse.
Solway Cross was quite moderate, and Ronnie eventually donated it for auction at a
charity night the twins had organised at The Cambridge Rooms on the A3 near New
Malden. With the twins spurring on the bidding, the landlord, encouraged by excess
alcohol "won" the horse, paid up, but then immediately put it up as a raffle prize.
Subsequently an actor won the horse in the raffle, but eventually Solway Cross returned
to The Grove, still in Mrs Kray's name, and having raised a considerable amount for
charity.

STINTON,   Beech Cottage   1868-1869

The arrangement for *James Martin* to train Mr. Partner's horses terminated in January
1868, they were subsequently described as "trained privately".From December 1868 to
July 1869, they were under the care of "Stinton" "Mr. Partner" was the name used by
Messrs. Roberts and Kingdom.
.

STRONG, W   Woodcote Lodge Stables   1893-1894

SUTCLIFFE, John E.   Ermyn Lodge   1966-1975
(1906-1975)

John E. Sutcliffe served with the Royal Marines, leaving as a Major in 1945. He
subsequently built up a company specialising in catering, and turned to racehorse
owning as a hobby, having racehorses with *Fred Winter*, Ryan Price, and Willie
Stephenson. He was instrumental in starting the training career of his son *John R.E.
Sutcliffe* in 1963, and then in 1966 he purchased Ermyn Lodge and applied for a training
licence for himself. In 1971 he trained Specify to win the Grand National. In the same
year he trained Cala Mesquida to win the Schweppes Gold Trophy, a race he won again
in 1973 with Indianapolis, when he also trained the second Volunteer.
He twice trained the winner of Royal Ascot's Wokingham Handicap, Plummett in 1973,
and Ginnies Pet in 1974. Ginnies Pet also won the FPA Gold Cup at York, the race

carrying a larger prize than the Wokingham. His fastest two-year-old was probably Streak who won the National Stakes, at that time a Group 3 race. Sutcliffe also played a pivotal role in saving Lingfield Park racecourse. He left an estate of £40,885.

SUTCLIFFE, John   Woodruff   1963-1993
(1940-

John Sutcliffe, (John Sutcliffe Junior) took out a trainer's licence at the age of 23, following a spell as pupil trainer with Ryan Price during which he won the Amateur Jockeys Championship; and was best man at Lester Piggott's wedding.

He trained Elan to win the Gloucestershire (now Supreme Novices') Hurdle in 1964, the following year he trained the same horse to win the Schweppes Gold Trophy, and Sutcliffe was fifth in the National Hunt Trainers Championship.

Success on the Flat came at a similar meteoric pace. In 1968 he trained Hard Water to win the Duke of York Stakes, and in the same year he had in the stable two outstanding horses: Jimmy Reppin and Right Tack. Both were unfashionably bred, cheap purchases but both were top class milers. Jimmy Reppin finished third in the 1968 2,000 Guineas behind Sir Ivor and Petingo, and won the Hungerford Stakes and the Waterford Crystal Mile, Right Tack won the Middle Park Stakes that year.

In 1969 Right Tack became the first horse to win the 2,000 Guineas and Irish 2,000 Guineas. Sutcliffe went desperately close to a clean sweep for owner Mr J.R. Brown, when Motionless finished third in the 1,000 Guineas and second in the Irish 1,000 Guineas. Right Tack also won the St James's Palace Stakes, and Jimmy Reppin won the Sussex Stakes, Hungerford Stakes, Valdoe Stakes, Queen Elizabeth II Stakes and the Prix Perth.

Jimmy Reppin and Right Tack both failed to make an impact at stud, but Sutcliffe's next star, Mummy's Pet who won the then Norfolk (now Flying Childers) Stakes, the Sceptre Stakes and the Temple Stakes, and finished second in the Middle Park Stakes, and Kings Stand Stakes, proved to be a prolific sire of sprinters.

Another outstanding sprinter trained by Sutcliffe was Mr. Stanley Powell's The Brianstan who won the 1969 Prince of Wales's Stakes, York, and the 1971 Duke of York Stakes.

Sutcliffe established a reputation as a 'handicap specialist' training the winners of the Royal Hunt Cup and the Bessborough Handicap on three occasions. Other handicap successes included the Ebor, the Wokingham, the Jubilee, and the Ayr Gold Cup.

In 1973 he achieved the rare distinction of winning a Pattern race with a horse making its racecourse debut when My Drifter won the Craven Stakes. His other Group race wins included Oscilight who won the 1978 Temple Stakes, and Tender King who won the 1981 Richmond Stakes, and was third in the 1981 Dewhurst Stakes. The following season Tender King finished second in the Irish 2,000 Guineas, third in the 2,000 Guineas, and third in the July Cup.

Judy Dick, daughter of the trainer *Dave Dick*, was a work rider for Sutcliffe in the early years, as was the former *Ted Smyth* apprentice Brian Rouse, who subsequently reapplied for his licence and rode a 1,000 Guineas winner. *Les Montague Hall*, who later trained at Epsom, was also a work rider for Sutcliffe, as was Newmarket trainer Ray McGhin. Trainers Mark Flower and Lynda Ramsden also worked for Sutcliffe.

When Kempton Park offered a £50,000 bonus for a horse to win three races at an evening meeting, Sutcliffe went for it and won it. The offer was not repeated. In 1990 he won the most valuable prize of his career the Schweppes Golden Mile with March Bird. Sutcliffe later had a brief spell as assistant to *Gary Moore*.

| SWIFT, Brian | Loretta Lodge | 1967-1985 |
| (1937-1985) | | |

Jack Swift was one of the leading bookmakers in the country in the immediate post-war period. He was also an enthusiastic racehorse owner who at various times had horses stabled with trainers *Dave Dick, Tommy Carey, Dick Thrale, Jack Reardon* and *Staff Ingham*. His son Brian frequently visited the stables and 'caught the racing bug'. He served an apprenticeship with *Jack Reardon* and rode 200 winners before increasing weight forced his retirement.

He briefly worked in his father's business, however the lure of racing proved too strong for Brian, and he returned to Epsom as *Staff Ingham*'s assistant.

Brian Swift's training career got off to the brightest start when he was given charge of a novice hurdler called Persian War. Brian trained the horse to win the Victor Ludorum at Haydock and the Daily Express Triumph Hurdle. However, owner Henry Alper proved to be a difficult man to train for, and following a dispute when the horse was entered for a race in France without Swift's knowledge the horse was moved to Colin Davies' stable at Chepstow where he won three Champion Hurdles.

In 1969, Brian enjoyed his first major success on the Flat with Tribal Chief who won three of his four two-year-old outings including the New Stakes and the Norfolk Stakes. In the same year Brian had another useful two-year-old in Decoy Boy who won five races, was second in the Nunthorpe Stakes and was rated superior to Tribal Chief. In 1973 he trained Supreme Gift to win the Portland Handicap, the horse was also third in the Prix de l'Abbaye.

In 1980 Swift enjoyed Group 1 success when the enigmatic Swan Princess won the Phoenix Stakes. A difficult horse to train, Swan Princess had intense nervous energy, and on more than one occasion burnt herself out by bolting to the start.

Swift had handicap success in the 1971 City and Suburban at Epsom with Tandy, and also won the Lincoln with The Hertford in 1976. Other handicap races won included the Stewards Cup and the Wokingham Handicap.

Swift's career then hit a sticky patch. The number of winners dropped to eight in 1981. A virus struck the horses, his marriage broke up, and the original plan for the M.25 saw it cutting across Swift's gallops and *Staff Ingham*'s gallops. (The motorway when finally built was 100 yards behind Loretta Lodge). One night when a group of Swift's lads were walking back from the Cock at Headley, they were involved in an accident, one of the lads David Brannigan was hit by a car and killed. Brannigan had come to Epsom from Glasgow, arriving at Loretta Lodge when the stable jockey was Jock Wilson, and the stable apprentice Jock Wilkinson; Brannigan thus became "Angus". Brian Swift arranged for a permanent memorial on the approach to the village, "Headley welcomes careful drivers, In memory of David Angus Brannigan."

In 1982 Brian was under bidder at 22,000 guineas for a foal who was a half-brother to Swan Princess by Dominion. By the following September the colt had developed as attractively as Swift anticipated, and this time he went to 146,000 guineas to secure the colt, Primo Dominie. In 1984 Primo Dominie won the Coventry Stakes, July Stakes and Richmond Stakes, thus becoming the first two-year old to win three Pattern races. Primo Dominie also finished third in the Middle Park Stakes.

Another star two-year-old emerged the same year with the cheaper Prince Sabo who won the Flying Childers Stakes.

Swift entered 1985 with potentially the two fastest horses in the country in his care, and his stable through the lean patch, however in February 1985 he suffered a massive heart attack and died a few days later. He left an estate of £649,223.

Primo Dominie went to Michael Stoute at Newmarket and eventually became a leading sire.

SWIFT, Sylvia	Loretta Lodge	1985

Brian Swift's wife Sylvia took out a licence on his death, training Prince Sabo to win the Palace House Stakes.

SYDNEY, Alfred E.H.		1880-81
(1841-1922)		

Sydney moved to Lewes in 1881, remaining there for the rest of his career.

TABOR, Charles Victor	Priam Lodge	1907-1908
(1873-1951)	Downs (Derby Arms)	1909-1910
	Holly Lodge	1911-1943

Victor Tabor was born on May 24th 1873, the son of an Essex farmer, he was educated at Uppingham School, and was for many years leading rider on the East Anglian circuit. He commenced training in 1907, advertising for an "experienced feeder" for his 20 horses, at Priam Lodge, he also used the stables near the Derby Arms, prior to moving to Holly Lodge at Kingswood. In 1916 he trained Furore to win the Irish Derby. The following year Furore won the Cesarewitch, the first of Tabor's three winners in that race, to be followed in 1928 with Arctic Star, and in 1937 with Punch. His best chaser was Airgead

Sios who won three valuable chases in 1936 culminating with the Champion Chase at Liverpool, and in 1938 won the King George VI Chase, and the Victory Steeplechase at Manchester. Tabor's wife *Ethel Woodland*, who died in 1941, was the sister of National Hunt stalwart *Percy Woodland*, and was a fine horsewoman who assisted Tabor throughout his career. Tabor left effects of £340.

| TAGG, Thomas Cheshire | Woodlands | 1920-1926 |
| (c.1866- 1946) | | |

Tagg was born c. 1866 in Newhall, Derbyshire, and is shown in the 1911 census as a professional coachman residing at Woodlands Stable, Barnes Common, Tagg features in Horses in Training 1920 based at Woodlands, Barnes Common. In Horses In Training Annual 1926, his address is listed as Woodlannds, Epsom, apparently bestowing the name of his Barnes stable on the property in Beaconsfield Road that he named Woodlands. When Stanley Wootton purchased the gallops in 1926, Tagg (with *McNaughton, Vere Barker*, and *Barnes* appeared on the draft schedule of trainers using the Downs, but was deleted from the final schedule).

Under the name Thomas Skelton he rode Old Joe to win the 1886 Grand National. He later drove the London to Dorking coach, and was master of the horse for Bertram Mills Circus. Tagg also appeared in the film "Dick Turpin" playing a coachman. He was living at Mortlake at the time of his death.

| TALBOT, Frederick W. | Headley Park Stables | 1894-1901 |
| (1861- ?) | | |

Born at Harwell, Berkshire, Talbot was a stable lad in Epsom at the time of the 1891 census, taking over Headley Park stables c. 1895. He is mentioned in The Sporting Life gallop reports from 21st March 1895. By 1911 he was out of racing and working as a coachman in Kensington.

| TAYLOR, Albert P. | Myrtle Cottage | 1954-1959 |
| (1916-1993) | | |

Former *Herbert Smyth* apprentice, after a spell at Myrtle Cottage, "Manch" Taylor retired from training, later making a brief comeback in the 1970s, when training at Headley Down, Hampshire.

| TAYLOR, John | Downs Lodge | 1900-1901 |
| (1866- 1925?) | | |

Born in Durham, trained at "Downs Lodge" in the 1911 census he is described as an "Unemployed horseman" living at Epsom Common.

TEAL, Roger   Thirty Acre Barn   2007-2015
(1967-

Roger Teal rode 15 winners as an amateur jockey, after which he joined Philip Mitchell's yard and was, from 1994, assistant trainer. During this period he took Running Stag to victories all over the world. Teal trained Highly Regal to win the 2009 London Mile Handicap, and Steele Tango, whose numerous good performances in top company included victory in the Group 3 Darley Stakes, and a valuable handicap in Dubai.
Teal moved to Berkshire where he enjoyed success with Tip Two Win, who won the Group 2 Al Biddah Mile, and was second in the 2018 2,000 Thousand Guineas.

THIRKELL, James   South Hatch   1857-1860
(1827- ?)   Smitham Bottom   1860

Thirkell was based at South Hatch as private trainer to Mr. Carew, subsequently moving to Smitham Bottom, prior to taking up an appointment in Asia.

THOMSON   1899, 1900

Training Intelligence in The Sporting Life 15th February 1900, lists him under Epsom Trainers. He appears in Sporting Life gallop reports in 1899.

THRALE, Peter   Startside   1945-1959
(1886-1959)

Thrale was a qualified veterinary surgeon who had served with the Royal Veterinary Corps during WWI. He commenced training in 1923 at Croydon, and subsequently moved to Woolgars Farm at East Horsley, some ten miles south west of Epsom. His successes while at East Horsley included Drintyre who won the Scottish Grand National, and Nitischin who won the 1932 Irish Oaks. Thrale established a reputation as a shrewd purchaser of cheap bloodstock, and an outstanding trainer under both codes.
In 1945 he moved to Epsom. His National Hunt successes during this period included Meritorious, and Amazon's Choice in the Triumph Hurdle. Thrale's other successes while based at Epsom included the Royal Lodge Stakes in 1950 with Khor Moussa, the New Stakes in 1949 with Master Gunner, and the Oxfordshire Stakes in 1954 with Umberto. In 1951 he trained Lady Godiva to finish second in the Irish 1,000 Guineas, and in the same year won the Cornwallis Stakes with Sir Phoenix. Thrale's stable jockey was his son-in-law *Ken Gethin*.
At his peak Thrale had horses in four yards in Langley Vale. He left £18,155 gross, and £11,010 net.

THRALE, Richard   Downs House   1953-1966
(1897-1973)

The cousin of *Peter Thrale*, Dick Thrale rode a lot of Peter Thrale's National Hunt horses before the war. He stayed on at the yard at Addington after Peter moved to East Horsley, breaking the two-year-olds, and in 1937 took out a licence to train there.
In 1953 he moved into Downs House, where he trained Indigenous who held the record of fastest horse when winning at Epsom on June 2nd 1960 at an average of 41.97 mph, this stood as the fastest time until electronic timing was introduced.
Richard Thrale's daughter Gillian is the mother of former National Hunt champion jockey Richard Dunwoody.

TOMLINSON, Jeffrey   Pitt Place   1868-1872
(1833- ?)

Tomlinson is listed in Ruff's Guide 1870 as private trainer and jockey at Pitt Place. His name appears on Training Reports in The Sportsman between 1868 and 1872.

TURNER, Charles   Carshalton   1839-1870
(1807- 1883)

An article in The Sporting Life, 2nd February 1870 regarding trainers using Farthing Downs, Smitham Bottom noted:

"veteran Mr C. Turner of Carshalton, was rather fortunate having trained Sir Felix, Jim Crow etc., besides that good steeplechase horse Curate, who was second To Chandler in the 1848 Grand national, being beaten by a head only, and won several races before he broke his back at Aintree the following. year".

Turner had runners at the Cheam/North Cheam meetings in 1839 and 1840.
In the 1841 census he is described as a trainer, and advertises as a trainer selling horses in Bells Life that year. He is later described as a veterinary surgeon. His son Charles Turner, (b.1829) was also a veterinary surgeon and keen sportsman.
Charles Turner died on 27th November 1883, leaving an estate of £3,425.

TURNER   1884

Noted in the Belfast News Letter on various dates in Spring 1884; under Epsom Training Notes:

"Turner's Knight of the Cross went a mile."

Turner also rode Knight Of The Cross for owner Mr East, but by the summer of 1884 the horse was under the care of *William Holt*.

VINCENT, George	The Cottage	1887-1895
(1858-?)		

George Vincent, born in Wallop, Hampshire, trained on a small scale from The Cottage stables. In 1893 he had four horses in training.

WAITING, Robert	Woodcote Grove	1888-1895
(1847-1912)		

Sometimes shown as Robert Warling or Whiting, he was born in Cumberland. The 1891 census lists his address as New Road (now known as Worple Road), and he appears to have been using the stables (known as The Shrubbery) attached to Woodcote Grove. At the baptism of his daughter in 1892, he is described as a "Private Trainer."
From 1881-1887 he was described as a "Coachman." In 1889 after working two horses on the trial ground, Robert "Whiting" described in court as "private trainer of racehorses to Mr Quarterman East" was approached by *John Nightingall* and told "They are not racehorses they are hacks. If you call this a trial you are a liar." Whiting/Waiting in turn called Nightingall a liar. In the altercation that followed Nightingall struck Waiting with his whip and was subsequently fined £1 for assault.
After retiring from training he farmed near Dorking, Surrey and died there in 1912 leaving effects of £4,308.

WALKINGTON, Spink Birdsall	1921
(1881-1940)	

Born in Bridlington, Yorkshire, Walkington was employed by William Nightingall at the time of the 1901 census. He won the 1906 Northumberland Plate riding Outbreak. He rode in the 1911 Derby for *George Barclay*, and had five mounts in the Grand National between 1910 and 1919. He served in the Army Veterinary Corps during World War I, based mainly in Egypt.

WALLINGTON, Harold G.	Sandown Lodge	1939-1940
(1898-1972)	Hillcrest	1947-1968

From 1945 to 1973, Hillcrest was used by the father, and subsequently by the son; Harold G. Wallington. Harold Wallington senior was a National Hunt jockey who rode with limited success during the 1920s. He then became head lad to the American-born trainer Morgan de Witt Blair who trained at Ewhurst in Surrey. In 1936 Blair trained Victor Norman to win the Champion Hurdle.

189

In 1937, Wallington bought a horse called St Andrews out of a seller, sold a quarter share to *Staff Ingham*, and a half share elsewhere. He stabled the horse at *John Nightingall's*, and employed Phillip Welsh who had recently left *Herbert Smyth* to 'train' the horse. Welsh wrote a book, *Stable Rat*, which describes his time with the Wallington family, and Herbert Smyth. Prior to racing in a handicap at Goodwood, St Andrews worked with three useful performers from *Walter Nightingall's* yard, with Welsh "taking a tug" despite having some lead secreted in his waistcoat. On the strength of this trial, Harold mortgaged his house and put the proceeds on St Andrews, Phil Welsh invested his life savings. The horse duly obliged, and thus Wallington's training career was born.

The coup caused some antagonism in Epsom, not least from *John Nightingall* in whose name the horse was trained, but also from *Walter Nightingall* who had been duped into providing galloping companions in good faith, and *Jack Reardon* who had £4,000 on his own horse in the race.

Wallington rented some boxes at Sandown Lodge, but his training plans were interrupted by the outbreak of war. The Epsom and Ewell Herald reported on 20th March 1942:

"Those engaged in the Epsom district in the horse racing industry will be still further affected by the restrictions on the race meetings. Horse racing will be restricted to a few courses with a view to economy in public transport.
Only five courses will be used. They are Newmarket, Salisbury, Windsor, Stockton and Pontefract. Only horses trained at Newmarket will be allowed to race there, with the exception of the Classic races and several important events usually held at Ascot. Only horses trained south of the Trent, Newmarket horses excluded, will be allowed to take part in the races decided at Windsor and Salisbury. The meetings to be held at Stockton and Pontefract will be confined to horses trained North of the Trent."

Harold Wallington moved to Malton to exploit the weaker racing at Stockton and Pontefract (fellow Epsom trainer *Cecil Ray* made a similar move).

The move proved beneficial because Wallington met some owners who proved to be the mainstay of his career and stayed with him after he moved back to Epsom, textile magnate Willie Satinoff, later to become a director of Manchester United, and killed in the Munich Air Disaster; and the Pacitto brothers who owned the ice cream parlours at Scarborough and Redcar. After returning to Epsom in 1945, Wallington was a frequent visitor to the north for his owners, notably when winning the 1952 Zetland Gold Cup at Redcar with Mid View.

He specialised in middle-distance handicaps winning the Victoria Cup, Cambridgeshire and Royal Hunt Cup. Wallington's best horse was probably Castelmarino who won the 1955 Solario Stakes.

WALLINGTON, Harold G.(jun.)Hillcrest   1969-1973
(1937-1976)

Harold Wallington junior succeeded his father in 1969. A trained veterinary surgeon, he had assisted his father for some years. In 1970 he trained Jukebox to win the Stewards Cup, (then the richest sprint in the Calendar) carrying topweight. Jukebox also won the Sceptre Stakes, and the Hackwood Stakes, before becoming a successful stallion, notably siring Music Boy, the champion juvenile of 1975.
In 1970 Wallington introduced Mon Plaisir, who after winning an Ascot handicap by an easy looking 15 lengths, finished third in the Irish 2000 Guineas, beaten in a photo finish by Decies and Great Heron. Mon Plaisir was essentially a spring horse that favoured some cut in the ground; he won the 1971 Victoria Cup and the Newbury Spring Cup in 1972 and 1973.
The future looked bright for Wallington, but his father's death had resulted in a large tax bill. As a result the yard at Hillcrest was sold, and subsequently demolished to allow access to Down Cottage and Hillcrest Close was built. Harold became secretary of the Racehorse Owners Association, but died six months later.

WALLS, Thomas	The Paddocks, Windmill Lane	1917,1919,
(1883-1949)		1922-27
	The Grange/The Looe	1928-39, 1943
		1947
	Warren Farm Stables	1937

Tom Walls started his working life by fulfilling a dream to be a locomotive driver, he then decided to become a detective. However, three months of pounding the beat as Metropolitan Police Constable 2510 "C" Division, was sufficient to dull the notion and he turned to acting.
His theatrical success commenced in 1922, when with fellow Epsom resident Ralph Lynn, he began a long run of 'farces' at the Aldwych Theatre, and these included Dirty Work, Tons Of Money, It Pays To Advertise, and A Cup Of Kindness.
Ben Travers, who was, in the main, the playwright of the farces, later observed: "Tom Walls was, without exception, the most extraordinary man I ever came across." Travers acknowledged the success of the farces owed much to Walls' "despotic" leadership, "in many ways he was a splendid man to work with, just as in some ways he was a vainglorious, implacable dunderhead." Walls eventually became a partner in the Aldwych Theatre, and directed several productions. He later bought the film rights to some of these productions, and directed some films.
He commenced training racehorses in 1917, and his combination of a full and varied show business career and his other career as a trainer, jockey, and huntsman attracted considerable public interest.

Walls explained that after appearing at Aldwych he was rarely in bed before 1.30 a.m. "It is a fuller day than most men's because of my twin interests - the stage and horses. My fifteen horses alone are enough to keep me fully employed. I always make a rule of saddling my own horse in a race. In wintertime I hunt on at least one day a week, and I usually manage to squeeze in one day shooting in every week in the season"

His major success as a trainer came with April The Fifth, a horse he owned in partnership with Mr Sidney McGregor. A late maturing two-year-old, April The Fifth had three unplaced runs as a two-year-old, but at three won the Lingfield Derby Trial, prior to winning the 1932 Derby at 100-6, making Walls the only Epsom based trainer to win an Epsom Derby in the twentieth century. The crowd was so large that despite Tom allowing 90 minutes for the two-mile journey from Ewell to Epsom Downs, the horse was forced to walk the last half-mile through the crowd.

In the Daily Mail, Eric Rickman reported:

"The success of April The Fifth, owned partly by Tom Walls the actor-manager and trained by him at Epsom was one of the most romantic triumphs in the long history of this great race. An actor who can get up early in the morning and train a Derby winner before he leaves for the managerial office or the film studio, an actor who never fails to amuse, and a keen, competent horseman liked and admired by all who meet him, such is the man who has won this Derby. No wonder the crowd cheered.

In The Daily Telegraph, Hotspur noted:

"Never have I seen a Derby winner come from behind as he did to make up so much ground. It was simply irresistible. After nearly a hundred years it has been demonstrated that a Derby winner can be trained at Epsom."

The Daily Express followed up with a story of how Walls "lay at death's door" the previous year after a hunting accident, and his faith in the horse's potential kept him involved with training.

"It is said the actor won £40,000 in bets alone yesterday, and apart from that any Derby winner is worth £40,000 in stud fees, in addition to the Derby stakes of £6,000."

Meanwhile, his son, Tom Walls junior was making his mark as a jockey, and father and son rode in the same race at Lewes on 31st August 1932. Tom Walls claimed that the highlight of his turf career was when his son rode Crafty Alice, (another Sidney McGregor-owned horse), to victory in the Grand Military Gold Cup. "Although I won the Derby with April The Fifth in 1932 there is no gold trophy. All my life I have wanted a gold trophy, and Young Tom has realised that ambition."

Walls expanded his business empire to include Wansford Quarry near Peterborough. His transition from stage to screen met with reduced success, and several of his business ventures were unsuccessful.

The purchase of the Fortune Theatre for £50,000 proved to be a drain on resources, and he lost £12,000 making a film of "Tons of Money", which he later described as a "cold flop." Ben Travers was persuaded to invest in the quarry, and the Fortune Theatre. He noted: "However gruesome was the appearance of his banking account at any given time, Tom always pursued a mode of life which was an unvarying pattern of glorious extravagance."

Tom Walls died on 27th November 1949. On the 21st and 22nd June 1950 the contents of his house, The Looe, Ewell, were sold en situ. In addition to the farm, garden, and stable equipment, there were 22 watercolours, nine oil paintings, six lots of table china, five lots of silverware, 12 lots of table glass, and a vast array of antique furniture. The billiard room alone yielded 45 lots.

However even after the realisation of the assets, and the payment of debts, his estate yielded only a few thousand pounds. He bequeathed his property to his son Thomas Kenneth Walls, "in the knowledge that he will always look after his mother and Aunt Minnie." Walls' lifestyle took a lot of financing, running a stable as an owner-trainer is an expensive business, and some of the show business ventures were not as profitable as he liked people to believe. Walls remains one of the most charismatic personalities the turf as seen, as one obituary writer observed: "He lived the life of three men, but spent the salary of six." His ashes were scattered by the winning post at Epsom.

WALSH, Jack   Rowland Lodge   1890-91
(?1867 – 1944)

Jack Walsh, (brother-in-law of Ayr trainer John McGuigan), served an apprenticeship at the Curragh before going to Scotland to ride the Duke of Montrose's jumpers.

The Sheffield Independent 7th October 1890 noted:

"Mr Soden, the well-known gentleman rider has taken Rowland Lodge, Epsom and engaged J. Walsh, late jockey with S. Darling as his private trainer."

After a brief training career at Epsom, Walsh moved to America. On his retirement he returned to Scotland. McGuigan was a friend of the Woottons and spent several holidays in Australia as a guest of *Richard Wootton.*

WALTERS,   1885

The Sheffield Independent 22nd December 1885 notes under gallop reports, Epsom, the exercise routines for Nightingall, Jones, Sherwood and Holt adding that *"Walters sent Iodine II a mile and a half".*

Possibly Alfred Walters, (born Shifnal 1853), he trained at Jevington, Sussex until c. 1881; and trained at Letcombe at the time of the 1891 and 1911 census return.

WARD, G. LAING   Heathcote House   1918-1919
(1883-1944)

George Laing Ward trained in Sussex in 1911, and had a brief stay at Heathcote House before moving to Winchester where his numerous successes included the 1924 Queen Anne Stakes.

WARREN, George   Portland House   1953-1954

The Yorkshire Post, 20th August 1954, reported:

"One thousandth of a grain of caffeine has resulted in George F. Warren, the Epsom trainer losing his licence. That according to the owner Mr P. Raymond, the London hair stylist, was all that was found by the analysts in the saliva test taken from Galsere after he won at Alexandra Park on July 26th. When Mr Warren was asked if his licence had been withdrawn, replied " Well they held me responsible, so, of course my licence has been withdrawn." Speaking from his London home. Mr. Raymond said," I feel very sorry for George Warren, I am sure he would never have done anything unsporting. I shall try to help him in every way I can and shall try to clear his name. George is not a rich man. He has not got a car, does not bet. He lives in a small bungalow at Epsom."

WARRINER. John   Reigate   1863
(1825-1877)   Lime Tree Cottage   1869-1877
                          Church Street

John Warriner was for many years private trainer for the owner Squire George Osbaldeston. He lost the job in 1861 for what was described by Osbaldeston as "the most gross misconduct", however the Squire was notably a difficult man to please. At this stage Warriner was training at stables in Compton, near Wantage. During the 1870s Warriner maintained stables at Newmarket, and at Lime Tree Cottage (also known as Down Lodge) in Church Street, Epsom. The Sporting Gazette 1871, lists S. Warrener as training 16 horses at Epsom.
At the time of his bankruptcy hearing in 1871, Warriner gave his address as Church Street, Epsom.
Warriner appears in Training Reports from Epsom in The Sportsman in 1870 and 1871, but as early as 1866 the horses are referred to as "The Squire's".

WATKINS,   Kingswood   1914-1915

Possibly Charles Watkins born in 1857 in Herefordshire.

WATKINSON,   1906-1908
.
WATTS, Thomas   Woodcote Green   1895-1896

Possibly Thomas Watts born Bury St Edmunds 1840, died Epsom 1902'. In 1886, Watts was advertising in The Sporting Life as a tipster, describing himself as a former resident of Epsom, and trainer and owner. Similar adverts appeared in 1895 and 1896. Epsom Gallop reports in the Sheffield Daily Telegraph record:

31ˢᵗ May 1895
Watts' Taurus went a mile at half speed. Gypsy Jack doing a brace of 5 and 6 furlong canters.
23rd July 1895
Watt's Gypsy Jack covered 5 furlongs at half speed.
21ˢᵗ September 1895
Watts', Talbot's and the remainder did useful work.

Also mentioned in The Sporting Life gallop reports from March 1895.

WELLER, James William K.   Sun Hotel, Kingston   1911
(1861-1925)

Kingston-born Weller, is listed in the 1911 census as a jockey and trainer based at Sun Hotel Tap, Kingston. He was based in Epsom at the time of his death.

WEST, Adam   Gastons, Headley   2016
                            Thirty Acre Barn   2017
                            Loretta Lodge   2017-

Following a riding career in Ireland, West worked for *John Akehurst*, and then as head lad to *Roger Teal*. He set up in 2013 running a horse transport business, and breaking difficult horses, prior to taking out a trainer's licence in 2016.

WEST   The Warren   1868

The Sporting Life 22th February 1868 notes that West is training *Mr. Ellam's* horses at The Warren.

WEST   1902

Mentioned in The Sporting Life gallop reports, notably 22nd March 1902.

WESTLAKE, James P.   1909
(1859-1941)

Born at the Curragh, Westlake rode in Ireland and Australia, returning to the Curragh to train between 1897 and 1907. He trained at Whatcombe in Berkshire in 1908, Epsom in 1909, and then trained in Lambourn until 1934.

WHEELER, Robert   Downs House (Sherwoods)1910
(c.1848-c.1921)

Born in Hastings, Robert Wheeler trained at Rottingdean in Sussex (based there in the censuses of 1881, 1891, and 1901). On 3rd January 1910 it was announced that he had rented stabling from *Tom Sherwood*, to train Mr. G. Astor's horse. After a brief stay at Epsom, he moved to Childrey, Berkshire in 1911.

WHELAN, Dermot   Mannamead   1955-1957
(1918-1999)   Lavandou   1958-1983

Jeremiah Dermot Whelan (better known as "Boggy"), spent five years working for *Bill Payne*, and then served in the Royal Armoured Corps, and was involved in action at Dunkirk and Alamein. He worked for *Ron Smyth* for ten years, before taking out a licence, and he moved to The Durdans in 1958. He extended the yard and changed the name to Lavandou. Whelan's first major success was with Rocky Royale who won the 1960 Jubilee Handicap, further success followed in 1962 with Tropic Star who won the Cheshire Oaks, and the Pretty Polly Stakes at The Curragh. His best horse was Tug Of War who won the Northumberland Plate in 1977 and 1978, and the Goodwood Cup in 1978. He came closest to classic success with Indian Melody who finished third in the 1,000 Guineas and second in the Irish Oaks in 1961.
He also had some good apprentices in his charge: the brothers John and Bob Curant who both made the grade as jockeys, and Clive Searle who later became a trainer in England and Australia. Whelan also bred a number of good horses. "Boggy" Whelan was an old friend of Vincent O'Brien, and most of O'Brien's Epsom runners, including Nijinsky, were stabled at The Durdans during their stay at Epsom.

WHITELEY, James	Marden Park, Caterham	1874
(1844-?)	Coulsdon	1879-81
	College Road, Epsom	1901

James Whiteley was born in Cambridgeshire, and rode as a steeplechase jockey from c. 1870 to c.1880. In 1873 he rode 19 winners, and was sixth in the National Hunt jockeys championship. He was based at Godstone, Surrey during the early part of his career. In 1874 Whitely was a steeplechase jockey based at Marden Deer Park, Caterham; sharing the mounts with W. Gregory. He trained Messager to win the 1874 Grand International Hurdle. He then returned to Royston, Cambridgeshire, later working with his brother William at Coulsdon from late 1879. He was based in Germany in the 1890s, prior to a spell at Epsom c. 1901. "Whiteley" was champion jockey in Germany in 1876.

| WHITELEY, William | Coulsdon | 1879-1881 |
| (1847-?) | | |

The younger brother of *James Whiteley*, he was born in Cambridgeshire in 1847.

| WHITFIELD, Charles | | 1898-1901 |
| (1869-?) | | |

Born in Hammersmith, Whitfield is referred to as an Epsom-based trainer in Charles Richardson's 1901 publication The English Turf. Whitfield later trained in Wiltshire, and at Portsmouth.

| WILDE/WILD, Herbert | Uplands | 1903-1907 |

Listed in trainers and their addresses, The Sporting Life, 31 March 1905.

| WILDMAN, William | Mickleham | c.1760-1771 |

Wildman, a wholesale butcher, and trainer based at Mickleham, purchased Eclipse from the Duke Of Cumberland, later selling the horse to *Dennis O'Kelly*.
Wildman also trained Gimcrack, a small grey horse who won 27 of his 36 races in a career spanning seven seasons, and later became a successful sire. Gimcrack is commemorated in a painting by Stubbs, and also by the Gimcrack Stakes that is staged at York every August. Wildman purchased the horse at the end of 1764 from Mr Green. Gimcrack won one race for Wildman at the Newmarket Spring meeting and he was subsequently sold to Lord Bolingbroke. He remained at Newmarket where he won several 500 guinea matches. Gimcrack was later sold to race in France, returning to England the following year.

197

Wildman had a stud and training stables with 38 boxes on his land at Gibbons Grove, where he also reared animals for the meat market at Smithfield.

WILLSON, Alfred Richard	Bruce Lodge	1889-1899
(1851-1904)		

Lord William Beresford V.C., spent much time in India where Paris-born Willson looked after his horses. Lord Beresford returned to England circa 1889, and brought Willson with him, setting him up as his private trainer at Bruce Lodge. Willson is listed in Kelly's Directory 1889 as a trainer at Bruce Lodge. Willson also trained in Berkshire 1899-1901. He died in Hertfordshire leaving effects of £1,843.

WILSON, David	Ermyn Lodge	1981-1983
(1940-	Shifnal Cottage	1984-1986
	Loretta Lodge	1987-1988
	Cedar Point	1987-1996

Formerly assistant trainer to *John E. Sutcliffe*, Wilson spent 15 years training before becoming an assistant trainer, most notably with *Gary Moore*. The best horse he trained was probably Gamblers Dream who won Goodwood's August Handicap in 1981.

WINFIELD, Jesse	Woodcote Road	1877-1891
(1846- ?)		

Jesse Winfield is listed in the 1881 census as a "Betting Agent". He was also a purveyor of Jesse Winfield's Epsom Embrocation, "No stable complete without it." In 1884 champion jockey Fred Archer was endorsing Winfield's Epsom Embrocation. "Sir, I find your embrocation the best I have ever used." In 1878 at his bankruptcy proceedings Winfield is described as occupying Maidstone House; his horse Maidstone was running from 1875, and it is possible that he was training from Maidstone House prior to moving to Woodcote Lodge. In 1882 he employed *W. Davies* as his private trainer. In December 1884, Jesse Winfield was charged with libel, but discharged after no prosecution evidence was offered.

In 1887, he was quoted in the Yorkshire Gazette, Saturday 17th December, under the heading Steeplechase and Hurdle Race Controversy:

"You can hunt in any country for a lifetime and never meet such obstacles as we now meet with every day. Ten years ago I was running many horses over country, and hurdles, one mile and a half hurdle races, and won fifty-seven races in two years and very seldom had an accident. One and a half mile races will impart that bit of "venom"

which Lord Beresford says is required, and I think he is right. Do away with the "big grave" and let the fences be as natural as possible."

WINTER, Frederick N.	Bredenbury	1930-1933
(1894- 1965)	Treadwell House	1934-1936
	Rowland Lodge	1937-1943

Fred Winter rode Cherimoya to win the 1911 Oaks at the age of 16. He was riding in Austria for the Kaiser in 1914 when war broke out, and he was arrested on September 14th 1914, and interned in Barrack 2 at Ruhleben Concentration camp (which ironically was Hoppengarten racecourse.) Winter was given 24 hours prior notice of his arrest, but was unable to leave the country. The United States Ambassador intervened in 1915 on behalf of the interned British civilians noting: *"Jockey Winter, an employee of the Royal Gradirz stables, who in consequence of his employment by the German government, should obtain his liberty, but should not be permitted to leave Germany.)* Winter was however interned for the duration. He wrote home complaining of the boredom, and on release his weight had increased, and he struggled to relaunch his career. After failing to obtain a licence to train at Newmarket, he settled in Epsom. In 1944 he moved to stables at Southfleet in Kent. His main win while at Epsom was with Strathcarron in the 1935 King George Stakes at Goodwood. He also won the last running of the Grand International Hurdle, (by now reduced in status), in 1940 with Carlton. Frederick Winter died at Highfield, Bury Road, Newmarket leaving an estate of £10,195.

His son Frederick T. Winter (1926-2004) was one of National Hunt's outstanding men. He was riding out on Epsom Downs at the age of five, and had his first public mount when aged 13. He was educated at Ewell Castle School, where Dave Dick Junior was his contemporary and subsequent lifelong friend. He spent four years in the Parachute Regiment, taking up his career as a National Hunt jockey when demobbed in 1948. He rode three Champion Hurdle winners, two Grand National winners, and two Gold Cup winners. Winter was champion jump jockey four times and top trainer on eight occasions. He is the only person to have won the Cheltenham Gold Cup, Champion Hurdle and Grand National as both jockey and trainer.

| WOOD, Daniel | Kingston-Upon-Thames | 1911 |
| (1882- ?) | | |

WOOD, James	Rowland Lodge	1907
(1876-1951)	The Cottage	1911-1914, 1916-1917
	Bruce Lodge	1916
	Badminton	1930-1933
	Tattenham Corner	1935-1936
	Warren Farm	1936-1940
	Downs House	1945-1951

Wood trained his first winner in 1899, ridden by his father Charles Wood, the former champion jockey. Charles Wood refused to let his son ride; hence the early start to James' training career.

At this stage Wood was training at Doncaster, he joined the army in 1914. When travelling to France, his ship was torpedoed and sunk; he was rescued after several hours in the water. The Newcastle Journal, 29th December 1916 recorded that having received an appointment from the Army Veterinary Department he was giving up Bruce Lodge stables. As a result of wartime injuries, his health suffered, and he did not train again until 1930. Good horses trained by Wood include Joan's Star, twice second in Cambridgeshire (beaten by Esquire in 1945 and Fairey Fulmar in 1946), and The Bite who won the 1949 Stewards Cup.

The Bloodstock Breeders Review in the obituary of Jimmy Wood said:

"Always neatly dressed in dark, sober clothes, JW never conformed in appearance to any popular picture of a trainer or horseman. Though of retiring disposition, his friends knew him as a genial and entertaining companion. His kindness was also extended to a great variety of animals for which Downs House was a sanctuary."

| WOODHOUSE, A. | | 1894-95 |

| WOODLAND, Edmund | Purley | 1898, 1903-1909 |
| (1871-1919) | | |

Eldest brother of *William* and *Percy Woodland*, Edmund trained and farmed on the Downs south of Croydon. He was living at Kingswood at the time of his death, leaving his estate of £423 to his sister Ethel May, wife of trainer *Charles Victor Tabor*.

| WOODLAND, Edward | Kenley | 1906 |
| (1839-1919) | | |

Edward Woodland, father of the three brothers and Mrs Ethel Tabor, was a successful trainer and jockey, specialising in the treatment of infirm horses. He died in Epsom in 1919.

WOODLAND, Miss Ethel May   Woodcote Rise   1906
(1880-1941)

The sister of *Percy Woodland*, she married Char*les Victor Tabor* in 1905. She was also assisting *William McAllister* around that time. The Sporting Life, September 11th 1906, recorded:

"Miss Woodland's training stable at Epsom were partially destroyed by fire last night. The fire was discovered about seven o'clock;, and attention was at once directed to rescuing the horses. This was successfully done, notwithstanding the fact that the stables were made of wood. The local fire brigade, succeeded in extinguishing the fire and saving part of the stables."

The implication is that McAllister (or Tabor) was the licence holder, but Ethel Woodland trained the horses at this time.
She was a valuable assistant trainer to Tabor in later years, notably purchasing top chaser Airgead Sios. She suffered periods of ill health, and was found dead at Holly Lodge in 1941; the death attributed to "gas poisoning."

WOODLAND, Percy Maurice   Bush House, Holly Lodge 1919-1920, 1935-1939
(1884-1958)

Woodland was an all-round brilliant horseman; he rode two Grand National winners, two Grande Steeplechase de Paris winners, and two French Derby winners, and later trained in France and Wiltshire. In 1906 he rode, trained and owned Fragilite, the winner of the Grande Course de Haies d'Auteuil. Woodland served in the Flying Corps during World War I. The Liverpool Echo 6th December 1916 reported that he had been killed in Egypt. However, it later transpired that he was a prisoner of war in Palestine, after the Turks shot down his plane. He briefly shared the facilities at Holly Lodge with *Victor Tabor*, who was married to Woodland's sister in 1919, leaving to take stables at Alfriston, Sussex. He returned to Lower Kingswood in 1935, and was living there at the time of his death, he left £4,337.

WOODLAND, William G.	Heath House	1895-1899
(1872-1921)	Priam Lodge	1896
	Purley	1905

Woodland appears in Ruff's Guide 1898 as training for Lord Shrewsbury. He was the brother of *Edmund Woodland* and *Percy Woodland*, a fourth brother Herbert Woodland trained in France. William Woodland was managing a stud at Winchester at the time of his death leaving £284.

WOOTTON, Frank L.   Treadwell House   1915, 1918,
(1893-1940)   1927-1931

The Australian-born Frank Wootton, eldest son of *Richard Wootton* enjoyed a meteoric rise to fame as a jockey. He rode his first winner, at the age of nine, in South Africa. He rode his first winner in Britain at the age of 13, and was champion jockey on four successive occasions before he was 20. He won the 1909 Oaks on Perola, and the 1910 St Leger on Swynford. He rode in India during the winter of 1911. In 1912 he rode seven winners at the Ascot meeting. At 15, he was the youngest jockey in turf history to have ridden a Classic winner, and be champion jockey.

S.Theodore Felstead in Racing Romance summarised:

"Frank Wootton jumped to the top with spectacular speed for two reasons-he had been marvellously well trained and he began to ride plenty of winners for his father. Perhaps I might also add that he possessed the inborn talent."

The newspapers in Britain and Australia were enthralled with the child prodigy, and stories such as "Frank Wootton falls off motor cycle", "Frank Wootton ill with sore throat", "Frank Wootton fined for speeding on motor bike in Epsom", "Frank Wootton fined for speeding in Croydon", together with tales of his riding successes, and wealth were seized on by the press in Australia and New Zealand. Shortly after the 1909 Oaks win Frank was kicked on the head in a race, he suffered concussion; his condition for some time causing anxiety, and was the start of a spate of illness and injury, which coupled with rising weight resulted in premature retirement, and premature death.
In 1910 he was suspended for two months after clashing with fellow jockey Danny Maher in a close finish.
On the 5th June 1912 the Hurst Park stewards suspended Frank; a decision that prompted Richard Wootton to announce that he would sell his horses and return to Australia at the end of the season. On the 3rd August 1912 the stewards at Liverpool suspended Frank for a month for reckless riding. On the 4th October 1912 the Queensland Times carried the story that Frank was retiring due to weight problems, followed by a denial five days later.
The Sydney Stock Journal noted the effects of the controversy and weight problems on 15th November 1912:

"Though F. Wootton recently contradicted that he was retiring next season, the chances are that he has nearly finished his career as a jockey. During his recent suspension he put on weight rapidly; and though he was working hard to get it off he turned the scale at 9st. 1 lb. A few days before he intended resuming his calling. Though he will only be 19 years old next December, Frank Wootton is already the possessor of a tidy fortune. It

is expected that he will take up training. The London "Sportsman" stated he and his brother assisted by a capable head lad will be in charge of the Treadwell House horses during the visit of Wootton senior to Australia at the end of the year.

During 1913 Frank was clearly losing the battle against increasing weight, and in November that year, the news that Frank and Stanley Wootton were both retiring from race riding and visiting Australia was announced.

Richard Wootton had his own ideas on Frank's future:

"I want Frank to go back with me to Australia and stay there, I am returning for good after next season. I've asked Frank to make a trip out there this Winter-to see people I know and have a look at the ranch. I want him to stay there with me if he cares to, and also his brother Stanley. But the boys have the game to play themselves. They may have different ideas from mine, and I don't think a father should interfere."

On the 6th January 1914 Frank and Stanley arrived in Sydney accompanied by the jockey W. Halsey.

The Otago Daily Times 9th January 1914, reported under the heading:

Fortune At Twenty
Frank Wootton's retirement

"Chapter one of the romance of Frank Wootton, the famous jockey, ends with his retirement from the saddle owing to excessive weight. It is romance when a jockey still in his teens can quit with a substantial fortune.
The largest sum he received was £2000 plus £100 expenses for winning the 1912 Grand Prix de Paris."

Frank told the Adelaide Chronicle on his arrival that despite his father's previous statement he was there for a five-week holiday, and to visit his father's ranch.
Frank returned to Epsom, stating that he intended to resume riding at a "welter-weight." However, the jockey career was not resumed, and Frank took out a training licence. In June 1914 he rented boxes at Ogbourne, and trained his first winner. War interrupted his training career, and Frank served in the Middle East where he was mentioned in dispatches.
Frank's early efforts at training had indicated that he lacked the discipline of his father, and his brother Stanley. After one post-war visit Richard Wootton observed that Frank "needed taking in hand," and speculation about a return to race-riding started, fuelled in part by Frank's riding successes in impromptu 'Jumps' meetings while serving in Mesopotamia, and Stanley's immediate success as a trainer.

9th January 1920

The Belgian Newspaper, "Sport-Elevage" reported that:

"Frank Wootton is to ride in obstacles in France this season and that he has signed an agreement with the Ambateielos stable controlled by C. Halsey at Chantilly."

20th February 1920 The N.S.W. Morning Mail noted:

"Frank Wootton, the famous jockey has returned to Epsom after war Service in Mesopotamia. His weight is now over 10st. 8 lbs., and he contemplates riding over jumps in England. His father will return to Australia later this year."

Press Association 14th August 1920

"Frank Wootton intends to ride over sticks this winter."

Australian Press Association 23rd November 1920

"A cable message from London mentions that the ex-Australian, Frank Wootton, has received a license to ride under National Hunt rules."

Frank rode nearly 200 winners over jumps. His finest victory was in the 1924 Imperial Cup on Noce d'Argent, trained by his brother *Stanley Wootton*. He also won the 1924 Liverpool Hurdle on Stuff Gown, owned by his bother Stanley, and trained by Tom Coulthwaite at Hednesford. He rode mostly in hurdle races, but had a mount in the 1921 Grand National. By early 1922 he was challenging for the Jockey's Championship.

Auckland Star 18th February 1922

"The race between Frank Wootton and F.B. Rees for the honour of heading the table of winning jockeys promised to cause much excitement, but unfortunately Wootton met with an accident at Findon whilst riding one of R. Gore's charges, and broke his collar bone. Up to this time both Wootton and Rees had earned 61 winning brackets this year. The mishap to Wootton was a bit more serious than at first anticipated for five distinct cracks were discovered, while a piece of bone had to be removed.
Rees remarked: "I would have liked to have seen Frank finish at the head of the list, as he would thus have achieved a memorable feat to have been leading jockey under both Rules of Racing.""

Auckland Star 12th April 1924

"Frank Wootton is to ride in Ireland at the end of this season."

By the end of the 1924-25 jumps season, Frank had retired (again), and apparently was returning to Australia permanently.

Evening Post 22nd July 1925

"In paying a farewell tribute to Frank Wootton the London Evening News remarks: FW was a brilliant horseman, akin in genius and entitled to rank with Fred Archer, George Fordham, and Danny Maher. He would have been even greater if his tempestuous temperament had not conflicted with the authorities. In a letter to his sisters recently, FW said that he was going to the Isle of Wight to ride his last winner before retiring. He duly did."

Frank reflected on his career in the Sunday Sportsman...

"Lure Of the Flat
Frank Wootton on his career

To Frank Wootton has fallen the lot of having achieved the very highest attainment of the jockey's art. As a rider on the Flat he headed the list of winning jockeys in 1909,1910,1911,and 1912. After serving in the war, he came back to his transcendent ability in the saddle over hurdle and steeplechase courses.
Frank Wootton recalled how he watched other horses in the race, to see if they were badly ridden, and told my father about them. He many times secured the mounts on them for me next time, and thus I was not only able to ride winners, but to assist in swelling the guvnor's bank account, for he always backed me if I thought I could win.
Frank Wootton added that he preferred Flat to Jumps racing, not only because of the weather invariably being better, but also because the thrills were more intense.
"I decided to discard riding in steeplechases because in my opinion you cannot do both properly. You cannot ride with the same perfect balance over hurdles if you ride in steeplechases. That is the reason why Duller attained the perfect balance which has made him stand out as the best rider of all time over the smaller obstacles.""

Auckland Star 15th August 1925

"Frank Wootton returned to Melbourne last week by the Orama. His last visit to Australia was made eleven years ago.
" I hope to stay in Australia permanently" Mr Wootton said, "but what I will do I have not yet decided. It may be taken for granted that I have retired from the saddle."

After two years Frank grew restless again.

Evening Post, 26th July 1927

"Frank Wootton, the once famous jockey has returned to the Old Country. Wootton has been in Australia for a couple of years now, but he prefers the racing in England, and he is returning there to join his brother, Stanley, one of England's leading trainers."

Frank travelled to Calcutta, and then via Durban reaching England on 11th August 1927.

The Adelaide News 10th September recorded that he had taken an establishment at Epsom, and would train jumpers for the coming steeplechase season.
For several years, Frank, shared the stables with his brother *Stanley Wootton*, with Frank concentrating on the National Hunt horses. During the winters of 1929 and 1931, he trained the jumpers while Stanley was in Australia.

The Sydney Referrer noted on 3rd April 1929:

"S. Wootton has moved from his old quarters at Treadwell House, Epsom, and his brother Frank is now installed there. S. Wootton has taken over the stables recently occupied by G. Bennett, and would appear to be going in for a smaller team. In February there were not more than 25 horses in his new quarters, whereas last year he won 88 races with 43 different horses, Throughout 1930 Stanley was in Australia, and during that year Frank trained 28 Flat winners, and 35 National Hunt winners. The arrangement whereby Frank handled the horses, and his brother the business side worked well."

Ill health set in shortly after...
The New South Wales Herald reported on 2nd April 1932

"Frank Wootton the horse trainer, is expected to return to Epsom in the middle of May. He is now convalescing at Madeira after serious lung trouble. He was at a London nursing home for two months. The mild climate of Madeira is proving beneficial for him".

Torn between life in Epsom and life in Australia, in 1933, Frank Wootton returned to Australia, once again. S.Theodore Felstead in Racing Romance noted:
"He never gave you the impression of being able to settle down to the humdrum hard-working life of a trainer. He went back to Australia with his father after the war, on the understanding that between them they would start a stable there. However, Frank continued to sigh for the lights of London and the friends he had there. In 1921 therefore, he came back and having no hankering for training took out a National Hunt

licence. In the whole history of the English Turf there is no parallel to a jockey of such eminence taking to jumping. The hurdles were his game, with quite a number of objections for bumping and boring. What irked him was being idle in the Summer, he eventually took out a trainer's licence but that bored him more than ever. Frank was a very likeable fellow, modest to a degree, and impatient of the numerous ruses a small trainer must adopt."

The early years that he had spent striving to ride at an unnatural weight, plus the injuries that were part of his career, had taken their toll on his health. On 6 April 1940 at Central Police Court, Sydney, he was convicted of drunkenness. Later that day he died of traumatic epilepsy.

WOOTTON, Richard R.	Down Cottage	1906-1907
(1867-1946)	Treadwell House	1907-1914.1916

The Sheffield Independent, 21st May 1906, announced that the arrival of Mr Richard Wootton, a well- known and much respected Australian owner-trainer was expected any day now for the purpose of racing a select stud in this country. Richard Wootton arrived in Epsom in 1906 with his wife Catherine, sons *Frank* and *Stanley*, and daughters Stella and Brenda, plus some Australian jockeys including W. McLachlan. The family had left Australia in 1902 for South Africa, where Frank Wootton rode his first winner shortly before his tenth birthday. After four years in South Africa, the Wootton family briefly returned to Australia before setting sail to England. They landed at London on the White Star Line ship 'Suevic', on the 10th June 1906.

When Wootton's chauffeur was summoned for speeding on the way back from Goodwood, Wootton was described as a trainer, of Down Cottage, Epsom. He subsequently purchased Treadwell House.

Wootton revisited South Africa in the winter of 1906-07 returning on 16th March to Southampton on the Union Castle Mail steamship 'Norman'. His son, the boy jockey Frank Wootton, and Wootton's betting agent from New South Wales, 'Deafy' Wilkinson accompanied him.

Without the backing of a substantial owner, Wootton set his fees at the lowest, relied on his eye for an animal's constitution, and let the results advertise his ability. In 1912 he trained more winners than any other trainer, and in 1913 he was champion trainer in prize-money terms. In 1913 he also provided the favourites for the Derby and the Oaks. In the Derby Shogun, ridden by Wootton's son Frank was the victim in the roughest Derby ever. Twice Shogun had challenged, and twice was denied a run.

In 1913 Wootton's successes included three winners on the first day of Ascot, and also the Ascot Stakes, plus the top two-year-old races at Epsom, Newmarket and York. By now, Wootton enjoyed the patronage of the millionaire publisher Sir Edward Hulton. His victories for Hulton included three successive Gimcrack Stakes winners at York with Lomond in 1911, Flippant in 1912 and Stornoway in 1913. Hulton had asked Wootton to train his horses, Wootton expressed reluctance considering some of them to be not as good as the owner believed. He eventually agreed to take them on a month's trial. At the end of the month he advised the owner to sell six immediately "They won't win a hundred pounds between them", and also advised Hulton he should back his next runner, writing out a cheque for £500 with the request "Put that on for me." The horse duly obliged, the disposed horses proved to be moderate, and the relationship was forged.

Wootton was also outstanding at teaching jockeys; following the success of *Frank Wootton;* the Huxley brothers (champion apprentices in 1912 and 1913), *William Smyth, and David Dick,* were taught the trade at Treadwell House. William Huxley rode the winners of the Oaks and the 1,000 Guineas in 1914.

Richard Wootton was also a fearless gambler, and by 1913 had sent back over £60,000 to Australia. Inevitably this created jealousy, and The Sporting Life editor, Meyrick Good, observed: "He was a good friend but a bad enemy."

Trainer Charles Morton, a long-time admirer of the Woottons, fell out after he and Wootton had the first two favourites in the same race. Dick Wootton told him: "I don't think much of mine", and then landed a touch. Morton eventually made up with Wootton recording: "There is no use keeping daggers drawn with one of your best friends even if he occasionally does take one for himself."

Wootton's career in England was punctuated by legal cases. In 1908, an accusation by Richard Wootton that fellow trainer *James Bell* was "training by deceit" i.e. he employed *James William Platt* as nominee trainer was referred to the High Court. While waiting for the hearing the two were involved in an altercation at Gatwick on 7th January 1909, and that night *Bell* claimed that while walking along Treadwell Road, Wootton rushed at him, knocked him to the ground and seized him by the throat.

Bell summonsed Wootton to Epsom Police Court asking that Wootton be bound over to keep the peace, as *Bell* believed that he was in danger of bodily injury. Wootton claimed that *Bell* kicked him after he requested that *Bell* stop following him. Wootton was bound over in the sum of £50.

In December 1910 Richard Wootton was back in court, on this occasion with fellow Epsom trainer, *Jonathan Riste*. Wootton had been with *George Duller* senior, watching some of their horses work together, according to Duller, he became aware of *Riste* watching their horses from the woods, and drew it to Wootton's attention. An exchange of words took place, *Riste* was subsequently summonsed for using bad language, and in turn cross-summonsed Wootton.

In evidence, Duller said he heard Wootton tell Riste: "Go away like a good fellow, we should not watch your horses." Wootton's evidence was similar, he claimed he told Riste: "I should not stop to see your horses, I wish you would go away like a good chap." Riste then became abusive, Wootton responded "No wonder you were flogged off Lewes Downs," and asked him not to swear in front of his daughter.

Riste's evidence was that it was a hot day, and that he was sheltering in the undergrowth to avoid the heat while waiting for his horses to come by. Wootton told him to "Get off", and accused him of being a tout. Riste responded: "What you villain, call me a tout, do you think I follow your game thieving and robbing." According to Riste, Wootton responded: "If I have any more of you I will set about you and treat you a dashed sight worse than I did *Jim Bell.*"

James Hayes appeared as a witness, alleging that while on a train he heard Riste recounting the incident and that he admitted calling Wootton: "A South African robber." Under cross-examination, Hayes stated that he knew Wootton from 20 years ago in Australia.

Wootton and Riste were bound over to keep the peace for six months. Additionally. Riste was fined £2. Both men contested the verdict before the court was cleared.

Richard Wootton divided opinion in England. Down under the journal New Zealand Truth covered the developments:

4th February 1911

"WOOTTON WORRIES.
Their English success arouses jealousy.

"Dick Wootton it would seem is not too popular with his fellow trainers at Epsom. There is no doubt that the success of the Woottons has caused a deal of jealousy in England. Dick was always a dashing bettor when he "knew something" and from all accounts he has shown some of the turfites in the Old Country many points that have not been appreciated."

The Racing Specialist on 26th March 1912 reported:

"It is stated that at the end of the year Richard Wootton will probably give up training, and join Jack Brewer on the sheep farm they jointly own in Australia.
Stanley Wootton who has been his father's right hand man at Epsom for some time past, reliquishes race riding, and will take over the Treadwell House stable."

The New Zealand Truth stated on 21st September 1912:

"Worries of the Woottons
Their success on the English Turf, has also been an excellent advertisement for Australia. By sheer force of merit Dick Wootton as a trainer, and his sons Frank and Stanley as riders, worked themselves to the very front. Only those who have experienced the crusted conservatism of England can understand the skill and determination necessary. Recently there appears to have been growing friction between the Wootton family and the English Jockey Club.
Following Stanley Wootton's suspension after the ride on Fairy King at York, Dick Wootton loudly protested, and boldly affirmed that the stewards are hounding his son off

the English Turf, and rather than submit to such an injustice he would sell off his stables and return to Australia.
In Britain The Daily News and the Morning Post were among papers that backed Wootton."

The New Zealand Truth continued,

"It has been said that the Wootton family would never succeed on the English Turf because they had not acquired the crawlsome habit that is demanded by English Turf magnates. If this be the reason the Wootton family are to be complimented on declining to act as footmen or flunkeys to please the English Jockey Club."

When Richard Wootton fell out with Robert Sievier, the argument was more acrimonious than the incidents with *Jim Bell* and *Jonathan Riste*. Sievier had trained Sceptre, who in 1903 had won the 1,000 and 2,000 Guineas, the Oaks and St. Leger. He was a fearless and reckless gambler, and he owned a racing newspaper called *The Winning Post*. He wrote a column under the title "Glasshouses" in which he attacked various racing and political figures. In 1912, he directed a campaign of innuendo against Richard Wootton; there were articles on May 4th, 11th, 18th and 25th 1912. In the issue for September 28th there were allegations about a "trainer's ring". On 2nd November 1912 The Winning Post published a 'competition' for readers that consisted of a mythical race where the 'jockeys' were *Frank* and *Stanley Wootton* and five other jockeys connected to Treadwell House. The 'trainers' were Richard Wootton, his former assistant Eddie de Mestre, and various friends including Charles Morton. The public were invited to select the winner, the implication being that Richard Wootton could manipulate the result. The next copy of The Winning Post announced that there had been only one person who attempted to solve the problem, and he was resident in a lunatic asylum. Richard Wootton issued a writ for libel on November 28th, but the attacks continued.
On the opening day of the case, Wootton's counsel Mr F.E. Smith told the court that Wootton had trained in New South Wales for 17 years, and then in 1902 took 26 horses to South Africa. Before leaving Australia he had taken an action for slander against a trainer named Pearce, regarding an allegation against the running of Wootton's horses, and the jury found for Wootton.
On the second day Richard Wootton explained some of his finances to the court. He said that he was unable to say how much he had won betting since 1907, although his auditors would know. His total earnings averaged £5,000 per year. He had bought 13 acres in Epsom for £1,500. He had bought an estate in Australia for £40,000; he had 29 houses in Sydney yielding £2,000 per annum, and had brought £19,000 with him to this country. He owed some money on mortgages but this would soon be paid off.
After three days of insults and accusations of "stopping" horses, and running horses unfit, the judge Mr Justice Darling feigned despair: "Will I ever get to the bottom of the

wickedness of this world?" F.E. Smith, representing Wootton offered some advice, "I am sure Mr Sievier will help you."

Sievier, summing up, told the court: "They were out for the gold that came from Australia as nuggets and returned as sovereigns." Holding up a farthing he suggested that was the true value of the damages. The jury found that the words complained of were not true in substance or in fact, that they were not fair and honest comment, but that they were published without malice. Mr Justice Darling awarded Wootton the damages of a farthing. Sievier intended to appeal, but withdrew the appeal in April 1914, by which time he had been back on an unconnected charge of blackmail.

Richard Wootton returned to Australia; while Frank and Stanley were both away on active service. Richard Wootton returned once more to England, and represented their training interests under authority.

The attacks on Wootton by Sievier persisted, and eventually with the help of private detectives and the best lawyers in the country he issued 20,000 copies of a document "Incidents in the public life of Robert Standish Sievier." The document described a list of unpaid debts, cheating, theft and sending indecent prints through the post; it concluded: "He has from time to time been publicly stated to be a swindler, a card sharper and a thief, and a man with whom no decent person would associate."

Wootton made allegations about cheating at cards that stretched back to 1892, and included an incident in the Victoria Club, Melbourne in 1897, when Sievier was based there.

Sievier sued for libel. It was 1920 before the case was heard. Sievier lost the case, but Wootton's attempt to close *The Winning Post* or have Sievier warned off failed. Sievier appealed but the appeal was dismissed on June 30th 1921.

Richard Wootton was also involved in legal action against owner Jack Joel at that time. In July 1919 lawyers acting for Wootton issued a writ against Mr Joel claiming £10,452 being the percentage of prize- money won by Richard Wootton's apprentices *Frank Wootton*, E. Huxley and W. Huxley. At the hearing of the summons it was stated that this referred to races in 1913.

Mr Joel's position was that he had for many years been on good terms with *Frank Wootton* without any claim mentioned, and he objected to an action being launched against him on behalf of *Frank Wootton* without Frank's consent.

In November 1919 application was made to add as a plaintiff, *Frank Leonard Wootton*. The reason for the delay in adding Frank Wootton was attributed to him being in Australia, and later serving in Mesopotamia.

Lord Justice Bankes: Where is he now?

Mr Givern (for Richard Wootton): I hope that he is on his way back from Basra.

Lord Bankes giving judgement on the objections ruled that in this case it was necessary for *Frank Wootton* to have sworn an affidavit supporting the claim. However, he ruled that the Judge at the original hearing had no jurisdiction to add a plaintiff without written consent.

The claim was eventually withdrawn in July 1921.

The battle between Sievier and Richard Wootton had lasted for ten years, and shortly after Richard Wootton returned once more to Australia. He took with him his daughters Stella and Brenda, and his son Richard who was born at Treadwell House in 1909. Wootton's wife Catherine had died in childbirth.

After a visit to England in 1924, Richard Wootton arrived in Adelaide on 23rd December, stating that he "intended to stay in Australia." He noted racing in England had depreciated since the war, and that Englishmen would have to start taking the business side more seriously.

On 2 February 1931 at St Jude's Church of England, Randwick, he married Frances Young, and had three more daughters by this marriage. He established R. Wootton Pty Ltd, hotel and picture theatre proprietors and property owners; his holdings included the Doncaster Hotel, Randwick, and the Doncaster and Vocalist theatres, and residential real estate at Kensington and Randwick. Wootton also bought an agricultural property, Kicatoo, at Condoblin, and developed his interest in racehorse breeding.

The Auckland Star 3rd March 1945 recorded:

"Old Man Wootton made race goers sit up and take notice
Of all the trainers I have known, I give the Woottons, Richard and his son Stanley, pride
of place for knowing how to make racing pay. Treadwell House at Epsom offers one of
the classic stories of the English turf. It began in 1906 when "Old Man Wootton", a tall,
dark-visaged and hard-bitten Australian came to this country, via South Africa. He
meant to strike a new note, the main idea being a stable full of budding jockeys who
would not only ride many winners for himself, but for other owners as well. Richard
Wootton arrived here q quite unknown, with no one of any consequence to give him any
horses. He had a son Frank, however, who soon began to advertise the fact that Dick
Wootton was a man to reckon with."

Richard Wootton died on 26th June 1946 at Randwick.

WOOTTON, Stanley T.	Treadwell House	1915, 1917, 1919-1932
	Shifnal Cottage	1931-1941
	Treadwell House	1949-1959
	Shifnal Paddocks	1960-1962

In a brief riding career, Stanley Wootton rode Elizabetta to win the Chester Cup (carrying 6st. 11lb), and the Northumberland Plate in 1910. He claimed to have ridden nearly 400 winners in Britain, France, Belgium and Germany. However, with increasing weight, and with his brother breaking records as a jockey Stanley eased himself into the role of assistant to his father. With his brother Frank, Stanley returned to Australia in November 1913, returning to the UK the following April for the Flat racing season. He first took out a training licence in 1915, but his career was interrupted by the outbreak of war. Stanley Wootton took part in the Battle of the Somme, and stories of his wounds received at the front emerged.

Evening Post 13th July 1916:

"Lt. Stanley Wootton of the 17th Royal Fusiliers has been wounded at the front."

Numerous papers Auckland Star, Northern Advocate, Dominion, Evening Post 29 July 1916 reported that Stanley Wootton had subsequently died from wounds. Then, two days later,

Evening Post 31st July 1916:

"Stanley Wootton Not Dead
A cable message on the reported death of Stanley Wootton brought the following reply from his father: "Cannot understand the cable. Stanley awarded Military Cross. Home, convalescent."

Stanley had been part of a four-man unit that undertook nocturnal raids behind enemy lines; he was awarded the Military Cross on 8th August 1916 by Queen Alexandra at Buckingham Palace.

The London Gazette 18th August 1916 reported the award of the Military Cross.
"Temp. Lt. Stanley Wootton, R.Fus.
For conspicuous gallantry when repeatedly attempting to force his way into the enemy's trenches. He was knocked down at least twice and severely shaken, and finally had to be led away"

He was later en route to Palestine when the boat was sunk, in addition to the many men lost, 500 horses drowned. He rescued the ship's ensign and brought it back to Epsom.
In 1919 Stanley Wootton returned to Treadwell House to continue training racehorses. He always bought his horses cheaply, and on three occasions between 1921 and 1926 he trained more winners in a season than any other trainer. He won several big handicaps including the Cambridgeshire, the Imperial Cup, and City and Suburban. By the mid-1920s Wootton had so many horses, (all owned by himself), that he expanded to use Shifnal Cottage as an additional stable. In 1928, he moved into Shifnal Cottage, he later stated that Treadwell House contained too many memories of his late mother and his sisters.

213

In 1924 Wootton was involved in a bizarre court case, when a man appeared in court, charged with stealing £105 by means of a trick, i.e. purporting to be Stanley Wootton. A man called Crowe met the victim Edward Moore near Marble Arch; he claimed to have "inside information" from "his friend Stanley Wootton". He later introduced the accused, James McMahon to Moore, who told him he was Stanley Wootton and that he had "something very good for Wednesday better than the last"; he was having £200 on it and asked Moore to give him £200 to place on it. In the event Moore could only raise £105; he went to Epsom, saw the horse finish third, and saw the real Stanley Wootton unsaddling the horse. McMahon placated Moore by telling him he had something better coming up; they met the following week by which time Moore had finally realised that a trick was perpetrated. McMahon offered his watch and cigarette case in part settlement, after Moore attempted to detain McMahon he was assaulted. Another man called James Saunders had been a previous victim of the trickery. McMahon was convicted of impersonating Stanley Wootton to obtain money by deception, and sentenced to 18 months imprisonment.

On 2nd March 1925, Stanley Wootton instructed his solicitors to write to the Epsom Grand Stand Association enquiring if they would be prepared to sell to him the training gallops on Six Mile Hill. The E.G.S.A. was in the process of buying Epsom Downs, and needed to sell the surplus land to raise finance. The negotiations, sometimes acrimonious, continued for 15 months.

In June 1926 the E.G.S.A. wrote to all Epsom trainers to confirm that Stanley Wootton had taken over the Six Mile Hill gallops on Walton Downs. The purchase price was £35,000. At the same time Wootton took a lease on the Winter Gallops, i.e. those within the racecourse.

In 1926, Wootton announced that he was sending a team from England to the United States:

Evening Post 24th February 1926

"Stanley Wootton the well-known Anglo-Australian trainer, is sending several members of his huge team to America to race. "I am confident that I will get a fair chance. The American Authorities were splendid to me during my tour.""

In 1930 Stanley Wootton left Epsom to take a six-week holiday in Australia. Edwin de Mestre, formerly assistant to *Richard Wootton,* was rumoured to be taking over at Treadwell House. This story was dismissed by Stanley: *"I am merely going on an extended holiday and the stable will be taken over by brother Frank."*

Younger brother Richard, and sister Brenda accompanied Stanley Wootton. They arrived at Brisbane via Singapore. At a press conference, Wootton explained the difference in riding and training techniques in Britain and Australia. He opined that there were "too many racecourses in such a small country", and that consequently public facilities were surprisingly poor in Britain. Adding that there was no meeting in the world to compare

214

to Ascot. He told the press this was his first visit to Australia since 1913, and that he needed a break from the rigours of managing a large stable, plus his apprentices. When asked if he had the largest stable in Britain, Wootton replied: "I know of none larger." On his return to Britain, Wootton gradually reduced the number of horses he had in training to concentrate on his expanding property interests. On 14th January 1938 he was appointed as a Justice of the Peace, serving on the bench at Epsom magistrate's court.

Auckland Star 22nd January 1938

"Emperor of Epsom" Cuts Down Stable.
An Australian who settled in Surrey 30 years ago took up the training of racehorses and became known as the "Emperor of Epsom" was this week sworn in as a magistrate. Mr Stanley Wootton has announced his decision to cut down his able to only a few horses.

The Sydney Morning Herald 17th January 1938

"In future I will have only a few horses and will devote myself to being a bad farmer and, I hope, a good honorary magistrate. I am more or less giving up racing."

The Sydney Morning Herald, 17th January 1938 reported on Stanley Wootton's wedding to Kathleen Griffiths at St. Joseph's Church, Epsom; *"It was a quiet wedding, only immediate family being present. Mr. Wootton's staff was not aware of the event."*

Stanley Wootton had proved to be the best tutor of jockeys in the 20th century. Although conditions were hard, and pay low, there was a waiting list of boys who wanted a place in Wootton's stable. The boys slept in dormitories above the stables, or three to a room at the house of a local landlady who reported to Mr Wootton on their behaviour. Competition was intense to get accepted for a place at Treadwell House, and Wootton favoured boys who had a brother who had already shown the right aptitude. The brothers Smyth, Dick, Cordell, Ingham, Smirke and Hunter passed through the system. (John Dick brother of David and Robert Dick, was killed in a riding accident on 16th September 1915, aged 11)

In the financially depressed 1920s and 1930s, small boys from large families in the cities were eager to join the 'Wootton Academy'. The number of apprentice jockeys in the country was at its highest in the 1920s peaking at 234 in 1926. Philip Welch recalls in his book *Stable Rat* that he had an introduction to Wootton because his father knew Charlie Smirke's father. He recalled that Wootton inspected him feeling his bones to anticipate how big he would grow before declaring that there would be "ten boys in front of him", and recommending that they approach *Herbert Smyth*.
Charlie Smirke was the most successful jockey to "graduate" from the stables. He rode four Derby winners, four St Leger winners, two 2,000 Guineas winners, and one 1,000

215

Guineas winner. In Ireland, he won the Oaks on four occasions, the Derby twice, the 2,000 Guineas twice and the 1,000 Guineas once. Wootton believed good jockeys needed to be tough and tenacious and staged impromptu boxing bouts to identify who had the right qualities. Other Wootton boys to ride Classic winners include *Vic Smyth* who won the 1923 Oaks, *Tommy Carey* who rode the 1943 Derby winner Straight Deal, *Bobby Dick* who won the 1936 2,000 Guineas, and Joe Marshall who won the 1929 Derby. When Zabara won the 1952 1,000 Guineas, both the jockey *Ken Gethin* and the trainer *Vic Smyth* had served an apprenticeship with Wootton.

Under National Hunt rules Billy Stott and Frenchie Nicholson were both champion jockeys who started from Treadwell House. Stott achieved the Cheltenham double in 1933, and was champion National Hunt jockey for five successive seasons in the years 1927 to 1932. Frenchie Nicholson rode the Champion Hurdle winner in 1936 and the Gold Cup winner in 1942, and was champion National Hunt jockey in 1945. Another 'graduate', Sean Magee, (the son of the Irish Rugby captain), rode the Champion Hurdle winner in 1940. Johnny Gilbert set a record by riding ten consecutive winners over a period of 22 days in September 1959; it was part of a sequence of 16 wins from 17 rides. He was later the first chief instructor at the British Racing School, and was awarded the MBE for his services to racing.

Victor Smyth was Champion Apprentice in 1916 and 1917, Charlie Smirke in 1925 and 1926, and Leslie Cordell in 1928.

Jack Crouch, another star apprentice, was jockey to King George VI, but died in a plane crash. Alfie Sharples was killed in an accident in a race at Windsor.

Staff Ingham, Jackie Sirett, Bobby Dick, Vic Smyth, Ken Gethin, Tommy Carey, Peter Ashworth, Dave Dick, William Smyth and *Mick Haynes* were all former Wootton boys who later trained at Epsom. Frenchie Nicholson trained at Cheltenham, and like his mentor Stanley Wootton, was an exceptional tutor of jockeys. Freddie Hunter, John Hunter, and Alec Jack were other Wootton boys who became trainers.

Other jockeys trained by Wootton included Tommy Hawcroft, Arthur Wragg, Frank Field, "Monkey" Morris, Billy Turtle, Archie Smirke, Bernard Rook, Dick Broadway, Pat O'Leary, Dennis Savage, and Maurice Hunter. South African Terry Ryan was sent over to Wootton's at the age of 12, having ridden 60 winners already.

Stanley Wootton ruled his 'academy' strictly. Breaches of discipline were dealt with by corporal punishment, or instant dismissal. Boys who showed promise, but a liking for Epsom's nightlife, were sent down to *Gil Bennett's* stables at Polegate for a month or two. Bennett had a reputation for being as strict as Wootton with the added advantage that his stables were in isolated countryside. In 1928 when Wootton suspected that one of his apprentices, Noel Carroll, was supplying information on the stable runners to a bookmaker, he immediately reported the boy to the Jockey Club, Carroll and the bookmaker concerned were both warned off. The previous year, Carroll had been involved in a serious accident, while riding his bicycle to Wootton's stable; a car knocked him down. He sustained a fractured skull, and was on the critical list for some time.

216

Wootton's teaching methods were much admired by his colleagues. Scottish trainer John McGuigan said: "The fairest, most conscientious and pain-staking trainer I know with regard to apprentices is Stanley Wootton, who has been rewarded by turning out so many useful jockeys."

"Confidence, obedience, cleanliness, -that could be described as the motto of the Wootton Academy, and results have proved there could not be a better one for turning out successful jockeys," recalled Charlie Smirke.

In his book, Memoirs of a Racing Journalist, Sydney Galtrey writes:

"Maybe Stanley Wootton would modestly disclaim to be ranked as a genius. Of all the prominent figures I have met and studied on the racecourse, Stanley Wootton is one of the most intriguing, His father, Dick Wootton, had the ability to train racehorses in his own enlightened way, and, having said that, I can justly add that in exploiting them he blended shrewdness, bluntness and boldness, while never hesitating to exploit such knowledge as came his way through the eminence of his son Frank as a jockey.
Stanley Wootton inherited the best of his father's virtues. He, too, has been a brilliant maker of jockeys. His success has been no less as a trainer. He simply must be a trainer in the highest class because his horses look marvellously well for hard condition and fitness. That they do not take part in classic races is because Stanley Wootton long since decided to specialise and answer only to himself, as an owner.
Stanley Wootton was born with much intelligence. He had done everything to develop it, to cultivate a distinctive personality and a breadth of outlook. His mind is logical and severely calculating. It is extremely well ordered . His coolness at all times seems unnatural. He seems to have his mental equipment under severe restraint as to be icily unemotional. There is no aggression, no uncontrolled exultation, and no evidence of untold relief in moments of success. He is much liked and much admired by all who can recognise cleverly used intelligence."

Wootton stopped training on the outbreak of war in 1939. He told his staff that he was selling his horses and volunteering for military service and that they should do the same. The Dundee Courier 28th June 1940 reported that he had rejoined the Army, taking up a commission with the King's Royal Rifles. He left in 1941 due to ill health, he observed there was a lack of demand for Cavalry Officers, and on the advice of his Commanding Officer could best help the war effort by farming. In October 1945 he flew to Australia to visit his father who was seriously ill; he told The Sydney Morning Herald, that because of low prize-money it was impossible for English owners to make it pay. Wootton stayed with his father until leaving for England on 21st May 1946. Wootton was in Australia again from late 1947 until 9th April 1948; he was at this time developing his bloodstock breeding in Australia, and had a few horses in training there with Maurice McCartan. He spent the winter of 1948-49 in South America, and on his return he took out a training

217

licence in January1949, telling the press that he intended to train 20 of his own horses and also have three or four apprentice jockeys. He moved back into Treadwell House in 1951.

His post-war success in Australia was first recorded in The Sydney Sunday Herald in April 1951, under the headline "Brilliant Donegal may get Stradbroke Start" the paper noted that owner Stanley Wootton purchased Donegal in France, the horse was an instant success in England, and now had a strong claim to be champion sprinter in Australia.

Back in England, the following year, with just ten horses, Wootton finished 20th in the Trainers Championship. The main contributor was Rawson who won six races including Ascot's Cumberland Lodge Stakes. In 1952, Rawson also won the Princess of Wales Stakes. Wootton continued to train on a small scale throughout the 1950s; at this time he invariably travelled to New York on the Queen Mary (1952-57) returning in April for the start of the Flat racing season. *Staff Ingham* in 1953, *Marjorie Nightingall* in 1947 and 1953, and *Walter Nightingall* in 1954 made the same trip, although their training careers necessitated an earlier return to England. Wootton's 1948-49 cruise to South America was apparently recommended to other Epsom trainers, with *Staff Ingham* making the trip in 1952 and 1954, and *Marjorie Nightingall* in 1950.

Staff Ingham trained most of Stanley Wootton's horses during this period, and provided mounts for the top boys like O'Leary, Broadway, Henry Jones and *Mick Haynes*.

Wootton extended his interests in Australia to include racehorse breeding. He purchased the horse Star King in 1950, following the horse's success in the Gimcrack Stakes, Richmond Stakes, Jersey Stakes and Greenham Stakes. Star King was known as Star Kingdom in Australia where he sired the first five winners of Sydney Turf Club's Golden Slipper Stakes, and three future stallions in Todman, Biscay and Bletchingley. The Canberra Times, 24th December 1956, described Todman as the "Best Colt Ever" noting that Stanley Wootton the breeder was in Australia when Todman smashed the record for fastest Australasian two-year-old on his racecourse debut at Randwick the previous day.

By the 1950s Wootton's business affairs attracted the attention of the Inland Revenue. The horse training business was showing a massive loss, year on year. In 1954 the tax inspector for Epsom wrote to the Chief Inspector of Taxes for guidance, pointing out that Wootton "enjoyed a substantial standard of living, but has paid no taxes during or since the war."

Wootton's explanation was that since 1940 he had won £375,000 betting.

The Chief Inspector of Taxes observed: "It is understood that Wootton has the reputation of betting on a grand scale, even so, the suggestion that he has acquired £375,000 by betting is extremely unusual."

Epsom's tax inspector observed that in 1952: "accountants noted that betting receipts and payments were recorded in detail."

The Chief Inspector concluded that Wootton "could be considered primarily as a successful backer who carries on training and farming as a sideline." However, if, he should be taxed on the profits of betting it would provide an opening for trainers to set betting losses against business profits, and the matter was dropped.

218

Stanley Wootton relinquished his training licence in 1962. In November 1967, after a somewhat uneasy truce of 40 years, the Epsom Grand Stand Association gave Wootton notice to quit some of the land on Epsom Downs that he was leasing from them. He contested the notice to quit on the grounds that agricultural land was outside of the landlord and tenant ruling. This was upheld in the courts, and Wootton promptly gave the Six Mile Hill gallops on Walton Downs to the Horserace Betting Levy Board on a 999-year lease, at the rent of "a peppercorn if required." Epsom and Walton Downs were now under one administration.

Stanley Wootton said: "In handing over the gallops, I have in mind what the people of England have given the Wootton family."

Wootton spent much of 1979 in Australia, near to his daughter Catherine. Writing to a friend in Epsom he said: *"Thanks to Catherine I now have a comfortable flat near her, she calls daily. We have just returned from 16 days up country looking at our very numerous bloodstock."*

Wootton returned to Australia for the winter of 1981, but subsequent winters were spent mainly at Javea in Spain, or Cannes in France, where he was taken ill during the journey, and had a pacemaker fitted in February 1984.

The Times, March 25th 1986, in Wootton's obituary, noted:

"The success of Epsom as a racehorse training centre owes much to his many years of outstanding service in saving and preserving the Downs for such a use."

Stanley Wootton left an estate valued at £596,650 in the United Kingdom.

WORTH, John	Church Street	1859
(c.1791-1861)		

John Worth is listed as a horse trainer, Church Street, in Kelly's Directory 1859.

WRIGHT, Edward/Edmund	Mickleham	1839-1842
(1811-1863)	Woodcote End	1843-1846

Wright appears in The York Herald 2nd March 1839 where he is listed as training four horses for Lord Albemarle, and one for Lord Tavistock at Epsom. The Sporting Gazette 1844, records that several runners for the Derby boarded at Wright's stable that year. During his career as a jockey he rode Tarantella to win the 1833 1,000 Guineas.

WYATT, Robert	Bruce Lodge	1881- 1883
(1850- 1889)		

Molesey-born Wyatt was a jockey attached to *James Potter* in the 1871 census. Also employed there was *John Sherrington,*. The two men were later related by marriage, having married the sisters, Jane and Ellen Blake. Wyatt's riding career ended circa 1879 after he broke a collarbone and sustained serious injuries when schooling a horse on the "back of Sherwood's" gallop.

In 1872 he bought Eclipse Cottage for £750, at the time the property was tenanted to *James Martin*. He bought 24 The Parade, Epsom, in 1874, and was living there at the time of his death from "progressive paralysis" in 1889.

Wyatt sold Eclipse Cottage circa 1877, presumably to finance the building of Bruce Lodge in Burgh Heath Road. He left effects of £290.

The Penny Illustrated Paper and Illustrated Times (London, England), Saturday, January 19, 1895 describes a visit to Epsom to visit trainer James "Jemmy" Adams, accompanied by an artist:

"On the day our artist visited the stable which poor Bobby Wyatt had built on the rise of the hill, lower than the late Jack Jones's establishment, whence Lord Marcus Beresford for the Prince of Wales sent out useful chasers."

WYCHERLEY, Henry	South Hatch Cottage	1846, 1853-55
(c.1816-1856)	Clay Hill	1851-53

Wycherley, born at Wem, Shropshire, is listed in Ruff's Guide 1852 as based in Epsom training for Capt. Powell, Mr Barnard, and Mr. J. Dolby; and in Ruff's Guide 1856 as training at South Hatch Cottage, for Mr J. Barnard, Mr T Barnard, and Mr H. Mayo. He is recorded in Kelly's Directory 1855 as John Wycherley "horse trainer, South Hatch". He died on January 8th 1856 at South Hatch Cottage, aged 40.

WYLDE. E.		1903-1907

Possibly *Herbert Wilde*. E. Wylde appears in gallop reports in The Sporting Life in 1904 and 1905.

WYNNE, Gerald O.	Heath House	1949-1950
(1924-1985)		

YOUNG, Charles Florance	Kirriemuir	1911-1915
(1865.1934)	Tangleycroft	1917-1919
	Burgh Heath Road	

Educated at Harrow and Trinity College, Cambridge, Young was managing director in the family business, Young's Brewery of Wandsworth. He trained at Lambourn between July 1906 and December 1911. In Epsom, he was based originally in Links Road, moving to Burgh Heath Road in 1917.

PART 3.

EPSOM'S RACING STABLES PAST AND PRESENT

ANDREWS CLOSE
Ascot House

The house still stands, but the yard and paddocks were replaced by housing in Andrews Close, and Wimborne Close circa 1959. The stables were last used by *Ron Smyth*.

ASHLEY ROAD
Seabright

Used as the main yard by *Sam Hanley* between the wars, and as Hanley's overflow yard after 1945. Situated next to the old Police Station, the stables were demolished in the late 1950s, and are now part of the site of Ashley Avenue.

The Cottage/Hovedene/Portland House Stables

Probably the same stable yard, but attached at different times to the two houses that the yard stood between. Prior to 1914, the yard, which was constructed of flint, was attached to The Cottage, (now known as 32 Ashley Road). From the 1920s, it was known as Portland House Stables and attached to the property of the same name. Both houses are still standing, but the stables were converted to Portland House Mews circa 1993.

BEACONSFIELD ROAD
St Margaret's (also known as The White House, and Burnside).

Partly converted to housing pre-1945, but the stables, known as The White House, were used by *George Duller* junior in the post-war period. *Jackie Sirett* re-named the stables Burnside. The stables were demolished in 1973 and are now the site of Saddlers Way.

Mannamead (also known as Gondola, possibly L'Etoile)

Percy Allden purchased the middle of three properties in Beaconsfield Road, a small farm, and changed the name to Gondola. *Bobby Dick* bought the property and renamed the stables Mannamead after the horse he rode to three victories in 1935. The horse Mannamead was sold to Hungary as a stallion, and was stolen during the Russian invasion.
In the early 1950s the Metropolitan Police bought the stable yard, and Mannamead House. The house was demolished, the paddocks replaced by housing, and police horses occupied the stables. From 1976 to 1991, one of the yards was again used for racehorse

training. In 1993 Mannamead Close was built on the site, and a smaller stable yard built behind Beaconsfield Road. In 1998 the "new" yard was demolished.

Startside (also known as Hazelwood, Woodlands)

Percy Allden's brother *George Allden* trained at Woodlands, and *Major Mairs* trained at Hazelwood in the 1930s.
Post-war, *Peter Thrale* improved the site, and Startside stables were established. After *Peter Thrale's* death, Sid *Dale* bought the stables. Startside was demolished in 1974, and is now the site of Spencers Close

Hillcot

The stables remain in some disrepair; they are unused since circa 1973. When last in use the stables housed Prix du Moulin winner Gold Rod trained by *Reg Akehurst.*

BRIGHTON ROAD, KINGSWOOD
Holly Lodge

Victor Tabor was the main occupant prior to 1939, and from here he trained an Irish Derby winner, a King George VI Chase winner, and three Cesarewitch winners. The stables had direct access to the Walton Heath gallops, but have not been used post-war. The site now houses a mobile homes park.

Mayfields

Tom Griffiths and *Peter Dawson* used the stables in the 1950s and 1960s. Since the early 1970s the stables were used as livery stables under the name of Clock House Stables. A planning application circa 2000 to develop the site was refused; the stables were demolished in 2010 and replaced by housing.

BURGH HEATH ROAD (formerly known as Church Street, Downs Road, or Downs Hall Road)
Mospey

The house (built circa 1882) remains, and is currently used as a retirement home. The stables and paddocks were developed circa 1964 and are now the site of Mospey Crescent. The property is famous as the base for *Victor Smyth*, the trainer of Zabara the 1,000 Guineas winner, and three Champion Hurdle winners. The name Mospey was given by the former owner Major Misa and is Epsom reversed.

Bruce Lodge

The house and stables date back to at least 1881, and *Robert Wyatt* probably built the property, and on his death, *James Adams* bought Bruce Lodge. Following Adams' financial problems, The Sporting Life 26 ᵗʰ February 1896 noted that Lord William Beresford had bought the property, was having it renovated, and would then install his private trainer. The stables were used between the wars by *Bill Larkin*, and subsequently by *Vic Smyth*. The Times 5th May 1934 recorded *"The Bruce Lodge training establishment has been sold to V. Smyth, the trainer. Bruce Lodge was owned by W.F. Larkin, who decided to sell owing to ill health. It adjoins Smyth's training stables."* The property is currently divided into flats, the stabling made way for Mospey Crescent and Burghfield, circa 1964.

Down Cottage

Originally the stables of Downs Hall, this property was known as Down Cottage from circa 1870.
The land was purchased in 1809 by *John Forth*. In 1824 he advertised the property in The Times:

"Comprising a newly erected and substantial brick built mansion, containing an entrance hall, dining, drawing, breakfast and housekeeper's room; 9 bedrooms, excellent domestic offices of every description attached, and supplied in all parts with good water, and is now in the occupation of the Earl of Oxford.
The detached buildings consist of very superior stabling for 24 horses, brick and slated, with good granary and lofts over, well supplied with excellent water by pipes underground. Also coach and chaise houses, brewhouse, cowhouse, dog kennels, piggery, and upwards of 36 acres of excellent meadow, pasture, and arable land. The above property is particularly desirable for any gentleman or nobleman fond of the field, being within a short distance of several packs of stag and foxhounds."

The yard and cottage were rebuilt in 1918, and demolished in 1972 and replaced by Hillcrest Close.

Hillcrest

The house was separated from the stables circa 1945, and still remains. The stables were demolished in 1972 to form 2 and 2A Treadwell Road, and the entrance to Hillcrest Close.

Priam Lodge

The property was known in the early part of the 19th century as Priam Cottage, Downs Cottage or Downs Farm. The stables have no known connection with the 1830 Derby winner Priam, but probably mark the year when the house was re-built. Used in the late 19th century by *John Jones* and *Arthur Nightingall* who both trained for the Prince of Wales. Following *John Jones'* death, Priam Lodge was sold in 1893 to Charles White, a bookmaker.

Victor Smyth used the yard from circa 1945 to 1959.

On his 25th birthday, Gay Kindersley inherited £750,000 from the estate of Ernest Guinness. He bought a farm and 80 acres near Beare Green, Dorking; and Priam Lodge. The house was converted to four flats, which at the time housed *Don Butchers*, two head lads, and stable jockey Alan Oughton.

Kindersley let Don Butchers train there rent-free in return for having two of his horses trained for no fee.

Eventually the Iveagh Trustees who managed the Guinness inheritance advised that the lifestyle was draining Kindersley's resources, and at the trustees' instigation he sold Priam Lodge and the Dorking farm, and bought premises at Lambourn.

Priam Lodge was bought by *Tommy Gosling's* father-in-law Hubert Vickery, and subsequently passed to Gosling's sons.

In 2018 the stables were demolished and replaced by a housing development known as College View.

Shifnal Cottage

The head lad's cottage for South Hatch in the 1890s, the property takes its name from the South Hatch- trained Grand National winner. It was inhabited by *Stanley Wootton* from c.1928 until c.1945, and then used by *"Snowy" Parker*. On Parker's retirement it was bought by *Stanley Wootton* as a cottage for his housekeeper. Wootton sold the property circa 1984, and subsequently the stables were used as an overflow yard for South Hatch, and rented by a number of trainers on a short-term basis during the 1990s.

The Chalet/Downs Lodge

Occasionally the stables have been referred to as Downs Lodge. For much of *Walter Nightingall's* career it was the third South Hatch yard. It was subsequently bought by *Stanley Wootton*, and sold by him circa 1984. The stables were let on a short-term basis during the 1980s.

Wendover

Formerly the "Top Yard" at South Hatch, bought by Heather and Arthur Pitt in 1969.

South Hatch

The name South Hatch dates back to the early Enclosure Acts of the 18th century; where the enclosed land ceased, there was a gate or hatch providing exit to the common grazing land, South Hatch was the last enclosure at the top of Burgh Heath Road prior to entry to the common land of Epsom Downs.
The property is linked with the Nightingall family, various members of whom trained there for 110 plus years. In *John Nightingall's* time "South Hatch" encompassed Shifnal Cottage, and The Chalet. During *Walter Nightingall's* time it included the land from South Hatch up to Wendover (including Beech Cottage), and The Chalet.
The property was advertised on 20th August 1857, as including 19 stables, four acres, and several cottages. On the 10th January 1862 it was re-advertised, by which time the neighbouring properties had been acquired, in addition to *John Nightingall* renting the 19 stables and cottages, a further range of stables was occupied by *William Burbridge*, and other stabling and land occupied by *Robert Sherwood*.
It was the revised, larger property that formed the core of South Hatch during the Nightingall era.
William Nightingall rebuilt the property in 1900, and the main yard with its hostel, flats, and cottage dates from that period.
The size of the property facilitates multiple occupations, and there are numerous examples of several trainers operating simultaneously from different yards on the site. Inevitably the old yard, and the hostel accommodation are showing signs of age. In 2004/05 a planning application that involved building a new yard and trainer's house in the paddock and replacing the old yard/hostel with housing was refused. A further application was submitted in October 2018.

CHALK LANE
Heathcote House Stables

The stables were used for training purposes from 1890; they were demolished circa 1968, and are now the site of Berkley Place. The 1900 Rate Book indicates that at that time they were owned by Walter Langlands, a family with a long association with training and racing on the Downs. When *David Hanley* was training in the United States, he drove to Canada for a holiday, while staying at a motel he got into conversation with the owner who told him "I know Epsom, I was stationed there before D Day." It transpired that the Canadian was billeted at Heathcote House, the stables where Hanley had been based for 25 years. Many of the Canadians left a lasting reminder by carving their initials in the wall outside The Durdans. "B.C." i.e. British Columbia is one of a number wistfully carved.

The Durdans

The Durdans, was originally constructed using materials from the demolished Nonsuch Palace in Ewell. In 1537 Henry VIII instigated the building of Nonsuch Palace at Ewell on the edge of the North Downs. The palace subsequently passed on to James I and then to Charles II. Epsom was the base for some of Charles' amorous affairs, and for a while he kept Barbara Villiers at Nonsuch, and Nell Gwyn at The King's Head in Epsom. Charles allegedly had a training stable built for Nell Gwyn adjacent to the King's Head, but she made little use of it, and persuaded Charles to move to Newmarket where she did not have to compete with Barbara Villiers. Charles gave Nonsuch to Barbara Villiers as compensation, and created the title for her "Duchess of Cleveland."
A painting by Knyff of The Durdans in 1631 shows the house in its full glory with formal gardens and a bowling green, and stables on the site of what subsequently became Heathcote House stables.
Diarist John Evelyn recorded a dinner on September 1st 1662, when fellow guests included Charles II, the Queen, and the future James II. In the 18th century the house was twice rebuilt.
Sir Gilbert Heathcote bred Amato, the 1838 Derby winner at The Durdans. Amato is one of four Derby winners buried in the grounds of The Durdans.
The fifth Earl of Rosebery bought the house in 1874. Although he had official residences in London, and other private homes, he favoured The Durdans as a place to escape from the pressures of public life.
Lord Rosebery held several junior posts in Gladstone's government, and was appointed Foreign Secretary in 1886. In 1890, Lady Rosebery died. Lord Rosebery dropped out of his active role in politics for a while. In 1892 he returned as Foreign Secretary. In 1894 Gladstone resigned, and Rosebery became Prime Minister for a year, he quit politics for good in 1905.
The fifth Earl of Rosebery rarely went racing, stating "So far as I am concerned the amusements of the Turf do not lie on the racecourse. They lie in the breeding of a horse, in watching the development of the foal, and the exercise of the horse at home." Rosebery combined the Rothschild stud at Mentmore with The Durdans. The 1894 Derby and Guineas winner Ladas, the 1895 Derby winner Sir Visto, and the 1905 Derby winner Cicero all retired to The Durdans and are buried in the grounds near Amato's grave.
There are four listed buildings on the site, including stable ranges from the 18th and 19th century. The feature is the indoor riding school, designed by George Devey, that was built in 1881 and is Grade 2 listed.
The stables were known as Lavandou during *Dermot Whelan's* tenure.

Maidstone House (also known as York House)

The original house was built for Lord Berkeley in the 17th century, and passed to Sir Edward Northey circa 1700. The current building is Grade 2 listed and is described by English Heritage as mid C18.

Jesse Winfield, commission agent, trainer, and dealer was resident at the time of his bankruptcy in 1878. Solicitor Herbert Grundtvig owned the house from c 1890 to c 1918, when it appears as a Northey family holding. Mrs Phyllis Nunneley, who married Hubert Nicholls, was in residence from 1930 to 1962 when the property was advertised for sale in Country Life, "instructions of Mrs Phyllis Nunneley" and during this period *Phillip Nunneley* briefly trained from the premises.

CHURCH STREET
Pitt Place

Used in the 19th century, notably by *Fothergill Rowlands* who was responsible for introducing Prince Albert to National Hunt racing. The Glasgow Herald, 5th March 1877 noted:

"Pitt Place where Scamp is trained, is one of the prettiest places near London, as indeed it should be, as I believe the rent is nearly £600 a year, and there are only nine acres of ground to it. It is the favourite resort of half the young "swells" connected with steeplechasing, and apparently Mr Fothergill Rowlands has to entertain half the Household Brigade. It is rare fun for them, as there are in stable nearly fifty horses; and the afternoon I was there we had about half a dozen hurdle races."

The stables do not appear to have been used in the 20th century. The house was demolished and replaced by a block of flats in the 1960s.

Nell Gwyn Stables/ New Stables/Horse and Groom Stables/ Farm Stables/Lime Tree Cottage

The stables stood adjacent to the King's Head. This was the site of the stables allegedly built by King Charles I for Nell Gwyn. On 25 October 1762, Philip Hall of East Bergholt sold, to Samuel Inman of the City of London, *"his copyhold message with the outhouses, gardens, grounds and appurtenances – in the occupation of Joseph Cooke and known by the sign of the Horse and Groom"*
The earliest mention of the New Stables appeared in 1701

London Gazette (London, England), 20 October 1701; Issue 3751 p2

The last Thursday, Friday and Saturday in November next, 3 Plates will be run for on the new Heat on Epsom Downs in Surrey; ..... The Horses to be entered at Devereux Watson's at the new Stables in Epsom.

On the death of Samuel Inman, and under his will dated 7 November 1775 the premises passed to his Executors and Trustees. They were formally admitted on 27 October 1777 when the occupier was named as *Robert Bloss*.

By 1797, the Horse and Groom property had become occupied by 'the widow Dilley'; mother of *John Dilly*, and widow of Thomas Dilly. The Racing Calendar for 1797, John Dilly advertised that he took in horses to train at the stables of his late father.

On 9 June 1800, Samuel Inman's son, Samuel Inman the younger of Gloucester Street, Queen Square, Middlesex, gained possession of the property; his mother and sister having surrendered their rights to him.

On 11 August 1815, the Rev Andrew Reed of Cannon Street Road, St. George's in the East, Middlesex, acquired the property for £680 and, from 12 October 1819, obtained a licence to let it to Sarah Watts of Epsom, widow, for 21 years. In 1822 *Thomas Scaith* was training at the stables. With Sarah Watts in occupation, on 25 October 1824, the premises were purchased by Rowland Stephenson, banker, Lombard Street, London, for £800. In the public auction on 6 October 1840, following Stephenson's bankruptcy, the Horse and Groom estate was purchased by George Cooper Ridge of Morden Park for £376.10.0. Ridge died intestate on 24 March 1842 and never completed the contract but his family were shown as owners for the 1843 Tithe return, with *George Dockeray* as occupier.

After Dockeray, George Hodgman was the tenant, leasing the property for seven years, (1855 – 1863) for £35 p.a. whilst leasing The Warren for 14 years from 1860. *Thomas Hughes* was at the Horse and Groom site by 1862 and purchased the premises 15 April 1863 for £1102. He is listed at Church Street to 1867, before Worple Road from 1875 – 1882. *Saxton* and *Holt* trained from Lime Tree Cottage. The Register of Electors for 1886 and 1887 shows the cottage as being in *Mr. Hughes'* yard.

John Coleman, Veterinary Surgeon, took over what became 'The Farm' from 1899 until his death in 1923. Subsequently it was the site of the Farm Garage, until development c. 1980.

COLLEGE ROAD
Rowland Lodge

Originally the main yard to Pitt Place, the stables take the name from *Fothergill Rowlands*. Rowland Lodge housed Moifaa the 1905 Grand National winner. Circa 1907 the property was referred to as "Uplands" by the trainer *James Phillips,* but with two properties of a similar name in Epsom, Rowland Lodge was re-instated. The stables were also used by *Victor Smyth*, and his brother *"Monty" Smyth*. The stables were demolished circa 1962, and are now the site of block of maisonettes of the same name, and Rosebery Avenue.

Burley Lodge

Burley Lodge was the base of the veterinary surgeon, auctioneer, bloodstock dealer and breeder *George Forbes*. The property was demolished circa 1972, and is now the site of Tintagel Close. The last stallion to stand at stud there was Tintagel.

DOWNS ROAD (formerly known as Grandstand Road)
Uplands

The Times, 13th December 1909 records the sale by auction of the *"Freehold training establishment at Epsom Downs known as the Uplands, Downs Road for £1,150"*. The house still stands, and was used as the Stable Lads Club in the 1950s. The Wootton family previously used the paddocks and stables, which were developed in 1962 to form The Ridings and Milburn Walk.

Clear Height

The name is particularly apt, the yard stands on virtually the highest point of the Downs, and on a clear day it affords an amazing view of London from the Thames Estuary to Heathrow Airport.
The house, and the three rows of brick built stables were built for *Ron Smyth* in 1957/58; the name of the property was taken from a moderate stalwart horse in the yard at the time.
In 2004, a separate yard, capable of housing approximately 25 horses was developed in the grounds, and refurbished in 2019.

EPSOM DOWNS
Derby Arms/Down House/Downs Stables/Downs Lodge

The stable block stood next to the Derby Arms, with living accommodation above the boxes. It was in use as a racing stable from circa 1860 to 1930. During the 19th century, *"John Armstrong*, The Downs" was sufficient to find the stables. It was then briefly called Downs House until that name was ascribed to Sherwood's Cottage, the house by the Derby start. In a state of disrepair, the property then suffered bomb damage circa 1943.

Downs House/Sherwood's Cottage/Melision Lodge

In the book "Ancient Epsom" by Reginald White, the author refers to O'Kelly having two large racing establishments, Clay Hill and Melision Lodge. He quotes,

"Within the circuit of the course, Col. O'Kelly has enclosed about ten acres of land and divided it into six paddocks for training of horses, which for its great convenience is allowed to be one of the best in England for that purpose. On the North side of this enclosure is a dwelling called "MELISION LODGE" at which a well whose depth is 395 feet, and the water is raised by an engine worked by hand. Known for many years as "Sherwood's" and now as "Downs House" it remains to this day very much as it was in the days of Eclipse and O'Kelly"

O' Kelly's training establishment 'on the Downs' descended through members of the family, passing to Charles Langdale through his marriage with Henrietta Grattan, daughter of Mary O'Kelly, who was the daughter of Andrew O'Kelly's cousin.
The property was occupied by the Sherwood family for over 100 years; but it was not until 1885 the family bought the freehold (from Charles Langdale.) By then the property was known as Sherwood's Cottage or simply Sherwood's.
The name persists today with the turf gallop and sand track at the rear of the property, (the site of the old course start), still known as Sherwood's. The Epsom and Ewell Borough Council purchased Downs House on 22nd February 1944, ensuring that Epsom's most historic training establishment was preserved for its original purpose.
The property was sold on leasehold during 2016, an application to refurbish the stables and house was made in October 2018.

THE GROVE
Grove Stables

The stables were demolished circa 1970 and replaced by housing. The stables were probably originally attached to The Grove, the Georgian house that remains and is now divided into apartments.

HEADLEY ROAD
Woodruff

The first record of the stables is during the 1930s when *Pat Donoghue* trained ponies on the site; subsequently his father Steve made an aborted attempt to train thoroughbreds there, before moving to Berkshire. The property was subsequently bought by *Tommy Carey*; and later sold to the Sutcliffe family. *John Sutcliffe* junior trained Right Tack the 1969 2,000 Guineas winner here. After Sutcliffe's retirement Woodruff House was separated from the stables.

Cedar Point

The house and stables were constructed on land adjacent to Woodruff during the 1980s.

Chalk Pit Stables

The stables and bungalow are built in the chalk pit opposite Woodruff, and was the base of *Brooke Sanders* until her retirement.

Condover

Condover Stables are currently in the same ownership as Chalk Pit Stables. The stables and the bungalow were built circa 2000 on the land behind Condover

HYLANDS ROAD
Woodcote Rise

Prior to 1895, the property was a stud owned by Mr. F. Horton. Following Horton's death in 1895, the property was advertised as having good stabling for 20, a residence and six acres of land. The property was used as a racing stables from circa 1900 to 1935. Digdens Rise was built on most of the site. "Digdens" was the ancient name for the Common Fields either side of Chalk Lane.

LONGDOWN LANE
Bredenbury

The house still stands, part of the stables remain as outbuildings, the site has been unused for racehorse training since 1947.

REIGATE ROAD
The Looe (aka. The Grange)

Tom Walls trained the 1932 Derby winner, April the Fifth here. The property was previously known as The Grange. The stables suffered some bomb damage during World War II. In the 1950s, the yard was used as the base of a horse transport business, and the stables for storage; but the barn and outbuildings are now in light industrial use.

Heath House, Burgh Heath

Burgh Heath was an archetypal hamlet. The roads from Sutton and Epsom to Reigate converge by a pond, this proved to be a popular watering hole for horses, and eventually two inns, a church, and two rows of cottages were built by the pond.

231

The Sporting Life, 19th January 1881 featured a" A Visit To Robert I'Anson". The article noted:

"A thorough scene of rural life is to be gained by a stroll round the cottages, in addition to Heath House , a few shops, and an inn in rejoicing in the name of The Sheepshearer's Arms, which comprise Burgh Heath. For nearly six years Robert I'Anson has lived at Burgh Heath, having taken the house with a lawn big enough for lawn tennis, and fruit and kitchen gardens to match. A half hour was spent in looking over the pictures which adorn the walls of the snug dining room, chief amongst these are Austerlitz and Shifnal (both grand National winners); the French Chaser Wild Monarch, and that grand favourite horse Becchus," Near the House I'Anson has a first class steeple-chase and hurdle-race course which Sir John Hartopp, to whom the property belongs, gave him permission to make.
The stabling at Burgh Heath is excellent, the boxes being lofty, dry and well ventilated. In the principal yard behind the house, where the most forward horses stand, there is accommodation for about a dozen, and a stone's throw further off a long range which John Day built for his visitors to Epsom in the palmy days of Danebury. I addition to these are scattered here and there smaller batches of stabling."

The yard had stabled winners of the Champion Hurdle, the Scottish Grand National, the Imperial Cup and the King's Stand Stakes. In 1969, The Sheepshearer's, Heath House, and the cottages were demolished and replaced by a development of town houses.

Surrey Yeoman, Burgh Heath

The public house stood opposite The Sheepshearer's. There is reference to stables at the "British" Yeoman at Burgh Heath, following a fire.

Sporting Intelligence
The Newcastle Courant, Friday 11th January 1867
"TOTAL DESTRUCTION OF JOHN DAY'S STABLE

Intelligence was on Friday night received by John Day of the whole range of his extensive stabling at Banstead, where his horses stand during the Epsom meeting, being burnt to the ground. The severity of the frost, as well as the state of the roads, prevented the engines being brought to the ground, and playing upon the fire with the energy they might have done had the weather being more favourable. We have not heard whether the buildings were insured; but, under any circumstance the loss to John Day will be very serious."
York Herald, Saturday 12th January 1867

"FIRE AT JOHN DAY'S STABLES AT BANSTEAD

The stabling at the rear of the British Yeoman, at Burgh Heath, near Epsom Downs, was recently destroyed by fire. These stables were the property of John Day, and were used by him for the Danebury horses during the Epsom meeting".

The Sheffield and Rotherham Independent, Tuesday January 15th 1867

"John Day it is gratifying to learn will only be a loser to the extent of £100 by the burning down of his stables at Banstead, as he was insured."

The British Yeoman was later known as The Surrey Yeoman. The 1871 census lists the proprietor as Frank May; his cousins Henry May, horse farrier born Mickleham 1843 and Edward May, horse farrier born Redbourne 1845, plus two stable lads were also resident. Henry and Edward's father *Harry E. May*, trainer of Grand National winners Little Charley and Anastsis, was training at Turf Cottage, Sutton in 1871, moving to Heath House, Burgh Heath in 1872.

ROSEBERY ROAD
Myrtle Cottage

The cottage still remains, but the yard is now the site of a block of maisonettes built circa 1960. Used as an additional yard by *Peter Thrale* in the early 1950s, last occupied by *Manch Taylor.*

RUSHETT LANE
Glanmire Farm

The house has been extended to form two semi-detached houses; the stables remain, but have been unused for thoroughbred training since *Dave Dick* retired. The extended and modernised yard is now used for livery.

SHEPHERDS WALK
The Limes/Larchfield

The stables were originally attached to Larchfield, the house that stands in Farm Lane and used by *Johnny Dines. John Benstead* took over the stables in 1960. The property, The Limes, became self-contained with a separate trainer's house, and access is via Shepherd's Walk.

Ermyn Lodge

The house and stables were constructed in the late 1920s and occupied by *Jack Reardon*. The yard was modernised and extended by *John Sutcliffe* in 1965, and further stabling built in the 1990s. The house was rebuilt and the stud buildings added circa 2005.

Thirty Acre Barn

Originally the Thirty Acre Farm; during the time of *Staff Ingham*'s and *Geoff Lewis'* occupations the paddocks and gallops extended to nearer 85 acres, providing a self-contained training centre with private gallops. On 4th July 1943 a RAF plane returning from a mission over Cologne in which it suffered extensive damage was forced to land at Thirty Acre Barn. With two engines out of use, the plane, (returning to RAF Breighton in East Yorkshire), was listing badly. Struggling to maintain a course and altitude, with most of the crew having bailed out, and the built up area of London approaching, the two pilots brought it down in the Thirty Acre Paddock. The plane ignited and was destroyed, the remaining crew members were unhurt.

Shepherds Walk stands on the site of Stane Street, and during *Staff Ingham*'s time there the address was given as Roman Road.

Staff Ingham extended the property building a second yard on rising ground behind the main yard,

Providing a total of 42 boxes, subsequently *Geoff Lewis* built an all-weather gallop around the perimeter of the main gallops.

Following *Geoff Lewis'* retirement, *Terry Mills* bought the main gallop and constructed a much larger all -weather gallop.

For many years, the horses travelling from Shepherds Walk to the Downs had to contend with the traffic in Langley Vale Road. In the 1990s Epsom and Ewell Council constructed a horse margin to provide safe access to the Downs.

SOUTH STREET
Abele Villas/South Street Stables

The stables stood behind the Abele Villas and Abele Cottages, incorporating what is now a builders yard on the corner of Dorking Road. The yard was used by a number of trainers pre-1930

The stables were probably the original stables to Abele Grove, which became a convent, and later a hotel/restaurant.

Bordeaux House

Used as a racing stable in the 19th century. The house stood between the town and what is now Rosebery Park.

TATTENHAM CORNER

The site was used for training stables prior to 1915, with trainers sometimes simply using "Epsom Downs" as the address. In 1961 the development of new racecourse stables at the top of Chalk Lane on land previously attached to The Durdans rendered the four-acre site at Tattenham Corner Stables redundant, and the E.G.S.A. applied for planning permission to demolish the stables and sell the land for housing. Epsom and Ewell Borough Council rejected the plans. Walter Nightingall on behalf of local trainers backed the objections, stating that the premises could play an important role in the future of racehorse training at Epsom. *Mick Haynes* used the stables for many years, and on his retirement, the property was renovated in 2005

THE WARREN

Situated at the top of Six Mile Hill gallops, the property owes its name to its hare coursing facilities, with coursing still taking place on the Downs in the 19th century.
According to the Council for British Architecture 1996, The Warren was built in 1666 as a hunting lodge, with 25 acres of land. No royal connection to the site is documented until 1744, when an advert in the London Advertiser refers to a greyhound being lost from the Prince of Wales' Hare Warren at Epsom, a reward of half a guinea is offered, and "no Questions asked". During the period when The Derby started behind Downs House, The Warren provided the saddling enclosure.
An advertisement in the Sporting Magazine 1805, offers nominations to the stallion Teddy the Grinder for five guineas *"at Mr Durand's Warren, Epsom Downs."* By 1860, The Warren was owned by a Mr Hodgman who employed *Ben Land,* (among others), as his private trainer.
Benjamin Ellam who owned a saddler's business in Piccadilly subsequently bought The Warren, and the 1866 Oaks winner Tormentor was bred here. In partnership with Jockey Club steward Prince Soltykoff, *Ellam* ran The Warren Stud, and conducted regular bloodstock sales at The Warren. Ellam made considerable improvements to The Warren, adding two large rooms, forty feet long, and used for entertaining guests during The Derby and the bloodstock sales. The Morning Post 26th September 1881 reported on an uneventful Warren Stud Sale marred by a clash with the Cobham Stud Company Sale which *"fairly took the wind out of Mr Ellam's sails",* *"there were not a dozen passengers by the special train from Waterloo, and scarcely a hundred spectators."* Of 46 lots only 9 changed hands. *"Three octogenarian local trainers were present, Ralph Sherwood who trained Amato winner of the Derby in 1835, Sirikol, Samarcand, Campanile and many other good horse-John Armstrong whom all Epsom expected to win the Derby with The Trapper in 1854; and the evergreen John Nightingall, father of "Steeplechase Jack."*

The property was still in use as a stud in 1885 when The Racing Calendar advertised *"The Warren Stud, Epsom Downs. Ethus at 15 guineas per mare. Apply to Mr Ellam, 213, Piccadilly; or the Stud groom, The Warren."*

Ellam died in 1910, and the property was sold to Epsom Grand Stand Association in 1913 for £9,000. The house fell into disrepair, was damaged by fire, and was subsequently demolished. The site is now overgrown, but the two gateposts are still visible in the woods, and part of the hare warren wall remains.

TILLEY LANE
Loretta Lodge

Originally known as Fourfields Farm, and used for training by *Ian Benstead*. The site was purchased by the Swift family circa 1966, completely rebuilt, and re-named Loretta Lodge. A motif of a swift is mounted on the stable yard entrance. The name was taken from *Brian Swift's* wife Loretta, the daughter of *Scobie Breasley*. An adjoining house, Headley Hill House, was constructed in 1981.

Following Swift's death, *Terry Mills* purchased the houses and stables, and extended the property to include a five-furlong circular all-weather gallop, with the property extending to 59 acres.

On the retirement of *Geoff Lewis, Mills* purchased 42 acres of land on the opposite side of Tilley Lane, bordered by Headley Road and Shepherd's Walk, and constructed a straight five-furlong all-weather gallop.

TREADWELL ROAD (formerly known as Link Road)
Treadwell House

Described in 1913 thus, "No racing establishment is known better throughout the world." The property is inextricably linked with the Wootton family. The house remains; but the lodge is now a separate property. Circa 1962, housing was built on the paddocks on either side of the stables; and Aston Way was built behind the stables separating them from the paddocks formerly known as the Rifle Butts gallops.

Circa 1982, the stables were demolished and replaced by the properties now known as 39-47 Treadwell Road, and 6-12 Aston Way. Ten years later the remaining small paddock was developed and Wootton Close was formed.

UPPER HIGH STREET (formerly known as Station Road)
Badminton House/East Hill House

Badminton House was used as a training stable for 50 years from 1880 and primarily associated with trainer Ted Goby. During the Derby meeting, Charles Morton stabled several of his Derby winners here. Situated opposite the old Epsom Station, the site was acquired by Epsom and Ewell Council c. 1962 and is now occupied by Upper High Street car park.

Rail was the primary means of transportation for horses in the 19th and early 20th century. In the mid-1920s, a local coach operator, Mr Richmond, had horseboxes built on the chassis of two former buses, and for the next 30 or so years, Richmond's of Epsom, and Hawkins from Ewell transported horses to the races, bloodstock sales, and stud. For long distance trips they transported the runners to the principal London rail termini. When the railways were nationalised, the transport of livestock by rail was prohibited, and so all journeys were done by road. Horseboxes were subjected to a speed limit of 30 M.P.H.; therefore the Northern fixtures became a three-day trip.

There was a livery yard on the site as early as 1852. When the Railway Hotel was sold in 1857 it was offered with stabling for 11 horses, plus five freehold building plots. Local estate agent Lawrence Langlands bought three of the plots for £183, and one of these became the site of East Hill House, later known as Badminton House. A. Templeman, based at the Railway Hotel, was training under Pony Turf Club rules in 1933, probably using the adjoining Badminton House stables.

WARREN ROAD, BANSTEAD
Warren Farm

John Soper, who worked for *Staff Ingham* in the 1950s, recalled a visit there in 1943 when *Jimmy Wood* was resident trainer.

"The yard was three sides of a square with a low wall facing the east side. Built of mostly flint and brick, the buildings had a slated roof, inside the stable buildings a cobbled corridor running around from which the loose boxes were divided by timber partition walls and on the corridor wood panelled with iron bars uppermost; the stables had half-doors. It was clear the boxes had been converted from ancient stalls. The partitions were below roof height and two double door exits into the central yard from each corridor, also the windows were placed on this side, making the whole airy in the summer and cosy in the winter. Ideal for racehorses."

WEST HILL
Clay Hill/Eclipse Cottage

A local historian, James Edwards, described a visit to O'Kelly's stud and stables at Clay Hill.

" In the front of the house is an elegant drawing room 40ft. by 12 ft. with gardens, shrubbery and stabling. There are 35 paddocks for his large stud of stallions, brood mares, colts and fillies. Here I was entertained with a sight of Eclipse."

James Edwards also mentioned the 35 paddocks being at the back of the 'beautiful range of stabling' on about 100 acres of land. In "Ancient Epsom" Reginald White wrote:
Whence and how all this has vanished, without leaving any trace with the exception of a few loose boxes which have probably been demolished? It seems almost incredible, and yet the establishment must have had an existence.

The part of the estate above Clay Hill Green had passed into the possession of Henry Grattan, M.P. through his wife Mary O'Kelly Harvey, daughter of Andrew O'Kelly's cousin. Little remains in Epsom to commemorate Eclipse. The Clay Hill stud and O'Kelly's fine house have disappeared. O'Kelly's house was replaced by a Victorian building that now houses Kingswood House School, and the infant school stands on part of the old stables. A groom's cottage called Eclipse Cottage is still standing today, the only link to the 18th century estate.

WILMERHATCH LANE
Woodcote Stud (Also known as Turbine Stud)

The stud was used for training purposes sporadically during the 20th century. *David Hanley* recalled that his father Sam had permission to use the grounds of the R.A.C. Club to reach the Downs from the stud.

WINDMILL LANE
Bush Lodge

The bush marked the border between Epsom and Ewell. Bush Lodge is still standing adjacent to the railway bridge in Windmill Lane. The stables are now housing. Occasionally the address was given as Chuters Grove, the road at the rear of Bush Lodge.

The Paddocks

Originally used by *Tom Walls,* the site is now housing probably occupied by Dorling Drive.

WOODCOTE

Several stables once stood on the Stone House estate, notably Althorp Lodge, Middle House, and Woodcote Lodge. There is no recorded use of these stables since 1914.

Althorp Lodge

The house and stables stood opposite Woodcote Green. The cottage attached to Stone House became known as Althorp Lodge. The 1900 Rate Book indicates that *Charles Arnull* was renting the property from Epsom Guardians. It subsequently became part of Epsom Workhouse. The site is now occupied by the outbuildings of Epsom Hospital; possibly the nurse's home.

Woodcote Lodge

These were also known as Mr Case Walker's stables; circa 1880 they were the private stables of racehorse owner Mr Thomas Case Walker. Circa 1930 the property was passed from Epsom Poor Law Institution to Surrey County Council, and became Epsom Hospital, Woodcote Lodge is now the main building of Epsom nurse's home.

Woodcote End

The ruins of a stable are located in the woods at The Durdans adjacent to the Derby winners' graves; this is probably the site of 19th century stables.

WORPLE ROAD
Caithness (Also known as Ashley Racing Stables)

The stables were used from circa 1887. In 1997, the stables and coach house were demolished, and replaced by housing. Possibly this was the site of *William Reeves'* Field House stables.

Sandown Lodge

Also known as "Boxall's" after the family that owned it, and sub-let various parts of the yard. In 1933, Roland Phillips, and Pat Donoghue were training under Pony Turf Club rules from on the site. The maximum height of a pony was 15 hands, and racing took place on 82 days between April and October at Northolt and Portsmouth.
The flats known as Sandown Lodge, (built circa 1960), now occupy the site.

TADWORTH PARK

In addition to the private racecourse on Walton Heath, used mainly by the *Nightingall* family; "Gales Weekly" records that during the period circa 1889-1890, *John Jones* used the schooling grounds at Tadworth Park (in some cases recorded as Tadworth Country). Other Epsom trainers, *Holt* and *Adams* are also recorded as occasionally using this facility.

TADWORTH COTTAGE

Tadworth Cottage was adjacent to Tadworth Lodge on Walton Heath. The stables had been the base for G. *"Tiny"* Milne. The Racing Indicator 1865 records: *"Sir Joseph Hawley has taken Tadworth Cottage once occupied by "Tiny Milne" and is building new boxes."* Hawley used the premises for stabling his runners during the Derby meeting. *Robert I'Anson* junior trained from Tadworth Cottage, as well as Heath House, possibly training Grand National winner Austerlitz here.

MICKLEHAM

Standing some four miles south of Epsom Downs, Mickleham lies at the foot of the North Downs where the Roman road, Stane Street, turns south to drop below the steep precipice of the North Downs known as Box Hill.

James Edwards, who trained at Newmarket for Lord Jersey, habitually moved his Derby entrants to Mickleham for the month prior to the Derby. On the downs above Mickleham, Edwards prepared three Derby winners, Middleton in 1825, Mameluke in 1827, and Bay Middleton in 1836. Other Derby winners prepared at Mickleham after walking from Newmarket include Priam and Cadland.

The Times, 113th May 1824 recorded,

"The King's horses left Newmarket at 3.00 this morning for Mickleham" (in preparation for the Derby.)

The Malton trainer John Scott also prepared his Derby winners at Mickleham. The 1843 winner Cotherstone was stabled at Leatherhead, but his subsequent winners were prepared at Mickleham.

William Wildman's stables at Mickleham, where Eclipse was first based, were used for racehorse training for much of the 19th century, *George Dockeray, R. Drewitt*, and *Robert L'Anson Senior* being the most successful.

An article in the Sporting Gazette, Sunday 19th May 1844 indicates the build-up to The Derby:

The lots will be located, so far as we can at present ascertain, as follow:
At Epsom- Sir G. Heathcote's, Mr Mostyn's, Gill's, Osborne's, I. Sadler's, I .Day's, Scott's (Ascot). Death's, Taylor's (Lord Chesterfield's), Lord Orford's, Stephens, Lord Stradbroke's, Mr Osbaldeston's, Dockeray's Chifney's, Lumley's and Smith's.
At Baron De Teissier's –Lord Exeter's.
At Wright's-Lord Albemarle's, Colonel Peel's, Lord Stradbroke's, Mr Osbaldeston's , and Hon. Mr Ongley's.
At Leatherhead Scott's and Planner's.

At Mickleham-Heseltine's and S.Day's.
At Headley-Duke of Richmond's, Lord G. Bentinck's, Rogers's and Treen's.
At Banstead-John Day's.
At Ashtead-Forth's.
HORSES EN ROUTE TO EPSOM. –On Wednesday last the following horses passed through York en route to Epsom; - Beaufort, April Noddy, and Inheritress. On Friday Boniface and Mountain Charles passed through York for the same place.
The report that Ratan passed through London on Thursday was premature; he sweated at Newmarket that morning, left on Friday and arrived at Leatherhead in the afternoon per van.

SMITHAM BOTTOM, COULSDON

The Red Lion at Smitham Bottom to the east of Epsom appears regularly as a training stable in the mid-19th century. It was also the site of *Sam Pearce's* stud; and a venue for trotting matches, boxing, athletics, and hunt meets. The hounds for the Mid-Surrey Staghounds, (formerly The Earl of Derby's Staghounds), were kennelled at Smitham Bottom.
The Red Lion with 14 acres of meadowland was advertised for sale by auction in The Standard 6th May 1843.
The property with a reduced meadowland of 6 acres was re-offered in March 1856.
The Sporting Life, Wednesday 2nd February 1870, under the headline "A Morning at Smitham Bottom" recorded:

Few persons are aware-even those connected with the details of racing-that there is within half an hour's railway journey an excellent piece of ground in every way suited for training racehorses and which has been for many years used for that purpose, whilst at present about sixty horses including some of high pretensions, are being prepared there for the approaching campaign. The place to which I allude is Smitham Bottom within four miles of Croydon on the Brighton road, and within one mile of Caterham Junction. I set out early this week, and arrived at the Red Lion at Smitham Bottom, which is now kept by George Milne, so well known to most frequenters of the Turf as the late trainer to the Marquis of Queensbury and others. Milne has also got a few horses in training himself, and has room for some more. The kennels and stables were built and fitted by Milne from whom they are rented. There are at present thirty two and a half couple of hunting hounds at Smitham Bottom.
The training ground is a tract of high land, about a quarter of a mile from the Red Lion called farthing Downs. It is extraordinary that with the great demand for racecourses in the metropolitan District no enterprising Clerk of the Course has set his eye on this place, as the turf is first rate with a straight gallop of three quarters of a mile, and one of three miles. Many good horses have been trained on Farthing Downs. One of the first to use them was Sam Pierce, a native of Bristol, who lived at the Red Lion, and

commenced training on the Downs more than forty-five years ago. W. Scott, who now trains at Holywell, also tried his hand here for a time, but in more recent times horses came over from Sutton, whilst the Epsom trainers have had many a spin on the quiet on farthing Downs. The right of training on the downs is attached to the lease of the red lion, and Milne charges for each horse galloped on it. Besides Milne trainers using these gallops are Henry May who trains at Sutton, William Burbridge , who formerly lived at the Red Lion, Mullinger and G. Prince. May has been particularly fortunate with steeplechasers, having won the Grand National with both Little Charley and Anatis, and been second two years in succession with Knight of Gwynne.

SUTTON
Turf Cottage

The lease was held by Mrs Lucy Balchin from 1852-c.1864, and then by *Ben Land, Harry May*, and *James Adams*, the site ceased to be used for training racehorses c. 1888. It was from these stables that *Charles Balchin* trained Jealousy to win the 1861 Grand National. The address was Banstead Road, Sutton, this later became Cotswold Road, and the site of the stables is now Bicknoller Close.

APPENDIX A. SOME MAJOR RACES WON BY EPSOM TRAINED HORSES
GROUP RACES WON BY EPSOM TRAINED HORSES SINCE 1971

YEAR	RACE	HORSE	TRAINER	STABLE
	GROUP 1			
1972	Irish Derby	Steel Pulse	A.E.Breasley	South Hatch
1975	Middle Park Stakes	Hittite Glory	A.E.Breasley	South Hatch
1980	Phoenix Stakes	Swan Princess	B.Swift	Loretta Lodge
1983	Grand Prix de Paris	Yawa	G.Lewis	Thirty Acre Barn
1984	Premio Roma	Yawa	G.Lewis	Thirty Acre Barn
1995	Prix de l Abbaye	Hever Golf Rose	T.J.Naughton	The Durdans
1995	July Cup	Lake Coniston	G.Lewis	Thirty Acre Barn
2002	Queen Elizabeth II	Where or When	T.Mills	Loretta Lodge
2016	St Leger	Harbour Law	L.Mongan	Condover
	GROUP 2			
1971	Temple Stakes	Mummys Pet	J. Sutcliffe jun.	Woodruff
1972	Geoffrey Freer	Sol Argent	T.Gosling	Priam Lodge
1975	Queen Mary Stakes	Rorys Rocket	P.Ashworth	Treadwell House
1975	Flying Childers	Hittite Glory	A.E.Breasley	South Hatch
1975	John Porter Stakes	Salado	P.Mitchell	Downs House
1977	Richmond Stakes	Persian Bold	A.Ingham	Thirty Acre Barn
1978	Temple Stakes	Oscilight	J. Sutcliffe jun.	Woodruff
1980	Queen Anne Stakes	Blue Refrain	C.J.Benstead	The Limes
1981	Richmond Stakes	Tender King	J. Sutcliffe	Woodruff
1984	Richmond Stakes	Primo Dominie	B.Swift	Loretta Lodge
1984	Flying Childers	Prince Sabo	B.Swift	Loretta Lodge
1994	Hardwicke Stakes	Bobzao	T.Mills	Loretta Lodge
1995	Goldene Peitsche	Hever Golf Rose	T.J.Naughton	The Durdans
1995	Premio Melton Memorial	Hever Golf Rose	T.J. Naughton	The Durdans
1999	Saratoga Breeders Cup H.	Running Stag	P.Mitchell	Downs House
1999	Brooklyn Handicap	Running Stag	P.Mitchell	Downs House
1999	Kings Stand Stakes	Mitcham	T.Mills	Loretta Lodge
2000	Massachusetts Handicap	Running Stag	P.Mitchell	Downs House
2005	Champagne Stakes	Close To You	T.Mills	Loretta Lodge
2017	Al Biddah Mile (Qatar)	Mr Scaramanga	S.Dow	Clear Height

GROUP 3

1971	Sandown Classic Trial	L'Apache	T.Gosling	Priam Lodge
1971	Duke Of York Stakes	The Brianstan	J. Sutcliffe jun.	Woodruff
1972	Earl of Sefton Stakes	Lord David	S.Ingham	Thirty Acre Barn
1972	Doncaster Cup	Biskrah	A.Breasley	South Hatch
1973	Craven Stakes	My Drifter	J. Sutcliffe jun.	Woodruff
1974	National Stakes	Streak	J.E. Sutcliffe	Ermyn Lodge
1974	Ormonde Stakes	Crazy Rhythm	S.Ingham	Thirty Acre Barn
1976	Coronation Stakes	Kesar Queen	A.Breasley	South Hatch
1976	Lingfield Oaks Trial	Heaven Knows	R.Smyth	Clear Height
1977	Horris Hill Stakes	Persian Bold	A.Ingham	Thirty Acre Barn
1977	Earl of Sefton Stakes	Heaven Knows	R.Smyth	Clear Height
1978	Goodwood Cup	Tug Of War	D.Whelan	Lavandou
1979	Cornwallis Stakes	Hanu	A.Breasley	South Hatch
1979	Jersey Stakes	Blue Refrain	C.J.Benstead	The Limes
1980	Queen Anne Stakes	Blue Refrain	C.J.Benstead	The Limes
1983	Duke Of York Stakes	Vorvados	M.Haynes	Tattenham Corner
1983	Cork and Orrery	Sylvan Barbarosa	P.Mitchell	Downs House
1984	Italian St Leger	Rough Pearl	G.Lewis	Thirty Acre Barn
1984	Coventry Stakes	Primo Dominie	B.Swift	Loretta Lodge
1984	Prix de Merano	Yawa	G.Lewis	Thirty Acre Barn
1984	July Stakes	Primo Dominie	B.Swift	Loretta Lodge
1985	Palace House Stakes	Prince Sabo	Mrs. S. Swift	Loretta Lodge
1986	American Express Stakes	Sylvan Express	P.Mitchell	Downs House
1987	Greenlands Stakes	Sylvan Express	P.Mitchell	Downs House
1988	Palace House Stakes	Perion	G.Lewis	Thirty Acre Barn
1989	Phoenix Sprint	Point Of Light	G.Lewis	Thirty Acre Barn
1990	Molecomb Stakes	Poets Cove	W.Carter	Loretta Lodge
1991	Sweet Solera	Pearl Angel	Miss B.Sanders	Chalk Pit
1992	Spreti Rennen	Karinga Bay	G.Lewis	Thirty Acre Barn
1993	Spreti Rennen	Karinga Bay	G.L.Moore	Ermyn Lodge
1993	Badener Meile	Karinga Bay	G.L.Moore	Ermyn Lodge
1993	Grosser Preis d Dortmund	Karinga Bay	G.L.Moore	Ermyn Lodge
1994	Prix du Meautry	Lake Coniston	G.Lewis	Thirty Acre Barn
1994	Hungerford Stakes	Young Ern	S.Dow	Clear Height
1994	Diadem Stakes	Lake Coniston	G.Lewis	Thirty Acre Barn
1994	Queens Vase	Silver Wedge	G.Lewis	Thirty Acre Barn
1994	Rose Of Lancaster	Urgent Request	R.Akehurst	South Hatch
1994	Prix du Palais Royal	Young Ern	S.Dow	Clear Height
1995	King George Stakes	Hever Golf Rose	T.J.Naughton	The Durdans
1995	Duke of York Stakes	Lake Coniston	G.Lewis	Thirty Acre Barn

1996	Benazet Rennen	Passion For Life	G.Lewis	Thirty Acre Barn
1995	Prix de Seine et Ost	Hever Golf Rose	T.J.Naughton	The Durdans
1995	Holsten Trophy	Hever Golf Rose	T.J.Naughton	The Durdans
1997	Prix de St George	Hever Golf Rose	T.J.Naughton	The Durdans
1997	Prix du Couvert	Hever Golf Rose	T.J.Naughton	The Durdans
1998	Prix Gontaut Biron	Running Stag	P.Mitchell	Downs House
2001	Somerville Stakes	Where or When	T.Mills	Loretta Lodge
2002	Cornwallis Stakes	Peace Offering	T.Mills	Loretta Lodge
2003	Holsten Trophy	Capricho	J. Akehurst	South Hatch
2004	Supreme Stakes	Mac Love	J.Akehurst	South Hatch
2004	Prix Eclipse	Imperial Applause	T.Mills	Loretta Lodge
2005	Laurent Perrier Champagne	Resplendent Glory	T.Mills	Loretta Lodge
2006	Grosser Preis Der Bremer	Birkspiel	S.Dow	Clear Height
2009	Thurley N. Darley Stakes	Steele Tango	R.Teal	Thirty Acre Barn

OTHER MAJOR RACES
Pre 1971

1781	Derby	Young Eclipse	D.O'Kelly	Melision Lodge
1784	Derby	Serjeant	D.O'Kelly	Melision Lodge
1838	Derby	Amato	Ralph Sherwood	Downs House
1840	Ascot Derby(King Edward VII	Bokhara	Ralph Sherwood	Downs House
1843	Ascot Derby(King Edward VII)	Amorinio	Ralph Sherwood	Downs House
1843	Coronation Stakes	La Stimata	Ralph Sherwood	Downs House
1846	Ascot Derby(King Edward VII)	Bravissimo	Ralph Sherwood	Downs House
1846	Ascot Trial St.(Queen Anne)	The Conjuror	G.Dockeray	Horse and Groom
1853	French Derby	Jouvence	Ralph Sherwood	Downs House
1853	French Oaks	Jouvence	Ralph Sherwood	Downs House
1862	Queens Stand (Kings Stand St)	Shillelagh	F.Balchin	The Warren
1869	Manchester Cup	Jove	G. Simpson	Woodcote Green
1869	New Stakes	Temple	Ralph Sherwood	Downs House
1875	All Aged St(Cork and Orrery)	Lowlander	W.Reeves	Ashley Road
1876	All Aged St(Cork and Orrery)	Lowlander	W.Reeves	Ashley Road
1876	Queens Stand (Kings Stand St)	Lowlander	W.Reeves	Ashley Road
1876	Ascot Stakes	Whitebait	W.Reeves	Ashley Road
1907	Duke of York Stakes	Simonson	Will. Nightingall	South Hatch
1911	Gimcrack Stakes	Lomond	R.Wootton	Treadwell House
1911	New Stakes (Norfolk)	Lomond	R.Wootton	Treadwell House

1912	Coventry Stakes	Shogun	R.Wootton	Treadwell House
1912	Gimcrack Stakes	Flippant	R.Wootton	Treadwell House
1913	Gold Vase (Queens Vase)	Shogun	R.Wootton	Treadwell House
1913	Alexandra Plate	Rivoli	R.Wootton	Treadwell House
1913	Ascot Trial St(Queen Anne)	Lomond	R.Wootton	Treadwell House
1913	Ascot Biennial Stakes	Stornoway	R.Wootton	Treadwell House
1913	Gimcrack Stakes	Stornoway	R.Wootton	Treadwell House
1913	Greenham Stakes	Shogun	R.Wootton	Treadwell House
1916	Irish Derby	Furore	C.V.Tabor	Holly Lodge
1926	Queen Anne Stakes	Bulger	S.Wootton	Treadwell House
1930	Irish Derby	Rock Star	W.Nightingall	South Hatch
1932	Queens Vase	Silvermere	W.Nightingall	South Hatch
1932	Lingfield Derby Trial	April The Fifth	T.Walls	The Looe
1932	Derby	April The Fifth	T.Walls	The Looe
1934	King George Stakes	Old Riley	T.Rintoul	Mannamead
1935	King George Stakes	Strathcarron	F.N.Winter	Treadwell House
1936	Imperial Stakes	Lovers Path	V.Smyth	Mospey
1936	Lingfield Derby Trial	Barrystar	W.Nightingall	South Hatch
1938	Lingfield Derby Trial	Blandstar	G.Duller	Heathcote House
1939	Molecomb Stakes	Allure	V.Smyth	Mospey
1941	Dewhurst Stakes	Canyonero	W.Nightingall	South Hatch
1942	Nunthorpe Stakes	Linklater	W.Smyth	Down Cottage
1943	Nunthorpe Stakes	Linklater	W.Smyth	Down Cottage
1943	Derby	Straight Deal	W.Nightingall	South Hatch
1943	Coventry Stakes	Orestes	W.Nightingall	South Hatch
1943	Middle Park Stakes	Orestes	W.Nightingall	South Hatch
1947	King George Stakes	Daily Mail	W.Nightingall	South Hatch
1947	Imperial Stakes	Henley In Arden	W.Nightingall	South Hatch
1947	Cornwallis Stakes	Straight Play	H.G.Smyth	Down Cottage
1948	Cheveley Park	Pambidian	W.Nightingall	South Hatch
1948	Nunthorpe Stakes	Careless Nora	J.Dines	Larchfield
1948	Princess Margaret Stakes	Azolla	W.Nightingall	South Hatch
1948	Greenham Stakes	Solar Slipper	H.G.Smyth	Down Cottage
1948	Champion Stakes	Solar Slipper	H.G.Smyth	Down Cottage
1949	Ribblesdale Stakes	Colonist	W.Nightingall	South Hatch
1949	Princess Margaret Stakes	Rose of Torridge	J.Dines	Larchfield
1949	Horris Hill Stakes	Lone Victress	W.Nightingall	South Hatch

1949	New Stakes (Norfolk)	Master Gunner	P.Thrale	Startside
1949	Queen Anne Stakes	Pambidian	W.Nightingall	South Hatch
1950	John Porter Stakes	Native Heath	V.Smyth	Mospey
1950	Gordon Stakes	Foxboro	V.Smyth	Mospey
1950	Greenham Stakes	Port O'Light	W.Nightingall	South Hatch
1950	King Edward VII Stakes	Babus Pet	G.Duller	The White House
1950	Lingfield Derby Trial	Tramper	W.Nightingall	South Hatch
1950	Jockey Club Cup	Colonist	W.Nightingall	South Hatch
1950	Royal Lodge Stakes	Khor-Mousa	P.Thrale	Startside
1950	Imperial Stakes	Clutha	V.Smyth	Mospey
1951	Horris Hill Stakes	H.V.C.	R.Smyth	Ascot House
1951	Sussex Stakes	Le Sage	T.Carey	Woodruff
1951	Oxfordshire St(Geoffrey Freer)	Le Sage	T.Carey	Woodruff
1951	Winston Churchill Stakes	Colonist	W.Nightingall	South Hatch
1951	Imperial Stakes	Zabara	V.Smyth	Mospey
1951	Cheveley Park	Zabara	V.Smyth	Mospey
1951	Cornwallis Stakes	Sir Phoenix	P.Thrale	Startside
1952	King Edward VII Stakes	Castleton	T.Carey	Woodruff
1952	Oxfordshire St (Geoffrey Freer)	Westinform	R.Smyth	Ascot House
1952	July Cup	Set Fair	W.Nightingall	South Hatch
1952	Diadem Stakes	Set Fair	W.Nightingall	South Hatch
1952	Gordon Stakes	Gay Time	W.Nightingall	South Hatch
1952	Cumberland Lodge Stakes	Rawson	S.Wootton	Treadwell House
1952	1.000 Guineas	Zabara	V.Smyth	Mospey
1952	Lingfield Oaks Trial	Zabara	V.Smyth	Mospey
1952	Coronation Stakes	Zabara	V.Smyth	Mospey
1952	Jockey Club Cup	Blarney Stone	V.Smyth	Mospey
1953	Oxfordshire St(Geoffrey Freer)	Harwin	J.Dines	Larchfield
1953	Queens Vase	Absolve	V.Smyth	Mospey
1953	Cherry Hinton Stakes	Eastern Venture	V.Smyth	Mospey
1953	Dewhurst Stakes	Infatuation	V.Smyth	Mospey
1953	Lowther Stakes	Crimson	H.E.Smyth	Down Cottage
1953	Princess of Wales Stakes	Rawson	S.Wootton	Treadwell House
1953	Royal Lodge Stakes	Infatuation	V.Smyth	Mospey
1954	Oxfordshire St(Geoffrey Freer)	Umberto	P.Thrale	Startside

247

1954	John Porter Stakes	Harwin	J.Dines	Larchfield
1954	Goodwood Cup	Blarney Stone	V.Smyth	Mospey
1954	Kings Stand Stakes	Golden Lion	C.Mitchell	Heath House
1954	Churchill Stakes	Prince Arthur	W.Nightingall	South Hatch
1954	Diadem Stakes	Set Fair	W.Nightingall	South Hatch
1954	Greenham Stakes	Infatuation	V.Smyth	Mospey
1955	Horris Hill Stakes	Clarification	V.Smyth	Mospey
1955	Solario Stakes	Castelmarino	H.Wallington	Hillcrest
1955	Sussex Stakes	My Kingdom	W.Nightingall	South Hatch
1955	Royal Lodge Stakes	Royal Splendour	W.Nightingall	South Hatch
1955	Coventry Stakes	Ratification	V.Smyth	Mospey
1955	Richmond Stakes	Ratification	V.Smyth	Mospey
1956	Sandown Classic Trail	Pearl Orama	S.Ingham	Thirty Acre Barn
1956	Cumberland Lodge	Le Pretendant	W.Nightingall	South Hatch
1956	Churchill Stakes	Le Pretendant	W.Nightingall	South Hatch
1956	Chesham Stakes	Dentivate	W.Nightingall	South Hatch
1956	Nunthorpe Stakes	Ennis	W.Nightingall	South Hatch
1956	Greenham Stakes	Ratification	V.Smyth	Mospey
1957	Lowther Stakes	Liberal Lady	P.Thrale	Startside
1957	Princess Margaret Stakes	Medina	S.Ingham	Thirty Acre Barn
1957	Challenge Stakes	Welsh Abbot	W.Nightingall	South Hatch
1958	Princess Royal Stakes	Mother Goose	W.Nightingall	South Hatch
1958	Diadem Stakes	Jack and Jill	W.Nightingall	South Hatch
1959	Diadem Stakes	Jack and Jill	W.Nightingall	South Hatch
1959	Geoffrey Freer Stakes	High Hat	W.Nightingall	South Hatch
1959	Jockey Club Cup	Prolific	W.Nightingall	South Hatch
1959	Princess Margaret Stakes	Lady Advocate	W.Nightingall	South Hatch
1959	Blue Riband	My Aladdin	W.Nightingall	South Hatch
1960	Blue Riband	Vienna	W.Nightingall	South Hatch
1960	Geoffrey Freer Stakes	High Hat	W.Nightingall	South Hatch
1960	Queens Vase	Prolific	W.Nightingall	South Hatch
1960	Jockey Club Stakes	Prolific	W.Nightingall	South Hatch
1960	Greenham Stakes	Filipepi	R.Smyth	Clear Height
1960	Lyons Maid Stakes	Apostle	S.Ingham	Thirty Acre Barn
1960	National Stakes	Kerrabee	S.Ingham	Thirty Acre Barn
1961	Cumberland Lodge Stakes	Hot Brandy	W.Nightingall	South Hatch
1961	Sandown Classic Trail	Just Great	S.Ingham	Thirty Acre Barn

248

1961	Princess of Wales Stakes	Apostle	S.Ingham	Thirty Acre Barn
1961	Jockey Club Cup	Apostle	S.Ingham	Thirty Acre Barn
1961	Lyons Maid Stakes	Vienna	W.Nightingall	South Hatch
1961	Aly Khan International Cup	High Hat	W.Nightingall	South Hatch
1961	Great Voltigeur Stakes	Just Great	S.Ingham	Thirty Acre Barn
1962	John Porter Stakes	Hot Brandy	W.Nightingall	South Hatch
1962	Prix d'Harcourt	Vienna	W.Nightingall	South Hatch
1962	Pretty Polly (Curragh)	Tropic Star	D.Whelan	Lavandou
1962	Cheshire Oaks	Tropic Star	D.Whelan	Lavandou
1962	Irish 1,000 Guineas	Lady Senator	P.Ashworth	Treadwell House
1963	Lyons Maid Stakes	Tacitus	W.Nightingall	South Hatch
1963	Solario Stakes	Penny Stall	W.Nightingall	South Hatch
1963	Coronation St(Brigadier Gerard)	Tacitus	W.Nightingall	South Hatch
1964	Coronation St (Brigadier Gerard)	Tacitus	W.Nightingall	South Hatch
1964	Westbury (Gordon Richards)	Tacitus	W.Nightingall	South Hatch
1964	Greenham Stakes	Excel	T.Gosling	Priam Lodge
1964	Queen Anne Stakes	Princelone	W.Nightingall	South Hatch
1965	Westbury (Gordon Richards)	Goupi	S.Ingham	Thirty Acre Barn
1965	Craven Stakes	Corifi	S.Ingham	Thirty Acre Barn
1965	Lingfield Oaks Trial	Quita	W.Nightingall	South Hatch
1965	2,000 Guineas	Niksar	W.Nightingall	South Hatch
1965	Irish 1,000 Guineas	Ardent Dancer	T.Gosling	Priam Lodge
1965	King Edward VII Stakes	Convamore	R.Smyth	Clear Height
1965	Hardwicke Stakes	Soderini	S.Ingham	Thirty Acre Barn
1965	John Porter Stakes	Soderini	S.Ingham	Thirty Acre Barn
1965	Jockey Club Cup	Goupi	S.Ingham	Thirty Acre Barn
1966	Coronation Cup	I Say	W.Nightingall	South Hatch
1967	King George Stakes	Right Strath	W.Nightingall	South Hatch
1966	Haydock Sprint	Be Friendly	C.Mitchell	Heath House
1966	Queen Anne Stakes	Tesco Boy	S.Ingham	Thirty Acre Barn
1967	New Stakes(Norfolk)	Porto Bello	S.Ingham	Thirty Acre Barn
1967	Imperial Stakes	Hametus	W.Nightingall	South Hatch
1967	Dewhurst Stakes	Hametus	W.Nightingall	South Hatch
1967	Greenham	Play High	W.Nightingall	South Hatch
1967	Kings Stand Stakes	Be Friendly	C.Mitchell	Heath House
1967	Haydock Sprint	Be Friendly	C.Mitchell	Heath House

249

1967	New Stakes (Norfolk)	Porto Bello	S.Ingham	Thirty Acre Barn
1968	Prix de L Abbaye	Be Friendly	C.Mitchell	Downs House
1968	Duke Of York Stakes	Hard Water	J. Sutcliffe jun.	Woodruff
1968	Hungerford Stakes	Jimmy Reppin	J. Sutcliffe jun.	Woodruff
1968	Seaton Delaval Stakes	Lady's View	P.Ashworth	Treadwell House
1968	Waterford Crystal Mile	Jimmy Reppin	J. Sutcliffe jun.	Woodruff
1968	Imperial Stakes	Right Tack	J..Sutcliffe jun.	Woodruff
1968	Middle Park Stakes	Right Tack	J. Sutcliffe jun.	Woodruff
1969	Yorkshire Cup	Quartette	T.Gosling	Priam Lodge
1969	Palace House Stakes	Be Friendly	C.Mitchell	Downs House
1969	Sceptre Stakes	Be Friendly	C.Mitchell	Downs House
1969	2,000 Guineas	Right Tack	J. Sutcliffe jun.	Woodruff
1969	Irish 2,000 Guineas	Right Tack	J. Sutcliffe jun.	Woodruff
1969	St.James Palace	Right Tack	J. Sutcliffe jun.	Woodruff
1969	Sussex Stakes	Jimmy Reppin	J. Sutcliffe jun.	Woodruff
1969	Hungerford Stakes	Jimmy Reppin	J. Sutcliffe jun.	Woodruff
1969	Queen Elizabeth II	Jimmy Reppin	J. Sutcliffe jun.	Woodruff
1969	Prix Perth	Jimmy Reppin	J.Sutcliffe jun.	Woodruff
1969	Select Stakes	Jimmy Reppin	J.Sutcliffe jun.	Woodruff
1969	Prince Of Wales Stakes	The Brianstan	J.Sutcliffe jun.	Woodruff
1969	New Stakes (Norfolk)	Tribal Chief	B.Swift	Loretta Lodge
1969	Norfolk St(Flying Childers)	Tribal Chief	B.Swift	Loretta Lodge
1970	Norfolk St (Flying Childers)	Mummys Pet	J. Sutcliffe jun.	Woodruff
1970	Prix du Moulin	Gold Rod	R.Akehurst	Hillcot
1970	King Edward VII Stakes	Great Wall	A.E.Breasley	South Hatch
1970	Greenham Stakes	Gold Rod	R.Akehurst	Hillcot
1970	Queens Vase	Yellow River	A.E.Breasley	South Hatch
1970	Prix de la Cote Normande	Gold Rod	R.Akehurst	Hillcot
1970	Nassau Stakes	Pulchra	J.Sirett	Burnside
1970	Lingfield Oaks Trial	Pulchra	J.Sirett	Burnside
1971	Coupe De Maisons Lafitte	Gold Rod	R.Akehurst	Hillcot

SOME MAJOR HANDICAPS WON BY EPSOM TRAINED HORSES

YEAR	RACE	HORSE	TRAINER	STABLE
1847	Royal Hunt Cup	Tragical	H.Bradley	Down Cottage
1850	Chester Cup	Mounseer	G.Dockeray	Horse and Groom

250

1852	Ebor	Adine	G.Dockeray	Horse and Groom
1853	Goodwood Stakes	Adine	G.Dockeray	Horse and Groom
1853	Chester Cup	Goldfinder	A.Sait	Old Wells
1863	Royal Hunt Cup	Victor	F.Balchin	The Warren
1864	Chester Cup	Flash-in-the=pan	D.Hughes	Horse and Groom
1868	Cesarewitch	Cecil	J.Nightingall	South Hatch
1865	Ebor	Verdant	F.Balchin	The Warren
1867	Chester Cup	Beeswing	J.Bentley	The Durdans
1873	Stewards Cup	Sister Helen	R.l'Anson Snr.	Walton Heath
1874	Royal Hunt Cup	Lowlander	W.Reeves	Ashley Road
1880	Lincoln	Rosy Cross	J.Martin	Bordeaux House
1895	Manchester November	Ivor	Wm. Nightingall	South Hatch
1900	City and Suburban	The Grafter	J.Brewer	Down Cottage
1901	City and Suburban	Australian Star	J.Hickey	Rowland Lodge
1905	Jubilee Handicap	Ambition	Wm. Nightingall	South Hatch
1911	Manchester Cup	Marajax	R.Wootton	Treadwell House
1912	Royal Hunt Cup	Eton Boy	H.Carter	Bruce Lodge
1913	Ascot Stakes	Rivoli	R.Wootton	Treadwell House
1917	Cesarewitch	Furore	C.V.Tabor	Holly Lodge
1925	City and Suburban	Greek Bachelor	S.Wootton	Treadwell House
1927	Liverpool Autumn Cup	Autocrat	T.Walls	The Looe
1927	Chesterfield Cup	Voltas Pride	W.Nightingall	South Hatch
1927	Cambridgeshire	Medal	S.Wootton	Treadwell House
1928	Goodwood Stakes	Arctic Star	C.V.Tabor	Holly Lodge
1928	Cesarewitch	Arctic Star	C.V.Tabor	Holly Lodge
1933	Goodwood Stakes	Prince Oxendon	V.Smyth	Mospey
1936	Cambridgeshire	Artists Prince	J.Dines	Larchfield
1936	Cesarewitch	Fet	H.Hedges	Grove Stables
1937	Cesarewitch	Punch	C.V.Tabor	Holly Lodge
1937	City and Suburban	William of Valence	H.G. Smyth	Down Cottage
1947	Portland Handicap	Good View	E.Parker	Shifnal Cottage
1949	Stewards Cup	The Bite	J.Wood	Downs House
1949	Manchester November	Fidonia	E.Parker	Shifnal Cottage
1951	Portland Handicap	Reminiscence	W.Nightingall	South Hatch
1951	Cesarewitch	Three Cheers	P.Thrale	Startside
1952	King George V Stakes	Giuliano	W.Nightingall	South Hatch
1952	Ascot Stakes	Flighty Frances	J.Dines	Larchfield

1952	Cambridgeshire	Richer	S.Ingham	Thirty Acre Barn
1952	Wokingham	Malkas Boy	W.Nightingall	South Hatch
1952	Zetland Gold Cup	Mid View	H.Wallington	Hillcrest
1953	Zetland Gold Cup	H.V.C.	R.Smyth	Ascot House
1953	Cesarewitch	Chantry	S.Ingham	Thirty Acre Barn
1954	Wokingham	The Plumbers Mate	H.E.Smyth	Down Cottage
1955	Victoria Cup	Alfs Caprice	H.Wallington	Hillcrest
1957	Goodwood Stakes	Persian Flag	W.Nightingall	South Hatch
1958	Portland Handicap	Welsh Abbot	W.Nightingall	South Hatch
1959	Victoria Cup	Alfs Caprice	H.Wallington	Hillcrest
1959	Royal Hunt Cup	Faultless Speech	H.Wallington	Hillcrest
1959	Stewards Cup	Tudor Monarch	W.Nightingall	South Hatch
1959	King George V Stakes	Suki Desu	W.Nightingall	South Hatch
1959	Zetland Gold Cup	Maddalo	P.Thrale	Startside
1959	Manchester November	Operatic Society	C.J.Benstead	The Limes
1959	William Hill Gold Cup	Faultless Speech	H.Wallington	Hillcrest
1960	Jubilee Handicap	Rocky Royale	D.Whelan	Lavandou
1960	Rosebery Stakes	Falls Of Shin	E.Parker	Shifnal Cottage
1960	Chester Cup	Hoy	L.S.Dale	Startside
1961	Ascot Stakes	Angazi	W.Nightingall	South Hatch
1961	King George V	Vinca	E.Parker	Shifnal Cottage
1961	Ayr Gold Cup	Klondyke Bill	C.J.Benstead	The Limes
1962	Wokingham	Elco	D.Whelan	Lavandou
1963	Wokingham	Marcher	D.Hanley	Heathcote House
1964	Cambridgeshire	Hasty Cloud	H.Wallington	Hillcrest
1965	King George V	Brave Knight	W.Nightingall	South Hatch
1965	Victoria Cup	Princelone	W.Nightingall	South Hatch
1965	Rosebery Stakes	Nooroose	E.Parker	Shifnal Cottage
1966	Stewards Cup	Patient Constable	R.Smyth	Clear Height
1967	Magnet Cup	Copsale	R.Smyth	Clear Height
1967	Ayr Gold Cup	Be Friendly	C.Mitchell	Heath House
1967	Victoria Cup	Hadrian	W.Nightingall	South Hatch
1967	Rosebery Stakes	Hotroy	W.Nightingall	South Hatch
1967	City and Suburban	Hotroy	W.Nightingall	South Hatch
1968	Vaux Gold Tankard	Quartette	T.Gosling	Priam Lodge
1969	Vaux Gold Tankard	Philoctetes	S.Ingham	Thirty Acre Barn
1969	Goodwood Stakes	Amberwood	C.J.Benstead	The Limes

1969	Rosebery Stakes	First Pick	H.Wallington Jnr.	Hillcrest
1970	Stewards Cup	Jukebox	H.Wallington Jnr.	Hillcrest
1970	Northumberland Plate	Philoctetes	S.Ingham	Thirty Acre Barn
1971	City and Suburban	Tandy	B.Swift	Loretta Lodge
1971	Victoria Cup	Mon Plaisir	H.Wallington Jnr.	Hillcrest
1971	Ayr Gold Cup	Royben	A.E.Breasley	South Hatch
1971	Portland Handicap	Royben	A.E.Breasley	South Hatch
1972	Cesarewitch	Cider With Rosie	S.Ingham	Thirty Acre Barn
1972	Ebor	Crazy Rhythm	S.Ingham	Thirty Acre Barn
1972	Wokingham	Le Johnstan	J.Sutcliffe jun.	Woodruff
1972	Jubilee Handicap	Grandrew	R.Smyth	Clear Height
1972	Goodwood Stakes	Biskrah	A.E. Breasley	South Hatch
1972	Royal Hunt Cup	Tempest Boy	J.Sutcliffe jun.	Woodruff
1972	Rosebery Stakes	Lord David	S.Ingham	Thirty Acre Barn
1973	Goodwood Stakes	Pamroy	A.Breasley	South Hatch
1973	Cesarewitch	Flash Imp	R.Smyth	Clear Height
1973	November Handicap	Only For Jo	R.Smyth	Clear Height
1973	Wokingham	Plummett	J.E.Sutcliffe	Ermyn Lodge
1973	Portland Handicap	Supreme Gift	B.Swift	Loretta Lodge
1974	Chester Cup	Attivo	C.Mitchell	Downs House
1974	Northumberland Plate	Attivo	C.Mitchell	Downs House
1974	Wokingham	Ginnies Pet	J.E.Sutcliffe	Ermyn Lodge
1974	Cesarewitch	Ocean King	A.Pitt	Wendover
1974	Ebor	Anji	J.Sutcliffe jun.	Woodruff
1974	Jubilee Handicap	Jumpabout	J Sutcliffe jun.	Woodruff
1975	William Hill Gold Cup	My Hussar	J Sutcliffe jun.	Woodruff
1975	Jubilee Handicap	Jumpabout	J Sutcliffe jun.	Woodruff
1975	Rosebery Stakes	William Pitt	S.Ingham	Thirty Acre Barn
1976	Ayr Gold Cup	Last Tango	J. Sutcliffe jun.	Woodruff
1976	Lincoln	The Hertford	B.Swift	Loretta Lodge
1977	Royal Hunt Cup	My Hussar	J Sutcliffe jun.	Woodruff
1977	Northumberland Plate	Tug Of War	D.Whelan	Lavandou
1978	Northumberland Plate	Tug Of War	D.Whelan	Lavandou
1978	Cambridgeshire	Baronet	C.J.Benstead	The Limes
1978	Stewards Cup	Ahonoora	B.Swift	Loretta Lodge
1979	Victoria Cup	The Adrianstan	J Sutcliffe jun.	Woodruff
1979	Wokingham	Lord Rochford	B.Swift	Loretta Lodge

1980	Jubilee Handicap	Blue Refrain	C.J.Benstead	The Limes
1980	Rosebery Stakes	Baronet	C.J.Benstead	The Limes
1980	Cesarewitch	Popsis Joy	M.Haynes	Tattenham Corner
1980	Cambridgeshire	Baronet	C.J.Benstead	The Limes
1980	Royal Hunt Cup	Tender Heart	J. Sutcliffe jun.	Woodruff
1982	Ascot Stakes	Popsis Joy	M.Haynes	Tattenham Corner
1982	Portland Handicap	Vorvados	M.Haynes	Tattenham Corner
1982	Lincoln	Kings Glory	P.Mitchell	Downs House
1982	City and Suburban	African Pearl	R.Simpson	South Hatch
1983	Cesarewitch	Bajan Sunshine	R.Simpson	South Hatch
1984	King George V	Rough Pearl	G.Lewis	Thirty Acre Barn
1984	City and Suburban	My Tony	G.Lewis	Thirty Acre Barn
1985	Victoria Cup	Tremblant	R.Smyth	Clear Height
1985	Cambridgeshire	Tremblant	R.Smyth	Clear Height
1985	City and Suburban	Redden	A.Pitt	Wendover
1986	City and Suburban	Nebris	R.Akehurst	South Hatch
1987	Ascot Vase	Inlander	R.Akehurst	South Hatch
1988	King George V	Thethingaboutitis	G.Lewis	Thirty Acre Barn
1989	Stewards Cup	Very Adjacent	G.Lewis	Thirty Acre Barn
1989	City and Suburban	Dismiss	R.Smyth	Clear Height
1989	Lincoln	Fact Finder	R.Akehurst	South Hatch
1989	Cesarewitch	Double Dutch	Miss B.Sanders	Chalk Pit
1990	Golden Mile	March Bird	J. Sutcliffe jun.	Woodruff
1991	Victoria Cup	Sky Cloud	R.Akehurst	South Hatch
1991	Golden Mile	Sky Cloud	R.Akehurst	South Hatch
1992	Golden Mile	Little Bean	G.Lewis	Thirty Acre Barn
1992	R.H.K. Jockey Club Trophy	Fire Top	R.Akehurst	South Hatch
1993	Tote Festival Handicap	Young Ern	S.Dow	Clear Height
1993	Ebor	Sarawat	R.Akehurst	South Hatch
1994	Victoria Cup	Face North	R.Akehurst	South Hatch
1994	Royal Hunt Cup	Face North	R.Akehurst	South Hatch
1994	R.H.K. Jockey Club Trophy	Knowth	R.Akehurst	South Hatch
1995	Tote Festival Handicap	Night Dance	G.Lewis	Thirty Acre Barn
1995	William Hill Cup	Silver Groom	R.Akehurst	South Hatch
1995	Wokingham	Astrac	R.Akehurst	South Hatch
1996	Ascot Stakes	Southern Power	R.Akehurst	South Hatch
1997	Victoria Cup	Tregarron	R.Akehurst	South Hatch
1997	Royal Hunt Cup	Red Robbo	R.Akehurst	South Hatch

2001	Tote Trifecta Handicap	Wannabearound	T.Mills	Loretta Lodge
2001	Rosebery Stakes	Gentleman Venture	J.Akehurst	South Hatch
2002	Hong Kong Jockey Club Sprint	Boleyn Castle	T.Mills	Loretta Lodge
2002	Royal Hunt Cup	Norton	T.Mills	Loretta Lodge
2002	Wokingham	Capricho	J.Akehurst	South Hatch
2005	Summer Stakes	Evaluator	T.Mills	Loretta Lodge
2009	Rosebery Stakes	Greylami	T.Mills	Loretta Lodge
2011	Master Collection (Dubai)	Steele Tango	R.Teal	Thirty Acre Barn

SOME MAJOR NATIONAL HUNT RACES WON BY EPSOM TRAINED HORSES

YEAR	RACE	HORSE	TRAINER	STABLE
1839	Grand National	Lottery	G.Dockeray	Mickleham
1839	Cheltenham Grand Annual	Lottery	G.Dockeray	Mickleham
1840	Grand National	Jerry	G.Dockeray	Mickleham
1841	Cheltenham Grand Annual	Lottery	G.Dockeray	Mickleham
1852	Grand National	Miss Mowbray	G.Dockeray	Church Street
1857	Grand National	Emigrant	C.Boyce	The Warren
1861	Grand National	Jealousy	C. Balchin	Sutton
1868	Sefton Chase	Roving Maid	W.Reeves	Down Cottage
1874	Liverpool Hurdle	Lowlander	W.Reeves	Field House
1875	Grand National	Pathfinder	W.Reeves	Field House
1876	Grand National Hurdle	Woodcock	J.Jones	Down Cottage
1876	Liverpool Hurdle	Whitebait	W.Reeves	Field House
1877	Grand National	Austerlitz	R.I'Anson jun.	Heath House
1877	Grand International Hurdle	Scamp	F.Adams	Pitt Place
1877	Grand National Hurdle	Citizen	W.Reeves	Field House
1877	Grand Sefton Chase	Citizen	W.Reeves	Field House
1877	Cheltenham Grand Annual	Chimney Sweep	J.Jones	Down Cottage
1878	Grand Sefton Chase	Chimney Sweep	J.Jones	Down Cottage
1878	Grand National	Shifnal	J.Nightingall	South Hatch
1879	Prince Of Wales Chase	High Priest	J.Jones	Down Cottage
1879	Scottish Grand National	Military	W.Reeves	Field House
1879	Kempton Park Grand Hurdle	Bacchus	R.I'Anson jun.	Heath House
1880	Kempton Park Grand Hurdle	Sign Manual	J.Jones	Down Cottage
1881	Grand International Hurdle	Lord Clive	J.Nightingall	South Hatch

255

1881	Champion Chase	Bacchus	R.I'Anson jun.	Heath House
1881	Sandown Grand Prize	Northfleet	J.Potter	York House
1882	Kempton Park Grand Hurdle	Theophrastus	J.Jones	Priam Lodge
1882	Grand National Hurdle	Theophrastus	J.Jones	Priam Lodge
1882	Prince Of Wales Chase	Mickey	R. I'Anson jun.	Heath House
1886	Liverpool Hurdle	Hungarian	J.Jones	Priam Lodge
1887	Liverpool Hurdle	Skyscraper	W.Holt	Church Street
1887	Sandown Grand Prize	Courtier	J.Nightingall	South Hatch
1888	Grand Sefton Chase	Magic	J.Jones	Priam Lodge
1889	Sandown Grand Prize	Castilian	J.Nightingall	South Hatch
1888	Grand International Hurdle	Freedom	J.Nightingall	South Hatch
1889	Lancashire Chase	Magic	J.Jones	Priam Lodge
1890	Grand National	Ilex	J.Nightingall	South Hatch
1890	Liverpool Hurdle	Toscano	Wm. Nightingall	South Hatch
1890	Lancashire Chase	Ilex	J.Nightingall	South hatch
1896	Grand Sefton Chase	Rory O'Moore	Wm. Nightingall	South Hatch
1901	Grand International Hurdle	Puerto	S.Ambler	Down Cottage
1903	Champion Chase	Rose Wreath	S.Ambler	Down Cottage
1904	Grand National	Moifaa	J.Hickey	Rowland Lodge
1905	Grand International Hurdle	Lucinda	Wm.Nightingall	South Hatch
1907	Grand International Hurdle	Rassendtyl	Wm.Nightingall	South Hatch
1907	Great Sandown Hurdle	Simonson	Wm.Nightingall	South Hatch
1908	Imperial Cup	Perseus	J.M.Bell	Priam Lodge
1914	Imperial Cup	Vermouth	J.M.Bell	Woodcote Rise
1915	Grand International Hurdle	Desmond's Song	J.M.Bell	Woodcote Rise
1915	Jubilee Hurdle	Fil d'Ecosse	F.Grundy	
1915	Lancashire Chase	Vermouth	J.M.Bell	Woodcote Rise
1916	Grand National	Vermouth	J.M.Bell	Woodcote Rise
1920	Two Thousand Hurdle	Trespasser	J.M.Bell	Woodcote Rise
1920	Imperial Cup	Trespasser	J.M.Bell	Woodcote Rise
1921	Imperial Cup	Trespasser	J.M.Bell	Woodcote Rise
1921	Grand International Hurdle	Morganatic Marriage	J.M.Bell	Woodcote Rise
1922	Imperial Cup	Trespasser	J.M.Bell	Woodcote Rise
1922	Grand International Hurdle	Forest Fire	J.M.Bell	Woodcote Rise
1922	Broadway Novices Chase	Victor Noir	H.G.Smyth	Downs House
1923	Scottish Grand National	Harrismith	W.Payne	Heath House
1924	Imperial Cup	Noce d'Argent	S.Wootton	Treadwell House

1924	Grand International Hurdle	Chartered	J.M. Bell	Woodcote Rise
1925	Imperial Cup	Scotch Pearl	Wm. Nightingall	South Hatch
1925	Gloucestershire Hurdle	Imprudence	W.Larkin	Bruce Lodge
1926	Imperial Cup	Peeping Tom	J.M.Bell	Woodcote Rise
1927	Imperial Cup	Zeno	Walt.Nightingall	South Hatch
1927	Jubilee Hurdle	Zeni	Walt. Nightingall	South Hatch
1927	Champion Hurdle	Blaris	W.Payne	Heath House
1928	Grand International Hurdle	Tide	J.M. Bell	Woodcote Rise
1929	Imperial Cup	Hercules	J.M.Bell	Woodcote Rise
1930	Liverpool Hurdle	Arctic Star	Walt. Nightingall	South Hatch
1931	Grand International Hurdle	Telegraphic	J.M. Bell	Woodcote Rise
1932	Scottish Grand National	Clydesdale	W.Payne	Heath House
1932	Imperial Cup	Last of the Dandies	W.Payne	Heath House
1932	Champion Chase	Colliery Band	W.Payne	Heath House
1933	Cotswold Chase	Ready Cash	W.Payne	Heath House
1933	Scottish Grand National	Libourg	W.Payne	Heath House
1934	Liverpool Hurdle	Advancer	Walt. Nightingall	South Hatch
1936	Victory Chase	Argental	W.Payne	Heath House
1936	Grand International Hurdle	Wheatley	W.Nightingall	South hatch
1937	Champion Chase	Airgeod Sios	C.V.Tabor	Holly Lodge
1937	Becher Chase	Airgeod Sios	C.V.Tabor	Holly Lodge
1937	Grand Annual Chase	Airgeod Sios	C.V.Tabor	Holly Lodge
1938	Becher Chase	Airgeod Sios	C.V.Tabor	Holly Lodge
1938	King George VI Chase	Airgeod Sios	C.V.Tabor	Holly Lodge
1939	Imperial Cup	Mange Toute	G.Duller	Heathcote House
1940	Grand International Hurdle	Carlton	F.Winter	Rowland Lodge
1940	Liverpool Hurdle	Celibate II	D.Dick	Glanmire Farm
1941	Champion Hurdle	Seneca	V.Smyth	Mospey
1942	Champion Hurdle	Forestation	V.Smyth	Mospey
1947	Champion Hurdle	National Spirit	V.Smyth	Mospey
1948	Grand Annual Chase	Clareman	Walt.Nightingall	South Hatch
1948	Champion Hurdle	National Spirit	V.Smyth	Mospey
1948	Gloucestershire Hurdle	Prince Rupert	H.G.Smyth	Down Cottage
1948	Champion Chase	Luan Casca	H.G.Smyth	Down Cottage
1948	Imperial Cup	Anglesey	S.Ingham	Thirty Acre Barn
1948	Lancashire Chase	Bronze Angel	V.Smyth	Mospey
1949	Oteley Hurdle	National Spirit	V.Smyth	Mospey

257

1950	Oteley Hurdle	National Spirit	V.Smyth	Mospey
1951	Gloucestershire Hurdle	Red Stranger	R.Smyth	Ascot House
1951	Imperial Cup	Master Bidar	R.Smyth	Ascot House
1952	Fielden Hurdle	Pont Cordonnier	V.Smyth	Mospey
1954	Tote Pattern H'cap Chase	Claude Duval	P.Thrale	Startside
1954	Triumph Hurdle	Prince Charlemagne	T.Carey	Woodruff
1955	Imperial Cup	Bon Mot	S.Wootton	Treadwell House
1957	Triumph Hurdle	Meritorious	P.Thrale	Startside
1958	Triumph Hurdle	Pundit	S.Ingham	Thirty Acre Barn
1959	Imperial Cup	Langton Heath	T.Griffiths	Mayfields
1960	King George VI Chase	Saffron Tartan	D.Butchers	Priam Lodge
1960	Cotswold Chase (Arkle)	Mazurka	R.Smyth	Clear Height
1960	Whitbread Gold Cup	Plummers Plain	L.S.Dale	Startside
1961	Agfa Diamond Chase	Carraroe	C.Mitchell	Heath House
1961	Cheltenham Gold Cup	Saffron Tartan	D.Butchers	Priam Lodge
1962	Fairlawne Chase	Hedgelands	C.Mitchell	Heath House
1962	Oteley Hurdle	Snuff Box	C.J.Benstead	The Limes
1962	Imperial Cup	Irish Imp	R.Smyth	Clear Height
1962	Kim Muir Memorial Ch.	Carrickbeg	D.Butchers	Priam Lodge
1964	Imperial Cup	Invader	L.S.Dale	Startside
1964	Gloucestershire Hurdle	Elan	J. Sutcliffe jun.	Woodruff
1965	Schweppes Gold Trophy	Elan	J. Sutcliffe jun.	Woodruff
1965	Triumph Hurdle	Blarney Beacon	R.Smyth	Clear Height
1965	Imperial Cup	Kildavin	J. Sutcliffe jun.	Woodruff
1966	Buchanan Whisky Hdle	Nikko	R.Smyth	Clear Height
1967	Fielden Hurdle	Secret Agent	C.J.Benstead	The Limes
1967	Triumph Hurdle	Persian War	B.Swift	Loretta Lodge
1968	Triumph Hurdle	Englands Glory	S.Ingham	Thirty Acre Barn
1969	Tote Placepot Hurdle	Rabble Rouser	R.Akehurst	Hillcot
1969	SGB Hire Shop Hurdle	Moyne Royal	R.Akehurst	Hillcot
1970	Buchanan Whisky H. Hdle	Cala Mesquida	J.E.Sutcliffe	Ermyn Lodge
1970	Holsten Diat Pils Hurdle	Moyne Royal	R.Akehurst	Hillcot
1970	Irish Sweeps Hurdle	Persian War	A.Pitt	Wendover
1970	SGB Hire Shop Hurdle	Bowies Brig	A.Pitt	Wendover
1971	Grand National	Specify	J.E.Sutcliffe	Ermyn Lodge
1971	Triumph Hurdle	Boxer	R.Smyth	Clear Height
1971	Compton Chase	Lucky Edgar	R.Smyth	Clear Height

1971	Schweppes Gold Trophy	Cala Mesquida	J.E.Sutcliffe	Ermyn Lodge
1972	Imperial Cup	Spy Net	L.S.Dale	Startside
1972	Buchanan Whisky H. Hdle	Moyne Royal	A.Pitt	Wendover
1973	Kirk And Kirk Ascot Hurdle	Moyne Royal	A.Pitt	Wendover
1973	Cheltenham Stayers Hdle	Moyne Royal	A.Pitt	Wendover
1973	Schweppes Gold Trophy	Indianapolis	J.E.Sutcliffe	Ermyn Lodge
1974	Greenham Group H. Hdle	Legal Tender	S.Ingham	Thirty Acre Barn
1974	Tote Placepot Hurdle	Supreme Halo	R.Smyth	Clear Height
1974	Mecca H'cap Hurdle	Supreme Halo	R.Smyth	Clear Height
1974	Imperial Cup	Flash Imp	R.Smyth	Clear Height
1974	Fielden Hurdle	Flash Imp	R.Smyth	Clear Height
1974	Triumph Hurdle	Attivo	C.Mitchell	Downs House
1975	Midlands Grand National	Rag Trade	A.Pitt	Wendover
1975	Buchanan Whisky H. Hurdle	Supreme Halo	R.Smyth	Clear Height
1975	Holsten Diat Pils Hurdle	William Pitt	S.Ingham	Thirty Acre Barn
1975	Premier Long Distance Hdl.	Moyne Royal	A.Pitt	Wendover
1981	Tote Placepot Hurdle	Ra Tapu	P.Mitchell	Downs House
1984	Summit Junior Hurdle	Beat The Retreat	J.Jenkins	Woodcote Stud
1984	Game Spirit Chase	Ragafan	R.Smyth	Clear Height
1985	Tolworth Hurdle	Wing And A Prayer	J.Jenkins	Woodcote Stud
1987	Swinton Handicap Hurdle	Inlander	R.Akehurst	South Hatch
1987	Imperial Cup	Inlander	R.Akehurst	South Hatch
1988	Tolworth Hurdle	Wishlon	R.Smyth	Clear Height
1988	Tote Placepot Hurdle	Russian Affair	R.Akehurst	South Hatch
1989	Swinton Insurance Hurdle	Inlander	R.Akehurst	South Hatch
1991	Summit Junior Hurdle	None So Brave	R.Akehurst	South Hatch
1992	Finale Junior Hurdle	Dare To Dream	R.Akehurst	South Hatch
1992	Summit Junior Hurdle	Dare To Dream	R.Akehurst	South Hatch
1993	Tote Placepot Hurdle	Amazon Express	R.Akehurst	South Hatch
1993	Summit Junior Hurdle	Admirals Well	R.Akehurst	South Hatch
1994	Sandown Chap Hurdle	Dark Honey	S.Dow	Clear Height
1994	Seagram Top Novices Hdle	Jazilah	R.Akehurst	South Hatch
1994	Dovecote Novices Hurdle	Jazilah	R.Akehurst	South Hatch
1994	Kennel Gate Hurdle	Gaasid	R.Akehurst	South Hatch
1996	Aintree Hurdle	Bimsey	R.Akehurst	South Hatch
1997	Book Of Music Nov. Chase	Chiefs Song	S.Dow	Clear Height
2013	Imperial Cup	First Avenue	L.Mongan	Condover

APPENDIX B
HORSES TRAINED AT EPSOM, MICKLEHAM AND SUTTON IN THE 19th CENTURY.

Sources:
- bl = Bell's Life in London &Sporting Chronicle
- era = The Era
- yh = York Herald
- sp = The Sportsman
- sg = Sporting Gazette
- sl = Sporting Life

bl	bl	bl	bl	bl	era	yh	yh bl	bl	bl	yh	bl

*Source indicates other horses were in the stable

	1839	1840	1841	1842	1843	1844	1845	1846	1847	1848	1849	1850
G.DOCKERAY	6*		6	12	8	8	8	8*	3*			10
R.SHERWOOD	12	11	11	11	12	13	14	15	11	11	11	
E.WRIGHT	5		3	9	5							
G.BOAST	3		2									
G.LAMBDEN	1								1*			
J.BALCHIN			5	7			5	5				
W.SMITH			7	1	10	7						
MAY				4								
S.DAY						9						
W.LUMLEY						3						8
R.DREWITT							3		6			
G.LANGRIDGE							5	4				
H.BRADLEY							2	6	9	9	6	
H.BELL											5	
J.REEVES												3

Sources: bl=   Bell's Life in London &Sporting Chronicle

	bl	bl	bl	bl	bl	bl	bl	bl	bl	bl
	1851	1852	1853	1854	1855	1856	1857	1858	1859	1860
G.DOCKERAY	11*		18							
R.SHERWOOD	12		6	7	3	4	3	14	9	3
W.LUMLEY			4	5	5			5		3
H.BRADLEY	6	7								
F.CROUCH	2									
W.& C. BALCHIN		6								
W.REEVES	9	2	11*	10			15	33	12	16
Down cottage										
H.J.WYCHERLEY		7	10							
W.MAY			3		4					
W.HOTHAM			4							
A.SAIT				4						
C.SEARLE				8			2	2	5	7
G.MILNE					4				5	8
J.ESCOTT							13			
C.BALCHIN								13		
H.PATTISON								16	3	
J.GREGORY								9	9	5
Private								14	6	6
J.ARMSTRONG								9		12
C.BOYCE								5		
J.HUGHES								11		
D.HUGHES										22
W.BURBRIDGE									5	8
MR. MELLISH										10
F.A. BALCHIN										12

261

Sources: bl=   Bell's Life in London &Sporting Chronicle
               yh=   York Herald
               sl=   Sporting Life

	yh bl	bl	bl sg	bl sg	bl sg	bl	bl sp	bl sp sl	bl sp	yh sp
	1861	1862	1863	1864	1865	1866	1867	1868	1869	1870
H.PATTISON	20									
R.SHERWOOD			2		5		6	9	17	13
B.LAND		15								
C.SEARLE	12			5						
Private				22				8		
J.ARMSTRONG	12		10					6		
J.HUGHES	26	23	21							
D.HUGHES									26	
T.HUGHES								17		15
W.REEVES	30	23	18	28	24	20	30	51	43	
Down Cottage										
G.MILNE		6						3		
W.BURBRIDGE				9				9	10	7
R.I'ANSON	17	12			10		14	18	9	
G.SIMPSON	9	6	9			3	5	3	6	10
John NIGHTINGALL	9	7	12	24	27	29	31	35	31	37
F.A.BALCHIN	20	3	18	32	43	41	20			
E.WRIGHT		2	2		10					
J.POTTER							4	7	21	
H.FORSTER								8	8	
W.REEVES								20	4	5
Field House										
J.BENTLEY								10	10	
O.REEVES								2		
W.PUTTRELL									3	6
J,CARTER									5	
J.SEARLE									3	
F.POOLEY										5
T.LEWIN										3
W.ROBINSON										2
J.MARTIN										10
T.BARTON										4
F.MARTIN										2
Jas. NIGHTINGALL										4
J.REEVES							3			

Sources: bl=   Bell's Life in London &Sporting Chronicle
yh=   York Herald
sp=   The Sportsman
sg=   Sporting Gazette

	sp / sg	bl	sg / bl	bl	yh / bl	yh	yh / sc	yh / sp	sp	bl
	1871	1872	1873	1874	1875	1875	1877	1878	1879	1880
R.& T. SHERWOOD	20				12					
R.SHERWOOD		18								
T.SHERWOOD								6		12
J.POTTER							2			
H.FORSTER			4							
W.REEVES	3		14		18	19	3			
Field House										
J.SEARLE							1	18		
J.MARTIN	6		12		7			14		
T.BARTON	2									
F.MARTIN	2									
Jas. NIGHTINGALL	6		14	11	12	10		12		
W.ROE	3									
S.WARRENER	14									
J.DEACON					3					
J.JONES	13		13	20	30		24			
H.E.MAY			20							
H.GIBSON	12									
J.HARRISON	5									
GOSLING & ANSLEY			18							
J.ARMSTRONG							9			
JOHN NIGHTINGALL	32	41	37	32	27		36			30
W.REEVES	18									
Down Cottage										
G.SIMPSON	16						3	4		
D.HUGHES							10			
R.I'ANSON							25		26	
W.GOSLING					27					
G.HILL					2					
J.ADAMS						8	6			
F.ADAMS							1	44		
E.CASWELL							13			
J.CHANDLER							5			
MR. CHILDERS							1			
W,REEVES										25
Field House										
C.LAWRENCE								10		8
W.COODE										13

263

Sources: bl = Bell's Life in London & Sporting Chronicle
sp = The Sportsman
sl = Sporting Life

	bl 1881	bl 1882	sl 1883	1884	sp 1885	sp 1887	sp 1888	1889	sl 1890
J.JONES	25	32			33				
R.WAITING							8		
J.WINFIELD						6	10		
J.MARTIN		3	2			6	1		
H.D.BARNES									4
J.NIGHTINGALL	43	39	28			33			44
T.SHERWOOD		4				6	13		
W.REEVES		11							
Field House									
C.LAWRENCE	7	11							
W.COODE			13						
R.WYATT		21	20						
W.DAVIES		7							

Sources: sl=Sporting Life
sp=The Sportsman
HiT=Horses in Training

	sl	sl	HiT sl	sl	sl	sl	sl		sp
	1891	1892	1893	1894	1895	1896	1897	1898	1899
E.GRAY			6						
D.MANNING			3						
T.SHERWOOD		17	27	21			22		26
W.HOLT			15		12	17	25		
A.NIGHTINGALL			8						
W.NIGHTINGALL		32	22			29	33		33
MR. H. HARPER			1						
J.ADAMS	29	41	27	18					
W,H.REDMAN	8		4						
G.VINCENT			4						
A.WILLSON							14		
J.FREEMAN							20		

APPENDIX C

TRAINERS AT EPSOM Since 1900

	1900	1901	1902	1903	1904	1905	1906	1907	1908	1909
BARNES, H.D.	x	x	x	x	5	2	6	4		
Althorp Lodge										
Bush Lodge 04										
COBB,Francis	x	x	x	x						
Heath House										
GIBSON,James	x	x	x	x						
Eclipse Cottage										
GREUSIL,Philip	x	x	x							
Humphrey Villas, Burgh Heath Road										
HICKEY,James	x	x	x	10	10					
Rowland Lodge										
HOLT,William	x	x	x	12	?	8	12	6	4	5
Heathcote House										
INGE,William	x	x	x	x						
The Cottage										
MITCHELL,C	x									
NIGHTINGALL,Arthur	x					x	x	x		
Priam Lodge 00, Badminton1905										
NIGHTINGALL,William	x	x	x	29	33	46	41	45	50	48
South Hatch										
ORRELL,J	x	x								
Heath House										
SHERWOOD,Thomas	x	x	x	30	25	11	12	8	?	x
Downs House										
TAYLOR,John	x	x								
Downs Lodge										
ADAMS,William	?	x								
The Cottage										
HALL,William		x								
The Grove										
MACKSEY,Henry	?	x	x	x	x	x				
Priam Lodge										

	1900	1901	1902	1903	1904	1905	1906	1907	1908	1909
HUMPAGE,William			x							
I'ANSON,Robert	?	?	x	x	x	x				
Priam Lodge										
LONGHURST			x							
ALFORD				x						
AMBLER,Sam				x	x	x	x			
Down Cottage, Uplands										
CLEMENTS,John A.				x	x					
Heath House										
COVINGTON,A				x						
Downs Lodge										
KELLY,Joseph				x	x	x	x	x	17	
Holly Lodge,Kingswood										
WILDE,H				x	?	10	x	x		
Uplands										
BLACKMORE					x					
Worple Road										
CALEY,H					x					
Ashtead										
CARTER,M.					x	x	x	3		
Treadwell House										
COLEMAN,John					x	x	x			
The Farm, Church Street										
DOWLING,C					x	?	13	4		
The Warren										
GREEN,G					x	x				
Seabright										
GULLY,G					x	20	12			
Heath House										
PARKES,J					x					
PLATT,A					x					

	1900	1901	1902	1903	1904	1905	1906	1907	1908	1909
PERSSE,H.S.					x	25				
Althorp Lodge										
SAWREY COOKSON,Ernest					x	14				
Ashtead										
SIFFLE,W					x					
WYLDE,E					x	x	x	x		
BATES,E						x	5	4	7	7
The Rhodrons										
Althorp Lodge										
BARCLAY,George Jnr.						x	x	5		
Ashtead										
FENNING,B						x	x			
FORRAN,J						x				
JACKSON, Captain						3	5	3		
Downs Lodge										
JOHNSON,Edward						x	11	x	x	?
Althorp Lodge										
LOVE,A.						4				
Downs Lodge										
LEARY,J.						5				
LONGTON,W						x				
Downs Lodge										
PARKES,A.W.						x	x	4		
The Cottage										
McALLISTER,William						x	x	13	17	18
Woodcote Rise										
PAGE,Dennis						4				
Rowland Lodge										
PHILLIPS,G						6				
The Paddocks										

	1900	1901	1902	1903	1904	1905	1906	1907	1908	1909
PLUMB,A						x				
The Warren										
RISTE,Jonathan						x	3	8	5	7
Priam Lodge										
WOOTTON,Richard							x	x	29	42
Treadwell House										
KELLY,T.							10	16		
Holly Lodge										
WATKINSON							x	x		
COVE,H.J.								x		
DICKENSON								x		
TABOR,C.Victor								x	x	12
Derby Arms										
GARRETT,Harry									4	
Bush Lodge										
PHILLIPS,Harry									x	3
PHILLIPS,J.									5	x
Woodcote										
DULLER,George									9	22
The Chalet										
GOBY,Ted									13	19
Badminton										
ARNOLD,J										6
GLEESON,P									x	14
Heath House										
GOODGAMES,R										3
BARCLAY,R.										x
GREEN,J										6
The Warren										
McKENNA,J										16
Down Cottage										
PLATT,James W.										8
Priam Lodge										
WESTLAKE,J										6

	1910	1911	1912	1913	1914	1915	1916	1917	1918	1919
BATES,E.	7	7	5	x	x					
Downs Lodge 10										
The Rhodrons										
BELL,James	x	x	x	9	6	9	x	x	x	x
Woodcote Rise										
BRITTLE,C.	14									
CARTER,H.	8	20	26	24	31	21				
Bruce Lodge										
DULLER,George Snr.	19	45	?	18	16	17	x	x		
The Chalet 1910,12-17										
Down Cottage 1911										
GLEESON,P.	12	8	x	4						
Heath House										
GOBY,Ted	12	26	17	7	10	11	x	x		
Heathcote House										
Badminton										
KELLY,Joseph	x	19	x	15	10	10	x			
Derby Arms										
KEMP,Robert	x	8	9	11	12	x				
Ashtead 1912										
The Downs										
McALLISTER,William	14	14					x			
Woodcote Rise										
MORGAN,Dick	14	12	8							
Badminton										
MORGAN,W.	5									
The Warren										
NIGHTINGALL,William	38	35	25	25	31	31	x	15	16	8
South Hatch										

	1910	1911	1912	1913	1914	1915	1916	1917	1918	1919
OLIVER,W.	3	x	x							
Althorp Lodge										
PHILLIPS,J.	13	10	5	6	9	7	?	4	2	
Rowland Lodge 1910,										
Woodcote Rise										
PLATT,Jim	x	x								
Priam Lodge										
RISTE,Jonathan	12	10	5	6	9	7	?	4	2	
Priam Lodge										
SHERWOOD,Tom	3									x
Downs House										
WHEELER,Robert	x									
Downs House										
WOOTTON,Richard	43	44	43	44	43		x			
Treadwell House										
BELL,Stuart		x	x							
Woodcote Rise										
EDWARDS		?								
Uplands										
HAYES		x								
Worple Road										
POOLE,A.		x	x	x			?			
NIGHTINGALL,John		11	5	6	7	9	x	?		
Beech Cottage										
SCHOFIELD,Thomas		3	5	8	17	x				
Ashley Road										
SHERWOOD,Robert H.		3								

	1910	1911	1912	1913	1914	1915	1916	1917	1918	1919
TABOR,C.Victor		25	39	38	24		x	24	x	x
Downs House (Derby Arms)										
Holly Lodge										
WOOD,John		x	10	8	11		x	x		
The Cottage										
HOGG,Thomas		x	x	19					x	x
Caithness, Uplands										
KENNEDY,G.			20	10	x	x	x			
Rowland Lodge										
MORGAN,Thomas			x	x	x		x			
RHODES, M.N.			x					x		x
PLATT,A.			x	x						
YOUNG, Charles F.		x	6	11	9	6	?	x	?	x
Burgh Heath Road										
HYAMS,George			x	13	17	18	x	18	15	18
Down Cottage										
HAMPSON,Alfred				x	8	10	x	10	9	9
Hillcrest										
PRIESTLY, Francis V.				x		x				
Caversham House										
BELL,Oswald			x	x	10	6				x
Priam Lodge, Grange										
DAY,John					x	x				
Heathcote House										
RINTOUL,Thomas				x	x	x		x	x	x
Heath House										
WATKINS					x	?				
Kingswood										
CULLEN,William P.						9				
Heathcote House										
GRUNDY,F.						39		?	?	
Heathcote House										
NIQUET, M.L.						7				

	1910	1911	1912	1913	1914	1915	1916	1917	1918	1919
WOOTTON,Stanley						37		x		x
Treadwell House										
WOOTTON,Frank						10			x	
Treadwell House										
STANTON							x			
COLEMAN, J.								x	x	
The Farm										
COTTRILL,Henry L.							x	37	x	
South Hatch										
BELL,Major Marmaduke								x	x	5
The Grange										
JACKSON,J.								x		
WALLS,Tom								x		2
The Paddocks										
HACKETT, James F.									x	9
Rowland Lodge										
HAVELOCK-ALLEN,								x	x	
Woodcote Rise										
LYNG,W.									x	
Priam Lodge										
NEWEY									x	
South Hatch										
RANDELL,Charles A.									x	x
SHERRARD,F.R.									x	21
Treadwell House										
BARNES,H.D.										x
CALDICOTT,E.J.										4
GODFREY,Edward S.									?	x
Bruce Lodge										
LAING WARD										20
Heathcote House										
BERG, Horace										?
The Downs										
	217	300	228	282	282	264		112	44	96

n.b. Figures from 1916-1919 incomplete

273

	1920	1921	1922	1923	1924	1925	1926	1927	1928	1929
BARNES, H.D. *Flint House*	x	x								
BELL,Jim *Woodcote Rise*	x	x	10	9	4	6	8	10	5	?
BELL,Marmaduke *The Grange*	9	9	3	3	3					
BERG,Horace *Downs (Derby Arms)*	14									
DAY,John *Heathcote House*	10									
GOBY,Ted *Badminton*	8	14	9	3	10	9	11	7	8	6
GODFREY, Edward *Bruce Lodge*	21									
GRAY, George *Headley*	?									
HAMPSON, Alfred *Hillcrest*	6									
HYAMS,George *Down Cottage*	31	19	11	7	15	12	11	11	8	6
MORGAN,Dick *The Durdans*	x	19						x		
NIGHTINGALL,Art.	6									
NIGHTINGALL,John *Beech Cottage*	10	7	3	2	1	4	8	7	7	5
NIGHTINGALL,Will. *South Hatch*	32	43	39	32	42	54	60			
RISTE,Jonathan *Priam Lodge*	4	2	6	1	6	x				

	1920	1921	1922	1923	1924	1925	1926	1927	1928	1929
TABOR,C.Victor	20	?	34	23	42	37	30	28	24	30
Holly Lodge										
WOOTTON,Stanley	27	23	30	39	53	52	52	58	25	61
Treadwell House and Shifnal Cottage										
GOODMAN,J.		3	x	1	x					
HANLEY,M.		x	x	2						
Downs (Derby Arms0										
LARKIN,Bill		4	4	18	15	15	13	15	26	12
Bruce Lodge										
McNAUGHTON,Bernard		14								
Hillcrest										
NEWMAN,C.		x								
REARDON,Dennis		x	x							
WALKINGTON,S.		x								
BARCLAY,George Jnr.		x	7	8	6	9	8	7		
Hillcrest										
BENNETT,Gilbert		x	20	31	40	50				
Downs Lodge										
DULLER,George Snr.		x	15	8	9	7	7	6	7	?
Ascot House										
KILLALEE,James		x	x	3	11	7	14	14	12	?
Portland House										
RINTOUL,Thomas	x	x								
Heath House										
TAGG,T		x			8	?	4			
Woodlands										
FITZGERALD,W.			3	6	3	4	7			
MARTIN,Teddy		x	x	17	28	25	32			
Rowland Lodge										
LANGLANDS, Cecil W.			5	9	10	3	3	5	4	7
Hazon House										

	1920	1921	1922	1923	1924	1925	1926	1927	1928	1929
SHERWOOD,Laurence			2	4						
Downs House										
SIMPSON,A.			x							
Priam Lodge										
SMYTH,Herbert G.			14	20	22	22	21	21	28	22
Downs (Derby Arms)										
ALLDEN,George			?	9						
Langley Bottom										
DONNELLY,W.	x	x	x	x	x					
Sandown Lodge,Priam Lodge										
KEMP,Robert			x	12	13	10	11	10	8	6
Heathcote House										
McKENNA,H.			x	3					?	?
Hazelwood 28/29										
PAYNE,Bill			x	19	29	34	35	33	36	29
Heath House										
WALLS,Tom			x	4	6	7	9	11	19	11
The Paddocks										
The Grange, North Looe 28										
CAMERON,Bill				1	6	5	5	3	2	2
Priam Lodge										
ELLIS,B.				2						
HEDGES,Harry				1	14	11	7	11	15	9
The Grove										
PENDARVES,Jack				4	3	9	12	14	28	42
The Birches/Church Street										
POOLE,W.				7						
Glanmire Farm										
REARDON,Jack				3	9	4	4	?		
Chelmer										
ALLDEN,Percy					6	13	7	7		11
Gondola										
CARY,W.					5					

	1920	1921	1922	1923	1924	1925	1926	1927	1928	1929
CRAVEN,E.S.					x	5				
Caithness										
DOWNES,J.					4					
HANLEY,Sam					8	2	3	?	?	x
Turbine Stud										
HYDE,Stuart					x	6				
Farm Stables, Church Street										
HANSON, F.T.						4	4			
REARDON, Michael						13	9	8	14	?
Abele Villas										
STEVENS, Charles						x				
Downs Lodge										
SMYTH,Victor							x	23	32	24
Mospey										
NIGHTINGALL,Walter								45	60	56
South Hatch										
WOOTTON,Frank								x	7	x
Treadwell House										
DOYLE,E.									10	x
FALLON,J.									x	
The Grange										
HENTON,R.									?	?
Caithness										
KELLY,J.									x	x
The Haven, College Road										
PICKLES,A.										x
Hillcrest										
DULLER, George Jnr.										x
Down Cottage										
Annual Total	198	157	215	311	431	439	395	354	385	339

Note x = trainer based at Epsom but numbers of horses unknown
Note ? =trainer believed to be based at Epsom

	1930	1931	1932	1933	1934	1935	1936	1937	1938	1939
ALLDEN,Percy	9	15	9	10	8	24				
Gondola										
BARCLAY,Geo Jnr.	x	6								
Hillcrest										
BARCLAY, Richard	x	x	12	11	6	x	2	x	x	4
Hillcrest										
BARNETT,C.	x	6								
Turbine Stud										
BELL,Jim	7	3	4	3						
Heathcote House										
DICK,David P.	x	x	x	9	10	x	3	9	9	10
Glanmire Farm										
GOBY,Ted	5	8								
Badminton										
HANLEY,Sam	x	x	12	10	?	6	8	4	7	4
Seabright										
HEDGES,Harry	15	30	7	9	11	7	12	10	12	17
The Grove										
HYAMS,George	1	?								
Down Cottage										
KELLY, J	x	x	x	3	x	x	x			
The Haven,College Road										
KILLALEE,James	x	x	x	6	8	x	x	x	x	x
Portland House										
LANGLANDS, Cec.	9	11	7	7	10	17	12	8	10	14
Thirty Acre Barn										
LARKIN,Bill	10	4	?	5	5					
Bruce Lodge										
NIGHTINGALL,Jn	6	4	4	3	3	5	5	4	x	4
Beech Cottage										
NIGHTINGALL,Walt	59	61	63	62	60	58	64	55	71	88
South Hatch										
PAYNE,Bill	19	x	30	34	41	32	15	11	16	16
Heath House										
PENDARVES,Jack	41	29	23	27	18	19	11	12		
The Birches, Priam Lodge 34										

	1930	1931	1932	1933	1934	1935	1936	1937	1938	1939
PICKLES,A.	4									
Hillcrest										
REARDON,Jack	x	9	9	11	12	9	9	11	12	8
Ermyn Lodge										
SMYTH,Herbert G.	22	25	17	18	15	19	19	26	33	23
The Downs (Derby Arms)										
Down Cottage										
SMYTH,Victor	30	34	27	32	52	45	50	57	53	60
Mospey										
SMYTH,William	7	12	13	7	8	6	8	8	9	
Woodcote Rise										
Down Cottage										
TABOR,C.Victor	29	31	22	26	25	16	21	27	31	33
Holly Lodge										
WALLS,Tom	22	18	5	14	8	8	15	16	15	20
The Looe										
WINTER,Fred N.	x	7	14	10	17	9	18	9	8	9
Bredenbury, Treadwell House34, Rowland Lodge 37										
WOOD,John	x	5	3	3	5	8	4	9	7	5
Badminton										
Warren Farm 34										
WOOTTON,Stanley	?	26	25	25	32	27	24	19	10	11
Treadwell House										
Shifnal Cottage 33										
RINTOUL,Tom		x	x	5	x					x
The Bungalow, Mannamead										
BOXALL, A.S.			x	4	2	?	1	x	3	6
Sandown Lodge										
FOSTER,T.			x	?	5					
St Margarets										
REARDON,Michael			x							
MAJOR D.MAIRS			x	?	x	x	9	6	7	
Hazelwood										
RUSSELL,J.			x	18						
Treadwell House										
ESCOTT, Anthony				x	6		x			5
Uplands										

279

	1930	1931	1932	1933	1934	1935	1936	1937	1938	1939
CAMERON,Bill				x	x					
Priam Lodge										
MORGAN,Frank				x	x	x				
NUNNELEY,Philip				x	12	15	11	9	11	
Myrtle Cottage, Langley Bottom farm 39										
DULLER,George E,					x	16	17	18	19	10
Heathcote House										
StMargarets 38										
READ, George					x					
Heathcote House										
LANGLANDS, Geo S.						x	x	x	x	17
Woodlands										
WOODLAND,Percy						x	x	x		
Holly Lodge										
ALLDEN,George							7	4		
Woodlands										
DICK,Bobby								12	14	9
Mannamead										
DINES,Johnny							x	12	25	31
Larchfield										
BIRCH.Arthur W.								x	5	5
HARDY,Gerry								x	6	10
The Paddocks										
Shifnal Cottage										
RAY,Cecil									x	12
Hillcot										
DONOGHUE,Steve									31	
Woodruff										
INGHAM,Staff										x
Bredenbury										
WALLINGTON,Harold										x
Sandown Lodge										
Annual Total	295	344	306	371	367	343	349	358	422	442

Note x = trainer based at Epsom but numbers of horses unknown

	1940	1941	1942	1943	1944	1945	1946	1947	1948	1949
DICK,David P.	8	6						9	6	9
Glanmire Farm										
DICK,Bobby	6	3	5	3	8	8	9			
Mannamead										
DINES,Johnny	17				10	22	20	25	31	22
Larchfield										
DULLER,George E.	12	4				6	16	10	13	6
St Margarets										
White House 48										
HEDGES,Harry	5				9	11	9	17	11	
Grove Stables										
NIGHTINGALL,Wal	56	43	44	49	52	68	61	55	58	51
South Hatch										
PARKER,Evan	x	x	x	x	x	x	x	x	x	x
Shifnal Cottage										
PAYNE,Bill	14	6	12	2	10	20	16	23		
Heath House										
REARDON,Jack	6	6	6	3	5	8	9	7	11	11
Ermyn Lodge										
SMYTH,Herbert G.	21	8	7	7	11	19	27	25	31	21
Down Cottage										
SMYTH,Victor	38	28	31	27	48	63	43	35	44	64
Mospey										
SMYTH,William	5	3	5	3	4					
Down Cottage										
WOOTTON,Stanley	6	4								21
Shifnal Paddocks										
Treadwell House49										
WOOD,John	4				10	19	22	16	13	14
Downs House 49										
TABOR, C.Victor	23	9	4	5						
Holly Lodge										

	1940	1941	1942	1943	1944	1945	1946	1947	1948	1949
HARDY,Gerry	6						7	11	24	
The Chalet										
The Paddocks										
BIRCH,Arthur	4	3	1			1	5			
West Hill										
RAY,Cecil	12	8	10							
Hillcot										
ESCOTT, Anthony	11									
Uplands										
WINTER,Fred N.	8	?	?	x						
Rowland Lodge										
LANGLANDS, Cec.	7									
Thirty Acre Barn										
BELL,Charlie		6	7	10	9	22	21	12	8	
Treadwell House										
MILLER,Michael		5	6							
Bredenbury										
NUNNELEY,Phillip				12	11	9	17	20	22	21
Ascot House										
Langley Bottom Farm										
WALLS,Tom				2				3		
The Looe										
SMITH, W.G.					x	24	32			
St Margarets										
Thirty Acre Barn 46										
BLACKMORE,Michael					x	24	5	24	28	23
Myrtle Cottage										
HANLEY,Sam						7	5	8	9	?
Seabright										
THRALE,Peter						11	15	20	26	25
Startside										
INGHAM,Staff								26	48	58
Thirty Acre Barn										

	1940	1941	1942	1943	1944	1945	1946	1947	1948	1949
WALLINGTON,Harold								18	23	21
Hillcrest										
CAREY,Tommy								11	9	17
Woodruff										
GRIFFITHS,Tom								11	16	13
Woodcote Stud										
BAILEY,Percy								1	?	x
The Grove										
FARMER,Tom									10	24
Mannamead										
SMYTH,Ron									5	12
Ascot House										
ISOM, H.C.									5	x
Holly Lodge										
LANGLANDS, George									x	
Woodlands										
HICKEY,J										x
The Paddocks										
WYNNE,G.										13
Heath House										
Annual Total	269	142	138	123	187	342	339	387	451	446

Note x = trainer based at Epsom but numbers of horses unknown

Note ? =trainer believed to be based at Epsom

283

	1950	1951	1952	1953	1954	1955	1956	1957	1958	1959
BAILEY,Percy	10	7	14	7	12					
Grove Stables										
CAREY,Tommy	17	19	23	29	28	18	17	21	16	10
Woodruff										
DICK,Dave P.	8	8	10	13	13	9	x	11	x	?
Glanmire Farm										
DINES,Johnny	20	15	14	23	23	19	16	12	6	
Larchfield										
DULLER,George E.	25	27	3	7	10	3	7	5	7	2
White House										
FARMER,Tom	x									
Mannamead										
GRIFFITHS,Tom	7	10	16	9	10	11	17	18	14	18
Woodcote Stud										
Mayfields 56										
HANLEY,Sam	25	21	13	21	22	25	24	28	20	25
Seabright and Heathcote House										
INGHAM,Staff	23	25	25	26	34	35	37	36	40	33
Thirty Acre Barn										
NIGHTINGALL,Walt	63	73	70	68	61	60	68	67	51	50
South Hatch										
PARKER,Evan	x	x	x	x	x	x	x	x	x	x
Shifnal Cottage										
REARDON,Jack	10	9	12	11	9	11	8	6	7	7
Ermyn Lodge										
SMYTH,Herbert G.	27									
Down Cottage										
SMYTH,Ron	24	32	40	38	35	41	36	43	43	42
Ascot House										
Clear Height 58										
SMYTH,Victor	59	74	66	68	62	46	35	45	24	17
Mospey										

	1950	1951	1952	1953	1954	1955	1956	1957	1958	1959
THRALE,Peter	65	54	54	67	63	56	59	53	52	46
Startside										
WALLINGTON,Harold	23	22	25	29	31	21	20	19	19	15
Hillcrest										
WOOD,John	12	7								
Downs House										
WOOTTON,Stanley	19	16	13	13	17	9	5	4	4	7
Treadwell House										
WYNNE, Gerry	10									
Heath House										
FANCEY,E.J.		16								
Portland House										
NUNNELEY,Phillip	?	7	13	9						
Maidstone House										
SMYTH,H.E."Ted"		27	26	25	26	23	25	25	25	27
Down Cottage										
MITCHELL,Cyril			17	20	20	23	19	17	13	16
Heath House										
THRALE,Dick				22	26	27	28	25	38	35
Downs House										
WARREN,George				18	12					
Portland House										
FORBES,George					2					
Burley Lodge										
SIRETT,Jackie					x	4	11	15	16	12
The Durdans 54										
Portland House 55										
TAYLOR,A.P."Manch"					x	11	16	9	8	8
Myrtle Cottage										
ASHWORTH,Peter						9	13	17	14	22
Grove Stables										
BENSTEAD,C.John						7	6			
Park Farm										

285

	1950	1951	1952	1953	1954	1955	1956	1957	1958	1959
MORLEY LAWSON,Vic.						4	4	3		3
Longdown House										
WHELAN,Dermot						10	21	28	31	30
Mannamead										
Lavandou 58										
BUTCHERS,Don							16	17	25	34
Priam Lodge										
BENSTEAD,Ian									6	12
Fourfields Farm										
Annual Total	447	469	454	523	516	482	508	524	479	471

Note x = trainer based at Epsom but numbers of horses unknown

Note ? =trainer believed to be based at Epsom

	1960	1961	1962	1963	1964	1965	1966	1967	1968	1969
ASHWORTH,Peter	13	25	26	27	31	20	30	22	30	28
Grove Stables										
Treadwell House 61										
BENSTEAD,C.John	21	24	28	35	38	39	36	38	37	36
Hillcot										
The Limes 61										
BENSTEAD,Ian	17	18	15	18	20	17	21			
Fourfields Farm										
BUTCHERS,Don	33	32	27	18						
Priam Lodge										
CAREY.Tommy	17	15	10							
Woodruff										
DALE, L.Syd	x	36	40	45	46	48	53	47	39	40
Startside										
DICK,Dave P	2	3								
Glanmire Farm										
EMERY, Rene	10	8	12							
Portland House										
GRIFFITHS,Tom	15	9								
Mayfields										
HANLEY,Sam	23	19								
Heathcote House' Seabright										
INGHAM,Staff	32	36	41	31	41	40	38	35	42	40
Thirty Acre Barn										
MITCHELL,Cyril	16	18	17	20	21	21	18	19	22	26
Heath House										
Downs House 68										
NIGHTINGALL,Walt	62	63	58	63	67	64	64	53	48	
South Hatch										
NIGHTINGALL,Marj									x	
South Hatch										
PARKER,Evan	x	10	15	x	8	11	x	x	x	
Shifnal Cottage										

287

	1960	1961	1962	1963	1964	1965	1966	1967	1968	1969
REARDON,Jack	7	6	8	8	1					
Ermyn Lodge										
SIRETT,Jackie	11	14	13	14	20	14	19	16	19	19
Treadwell House 60										
Burnside 61										
SMYTH,H.E. "Ted"	34	27	28	25	26	25	25	25	28	22
Down Cottage										
SMYTH,Ron	40	50	43	41	39	53	46	47	47	51
Clear Height										
SMYTH,Victor	21	19	12	17	12					
Mospey										
THRALE,Dick	37	34	31	31	26	20	22			
Downs House										
WALLINGTON,H	22	22	23	25	22	26	18	18	20	
Hillcrest										
WHELAN,Dermot	38	38	46	47	47	46	50	37	43	37
Lavandou										
WOOTTON,Stanley	4	7	7							
Shifnal Paddocks										
GETHIN,Ken		8	8	6	6	9	10			
Hillcote										
HANLEY,David		7	28	32	33	40	39			
Heathcote House										
MORLEYLAWSON,V	?	3	3	2						
Longdown House										
STEVENS,Joe		12	11	9	10	13	13	16	8	?
Grove Stables										
DAWSON,Peter			17	16	19	23	19	25	25	26
Mayfields										
GRIFFITHS,D.J.		?	8							
Park Farm										
PAY,F.W.			2							
Copthill										

	1960	1961	1962	1963	1964	1965	1966	1967	1968	1969
SUTCLIFFE,J (Jnr)				25	47	47	42	x	39	41
Woodruff House										
HOWE, G.M.				1						
Hunters Chase, Walton										
GOSLING,Tommy					17	26	26	24	28	30
Priam Lodge										
SMYTH,Paul						16	16	19	18	20
Caithness										
EUSTACE,Ken							9	8	5	5
The Hermitage										
PITT,Arthur							7	17	18	21
Manor Farm Stables										
Wendover 69										
SUTCLIFFE,J. E.(Snr)							21	18	17	13
Ermyn Lodge										
SWIFT,Brian								26	26	36
Loretta Lodge										
MAHONEY,Pat								8	10	15
April Cottage, Sturts Lane										
AKEHURST,Reg									14	19
Hillcote										
BREASLEY.Arthur										28
South Hatch										
WALLINGTON,H Jnr.										16
Hillcrest										
Annual Total	475	563	577	556	597	618	642	518	583	569

Note x = trainer based at Epsom but numbers of horses unknown

Note ? =trainer believed to be based at Epsom

289

	1970	1971	1972	1973	1974	1975	1976	1977	1978	1979
AKEHURST,Reg	22	25								
Hillcote										
ASHWORTH,Peter	23	21	28	31	17	15	17	12	20	18
Treadwell House										
BENSTEAD,C.John	36	31	36	41	36	24	25	28	24	30
The Limes										
BREASLEY,A.:Scobie	37	45	34	51	48	48				25
South Hatch										
Derby Stables 79										
DALE,L.Syd	30	29	34	25						
Startside										
DAWSON,Peter	20	27								
Mayfields										
GOSLING,Tommy	25	30	23	22	25	19	15	12	13	12
Priam Lodge										
INGHAM,Staff	45	33	33	35	38	29	37			
Thirty Acre Barn										
MITCHELL,Cyril	22	19	19	19	21					
Downs House										
PITT,Arthur	20	23	19	26	34	29	36	27	17	25
Wendover Stables										
SIRETT,Jackie	16	14	13	11						
Burnside										
SMYTH,H.E."Ted"	22	27	22	21	22	14	12			
Down Cottage										
SMYTH,Paul	21	16	18	20	17					
Caithness										
SMYTH,Ron	49	45	50	46	45	50	51	49	45	38
Clear Height										
STEVENS,Joe	10	11								
Grove Stables										

	1970	1971	1972	1973	1974	1975	1976	1977	1978	1979
SUTCLIFFE,J. E(Snr)	21	23	27	28	21	26				
Ermyn Lodge										
SUTCLIFFE,J.(Jun)	59	52	49	57	45	41	43	39	39	47
Woodruff House										
SWIFT,Brian	39	38	37	45	46	43	42	46	41	53
Loretta Lodge										
WHELAN,Dermot	32	30	22	27	21	19	15	16	20	21
Lavandou										
EUSTACE,Kenneth	?	7								
The Hermitage										
WALLINGTON,H Jnr	13	18	16	17						
Hillcrest										
HAYNES,Mick					19	15	21	27	23	23
Tattenham Corner Stables										
MITCHELL,Philip						17	14	24	16	14
Downs House										
GOSWELL,Mick							12	9	10	
Mannamead										
INGHAM,Tony								31	21	26
Thirty Acre Barn										
Annual Total	562	564	480	522	455	389	340	320	289	332

291

	1980	1981	1982	1983	1984	1985	1986	1987	1988	1989
ASHWORTH,Peter	8	9	7	8						
Treadwell House, The Chalet 82										
BENSTEAD,C.John	33	35	42	44	45	43	46	34	27	27
The Limes										
BREASLEY,A."Scobie"	40									
South Hatch										
GOSLING,Tommy	14	8	9							
Priam Lodge										
HAYNES,Mick	30	21	25	28	27	34	32	25	29	24
Tattenham Corner										
INGHAM,Tony	23	17	21	23	18	14	15	17	15	9
Mannamead										
LEWIS, Geoff	26	41	46	56	55	55	60	50	48	60
Thirty Acre Barn										
MITCHELL,Philip	20	29	41	37	52	51	45	37	33	30
Downs House										
PITT,Arthur	31	29	27	17	20	15	12			
Wendover										
SMYTH,Ron	42	51	51	37	41	43	44	41	39	27
Clear Height										
SUTCLIFFE,John R.E.	44	35	48	46	44	46	43	35	36	28
Woodruff House										
SWIFT,Brian	47	39	41	40	42	37				
Loretta Lodge										
SWIFT,Sylvia						x				
Loretta Lodge										
WHELAN,Dermot	x	27	17	11						
Lavandou										
WILSON,David		14	25	21	21	17	12	23	36	20
Ermyn Lodge, Shifnal Cottage84										
Loretta Lodge 87,Cedar Point89										

	1980	1981	1982	1983	1984	1985	1986	1987	1988	1989
SANDERS,Brooke			2	2	?	?	2	13	24	43
Nohome Cottage, Chalk Pit Stables 87										
SIMPSON,Rodney			17	34						
South Hatch										
JENKINS,John					38	46	61	48		
Woodcote Stud										
AKEHURST,Reg						14	29	44	65	72
South Hatch										
HOWE,Ray						x				
Priam Lodge										
DAVIES,Jeff							25	x		
Ermyn Lodge,Shifnal Cottage87										
HUTCHINSON,Ray						x				
The Chalet										
KING,Walter						3				
Headley Park Stables										
GONSALVES, Anson									5	
Cedar Point										
DOW,Simon									19	30
Wendover										
CARTER,Walter										29
Loretta Lodge										
CURTIS,Roger										45
Ermyn Lodge										
Annual Total	358	355	419	404	403	418	426	367	376	444

	1990	1991	1992	1993	1994	1995	1996	1997	1998	1999
AKEHURST,Reg	76		71	59	76	82	69	71		
South Hatch										
AKEHURST,John		17					14	x	43	24
South Hatch 91,98,99										
Shifnal Cottage96,97										
BENSTEAD,C.John	31	25	20	18	20	20	15	15	12	
The Limes										
CURTIS,Roger	43	47	33							
Ermyn Lodge										
DENSON,Andrew	12	12		14						
The Chalet, Ashely Stables 93										
DOW,Simon	55	42	41	33	53	57	71	63	70	53
Wendover, Clear Height 92										
HAYNES,Mick	25	17	23	8	12	15	20	22	20	23
Tattenham Corner										
LEWIS,Geoff	47	51	59	67	54	50	52	63	42	31
Thirty Acre Barn										
MITCHELL,Philip	33	36	26	24	21	30	26	23	18	21
Downs House										
SANDERS,Brooke	36	34	26	20	18	16	14	16	12	17
Chalk Pit Stables										
SMYTH,Ron	29	26								
Clear Height										
SUTCLIFFE,John R.E.	19	x	x	x						
Woodruff House										
WILSON,David	16	27	23	14	18	?	9			
Cedar Point										
CARTER,Wally	48	49	39							
Loretta Lodge										

	1990	1991	1992	1993	1994	1995	1996	1997	1998	1999
DIXON,Mark			10	14	12	12				
Ermyn Lodge										
NAUGHTON,T.J."Joe"			31	26	31	37	63	56	24	29
The Durdans										
INGRAM,Roger				13	16	18	17	15	19	20
Shifnal Cottage, Wendover 94										
MILLS,Terry				26	24	32	24	23	25	35
Loretta Lodge										
MOORE,Gary				x	44	62	52			
Ermyn Lodge and Woodruff House										
W.GUEST					x					
Shifnal Cottage										
HALL,Les Montagu							12	14	13	6
Chartwell Stables										
MORRIS,Derek								x	6	x
Ermyn Lodge										
MOONEY,Peter							x	x		
Ermyn Lodge										
JOHNSTON,Brett									x	12
Cedar Point										
Shifnal Cottage 99										
McNAE,Angus									x	21
Ermyn Lodge										
O'SULLIVAN,Roland										19
Cedar Point										
HAMILTON,Nigel										x
South Hatch										
Annual Total	470	383	402	336	399	431	458	381	304	311

Note x = trainer based at Epsom but numbers of horses unknown

Note ? =trainer believed to be based at Epsom

RACEHORSE TRAINERS BASED AT EPSOM IN THE 21st CENTURY

	2000	2001	2002	2003	2004	2005	2006	2007	2008	2009
AKEHURST, John	22	28	28	26	25	38	32	39	31	26

South Hatch
Tattenham Corner 05,
Clear height 2008

DOW,Simon	68	54	54	47	26	24	20	25	24	22

Clear Height

HALL, Les Montague	14	14	14	12	10	x	8	x	x	7

Chartwell
Ermyn Lodge 01
Clear Height 05
Chalk Pit 07

HAYNES, Mick	10	14	11	12	7					

Tattenham Corner

INGRAM,Roger	17	20	20	15	19	20	21	20	18	19

Wendover

JOHNSON, Brett	11	13	14	11	13	9	7	12	13	8

Shifnal Cottage
Little Woodruff 01

MILLS,Terry	42	41	43	49	41	40	38	27	24	25

Loretta Lodge

MITCHELL,Philip	26	17	25	25	22	25	19	17		

Downs House

NAUGHTON, T.J."Joe"	31	28								

The Durdans

O'SULLIVAN,Roland	12	11	x	x						

Cedar Point

SANDERS,Brooke	11	10	11	17	15	18	13			

Chalk Pit Stables
Thirty Acre Barn 2006

HAMILTON,Nigel	x	x	x							

South Hatch

BOYLE,Jim			12	18	33	34	31	43	56	55

South Hatch

MONGAN,Laura			x	x	x	9	17	19	18
Condover									
PHELAN, Pat							4	4	25
Ermyn Lodge									
TEAL, Roger							x	17	7
Thirty Acre Barn									
ATTWATER, Michael							x	6	20
Racecourse Stables									
Tattenham Corner 2008									
SMITH, J									?
Tattenham Corner									
MILLS,Robert									
Loretta Lodge									x
Annual Total	264	250	232	232	211	208	198	194	212	232

	2010	2011	2012	2013	2014	2015	2016	2017	2018	2019
AKEHURST, John *Clear Height*	20	10	6							
ATTWATER, Michael *Tattenham Corner*	20	28	27	23	30	27	30	30	35	31
BOYLE, Jim *South Hatch*	52	48	45	7*	24	21	23	22	22	19
DOW, Simon *Clear Height*	32	36	27	24	23	31	25	21	24	35
HALL, Les Montague *Chalk Pit*	8	8								
INGRAM, Roger *Wendover*	9	13	9	14	12	12	12	15	14	8
JOHNSON, Brett *Woodruff 10, The Durdans*	9	18	12	14	14	7	14	10	15	12
MILLS, Robert *Loretta Lodge*	24	27	25	11	14	10				
MONGAN, Laura *Condover*	17	17	13	15	22	22	21	28	29	21
PHELAN, Pat *Ermyn Lodge*	21	19	17	19	19	25	25	12	20	21
SMITH, Ralph *Tattenham Corner,* *Woodruff 16*	9	6					?	8	9	
TEAL, Roger *Thirty Acre Barn*	7	20	20	18	22	17				
MAYLAM, Olivia *Chalk Pit*		?	11	10						
CARTER, Lee *Clear Height*			x**	10	20	22	21	23	12	11
PATTINSON. Mark *Tattenham Corner*							x	3	7	8
WEST, Adam *Gastons, Thirty Acre Barn* *Loretta Lodge*							x	13	28	45
	228	250	212	158	200	194	174	185	215	201

*J.Boyle website later showed figure as 30. **Succeeded J.Akehurt March 201

APPENDIX D. Trainers- Leading Prize Money Winners

FLAT RACING	Wins	Prize Money	Position	JUMPS RACING	Wins	Prize Money	Position
1901							
Will. Nightingall	19	3,275					
1902							
R. I'Anson	14	3,049					
Will. Nightingall	20	2,856					
1903							
Will.Nightingall	22	5,203					
1904							
Will.Nightingall	10	4,277					
1905							
Will.Nightingall	22	6,120					
1906							
Will.Nightingall	23	3,845					
1907							
R.Wootton	14	3,133					
Will.Nightingall	18	3,169					
1908							
R.Wootton	36	6,703	16				
Will.Nightingall	16	4,377					
1909							
R.Wootton	48	11,507	12				
Will.Nightingall	12	2,559					
1910							
R.Wootton	45	10,013	10				
1911							
R.Wootton	48	14,815	7				
1912							
R.Wootton	63	19,930	3				
1913							
R.Wootton	66	27,969	1				
H.Carter	10	4,602					

	Wins	Prize Money	Position
1914			
R.Wootton	49	17,581	3
1915			
Will.Nightingall	4	871	
1916			
C.V.Tabor	19	3,459	10
1919			
C.V.Tabor	40	7,926	16
S.Wootton	22	7,304	19
R.Wootton	10	2,658	
1920			
S.Wootton	14	4,283	
Will.Nightingall	9	2,615	
1921			
C.V.Tabor	16	3,722	
Will.Nightingall	16	3,626	
1922			
S.Wootton	25	5,078	
1923			
S.Wootton	45	11,791	
1924			
S.Wootton	58	13,633	
Will.Nightingall	35	9,446	
1925			
S.Wootton	59	14,808	8
Will.Nightingall	25	5,882	
1926			
S.Wootton	83	22,828	6
1927			
S.Wootton	77	22,515	5
Wltr.Nightingall	55	16,017	
1928			
S.Wootton	88	23,564	7
Wltr.Nightingall	36	12,337	

	Wins	Prize Money	Position
1929			
S.Wootton	76	18,259	
Wltr.Nightingall	34	9,104	
1930			
Wltr.Nightingall	29	7,189	
1931			
Wltr.Nightingall	43	10,266	15
V.Smyth	41	7,011	
S.Wootton	30	6,557	
1932			
Wltr.Nightingall	51	14,485	9
S.Wootton	32	11,212	11
T.Walls	7	11,119	12
1933			
V.Smyth	49	10,012	17
Wltr.Nightingall	34	8,919	
1934			
V.Smyth	47	9,146	
Wltr.Nightingall	25	6,529	
S.Wootton	27	4,935	
1935			
Wltr.Nightingall	41	11,710	
V.Smyth	37	8,645	
1936			
V.Smyth	38	18,578	7
S.Wootton	34	6,040	
Wltr.Nightingall	25	5,916	
1937			
V.Smyth	27	11,262	
Wltr.Nightingall	35	6,813	
1938			
Wltr.Nightingall	39	12,026	
V.Smyth	31	6,408	

	Wins	Prize Money	Position
1939			
V.Smyth	31	7,787	
Wltr.Nightingall	24	5,824	
1940			
Wltr.Nightingall	23	4,728	7
V.Smyth	23	4,220	9
1941			
Wltr.Nightingall	17	3,533	
V.Smyth	18	2,998	
1942			
V.Smyth	15	3,381	
Wltr.Nightingall	12	2,881	8
1943			
Wltr.Nightingall	29	13,833	1
V.Smyth	5	2,089	
1944			
V.Smyth	21	6,976	8
Wltr.Nightingall	24	6,865	9
1945			
Wltr.Nightingall	22	8,924	9
V.Smyth	20	6,789	13
1946			
Wltr.Nightingall	48	13,696	
V.Smyth	40	11,393	
1947			
Wltr.Nightingall	52	30,440	5
V.Smyth	41	16,114	
1948			
Wltr.Nightingall	30	16,557	16
V.Smyth	30	15,414	
1949			
Wltr.Nightingall	23	26,364	10
V.Smyth	37	15,436	

	Wins	Prize Money	Position
1940-41			
V.Smyth	9	1,132	3
Wltr.Nightingall	12	987	
1941-42			
V.Smyth	8	1,202	2
1947-48			
Wltr.Nightingall	4	1,643	
G.Duller	4	1,564	
1948-49			
V.Smyth	18	4,976	

	Wins	Prize Money	Position		Wins	Prize Money	Position
1950				1949-50			
Wltr.Nightingall	38	25,183	7	V.Smyth	12	3,288	
V.Smyth	37	23,488	9	P.Thrale	12	2,287	
1951				1950-51			
Wltr.Nightingall	49	28,668	8	R.Smyth	5	3,008	
P.Thrale	49	23,525	12				
V.Smyth	36	22,884	13				
1952				1951-52			
V.Smyth	23	31,299	5	P.Thrale	13	3,068	
Wltr.Nightingall	35	31,243	6	V.Smyth	10	1,901	
T.Carey	23	23,241	9				
P.Thrale	38	21,498	11				
1953				1952-53			
V.Smyth	36	21,506	11	Wltr.Nightingall	8	2,407	
Wltr.Nightingall	39	17,614					
1954				1953-54			
P.Thrale	43	19,889		P.Thrale	19	4,433	
Wltr.Nightingall	37	17,879					
1955				1954-55			
W.Nightingall	43	27,798	7	R.Smyth	11	2,038	
V.Smyth	31	17,307					
1956				1955-56			
W.Nightingall	42	25,425	7	P.Thrale	13	2,980	
S.Ingham	38	17,366					
1957				1956-57			
S.Ingham	51	28,918	6	P.Thrale	18	5,739	
W.Nightingall	37	19,428					
1958				1957-58			
W.Nightingall	20	16,835		D.Butchers	28	6,119	
S.Ingham	26	12,320					
1959				1958-59			
W.Nightingall	25	26,388	9	D.Butchers	13	5,736	12
S.Ingham	57	16,589					

303

	Wins	Prize Money	Position		Wins	Prize Money	Position
1960				1959-60			
W.Nightingall	17	27,897	11	L.S.Dale	8	10,143	8
S.Ingham	25	25,321		D.Butchers	32	8,426	10
1961				1960-1			
S.Ingham	51	41,800	5	D.Butchers	36	16,605	3
W.Nightingall	39	39,428	8				
1962				1961-62			
W.Nightingall	27	20,099		R.Smyth	9	4,669	
				D.Butchers	20	4,764	
1963				1962-63			
W.Nightingall	35	26,592		J.Sutcliffe jun	16	3,485	
S.Ingham	28	19,178					
1964				1963-64			
W.Nightingall	36	25,585		J.Sutcliffe jun	23	7,552	
S.Ingham	25	17,669					
1965				1964-65			
W.Nightingall	34	57,341	5	R.Smyth	5	3,689	
S.Ingham	34	43,633	10				
1966				1965-66			
S.Ingham	35	32,965	12	L.S.Dale	11	3,662	
W.Nightingall	21	28,301	20				
1967				1966-67			
W.Nightingall	18	30,956	9	B.Swift	5	6,890	
S.Ingham	25	19,427					
1968				1967-68			
J.Sutcliffe jun	31	42216	4	S.Ingham	3	4,566	
				L.S.Dale	14	3,570	
1969				1968-69			
J.Sutcliffe jun	31	84,509	7	R.Akehurst	7	4,635	
S.Ingham	34	41,741	20				
1970				1969-70			
J.Sutcliffe jun	32	23,420		R.Smyth	9	4,416	
A.Breasley	23	21,352					

	Wins	Prize Money	Position
1971			
J. Sutcliffe jun	26	23,042	
S.Ingham	29	20,464	
1972			
S.Ingham	18	33,891	
A.Breasley	29	26,993	
1973			
R.Smyth	33	34,935	
A.Breasley	20	23,000	
1974			
J.Sutcliffe jun	30	46,325	
J.E.Sutcliffe	17	27,071	
1975			
A.Breasley	45	67,888	11
J.Sutcliffe jun	21	38,038	
1976			
J. Sutcliffe jun	24	50,639	
B.Swift	16	41,074	
1977			
A.Ingham	19	46,504	
R.Smyth	19	39,810	
1978			
B.Swift	22	51,727	
C.J.Benstead	18	48,347	
1979			
B.Swift	24	65,793	
J.Sutcliffe jun	21	52,685	
1980			
C.J.Benstead	17	83,297	
B.Swift	22	60,976	
1981			
J.Sutcliffe jun	24	80,143	
C.J.Benstead	19	55,903	

	Wins	Prize Money	Position
1970-71			
J.E.Sutcliffe	9	26,114	
R.Smyth	13	13,917	
1971-72			
L.S.Dale	8	10,852	
R.Smyth	11	6,245	
1972-73			
J.E.Sutcliffe	12	16,020	
A.Pitt	8	6,665	
1973-74			
C.Mitchell	8	15,706	
R.Smyth	8	14,244	
1974-75			
R.Smyth	9	12,660	
1975-76			
R.Smyth	13	8,866	
1976-77			
S.Ingham	5	7,823	
1977-78			
A.Pitt	11	7,628	
1978-79			
A.Pitt	8	8,147	
1979-80			
R.Smyth	10	12,234	
1980-81			
P.Mitchell	13	11,764	

	Wins	Prize Money	Position		Wins	Prize Money	Position
1982							
J.Sutcliffe jun	20	68,702					
1983				**1982-83**			
G.Lewis	27	57,034		R.Smyth	8	11,450	
J.Sutcliffe jun	17	46,003					
1984				**1983-84**			
B.Swift	27	164,018		J.Jenkins	69	69,663	
G.Lewis	34	124,991		R.Smyth	6	20,569	
1985				**1984-85**			
G.Lewis	29	88,187		J.Jenkins	76	136,758	
R.Smyth	17	97,968					
1986				**1985-86**			
G.Lewis	25	68,774		J.Jenkins	63	91,560	
R.Akehurst	16	63,221					
J.Sutcliffe jun	16	60,996					
1987				**1986-87**			
G.Lewis	25	92,453		R.Akehurst	23	85,332	
R.Akehurst	27	86,051		J.Jenkins	41	62,433	
1988				**1987-88**			
G.Lewis	32	280,732	17	R.Akehurst	21	57,746	
R.Akehurst	25	139,633		B.Sanders	9	13,021	
1989				**1988-89**			
R.Akehurst	33	273,967		R.Akehurst	43	128,124	19
G.Lewis	23	268,573		B.Sanders	8	39,333	
1990				**1989-90**			
R.Akehurst	34	232,240		R.Akehurst	30	132,962	
G.Lewis	29	191,938		S.Dow	6	47,903	
1991				**1990-91**			
G.Lewis	43	266,405		R.Akehurst*	35	215,621	16
S.Dow	15	84,613		R.Curtis	12	42,514	
1992				**1992-3**			
G.Lewis	53	367,088	17	R.Akehurst*	18	123,757	
R.Akehurst	30	215,899		S.Dow	24	49,010	

*At Epsom for part of year

306

	Wins	Prize Money	Position		Wins	Prize Money	Position
1993				**1992-93**			
R.Akehurst	48	357,641		R.Akehurst	13	88,401	
T.Mills	9	347,140		B.Sanders	9	57,125	
1994				**1993-94**			
R.Akehurst	51	562,141	17	S.Dow	19	93,146	
G.Lewis	45	340,235		R.Akehurst	17	84,621	
1995				**1994-95**			
R.Akehurst	55	580,977	14	R.Akehurst	8	50,845	
G.Lewis	46	480,985	20	S.Dow	7	35,172	
1996				**1995-96**			
R.Akehurst	32	298,645		R.Akehurst	11	68,294	
G.Moore	33	199,438		S.Dow	4	58,748	
1997				**1996-97**			
R.Akehurst	28	314,584		R.Akehurst	6	86,873	
G.Lewis	26	202,508		G.Moore*	13	72,398	
				*At Epsom part of year			
1998				**1997-98**			
S.Dow	22	118,688		S.Dow	3	31,262	
G.Lewis	12	109,010					
1999				**1998-99**			
T.Mills	22	260,120		S.Dow	10	58,946	
S.Dow	21	179,365					
2000				**1999-2000**			
T.Mills	23	118,881		S.Dow	8	59,855	
S.Dow	17	118,507		J.Akehurst	5	41,511	
2001				**2000-01**			
T.Mills	34	391,529		S.Dow	8	47,483	
J.Akehurst	13	134,997					
2002							
T.Mills	35	713,855	18				
S.Dow	26	218,395					
2003							
T.Mills	27	353,306					
J.Akehurst	16	133,181					

	Wins	Prize Money		Wins	Prize Money
2004					
J.Akehurst	14	196,637			
T.Mills	19	173,633			
2005					
T.Mills	32	390,560			
J.Akehurst	18	206,644			
2006					
T.Mills	30	281,365			
J.Akehurst	17	229,195			
2007					
J.Boyle	40	195,294			
T.Mills	14	156,691			
2008			2007-08		
J.Boyle	50	224,632	L.Mongan	4	50,130
T.Mills	16	146,795			
2009			2008-09		
J.Boyle	59	318,879	L.Mongan	3	30,746
T.Mills	13	150,233			
2010			2009-2010		
R.Teal	12	168,845	P.Phelan	4	30,140
J.Boyle	30	145,119			
2011			2010-11		
J.Boyle	29	118,631	L.Mongan	5	20,706
R.Mills	11	116,984			
2012			2011-12		
M.Attwater	17	110,284	L.Mongan	3	16,818
J.Boyle	27	100,091			
2013			2012-13		
S.Dow	19	104,384	L.Mongan	1	50,187
M.Attwater	13	97,929			
2014					
M.Attwater	12	167,060			
S.Dow	18	127,044			
L.Carter	26	112,796			

2015			2014-15		
M.Attwater	13	123,021	L.Mongan	7	46,505
S.Dow	21	118,041			
2016					
L.Mongan	13	479,838			
S.Dow	14	109,023			
J.Boyle	20	103,259			
2017					
S..Dow	19	169,494			
M.Attwater	25	124,674			
2018					
S.Dow	18	179,828			
J.Boyle	15	127,322			
2019 to 01/09/19					
S.Dow	18	168,181			
M.Attwater	19	162,308			

BIBLIOGRAPHY

BOOKS

Epsom Censuses 1841-1891	Barbara Abdy
The Breedon Book of Horse Racing Records	Edward Abelson & John Tyrrel
Ringers and Rascals	David Ashforth
The Daily Telegraph Chronicle of Horse Racing	Norman Barrett(edited by)
The History of Steeplechasing	W.C.A.Blew
A Biographical Dictionary of Racehorse	David Boyd
Trainers in Berkshire	
Chasing A Dream	Les Carlyon
Jack Of His Own Trade	Susan Colling
Henry Custance in his book "Riding Recollections and Turf Stories"	
The Complete Record	Paul Davies
Donoghue Up	Steve Donoghue
The Wootton Family-Australia to Epsom	Bill Eacott
Racing Romance	S. Theodore Felstead
Memoirs of a Racing Journalist	Sydney Galtrey
Queen of The Turf	Quintin Gilbey
Good Days	Meyrick Good
The Lure Of The Turf	Meyrick Good
History of Newmarket and Annals of The Turf	J.P. Hore
Horseracing and the British 1919-39	Mike Huggins
Derby Day	David Holloway
Epsom Racecourse	David Hunn
Men and Horse I Have Known	The Hon. George Lambton
A Trainer's Memories	John McGuigan
Biographical Encyclopaedia of	Roger Mortimer, Richard
Flat Racing	Onslow & Peter Willett
My Sixty Years Of The Turf	Charles Morton
The Duke	David Nicholson
Calling The Horses	Peter O'Sullevan
Crooks, Horses and Jockeys	Arthur Sarl
Finishing Post	Charlie Smirke
Belmont- A Century Ago	Roland Sparkes
Neck Or Nothing	John Welcome
Stable Rat	Philip Welsh
Ancient Epsom	Reginald White
Bull	Howard Wright
The Derby	Michael Wynn Jones
Gentlemen of the Australian Turf	
Luck of the Game	
Kelly's Street Directory	

RACING ANNUALS

Timeform Racehorses, Raceform Horses In Training, Sporting Chronicle Horses In Training, The Sportsman Horses In Training, Sporting Chronicle Form Books, Raceform-Up-To-Date, Raceform, Chaseform, Cope's Racing Encyclopaedia, Tote Racing Annual, Ruff's Guide, Ward Hill Racing Annual, Directory of the Turf

NEWSPAPERS AND MAGAZINES

The Sporting Life, The Racing Post, Silks, Epsom & Ewell Herald, Racing Illustrated, Lotinga's Weekly, The European Racehorse, The British Bloodstock Breeder's Review, The Illustrated Sporting and Dramatic News, Sports Pictures, Bells Life, Bailys Magazine of Sports and Pastimes, Gale's Weekly, Racing Indicator, The York Herald, The Era.

Many thanks to the volunteers who manage and contribute to epsomandewellhistoryexplorer, and the staff at Bourne Hall Museum, Ewell.

Thanks also to Tim Cox for his help, encouragement, and access to his library.
Thanks to David Boyd fir his research on Berkshire Trainers and Newmarket Trainers.
Thanks to Roland Sparkes for his work on Turf Cottage, Sutton;
 Paul Matthieu for his work on Albert Parkes
;and William Morgan for his research into racing at Banstead.

I was also fortunate to interview Ben Cooksey, David Hanley, Mick Dillon, and Muddy King before they "weighed in" for the final time. Thanks also to John Benstead, Catherine Remond, Brian Jago, Chris Dwyer, John Keller, Judy Dick,Sean O'Byrne and many others who supplied me with their memories.